T0183307

Lecture Notes in Computer Science   12028

Founding Editors

Gerhard Goos
  Karlsruhe Institute of Technology, Karlsruhe, Germany
Juris Hartmanis
  Cornell University, Ithaca, NY, USA

Editorial Board Members

Elisa Bertino
  Purdue University, West Lafayette, IN, USA
Wen Gao
  Peking University, Beijing, China
Bernhard Steffen 🆔
  TU Dortmund University, Dortmund, Germany
Gerhard Woeginger 🆔
  RWTH Aachen, Aachen, Germany
Moti Yung
  Columbia University, New York, NY, USA

More information about this series at http://www.springer.com/series/7407

Huaikou Miao · Cong Tian ·
Shaoying Liu · Zhenhua Duan (Eds.)

Structured Object-Oriented Formal Language and Method

9th International Workshop, SOFL+MSVL 2019
Shenzhen, China, November 5, 2019
Revised Selected Papers

 Springer

Editors
Huaikou Miao
School of Computer Engineering
and Science
Shanghai University
Shanghai, China

Cong Tian
Institute of Computing Theory
and Technology
Xidian University
Xi'an, China

Shaoying Liu
Hosei University
Tokyo, Japan

Zhenhua Duan
Xidian University
Xi'an, Shaanxi, China

ISSN 0302-9743   ISSN 1611-3349 (electronic)
Lecture Notes in Computer Science
ISBN 978-3-030-41417-7   ISBN 978-3-030-41418-4 (eBook)
https://doi.org/10.1007/978-3-030-41418-4

LNCS Sublibrary: SL1 – Theoretical Computer Science and General Issues

© Springer Nature Switzerland AG 2020
This work is subject to copyright. All rights are reserved by the Publisher, whether the whole or part of the material is concerned, specifically the rights of translation, reprinting, reuse of illustrations, recitation, broadcasting, reproduction on microfilms or in any other physical way, and transmission or information storage and retrieval, electronic adaptation, computer software, or by similar or dissimilar methodology now known or hereafter developed.
The use of general descriptive names, registered names, trademarks, service marks, etc. in this publication does not imply, even in the absence of a specific statement, that such names are exempt from the relevant protective laws and regulations and therefore free for general use.
The publisher, the authors and the editors are safe to assume that the advice and information in this book are believed to be true and accurate at the date of publication. Neither the publisher nor the authors or the editors give a warranty, expressed or implied, with respect to the material contained herein or for any errors or omissions that may have been made. The publisher remains neutral with regard to jurisdictional claims in published maps and institutional affiliations.

This Springer imprint is published by the registered company Springer Nature Switzerland AG
The registered company address is: Gewerbestrasse 11, 6330 Cham, Switzerland

Preface

In spite of extensive research on formal methods and many efforts on transferring the technology to industry over the last three decades, how to enable practitioners to easily and effectively use formal techniques still remains challenging. The Structured Object-Oriented Formal Language (SOFL) has been developed to address this challenge by providing a comprehensive specification language, a practical modeling method, various verification and validation techniques, and tool support through effective integration of formal methods with conventional software engineering techniques. SOFL integrates Data Flow Diagram, Petri Nets, and VDM-SL to offer a visualized and formal notation for constructing specification; a three-step approach to requirements acquisition and system design; specification-based inspection and testing methods for detecting errors in both specifications and programs; and a set of tools to support modeling and verification. The Modeling, Simulation and Verification Language (MSVL) is a parallel programming language. It enables users to model a system as an MSVL program, to execute the program for simulating the behavior of the system, and to verify properties of the system. Its supporting toolkit MSV including MSVL compiler, interpreter, and several types of model checkers has been developed for automatic program verification. In particular, to verify C and Verilog/VHDL programs in large scale, some translators such as C2M and V2M, and a run time verification tool in code level have also been built to facilitate modeling, simulating, and verifying large systems in a formal manner.

Following the success of the previous SOFL+MSVL workshops, the 9th International Workshop on SOFL+MSVL for Reliability and Security (SOFL+MSVL 2019) was jointly organized in Shenzhen with the aim of bringing together industrial, academic, and government experts and practitioners of SOFL or MSVL to communicate and to exchange ideas. The workshop attracted 43 submissions on specification-based testing, specification inspection, model checking, formal verification, formal semantics, and formal analysis. Each submission was rigorously reviewed by two or more Program Committee (PC) members on the basis of technical quality, relevance, significance, and clarity, and 23 papers were accepted for publication in the workshop proceedings. The acceptance rate was 53%.

We would like to thank ICFEM 2019 for supporting the organization of the workshop, all of the PC members for their great efforts and cooperation in reviewing and selecting the papers, and our postgraduate students for all their help. We would also like to thank all of the participants for attending presentation sessions and actively joining discussions at the workshop. Finally, our gratitude goes to the editors at Springer for their continuous support in publishing the workshop proceedings.

December 2019

Huaikou Miao
Cong Tian
Shaoying Liu
Zhenhua Duan

Organization

Program Committee

Shaoying Liu (General Chair)	Hosei University, Japan
Zhenhua Duan (General Chair)	Xidian University, China
Huaikou Miao (Program Co-chair)	Shanghai University, China
Cong Tian (Program Co-chair)	Xidian University, China
Yuting Chen	Shanghai Jiao Tong University, China
Busalire Emeka	Hosei University, Japan
Colin Fidge	Queensland University of Technology, Australia
Weikai Miao	East China Normal University, China
Fumiko Nagoya (Program Co-chair)	Nihon University, Japan
Shin Nakajima	National Institute of Informatics, Japan
Kazuhiro Ogata	JAIST, Japan
Shengchao Qin	Teesside University, UK
Wuwei Shen	Western Michigan University, USA
Xinfeng Shu	Xi'an University of Posts and Telecommunications, China
Rong Wang	Hosei University, Japan
Xi Wang	Shanghai University, China
Jinyun Xue	Jiangxi Normal University, China

Contents

Software Analysis and Evolution

Software Analysis and Testing

Testing and Debugging

Analysis and Remodeling of the DirtyCOW Vulnerability by Debugging and Abstraction

Yanjun Wen$^{(\boxtimes)}$ and Ji Wang

College of Computer, National University of Defense Technology,
Changsha 410073, China
yjwen@nudt.edu.cn, jiwang@ios.ac.cn

Abstract. It is hard to understand clearly the principle of DirtyCOW vulnerability of Linux operating system, even for many experienced kernel developers. An approach is presented to rebuild the design model of the related Linux system calls, which gives an insight into the vulnerability. The remodeling, i.e. model-rebuilding, is done by first constructing a control flow diagram based on the debugging and analysis of the OS kernel, and then turning the control flow diagram to an abstract program based on abstraction to the observed concrete states. The approach provides an effective way for the comprehension of complex legacy software.

Keywords: Program comprehension · Operating system · Software remodeling · Vulnerability analysis · Software abstraction

1 Introduction

DirtyCOW [3] is a famous privilege escalation vulnerability in the Linux kernel, by which an unprivileged local user could gain the access right of the "root" user. The attack is due to a particular race condition, which can be led to by exploitation of the bug. It is difficult to understand the attack procedure of the bug even for many experienced kernel developers, because it involves a special interleaving execution of several concurrent threads. Besides, complex data structures and nested function calls are also obstacles.

Some kernel hackers [5] made excellent analysis to the bug, but the report involves so many OS details that it is also difficult to understand their description unless you are also a kernel hacker.

The paper presents an approach to rebuild the design model of the related Linux system calls of the bug, from which the attack procedure becomes very clear. The model helps us look insight into the vulnerability because it explicitly describes the design, which may only exist in the brain of some kernel developers before.

Supported by National Key Research and Development Program of China (No. 2017YFB1001802 and 2018YFB0204301).

© Springer Nature Switzerland AG 2020
H. Miao et al. (Eds.): SOFL+MSVL 2019 Workshop, LNCS 12028, pp. 3–12, 2020.
https://doi.org/10.1007/978-3-030-41418-4_1

The remodeling includes two steps. Firstly, reproduce the fault using Proof of Concept (POC) of the vulnerability, and debug the OS kernel to analyze the concrete-state transformations at some key control points (program points) in the interleaving path, and then build the control flow diagram (CFD) involving those control points. Secondly, abstract the observed concrete states, and analyze the abstract-state transformations between the adjacent control points in the CFD; after turning the transformations into statements, models can be gotten from the CFD.

This paper makes the following contributions:

– We build a model for the system calls related to DirtyCOW for the first time, which can help to understand clearly the vulnerability and its patch.
– We present a remodeling approach for legacy software, which could be used to comprehend those software and fix their complicated bugs.

The rest of the paper is organized as follows. After Sect. 2 gives some introduction to the DirtyCOW vulnerability, our analysis and debugging of the bug are described in Sect. 3. Then, Sect. 4 shows how to make abstraction and rebuild the model. Section 5 discusses the related work. The conclusion is made finally.

2   The DirtyCOW Vulnerability

The DirtyCOW vulnerability is a race condition that can be triggered when the Linux kernel's memory subsystem handles the copy-on-write (COW) breakage of private read-only memory mappings, which may cause normal users to own the "root" user's privilege. The bug has existed since the kernel version of around 2.6.22 (released in 2007) and was fixed late on Oct 18, 2016 [3].

The POC of DirtyCOW is a sample attack program [3], whose framework is shown in Fig. 1. The attack code is executed by an unprivileged user, but it can write to a read-only file, e.g. the password file "/etc/passwd" (used as example in the below).

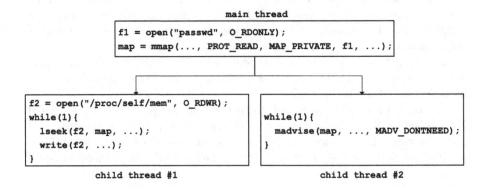

Fig. 1. Program framework of the POC

The attack program works as below.

1. The main thread opens the read-only file, and maps the file to a virtual memory area (VMA). Then it creates two child threads.
2. The child thread #1 writes repeatedly to the VMA by a special file "/proc/self/mem", which represents the whole virtual memory of a process. Since the file "passwd" is read-only, the kernel ensures that the writing only affect the memory, not the mapped file, by the COW mechanism.
3. At the same time, the child thread #2 repeatedly calls madvise() to clear the page table entry (PTE) of the VMA page that is being written by the child thread #1. The system call madvise notifies the kernel that the page is not needed further. If the process accesses that page later again, the content will be reloaded from the disk (or page cache) if it is a file-backed mapping. So the call to madvise should not lead to the modification of the mapped file.

3 Our Analysis of DirtyCOW

We analyze the bug by debugging the OS kernel. Firstly, we reproduce the Dirty-COW attack in a qemu virtual machine (VM) which runs Linux kernel 4.4.6. Then we debug the OS kernel by qemu and gdb to analyze the attack path. The debug is done by setting some breakpoints in the key control points, such as the entrance and exit of a function, and observing the kernel states when the breakpoints are caught each time.

3.1 The Attack Path

We find that the attack runs along the path shown in Fig. 2, in which each line is one event (e.g. "main{") or two events (e.g. "mmap{}"). The main thread maps the file and creates two child threads. Then child thread #1 executes the system call write to modify the virtual memory at the mapped address. To access directly the virtual memory of a process (may not be the current process), it is a little complicated. Firstly, the function __get_user_pages is called (Line 11) to get the pages frames by simulating the paging procedure. Secondly, access the gotten page frames (Line 51).

It is the paging simulation that makes the program complicated. The simulation includes two parts: page table lookup (e.g. Line 13) and page fault handling (e.g. Lines 15–19). If no page fault is detected in the lookup, no page fault is handled next correspondingly (e.g. line 49). Moreover, if a page fault was detected in the lookup, it would be handled, and after that, the lookup and page fault handling would be done again! So it can be found that, in the path, the paging actions happen 4 times (Lines 13–19, 21–28, 40–46, 48–49)[1]. At the last lookup (Line 48), no page fault is detected. So __get_user_pages ends next (Line 50).

---

[1] The function __get_user_pages calls follow_page_pte only once, therefore the events in Line 13, 21, 40, 48 correspond to the same control point. The multiple occurrences of faultin_page are similar.

```
 1 //main thread:
 2 main{      //main() starts
 3   mmap{}      //mmap() starts and ends
 4   pthread_create{}
 5   pthread_create{}
 6
 7 //child thread #1:
 8 write{
 9   sys_write{  //impl. func of the system call, in kernel mode
10     mem_rw{  //access file in the 'proc' file system
11       __get_user_pages{
12         cond_resched{}        //called at gup.c:510
13         follow_page_pte{}      //page table lookup
14         //page fault detected
15         faultin_page{          //page fault handling
16    ①    handle_pte_fault{
17              do_cow_fault{}    //do COW
18            }handle_pte_fault  //handle_pte_fault() ends
19         }faultin_page
20         cond_resched{}
21         follow_page_pte{}      //lookup again
22         //page fault detected
23         faultin_page{
24            handle_pte_fault{
25    ②        do_wp_page{}
26            }handle_pte_fault
27            *flags &= ~FOLL_WRITE; //gup.c:355, modify the flag!
28         }faultin_page
29         cond_resched{  //called at gup.c:510
30           __schedule{  //process scheduling
31             __switch_to{
32               //childe thread #2:
33               madvise{
34                 sys_madvise{}     //pte cleared
35               }madvise
36               //child thread #1 resumed
37             }__switch_to
38           }__schedule
39         }cond_resched
40         follow_page_pte{}    //lookup at the third time
41         //page fault detected
42         faultin_page{
43    ③    handle_pte_fault{
44              do_read_fault{}
45            }handle_pte_fault
46         }faultin_page
47         cond_resched{}
48         follow_page_pte{}    //lookup at the fourth time
49    ④    //no page fault detected
50       }__get_user_pages
51       //access the pages that are gotten
52     }mem_rw
53   }sys_write
54 }write
```

Fig. 2. The attack path

Moreover, because the paging action may take a long period of time, process scheduling (e.g. Lines 29–39) is allowed before each page table lookup, which may trigger process switch. So the child thread #2 may run (Lines 32–35) between the second and third paging actions.

Besides the events such as the entrance and exit of functions, we also need to observe the kernel state transformation along the attack path.

3.2   Concrete State Transformation

Figure 3(a) shows the kernel state when the event "}mmap"[2] (line 3 of Fig. 2) happens. At this time, the file "passwd" has been mapped to the VMA starting from the virtual address (VA) 0xb7ffc000[3], but the PTE of the VA is still empty. Besides, several kernel objects has been created:

page 66c3 One page of the file "passwd" has been prefetched to memory and put in the page frame 0x66c3[4]. This page frame is a file-backed page.

address_space c68b36cc This object is used to record the pages of the file that are cached in memory. Its VA is 0xc68b36cc. Only one page of the file is in memory at this time.

file "passwd" It represents the file "passwd" opened previously.

vm_area_struct c6281318 It represents the VMA starting from 0xb7ffc000.

Figure 3(b) shows the state when the event "}do_cow_fault" (Line 17 of Fig. 2) happens. At this time, a COW has been performed. A new page frame (**page 7bc3**) is allocated, whose content is copied from the cached page frame **page 66c3** of the file. The PTE of the VA 0xb7ffc000 has also been set to use the newly allocated page frame. The new page frame is not in the cache of any file. So it is not a file-backed page, but an anonymous page, and reversely maps to a anon_vma object.

Figure 3(c) is the state when the event "}sys_madvise" (Line 34 of Fig. 2) happens. At this time, the PTE has been cleared, and the page frame 7bc3 is put back and becomes unused. At this time, the FOLL_WRITE bit of the flag has been cleared (at Line 27 of Fig. 2), which means that the aim of __get_user_pages is to read the pages, not to write. However, its aim is actually to *write* in this scenario. The code at Line 27 tries to *cheat* the page-table lookup function follow_page_pte [5]!

Figure 3(d) is the state when the event "}do_read_fault" (Line 44 of Fig. 2) happens. The PTE points to the page frame 66c3, which is a file-backed page. Since the flag has been modified to "read", the next page table lookup at Line 48 would not produce page fault. The file-backed page frame 66c3 would be gotten at Line 50 and be written at Line 51, which means the "read-only" file is modified!

---

[2] "}mmap" means the event "Function mmap() ends".

[3] In different tests, the virtual address may vary, and the addresses of other kernel objects may also be different with those in this paper.

[4] This is page frame number, and the corresponding physical address is 0x66c3000.

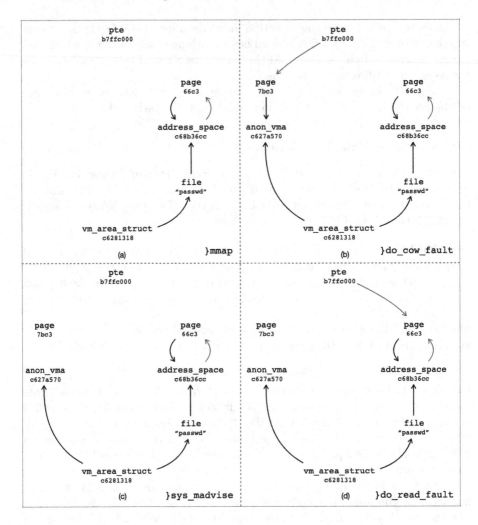

Fig. 3. The state transformation

3.3   Rebuilding of Control Flow Diagram

Each event in the attack path corresponds indeed to a control point in the source code. The CFD between these control points can be built by analyzing the source code and attack path, as shown in Fig. 4.

```
 1 sys_write{  //impl. func of the system call, in kernel mode
 2   mem_rw{   //access file in the 'proc' file system
 3     __get_user_pages{
         while(){
 4           cond_resched{}
 5           follow_page_pte{}        //page table lookup
           if(){
 6             //no page fault detected
             break;
           }
 7           //page fault detected
 8           faultin_page{        //page fault handling
 9             handle_pte_fault{
               if()
10                 do_cow_fault{}
               else if()
11                 do_wp_page{}
               else if()
12                 do_read_fault{}
13             }handle_pte_fault
             if()
14               *flags &= ~FOLL_WRITE;
15           }faultin_page
         }
16     }__get_user_pages
17     //access the pages that are gotten
18   }mem_rw
19 }sys_write
```

Fig. 4. The rebuilt CFD

There are 24 control points in the 19 numbered lines in the figure. In some lines (e.g. cond_resched{}), there are two control points. The flows between the control points are described by some newly-added conditional statements (e.g. the "while" statement in the fourth line). The conditions in the statements are all absent, because they concern some concrete variables, which may be complicated. Therefore, abstracting them would be helpful.

4 Remodeling of Related System Calls

4.1 State Abstraction

Let's take two abstract state variables (pte and flag) as examples.

"pte" represents the PTE for the mapped virtual address. In our VM, it is a 32-bit memory unit. We abstract it to the set {none, file_page, anon_page}. The meaning of each abstract value is:

none The PTE is empty.
file_page The PTE is mapped to a file-backed page.
anon_page The PTE is mapped to an anonymous page.

"flag" represents the local variable foll_flags (type unsigned_int) of the function __get_user_pages. We abstract it to the set {FOLL_WRITE, FOLL_READ}. FOLL_WRITE means that "(foll_flags & 0x01) == 1" is true, and FOLL_READ means that the condition is false.

4.2   The Model Rebuilt

Following the steps below, we can get the model of the system call write and madvise.

1. For each transition edge of the CFG, analyze what action would be taken on the abstract state if that transition happened:
   - The action may be a test of conditions, and in this case we can label the transition edge with a condition on abstract variables.
   - Or, the action may be a modification to the states, and in this case we can label the transition edge with an assignment statement on abstract variables.
2. Turn the CFG labelled with actions to an equivalent abstract program. Specifically, the conditions on edges would become conditions in conditional statements. All events in the CFG of Fig. 4 will be commented out, since they just mean control points, not statements.

The model (abstract program) is described in C language, and includes only abstract variables. The final model is shown in Fig. 5. It can be seen clearly that the read-only file would be modified if the child thread #2 was switched to in the schedule() statement after "cheat" has been set to "true".

5   Related Work

There is much work on the analysis of DirtyCOW. Most of them, e.g. [5,10], are from kernel hackers. They analyze the bug in a concrete level, which involves many OS details. Farah et al. [1] and Saleel et al. [8] analyze the POC source code of the vulnerability statically and do not construct the design model. In the domain of remodeling, many works, e.g. [4], build models in UML, while this paper describes the model in C language with abstract variables. In the domain of program comprehension, we adopt the Pennington bottom-up comprehension model [7], and this work is close to those on design and architecture recovery [6,9] in program comprehension through dynamic analysis [2], but we focus on different aspect of design and use a different form (abstract programs) to describe the design.

```
/* initial state after mmap */
// main{           //beginning of function main()
// }mmap          //end of function mmap()
enum {none, file_page, anon_page} pte = none; //pte of the mmaped page
enum {FOLL_WRITE, FOLL_READ} flag; //follow-flag for page-table lookup
bool vma_writable = false;    //PROT_READ in the parameters of mmap()
bool cheat;  //whether to cheat the page-table lookup function
bool page_fault_detected;  //whether page fault is detected

void sys_write(){
  // mem_rw{
  /* get the page frames to be written */
  // __get_user_pages{
  flag = FOLL_WRITE;       //this is in syscall "write"
  while(true) {
    /* allow other processes to exec */
    // cond_resched(); //gup.c:510
    schedule();
    /* page-table lookup */
    // follow_page_pte{
    if (pte != none && (vma_writable || flag != FOLL_WRITE))
      page_fault_detected = false;
    else
      page_fault_detected = true;
    // }follow_page_pte
    if (!page_fault_detected)
      break;
    /* page fault detected */
    /* page fault handling */
    // faultin_page{
    cheat = false;
    // handle_pte_fault{
    if (pte == none) {
      if (flag == FOLL_READ)
        /* map to the file-backed page frame directly */
        // do_read_fault{
        pte = file_page;
        // }do_read_fault
      else if (flag == FOLL_WRITE)
        /* do COW, and map to the newly-allocated anonymous page frame */
        // do_cow_fault{
        pte = anon_page;
        // }do_cow_fault
    }else {
      // do_wp_page{
      if (pte == file_page)
        /* do COW too */
        pte = anon_page;
      else if (pte == anon_page) //should hold
        /* already mapped to an anonymous page frame, safe to access it,
           so change the flag directly */
        cheat = true;
      // }do_wp_page
    }
    // }handle_pte_fault
    if (cheat)
      // *flags &= ~FOLL_WRITE;  //gup.c:355
      flag = FOLL_READ;  //!!!
    // }faultin_page
  }
  // }__get_user_pages
  /* access the pages that are gotten */
  if (pte == anon_page)
    modify(anon_page); //only mem is modified
  else if (pte == file_page) //should hold
    modify(file_page);  //the file will also be modified!
  // }mem_rw
}
void sys_madvise() {
  pte = none;  //clear the pte
}
```

Fig. 5. The model of related system calls

6 Conclusion

The DirtyCOW vulnerability is analyzed deeply in this paper. The attack path and kernel state transformation are presented in detail. Furthermore, the model of the related system calls is rebuilt based on the analysis and abstraction, which makes the attack principle very clear. The remodeling approach could be used to comprehend and fix the complex bugs in a lot of legacy software. Formal verification on the models would also be meaningful, which is our next research interest.

References

1. Alam, D., Zaman, M., Farah, T., Rahman, R., Hosain, M.S.: Study of the Dirty Copy on write, a Linux kernel memory allocation vulnerability. In: 2017 International Conference on Consumer Electronics and Devices (ICCED), pp. 40–45, July 2017. https://doi.org/10.1109/ICCED.2017.8019988
2. Cornelissen, B., Zaidman, A., Deursen, A.V., Moonen, L., Koschke, R.: A systematic survey of program comprehension through dynamic analysis. IEEE Trans. Softw. Eng. **35**(5), 684–702 (2009)
3. CVE-2016-5195. https://dirtycow.ninja
4. Garde, S., Knaup, P., Herold, R.: Qumquad: a UML-based approach for remodeling of legacy systems in health care. Int. J. Med. Inf. **70**(2–3), 183–194 (2003)
5. Github: Dirty COW and why lying is bad even if you are the linux kernel. https://chao-tic.github.io/blog/2017/05/24/dirty-cow
6. Kai, K., Mössenböck, H.: Scene: using scenario diagrams and active text for illustrating object-oriented programs. In: International Conference on Software Engineering (1996)
7. Mayrhauser, A.V., Vans, A.M.: Program comprehension during software maintenance and evolution. Computer **28**(8), 44–55 (1995)
8. Saleel, A.P., Nazeer, M., Beheshti, B.D.: Linux kernel OS local root exploit. In: 2017 IEEE Long Island Systems, Applications and Technology Conference (LISAT). IEEE (2017)
9. Yan, H., Garlan, D., Schmerl, B.R., Aldrich, J., Kazman, R.: Discotect: a system for discovering architectures from running systems. In: International Conference on Software Engineering (2004)
10. ZDNet: The Dirty Cow Linux bug: a silly name for a serious problem. https://www.zdnet.com/article/the-dirty-cow-linux-security-bug-moos/

A Formal Technique for Concurrent Generation of Software's Functional and Security Requirements in SOFL Specifications

Busalire Emeka$^{(\boxtimes)}$ and Shaoying Liu

Hosei University, Tokyo, Japan
onesmusemeka93@gmail.com, sliu@hosei.ac.jp

Abstract. Formal methods offer a precise and concise way of expressing system requirements which can be tested and validated with formal proofs techniques. However, their application in the development of security aware industrial systems have been associated with high costs due to the difficulty in integrating the functional and security requirements which are generated in an ad hoc manner. Reducing this cost has been a subject of interest in software requirements engineering research. In this paper we propose a formal technique for concurrent generation of functional and security requirements that can help provide a systematic way of accounting for security requirements while specifying the functional requirements of a software. With this technique, the functional behaviors of the system are precisely defined using the Structured Object-Oriented Formal Language (SOFL). The security rules are systematically explored with the results incorporated into the functional specification as constraints. The resultant specification then defines the system functionality that implies the conformance to the security rules. Such a specification can be used as a firm foundation for implementation and testing of the implementation. We discuss the principle of integrating security rules with functional specifications and present a case study to demonstrate the feasibility of our technique.

1 Introduction

The widespread use of software applications in the fields of transport, education, logistics, finance etc. has made the techniques applied to preserve the security of data handled and stored by these applications to be a critical factor during their design phase. However, most software engineering methodologies have a bias of taking the standard approach of analysis, design and implementation of software system without considering security, and then add security as an afterthought [1]. A review of recent research in software security reveal that such approach may lead to a number of security vulnerabilities that are usually identified after system implementation. Fixing such vulnerabilities calls for a "patching" approach since the cost associated with redevelopment of the system at such a point may be too high. However, the "patching" approach is an anti-pattern in the development of high-risk software systems.

© Springer Nature Switzerland AG 2020
H. Miao et al. (Eds.): SOFL+MSVL 2019 Workshop, LNCS 12028, pp. 13–28, 2020.
https://doi.org/10.1007/978-3-030-41418-4_2

To solve the challenge of integrating security attributes into software system requirements, we have developed a requirement engineering methodology that promotes a systematic integration of security requirements into the software design process. Our approach pushes for: (1) Availing to the developer a variety of security methods and their tradeoffs. (2) Providing a systemic methodology for concurrent generation of security requirements and functional requirements in the software design process. This technique advocates for a security aware software development process that combines a selected standard software development methodology, formal methods techniques, and standard security functions [2].

Our proposed technique works by adopting the secure by design [3] software development approach through provision of a formal model for interweaving security and functional requirements. We achieve this by integrating process trees and attack trees [4] security analysis methodologies with a formal design process of functional requirement analysis and specification using Structured Object-Oriented Formal Language (SOFL) [5, 6]. The process tree offers the benefit of a bounded scope, enabling the traversal of all the application's processes from the root node to the forked child processes at the sub-nodes and end-nodes. While traversing through the nodes of the process tree, we conduct an attack tree analysis at each process node to identify potential vulnerabilities and define their mitigation strategies as additional security requirements.

The main contributions of these paper are:

- Provide a formal verifiable model for integrating security and functional software requirements
- Mitigate security threats [7] with proper security mechanisms by formally identifying, defining and expressing potential software vulnerabilities and their related countermeasure strategies.

The rest of the paper has the following organization. Section 2 focuses on related existing research on secure by design security requirement engineering approaches. Section 3 provides the basic concepts of our proposed technique for concurrent generation of functional and security requirements. To demonstrate the feasibility of our proposed approach, we present in Sect. 4, a case study through which we used the technique to generate, analyze and integrate security and functional requirements of an online banking application. Finally, Sect. 5 concludes the paper by sharing our experience of the case study, lessons learnt and the future direction of our research.

2 Related Works

A number of researchers have worked on models targeting the integration of software security attributes at the requirements levels. Epstein et al. [8], proposed a framework for network enterprise utilizing UML notations [9] to describe Role Based Access Control model (RBAC). Shin et al. [10] offered a similar proposal focusing on the representation of access control such as MAC and RBAC using UML. Jurjens [11] proposed an extension of UML, called UMLsec which focusses more on multi-level security of messages in UML sequence and state interaction diagrams. Similarly,

Lodderstedt et al. [12] introduce a new meta-model components and authorization constraints expressed for Role Based Access Control. These attempts leveraged on extending UML to incorporate security concerns into the functionalities provided by the software system.

Logic based approaches [13] have also been proposed for security aware requirement engineering techniques. Mouratidis et al. [14] proposed the Secure Tropos methodology, which is based on the principle that security should be given focus from the early stages of software development process, and not retrofitted late in the design process or pursued in parallel but separately from functional requirements. However, to the best of our knowledge, the existing security requirement engineering approaches address different security concepts and take different viewpoints on matters security. Each modeling approach can express certain aspects but may lack conceptual modeling constructs to interweave security requirements with their associated functional requirements from the early stages of requirements engineering.

This paper seeks to contribute to this gap by presenting and discussing the application of a software engineering methodology, which supports the idea of secure by design approach by analyzing software vulnerabilities and incorporating recommended security considerations at the requirements engineering phase.

3 Our Proposed Methodology

Our methodology for concurrent generation of security and functional requirements works by integrating functional requirements written in SOFL [6] and standard security requirements drawn from the Common Criteria for Information Technology Security Evaluation [15], the AICPA's generally accepted privacy principles and the BITS

Table 1. Sample standard security requirement

Requirement ID: SR-IDEN-010	Category: Security
Subcategory tags	Identification, User ID, Login, Backdoor prevention
Name	Backdoor prevention
Requirement	All interfaces of software that are accessed for performing any action shall have the capacity to recognize the user ID
Use Case(s)	Initial login to the system, batch jobs, API calls, network interface
Rationale	Identification must be applied across all system interfaces. In the event that a "backdoor" exists through which access is granted with no identification, the security of the system shall be compromised
Priority	Critical/**High**/Medium/Low
Constraints	N/A
Comments	The terms "interface" refers to the point of entry into a system. It can be a network interface, user interface, or other system interface as appropriate
Test Case Ref #	STC-IDEN-010-1

Master Security Criteria [16]. We elicit these standard security requirements using SQUARE [17] methodology. SQUARE encompasses nine steps, which generate a final deliverable of categorized and prioritized security requirements. The outcome of the SQUARE methodology is a set of standard security requirements, broadly be classified into: Identification requirements, Authentication requirements, Authorization requirements, Security auditing requirements, Confidentiality requirements, Integrity requirements, Availability requirements, Non-repudiation requirements, Immunity requirements, Survivability requirements, System maintenance security requirements and Privacy requirements. Table 1 below showcases a sample identification requirement for preventing backdoors in authentication systems, elicited using SQUARE methodology.

Our key focus is to provide a framework that can holistically integrate functional and security requirements of a system software, and eventually yield software requirements that satisfy the required security requirements. The principle of integration is a basic conjunction between a functional requirement and its associated security requirement, expressed as follows.

$$S' = F \wedge S$$

Where S' is the defined software requirement, F the functional requirement and S the standard security requirement related to the functional requirement. Figure 1 below highlights a conceptual schema of our proposed technique.

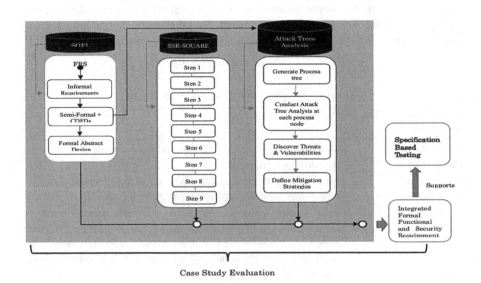

Fig. 1. Conceptual schema of our proposed technique

3.1 The Proposed Technique in Details

Figure 2 below shows a conceptual meta-model of our proposed framework. It illustrates the process through which we achieve concurrent generation standard security requirements and functional requirements specification written in SOFL formal language given by the following steps:

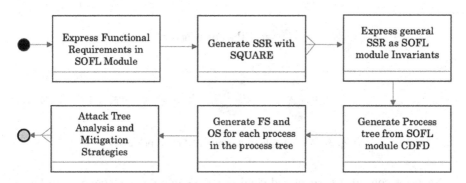

Fig. 2. A conceptual meta-model of our proposed technique

First, we generate the software's functional requirement specification by expressing the requirements as a SOFL module alongside its associated Conditional Dataflow Diagram. Our key goal here is to define and formerly express all the functional behaviors as a complete set of functional requirements. After defining the functional requirements, we generate relevant standard security requirements based on client specifications and application's operating environment. We achieve this by applying the SQUARE methodology. We then express the general standard security requirements as SOFL module invariants thereby achieving the first integration of security and functional requirements.

The next step focusses on generating the application's process tree. A process tree provides a hierarchical organization of parent processes and child processes spawned from the parent process. The generation of the process tree is achieved by converting the top level CDFD process of our SOFL module into a process root and the decomposed CDFD's processes into child processes. The mapping of the decomposed

CDFD to a process tree follows a one to one mapping in the sense that the lowest level CDFDs are mapped as child processes while the intermediate level CDFDs are mapped as parent processes (Fig. 3).

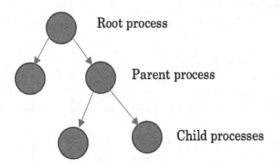

Fig. 3. An example of a parent and child process

Next, we convert the parent and child processes into one or more System Functional Scenario forms. A System Functional Scenario form is a sequence of operations given by:

$$d_i[OP_1, OP_2, \ldots OP_n]d_o$$

Where d_i is a set of input variables of the system behavior, d_o is the set of output variables and each $OP_i (i \in \{1, 2, 3, \ldots n\})$ defines an operation. This System Functional Scenario defines a behavior that transforms the input data item d_i into the output data item d_o through a sequence of operations OP_1, OP_2, ... OP_n. contained in a parent process or a child process at any given node of the process tree.

We then derive Operation Scenarios for the generated System Scenarios. To derive an operation scenario, we transform the pre- and post-condition of an operation into Operational Functional Scenario form consisting of operations such as

$$\left(OP_{pre} \wedge C_1 \wedge D_1\right) \vee \left(OP_{pre} \wedge C_2 \wedge D_2\right) \vee \cdots \left(OP_{pre} \wedge C_n \wedge D_n\right)$$

Where C_i $(i = 1, \ldots n)$ is called a guard condition containing only input variables and D_i $(i = 1, \ldots n)$ is known as **defining condition** containing at least one output variable. Based on the derived Operational Functional Scenario, the final step focusses on eliciting potential vulnerabilities for each of the derived Operational Functional Scenario. We employ attack tree analysis [17] as a technique for identifying the potential vulnerabilities exhibited by each Operational Functional Scenario and further define a mitigation strategy for each of the identified potential vulnerabilities as part of the Operation Function Scenario guard condition C_n or as an invariant of the SOFL module.

These mitigation strategies qualify as additional security requirements that are intertwined with their related functional requirements.

3.2 Adopted Attack Tree Analysis Algorithm

We conduct attack tree analysis through a goal oriented approach where we first identify a primary goal X representing a set of system assets or resources that may be targeted by an attacker i.e. $X = \{X_1, X_2, ..., X_n\}$. Our interest here is to have an attacker's mindset by considering what can make a functional requirement of an application fail when attacked. We then divide the primary goal into sub-goals noting that either all or some of them are required to materialize the primary goal i.e. $S \subseteq X$. We further select a permutation α of S, and based on the sub tree and permutation α, we compute the expected outcome. Our algorithm for the attack tree analysis is illustrated as follows (Fig. 4):

Require : The set elementary attack goal $X = \{ X_1, X_2, ..., X_n \}$ and permutation $\alpha \in Sn$
1: **for** $i := 1$ to n **do**
2:     Consider $X_{\alpha(i)}$
3:     **if** success or failure of $X_{\alpha(i)}$ has no effect in the success or failure of
4:     the root node **then**
5:         Skip $X_{\alpha(i)}$
6:     **else**
7:         Try to perform $X_{\alpha(i)}$
8:         **if** the root node succeeds or fails **then**
9:             Stop
10:        **endif**
11:    **endif**
12: **endfor**

Fig. 4. Attack tree analysis algorithm

4   Case Study

In this section, we demonstrate a case study from which we display a practical scenario of how our methodology achieves the concurrent generation of functional and security requirements. We consider a typical online banking web application where a customer can perform several financial transactions including but not limited to viewing of account balance, accessing a history of past transactions, transfer money between authorized accounts, and pay utility bills. To preserve the integrity of the web application, several standard security requirements such as authentication, identification, authorization etc. need to be incorporated into the system. Figures 5, 6 and 7 showcases the top level and decomposed CDFDs of the online banking application.

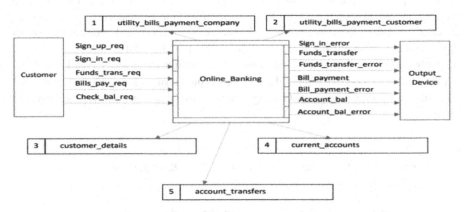

Fig. 5. Top level CDFD – online banking application

From the decomposed CDFD. We can generate a process tree similar to one displayed below.

The transformation from decomposed CDFD to a process tree follows a one-to-one mapping in the sense that, if the CDFD is decomposed further into more sub-processes for a given process, then the node depicting that process shall yield additional sub-processes as its children. For the sake of brevity and clarity, we shall only highlight how we interweaved a standard authentication requirement for the *SignUp* processes whose SOFL formal specifications can be expressed as shown below.

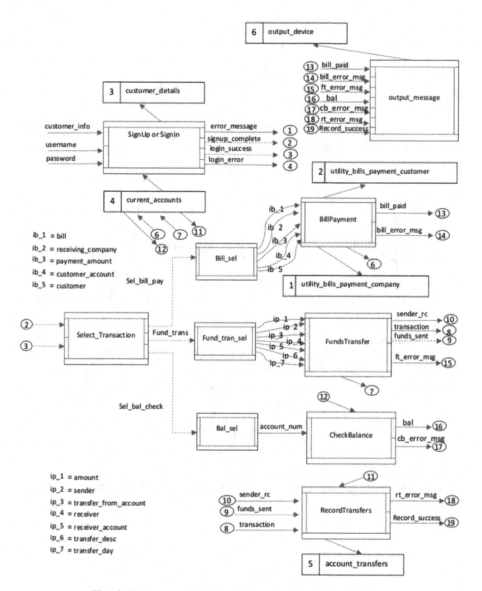

Fig. 6. Decomposed CDFD of the online banking application

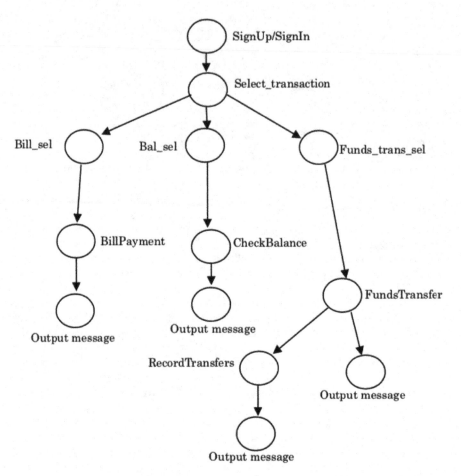

Fig. 7. The online banking application process tree generated from decomposed CDFD

```
/* Online banking Formal Abstract Design Specifications */
module SYSTEM_ONLINEBANKING;
const
/*Omitted for the sake of brevity */
type
CustomerProfile = composed of
                    full_name: CustomerName
                    email_address: string
                    national_id_num: string
                     password: string username: string
                    end;
CustomerName = string; /* customer full name */
 .

 .
 .

CurrentAccount = composed of
                    account_name: CustomerName account_number: nat0
                    account_balance: nat0 /* The unit is USD */ account_created: Date
                    bank_name: string
                    bank_branch: string
                    transaction_history: seq AccountTransactions current_accounts_status: bool /* True for Active, False
                    for Disabled */
                    end;
CurrentAccountFile = map CustomerProfile to CurrentAccount;

Date = Day * Month * Year; Day = nat0;
Month = nat0;
Year = nat0;
var

ext #customer_details: set of CustomerProfile
ext #current_accounts: set of CurrentAccountFile;

inv

forall[x: CurrentAccount ] | not exists [y: CurrentAccount ] | x.account_number = y.account_number;
/* Each customer account is unique */
forall[ x: CustomerProfile ] | not exists [y: CustomerProfile ] |
x.email_address = y.email_address => x.national_id_num < > y.national_id_num
/* Each customer has a unique email address and national ID number and each customer profile is unique */

process SignUp(customer_info: CustomerProfile) signup_complete:string | error_message: string

ext wr customer_details
pre customer_info notin customer_details and not exists[x:CustomerProfile] | x.email_address =
        get(customer_details).email_address and x.national_id_num = get(customer_details).national_id_num
        Comment
        Each customer profile is unique and each customer profile has a unique email address and national identification
        number

post if bound(signup_complete)
            then customer_details = union(~customer_details, {customer_info})
            and signup_complete = "Signup Successful"
            else error_message = "Either the provided email or National ID number already exists in customer
            records"
end_process;
```

SOFL Formal Abstract Specification for the SignUp process of an online banking application

The above SOFL specifications represent the functional behavior exhibited by our online banking application during a user sign up process. The process takes an object of customer profile information *{full_name, username, password, national_id_num, email_address}* and creates a new record of the customer if and only if the supplied customer information does not already exist in the external *#customer_details* database file where all the records of customer's profile are stored. Otherwise, it returns an error message indicating an existence of a similar record. For the login process, a user supplies a set of username and password, which are matched with those stored in the system's database.

4.1 Converting the SignUp Process into Its Equivalent System Functional Scenario Form

Given a set of customer information *{full_name, username, password, national _id_num, email_address}* as inputs, a *SignUp* process and an *error_message* as output we can generate a System Functional Scenario Form;

    {full_name,username,password,national_id_num,email_address}   *[SignUp,...]*
{error_message}

Other data items are used or produced within the process of executing the entire system scenario, but we have intentionally left them out. The next step involves deriving Operation Scenarios from our generated System Functional Scenario(s).

4.2 Deriving Operational Scenarios

To derive Operation Scenario(s), we take a Functional Scenario Process i.e. SignUp and express it in the form of a chain of logical disjunction of a set of its individual conjunctive elements made up of a precondition, a guard condition containing only the input variables, and a defining condition containing at least one output variable i.e.

*($\exists_x \in$ current_accounts | x **not inset** current_accounts $\wedge$ (dom(x).full_name = full_name $\wedge$ dom(x).username = username $\wedge$ dom(x).password = password $\wedge$ dom(x).national_id_num = national_id_num $\wedge$ dom(x).email_address = email_address) $\wedge$ signup_complete = "Signup Successful")*
OR
*($\exists_x \in$ current_accounts | x **inset** current_accounts $\wedge$ (dom(x).full_name = full_name $\wedge$ dom(x).username = username $\wedge$ dom(x).password = password $\wedge$ dom(x).national_id_num = national_id_num $\wedge$ dom(x).email_address = email_address) $\wedge$ error_message = "Similar Records exist in the database already")*

    This formalized *SignUp* expression checks for the existence of similar user records before signing up a new user with the same set of record inputs. Otherwise, it returns an error message depicting the existence of a similar record with the provided set of inputs.

4.3 Eliciting Potential Vulnerabilities for Each of the Derived Operational Scenarios

Eliciting potential vulnerabilities that may be associated with our derived Operational Scenarios, involves conducting an attack tree analysis on a behavior depicted by the SignUp process node in our process tree. To figure this out, we identify a goal or resource that is part of our derived Operational Scenario and may be a subject of an attack as well as consider a standard security requirement for the same.

The functional behavior depicted by the SignUp process, involves getting a set of inputs including a username and a password and storing them in a database file to be utilized by the *SignIn* process. A typical attack tree analysis on the *SignUP* process aimed at obtaining the stored username and password or identities of their equivalent yields 4 different paths i.e. direct access to the database, brute force login, threatening the user or shoulder surfing. Whereas paths such as threatening the user or shoulder surfing can be mitigated through management controls, gaining direct access to database and brute force login may not be effectively mitigated through management controls (Fig. 8).

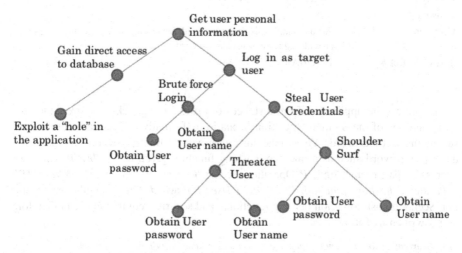

Fig. 8. Attack tree analysis showcasing paths that can be manipulated to obtain customer's personal information

To eliminate brute force login attack path, we need to interweave an authentication requirement with the functional requirements responsible for user credentials creation and storage. An authentication requirement is any security requirement that specifies the extent to which a business, application, component, or center shall verify the identity of its externals before interacting with them. Table 1 below describes a standard authentication requirement for credentials security [18] (Table 2).

Table 2. Credential security

Requirement ID: SR-OBA-001	Category: Security
Subcategory tags	Authentication, Credentials, Password, Hashing
Name	Credential security
Requirement	The system shall store the information used for authentication in a secure manner using public and widely accepted crypto algorithms
Use Case(s)	Password storage
Rationale	Authenticating information must be stored in such a way so that a third party without authorization to do so cannot easily obtain it. For example, static passwords should be passed through a one hash function and only the hash should be stores
Priority	Critical/**High**/Medium/Low
Constraints	N/A
Comments	Per-user salting is recommended for storing password hashing to provide additional level of security
Test Case Ref #	TC-OBA-001

To protect the application from instances of brute force attacks, we strengthen the post condition of the SignUp Operation Scenario by formally defining a secure way of storing the user password. We achieve this by formally defining a secure way of storing the user password such as a one way hashing function given by $f(r, h(P'))$ which we express as part of the *SignUP* Operation Scenario where, $r = random\ number$, $h(P')$ = *Password hashing function*, P' = *Stored User Password*. Our strengthened Operation Scenario post-condition bearing functional and security requirements can therefore be re- written as follows:

($\exists_x \in current_accounts \mid x\ not\ inset\ current_accounts \wedge (dom(x).full_name = full_name \wedge dom(x).username = username \wedge dom(x).password = password \wedge dom(x).national_id_num = national_id_num \wedge dom(x).email_address = email_address) \wedge signup_complete = "Signup Successful") \wedge dom(x).password = f(r, h(\sim dom(x).password))))

OR

($\exists_x \in current_accounts \mid x\ inset\ current_accounts \wedge (dom(x).full_name = full_name \wedge dom(x).username = username \wedge dom(x).password = password \wedge dom(x).national_id_num = national_id_num \wedge dom(x).email_address = email_address) \wedge error_message = "Similar Records exist in the database already")

5   Discussions and Conclusions

Our experience with the proposed framework can be summarized as follows: The methodology requires some software security expertise in addition to requirement engineering skills since it focusses towards achieving the integration of security analysis into the software requirement engineering process. Moreover, knowledge and skills of applying SOFL specification language in writing software requirements is a prerequisite. Even though our proposed methodology cannot guarantee the development of a completely secure system, we are confident that the application of our methodology can assist in the development of a system that is more secure compared to a system whose SRE process were done in an ad hoc manner.

This paper presents our experiences from the application of a methodology that encourage concurrent generation of functional and security requirements. We document our experience by applying the methodology in the development of an online banking application. Our findings indicate that the use of our approach supported the development of a software system that meets its security requirements and offers an early focus on security. Our experience on the other hand also indicated some issues for consideration, such as potential complexity of using formal notations in generating readable security requirements as well development of a supporting tool for the methodology. Resolving these issues is our main concern for future works.

References

1. Mouratidis, H., Giorgini, P.: Integrating Security and Software Engineering: Advances and Future Visions. Idea Group, Hershey (2006). https://doi.org/10.4018/978-1-59904-147-6
2. Khan, K.M.: Developing and Evaluating Security-Aware Systems, pp. 14–24. IGI Global, Hershey (2012) ISBN 1-59904-149-9
3. Mouratidis, H.: Integrating Security and Software Engineering: Advances and Future Visions, pp. 14–24. IGI Publishing, Hershey (2007) ISBN 1-59904-149-9
4. Nagaraju, V., Fiondella, L., Wandji, T.: A survey of fault and attack tree modeling and analysis for cyber risk management, pp. 1–6 (2017)
5. Nagoya, F., Liu, S., Hamada, K.: Developing a web dictionary system using the SOFL three-step specification approach. In: 2015 5th International Conference on IT Convergence and Security (ICITCS), pp. 1–5 (2015)
6. Liu, S.: Formal Engineering for Industrial Software Development Using SOFL Method. Springer, Heidelberg (2004). https://doi.org/10.1007/978-3-662-07287-5. ISBN 3-540-20602-7
7. Huang, H.C., Zhang, Z.K., Cheng, H.W.: Web application security: threats, countermeasures, and pitfalls. Computer **50**, 81–85 (2017)
8. Epstein, P., Sandhu, R.: Towards a UML based approach to role engineering. In: Proceedings of the 4th ACM Workshop on Role-Based Access Control, pp. 75–85 (1999)
9. Huget, M.P.: Agent UML notation for multiagent system design. IEEE Internet Comput. **8**, 63–71 (2004)
10. Shin, M, Ahn, G.: UML-based representation of role-based access control. In: 9th International Workshop on Enabling Technologies: Infrastructure for Collaborative Enterprises, pp. 195–200 (2000)
11. Kammüller, F., Augusto, J.C., Jones, S.: Security and privacy requirements engineering for human centric IoT systems using eFRIEND and Isabelle. In: 2017 IEEE 15th International Conference on Software Engineering Research, Management and Applications (SERA) (2017)

12. Lodderstedt, T., Basin, D., Doser, J.: SecureUML: a UML-based modeling language for model-driven security. In: Jézéquel, J.-M., Hussmann, H., Cook, S. (eds.) UML 2002. LNCS, vol. 2460, pp. 426–441. Springer, Heidelberg (2002). https://doi.org/10.1007/3-540-45800-X_33
13. Amini, M., Jalili, R.: Multi-level authorisation model and framework for distributed semantic-aware environments. IET Inf. Secur. **4**, 301–321 (2010)
14. Ouedraogo, M., Mouratidis, H., Khadraoui, D., Dubois, E.: An agent-based system to support assurance of security requirements. In: 2010 Fourth International Conference on Secure Software Integration and Reliability Improvement, pp. 78–87 (2010)
15. Common Criteria Part 2: Security Functional Requirements. The Common Criteria Portal. https://www.commoncriteriaportal.org/cc/. Accessed 28 July 2019
16. Security Criteria : BITS/Financial Services Roundtable. http://www.bitsinfo.org/security-criteria/. Accessed 28 July 2019
17. Kumar, R., Stoelinga, M.: Quantitative security and safety analysis with attack-fault trees. In: 2017 IEEE 18th International Symposium on High Assurance Systems Engineering (HASE), pp. 25–32 (2017)
18. Merkow, M.S., Raghavan, L.: Secure and Resilient Software, Requirements, Test cases and Testing Methods, p. 71. Auerbach Publications, Boston (2011)

Distortion and Faults in Machine Learning Software

Shin Nakajima[✉]

National Institute of Informatics, Tokyo, Japan
nkjm@nii.ac.jp

Abstract. Machine learning software, deep neural networks (DNN) software in particular, discerns valuable information from a large dataset, a set of data, so as to synthesize approximate input-output relations. The outcomes of such DNN programs are dependent on the quality of both learning programs and datasets. However, the quality assurance of DNN software is difficult. The trained machine learning models, defining the functional behavior of the approximate relations, are unknown prior to its development, and the validation is conducted indirectly in terms of the prediction performance. This paper introduces a hypothesis that faults in DNN programs manifest themselves as distortions in trained machine learning models. Relative distortion degrees measured with appropriate observer functions may indicate that the programs have some hidden faults. The proposal is demonstrated with the cases of the MNIST dataset.

1 Introduction

Machine learning software, deep neural networks (DNN) software [3], is based on statistical inductive methods to discern valuable information from a given vast amount of data so as to synthesize approximate input-output relations. The quality of DNN software is usually viewed from the predication performance that the obtained approximate relations, or inference programs, exhibit for incoming data.

The quality assurance of DNN software is, however, difficult [8]. The functional behavior of the inference programs is defined by the trained machine learning models, which DNN learning programs calculate with the training datasets as their inputs. The quality of DNN software is dependent on both the learning programs and training datasets; either or both is a source of the degraded quality. The learning programs, if not implemented faithfully in view of well-designed machine learning algorithms, result in inappropriate trained machine learning models. Moreover, inappropriate datasets, suffering from sample selection bias [12] for example, have negative impacts on the trained machine learning models.

The learning programs and datasets are potential root causes to affect the quality of inference programs, but their effects are more or less indirect. Although trained machine learning models have direct impacts on the overall quality,

© Springer Nature Switzerland AG 2020
H. Miao et al. (Eds.): SOFL+MSVL 2019 Workshop, LNCS 12028, pp. 29–41, 2020.
https://doi.org/10.1007/978-3-030-41418-4_3

research works on the machine learning quality have not considered the trained models as *first-class citizens* to study. In those works, the trained models are regarded as an *intermediate* collection of numeric data, that are synthesized by the learning programs, and then are embedded in the inference programs to provide their functional behavior.

This paper adapts a hypothesis that *distortions* in the trained machine learning models manifest themselves as faults resulting in the quality degradation. Although such distortion is difficult to be measured directly as they are, relative distortion degrees can be defined. Moreover, this paper proposes a new way of generating datasets that show characteristics of the dataset diversity [9], which is supposed to be effective in testing machine learning software from various ways [10]. As far as we know, this work is the first proposal to consider the trained machine learning models as *first-class citizens* to study the quality issues of DNN software.

2   Machine Learning Software

2.1   Learning Programs

We consider supervised machine learning classifiers using networks of perceptrons [4] or deep neural networks [3]. Our goal is to synthesize, inductively from a large dataset, an input-output relation approximately classifying a multidimensional vector data $\boldsymbol{a}$ into one of C categories. The given dataset LS is a set of N number of pairs, $\langle \boldsymbol{x}^n, t^n \rangle$ $(n = 1, \cdots, N)$, where a supervisor tag t^n takes a value of c $(c \in [1, \cdots, C])$. A pair $\langle \boldsymbol{x}^n, t^n \rangle$ in LS indicates that the classification result of $\boldsymbol{x}^n$ is known to be t^n.

Given a learning model $y(W; \boldsymbol{x})$ as a multi-dimensional non-linear function, differentiable with respect to both learning parameters W and input data $\boldsymbol{x}$. Learning aims at obtaining a set of learning parameter values (W^*) by solving a numerical optimization problem.

$$W^* = \underset{W}{argmin}\, \mathcal{E}(W; X), \quad \mathcal{E}(W; X) = \frac{1}{N} \sum_{n=1}^{N} \ell(y(W;\ \boldsymbol{x}^n),\ \boldsymbol{t}^n)$$

The function $\ell(\_, \_)$ denotes distances between its two parameters, representing how much a calculated output $y(W; \boldsymbol{x}^n)$ differs from its accompanying supervisor tag value $\boldsymbol{t}^n$.

We denote a function to calculate W^* as $\mathcal{L}_f(LS)$, which is called a learning program to solve the above optimization problem with its input dataset LS. Moreover, we denote the empirical distribution of LS as ρ_{em}. W^* is a collection of learning parameter values to minimize the mean of ℓ under ρ_{em}.

From viewpoints of the software quality, $\mathcal{L}_f(LS)$, a learning program, is concerned with the product quality, because it must be a faithful implementation of some well-designed machine learning algorithm, the supervised machine learning method for this case.

2.2   Inference Programs

We introduce another function $\mathcal{I}_f(\boldsymbol{x})$, using a set of trained learning parameters W^* or a trained machine learning model $y(W^*; \boldsymbol{x})$, to calculate inference results of an incoming data $\boldsymbol{x}$.

For classification problems, the inference results are often expressed as probability that a data $\boldsymbol{a}$ belongs to a category c. $Prob(W, \boldsymbol{a}; c)$, a function of c, is probability such that the data $\boldsymbol{a}$ is classified as c. This $Prob$ is readily implemented in $\mathcal{I}_f(x)$ if we choose *Softmax* as an activation function of the output layer of the machine learning model.

The prediction performance of $\mathcal{I}_f(\boldsymbol{x})$ is, indeed, defined compactly as the accuracy of classification results for a dataset TS that is different from LS used to calculate W^*; $TS = \{\langle \boldsymbol{x}^m, \boldsymbol{t}^m \rangle\}$. For a specified W, $Correct$ is a set-valued function to obtain a subset of data vectors in TS.

$$Correct(W; TS) \equiv \{\ \boldsymbol{x}^m \mid c^* = \underset{c \in [1, ..., C]}{argmax}\ Prob(W, \boldsymbol{x}^m; c) \wedge \boldsymbol{t}^m = c^*\ \}$$

If we express $\mid S \mid$ as a size of a set S, then an accuracy is defined as a ratio as below.

$$Accuracy(W; TS) = \frac{\mid Correct(W; TS) \mid}{\mid TS \mid}$$

Given a W^* obtained by $\mathcal{L}_f(LS)$, the predication performance of $\mathcal{I}_f(LS)$ is defined in terms of $Accuracy(W^*; TS)$ for a dataset TS different from LS. For an individual incoming data $\boldsymbol{a}$, a function of c, $Prob(W^*, \boldsymbol{a}; c)$, is a good performance measure.

2.3   Quality Issues

Loss and Accuracy. An NN learning problem is non-convex optimization, and thus reaching a globally optimal solution is not guaranteed (e.g. [4]). The learning

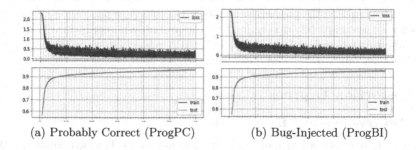

(a) Probably Correct (ProgPC)   (b) Bug-Injected (ProgBI)

Fig. 1. Loss and accuracy: MNIST dataset

program $\mathcal{L}_f(LS)$ is iterated over epochs to search for solutions and is taken as converged when the value of the loss ($\mathcal{E}(W; LS)$) is not changed much between two consecutive epochs. The learning parameter values at this converged epoch are taken as W^*. The derived W^* may not be optimal, and thus an accuracy is calculated to ensure that the obtained W^* is appropriate.

In some undesirable cases, W^* may be over-fitted to the training dataset LS. In the course of the iteration, at an epoch e, the learning parameter values $W^{(e)}$ are extracted. The iteration is continued until the accuracy becomes satisfactory. Both $Accuracy(W^{(e)}, LS)$ and $Accuracy(W^{(e)}, TS)$ are monitored to ensure the training process goes as desired. If the accuracy of TS is not much different from the accuracy with LS, we may think that the learning result does not have the over-fitting problem.

Figure 1 shows loss and accuracy graphs as epochs proceed measured during experiments[1]. The graphs, for example in Fig. 1(a), actually demonstrate that the search converges at a certain desirable point in the solution space because the loss decreases to be almost stable below a certain threshold, and the accuracies of both TS and LS reach a satisfactory level of higher than 0.95. Figure 1 shows that the loss together with the accuracy may be good indicators to decide whether NN training processes behave well or not.

Sources of Faults. Intuitively, NN machine learning software shows good quality if the prediction performance of $\mathcal{I}_f$ is acceptable. The graphs in Fig. 1, however, depict that there is a counterexample case as discussed in [9], in which the learning task uses the MNIST dataset, for classifying hand-written numbers.

Figure 1(a) are graphs of the loss and accuracy of a probably correct implementation of NN learning program, while Fig. 1(b) are those of a bug-injected program. The two graphs for the loss are mostly the same to be converged. The two accuracy graphs are similar as well, although the learning program of Fig. 1(b) has faults in it.

The MNIST dataset is a standard benchmark and is supposed to be well-prepared, free from any sample selection bias. A bug-injected program $\mathcal{L}_f$ accepts a training dataset LS of MNIST and calculates a set of trained learning parameters W^*. Intuitively, this W^* is inappropriate, because it is a result of the bug-injected program. However, the two accuracy graphs show that there is no clear sign of faults in the prediction results of the inference program $\mathcal{I}_f$, although its behavior is completely determined by the probably inappropriate W^*.

A question arises how faults in $\mathcal{L}_f$ affect W^*, which follows another question whether such *faults* in W^* are observable.

3   Distortion Degrees

3.1   Observations and Hypotheses

Firstly, we introduce a few new concepts and notations. For two datasets DS_1 and DS_2, a relation $DS_1 \preceq DS_2$ denotes that DS_2 is more distorted than DS_1.

---

[1] We return to the experiment later in Sect. 4.

For two sets of trained learning parameters W_1^* and W_2^* of the same machine learning model $y(W; \_)$, a relation $W_1^* \preceq W_2^*$ denotes that W_2^* is more distorted than W_1^*.

A question here is how to measure such degrees of the distortion. We assume a certain observer function obs and a relation $\mathcal{R}_{obj}$ with a certain small threshold ϵ_{obs} such that $\mathcal{R}_{obj} = (|obs(W_1^*) - obs(W_2^*)| \leq \epsilon_{obs})$. The distortion relation is defined in terms of $\mathcal{R}_{obj}$, $W_1^* \preceq W_2^* \Leftrightarrow \neg \mathcal{R}_{obj}(W_1^*, W_2^*)$. We introduce below three hypotheses referring to these notions.

[Hyp-1]   Given a training dataset LS, a machine learning program $\mathcal{L}_f(LS)$, either correct or faulty, derives its optimal, or near-optimal, solution W^*. For the training dataset LS and a testing dataset TS, if both are appropriately sampled or both follows the same empirical distribution, then $Accuracy(W^*, TS)$ is almost the same as $Accuracy(W^*, LS)$.

[Hyp-2] For a training program $\mathcal{L}_f$ and two training datasets LS_j ($j = 1$ or 2), if $W_j^* = \mathcal{L}_f(LS_j)$, then $LS_1 \preceq LS_2 \Rightarrow W_1^* \preceq W_2^*$.

[Hyp-3] For two training datasets LS_j ($j = 1$ or 2) such that $LS_1 \preceq LS_2$ and a certain appropriate obs, if $\mathcal{L}_f$ is correct with respect to its functional specifications, then two results, $W_j^* = \mathcal{L}_f(LS_j)$, are almost the same, written as $W_1^* \approx W_2^*$ (or $obs(W_1^*) \approx obs(W_2^*)$). However, if $\mathcal{L}_f'$ is a faulty implementation, then $W_1'^* \prec W_2'^*$.

The accuracy graphs in Fig. 1 show an instance of [Hyp-1]. In Fig. 1(a), the accuracy graphs for TS and LS are mostly overlapped, and the same is true for the case of Fig. 1(b). It illustrates that the accuracy is satisfactory even if the learning program is buggy.

Moreover, the example in [9] is an instance of the [Hyp-2] because of the followings. A training dataset $LS^{(K+1)}$ is obtained by adding a kind of disturbance signal to $LS^{(K)}$ so that $LS^{(K)} \preceq LS^{(K+1)}$. With an appropriate observer function obs_d, $\mathcal{R}_{obs_d}(W^{(K)*}, W^{(K+1)*})$ is falsified where $W^{(J)*} = \mathcal{L}_f(L^{(J)})$, and thus $W^{(K)*} \preceq W^{(K+1)*}$ is true.

3.2 Generating Distorted Dataset

We propose a new test data generation method. We first explain the L-BFGS [14], which illustrates a simple way to calculate adversarial examples.

Given a dataset LS of $\{\langle x^n, t^n \rangle\}$, $W^* = \mathcal{L}_f(LS)$. An adversarial example is a solution of an optimization problem;

$$x^A = \underset{x}{argmin}\, A_\lambda(W^*; x_S, t_T, x),$$

$$A_\lambda(W^*; x_S, t_T, x) = \ell(y(W^*; x), t_T) + \lambda \cdot \ell(x, x_S).$$

Such a data x^A is visually close to a seed x_S for human eyes, but is actually added a faint noise so as to induce miss-inference such that $y(W^*; x^A) = t_T$ for $t_T \neq t_S$ where $y(W^*; x_S) = t_S$.

Consider an optimization problem, in which a seed x_S is x^n and its target label t_T is t^n.

$$x^{n*} = \underset{x}{argmin}\ A_\lambda(W^*; x^n, t^n, x).$$

The method is equivalent to constructing a new data x^{n*} to be added small noises. Because the inferred label is not changed, x^{n*} is not adversarial, but is *distorted* from the seed x^n. When the value of the hyper-parameter λ is chosen to be very small, the distortion of x^{n*} is large from x^n. On the other hand, if λ is appropriate, the effects of the noises on x^{n*} can be small so that the data is close to the original x^n.

By applying the method to all the elements in LS, a new dataset is obtained to be $\{\langle x^{n*},\ t^n \rangle\}$. We introduce a function T_A to generate such a dataset from LS and W^*.

$$T_A(\{\langle x^n, t^n \rangle\}, W^*) = \{\ \langle \underset{x}{argmin}\ A_\lambda(W^*; x^n, t^n, x),\ t^n \rangle\ \}.$$

Now, $LS^{(K+1)} = T_A(LS^{(K)}, \mathcal{L}_f(LS^{(K)}))$ (for $K \geq 0$ and $LS^{(0)} = LS$).

Note that the noises or perturbations introduced with the above mentioned method may affect the inference results in certain ways; the miss-inferences for the adversarial cases and the inferences as expected for the distorted cases. We collectively call such perturbations as *semantic* noises as compared with *white* noises generated randomly.

3.3 Some Properties

This section presents some properties that generated datasets $LS^{(K)}$ satisfy; $LS^{(K)} = T_A(LS^{(K-1)}, \mathcal{L}_f(LS^{(K-1)}))$ where $LS^{(0)}$ is equal to a given training dataset LS.

[Prop-1] $LS^{(K)}$ serves the same machine learning task as LS does.

We have that $W^{(0)*} = \mathcal{L}_f(LS)$. As the optimization problem (Sect. 3.2) with $W^{(0)*}$ indicates, $x^{(n)*}$, an element of $LS^{(1)}$ does not deviate much from $x^{(n)}$ in LS, and is almost the same as $x^{(n)}$ in special cases. Therefore, $LS^{(1)}$ serves as the same machine learning task as LS does. Similarly, $LS^{(K)}$ serves as the same machine learning task as $LS^{(K-1)}$ does. By induction, $LS^{(K)}$ serves as the same machine learning task as LS does, although the deviation of $LS^{(K)}$ from LS may be large. □

[Prop-2] $LS^{(K)} \preceq LS^{(K+1)}$

The distortion relation is satisfied by construction using T_A if we take $LS^{(K)}$ as a starting criterion. □

[Prop-3] $LS^{(K)}$ is more over-fitted to $W^{(K-1)*}$ than $LS^{(K-1)}$ is.

In the optimization problem, if the loss $\ell(y(W^{(K-1)*}; x^*), t_T)$ is small, x^* in $LS^{(K)}$ can be considered to be well-fitted to $W^{(K-1)*}$ because the data x^* reconstruct the supervisor tag t_T well. We make the loss to be so small as above by choosing carefully an appropriate λ value. □

[Prop-4] There exists a certain K_c such that, for all K to satisfy a relation $K \geq K_c$, $Accuracy(W^{(K)*}, TS) \approx Accuracy(W^{(K_c)*}, TS)$ and $Accuracy(W^{(0)*}, TS) \geq Accuracy(W^{(K_c)*}, TS)$. TS is a dataset different from LS, but follows the same empirical distribution ρ_{em}.

From Prop-3, we can see $LS^{(K)}$ is over-fitted to $W^{(K_c)*}$ if $K = K_c + 1$. Because $W^{(K)*} = \mathcal{L}_f(LS^{(K)})$ and both LS and TS follow the empirical distribution ρ_{em}, we have $Accuracy(W^{(K)*}, TS) \approx Accuracy(W^{(K_c)*}, TS)$. Furthermore, $LS \preceq LS^{(K_c)}$ implies $Accuracy(W^{(0)*}, LS) \geq Accuracy(W^{(K_c)*}, LS)$ and thus $Accuracy(W^{(0)*}, TS) \geq Accuracy(W^{(K_c)*}, TS)$. □

[Prop-5] The dataset and trained machine learning model reach respectively LS^∞ and $W^{(\infty)*}$ if we repeatedly conduct the training $\mathcal{L}_f$ and the dataset generation T_A in an interleaving manner.

If we choose a K to be sufficiently larger than K_c, we have, from Prop-4, $Accuracy(W^{(K)*}, LS^{(K)}) \approx Accuracy(W^{(K_c)*}, LS^{(K)})$, which may imply that $Accuracy(W^{(K)*}, LS^{(K)}) \approx Accuracy(W^{(K+1)*}, LS^{(K+1)})$. From Prop-3, $LS^{(K+1)}$ is over-fitted to $W^{(K)*}$, and thus we have $LS^{(K)} \approx LS^{(K+1)}$, which implies that we can choose a representative $LS^{(\infty)}$ from them. Using this dataset, we have that $W^{(\infty)*} = \mathcal{L}_f(LS^{(\infty)})$, and that $W^{(\infty)*}$ is a representative. □

4   A Case Study

4.1   MNIST Classification Problem

MNIST dataset is a standard problem of classifying handwritten numbers [6]. It consists of a training dataset LS of 60,000 vectors, and a testing dataset TS of 10,000. Both LS and TS are randomly selected from a pool of vectors, and thus are considered to follow the same empirical distribution. The machine learning task is to classify an input sheet, or a vector data, into one of ten categories from 0 to 9. A sheet is presented as 28×28 pixels, each taking a value between 0 and 255 to represent gray scales. Aggregates of the pixel values represent handwritten strokes, and a number appears as a specific pattern of these pixel values.

In the experiments, the learning model is a classical neural network with a hidden layer and an output layer. Activation function for neurons in the hidden layer is *ReLU*; its output is linear for positive input values and a constant zero for negatives. A *softmax* activation function is introduced so that the

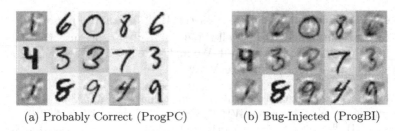

(a) Probably Correct (ProgPC)   (b) Bug-Injected (ProgBI)

Fig. 2. Distorted data

inference program $\mathcal{I}_f$ returns probability that an incoming data belongs to the ten categories.

4.2 Experiments

We prepared two learning programs $\mathcal{L}_f^{PC}$ and $\mathcal{L}_f^{BI}$. The former is a probably correct implementation of a learning algorithm, and the latter is a bug-injected version of the former. We conducted two experiments in parallel, one using $\mathcal{L}_f^{PC}$ and the other with $\mathcal{L}_f^{BI}$, and made comparisons. Below, we use notations such as $\mathcal{L}_f^{MD}$ where MD is either PC or BI.

Training with MNIST Dataset. We conducted trainings with the MNIST training dataset $LS^{(0)}$; $W_{MD}^{(0)*} = \mathcal{L}_f^{MD}(LS^{(0)})$. Figure 1 in Sect. 2.3 illustrates several graphs to show their behavior, that are obtained in the training processes. The two accuracy graphs in Fig. 1 show that $Accuracy(W_{MD}^{(0)*}, LS)$ and $Accuracy(W_{MD}^{(0)*}, TS)$ are mostly the same. In addition, $Accuracy(W_{PC}^{(0)*}, \_)$ and $Accuracy(W_{BI}^{(0)*}, \_)$ are indistinguishable. The above observation is consistent with [**Hyp-1**].

Generating Distorted Datasets. We generated distorted datasets with the method described in Sect. 3.2. We introduce here short-hand notations such as $LS_{MD}^{(K)}$; $LS_{MD}^{(1)} = T_A(LS^{(0)}, \mathcal{L}_f^{MD}(LS^{(0)}))$.

Figure 2 shows a fragment of $LS_{MD}^{(1)}$. We recognize that all the data are not so clear as those of the original MNIST dataset and thus are considered distorted. We may consider them as $LS \preceq LS_{MD}^{(1)}$, which is an instance of [**Prop-2**]. Furthermore, for human eyes, Fig. 2(b) for the case with $\mathcal{L}_f^{BI}$ is more distorted than Fig. 2(a) of $\mathcal{L}_f^{PC}$, which may be described as $LS_{PC}^{(1)} \preceq LS_{BI}^{(1)}$.

Training with Distorted Datasets. We then conducted trainings with the distorted dataset $LS_{MD}^{(1)}$; $W_{MD}^{(1)*} = \mathcal{L}_f^{MD}(LS_{MD}^{(1)})$. Figure 3 shows loss and

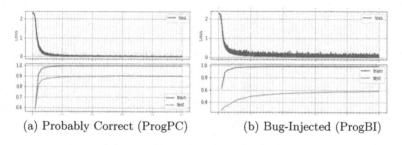

(a) Probably Correct (ProgPC)   (b) Bug-Injected (ProgBI)

Fig. 3. Loss and accuracy: distorted training dataset

accuracy graphs in their learning processes. Comparing Fig. 3 with Fig. 1 leads to the following observations.

Firstly, the overall loss values of Fig. 3 are smaller than those of Fig. 1 counterparts. The metrics concerning with the differences $(\ell(\_,\_))$ are small for the distorted dataset cases.

Secondly, for the MNIST testing dataset TS, $Accuracy(W_{MD}^{(1)*}, TS)$ is lower than $Accuracy(W_{MD}^{(0)*}, TS)$, while $Accuracy(W_{MD}^{(1)*}, LS_{MD}^{(1)})$ reaches close to 100%. Together with the fact of $LS \preceq LS_{MD}^{(1)}$, the above implies $W_{MD}^{(0)*} \preceq W_{MD}^{(1)*}$, which is consistent with [**Hyp-2**].

Thirdly, we consider how much the accuracies differ. We define the relation $\mathcal{R}_{obs}$ where $obs(W^*) = Accuracy(W^*, TS)$. Let $\mathcal{R}_{obs}^{MD}$ be defined in terms of $Accuracy(W_{MD}^{(0)*}, TS)$ with a certain ϵ_{MD}. Comparing the graphs in Figs. 1(a) and 3(a), we observe, for $\mathcal{L}_f^{PC}$, ϵ_{PC} is about 0.1. Contrarily, for $\mathcal{L}_f^{BI}$ from Figs. 1(b) and 3(b), ϵ_{BI} is about 0.4. If we choose a threshold to be about 0.2, the two cases are distinguishable.

Moreover, we define the $\approx$ relation for ($\epsilon < 0.2$). As we know that $\mathcal{L}_f^{PC}$ is probably correct and $\mathcal{L}_f^{BI}$ is bug-injected, we have followings. (a) $W_{PC}^{(0)*} \approx W_{PC}^{(1)*}$, and (b) $W_{BI}^{(0)*} \prec W_{BI}^{(1)*}$. These are, indeed, consistent with [**Hyp-3**].

Accuracy for Distorted Testing Datasets. We generated distorted datasets from the MNIST testing dataset TS; $TS_{MD}^{(1)} = T_A(TS, \mathcal{L}_f^{MD}(LS))$. We, then, checked the accuracy $Accuracy(W_{MD}^{(1)}, TS_{MD}^{(1)})$, whose monitored results are shown in Fig. 4. $Accuracy(W_{MD}^{(1)}, TS_{MD}^{(1)})$ and $Accuracy(W_{MD}^{(1)}, LS_{MD}^{(1)})$ are not distinguishable, because both $LS_{MD}^{(1)}$ and $TS_{MD}^{(1)}$ are constructed in the same way with $T_A(\_, \mathcal{L}_f^{MD}(LS))$ and thus their empirical distributions are considered the same. The graphs are consistent again with [**Hyp-1**].

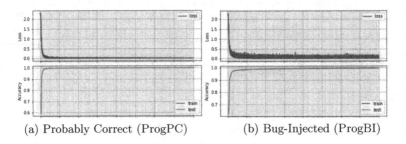

(a) Probably Correct (ProgPC)   (b) Bug-Injected (ProgBI)

Fig. 4. Loss and accuracy: distorted testing dataset

5   Discussions

5.1   Neuron Coverage

As explained in Sect. 3.1, the distortion relation ($\_\preceq\_$) between trained learning parameters is calculated in terms of observer functions. However, depending on the observer, the resultant distortion degree may be different. In an extreme case, a certain observer is not adequate to differentiate distortions. A question arises whether such distortion degrees are able to be measured directly. We will study *neuron coverage* [11] whether we can use it as such a measure.

A neuron is said to be *activated* if its output signal *out* is larger than a given threshold when a set of input signals in_j is presented; $out = \sigma(\sum w_j \times in_j)$. The weight values w_js are constituents of the trained W^*. *Activated Neurons* below refer to a set of neurons that are activated when a vector data a is input to a trained machine learning model, $y(W^*; a)$.

$$Neuron\ coverage\ (NC) = \frac{|\ Activated\ Neurons\ |}{|\ Total\ Neurons\ |}$$

In the above, $|\ X\ |$ denotes the size of a set X. Using this neuron coverage as a criterion is motivated by an empirical observation that different input-output pairs result in different degrees of neuron coverage [11].

Results of Experiment. We focus on the neurons constituting the penultimate (the last but one) layer, or the hidden layer for the current in NN learning model. As its activation function is *ReLU*, we choose 0 as the threshold. Figure 5 is a graph to show the numbers of input vectors leading to the chosen percentages of inactive neurons, $(1 - NC)$. These input vectors constitute the MNIST testing dataset TS of the size $10,000$.

According to Fig. 5, the graph for the case of ProgPC, the ratio of inactive neurons is almost 20%; namely, 80% of neurons in the hidden layer are activated to have effects on the classification results. However, the ProgBI graph shows that about 60% of them are inactive and do not contribute to the results. To put it differently, this difference in the ratios of inactive neurons implies that

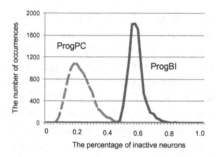

Fig. 5. Frequencies of inactive neurons

the trained learning model W_{BI}^* of ProgBI is distorted from W_{PC}^* of ProgPC, $W_{PC}^* \preceq W_{BI}^*$.

From the generation method of the distorted dataset, we have $LS \preceq LS_{PC}^{(1)}$ and $LS \preceq LS_{BI}^{(1)}$. $LS_{PC}^{(1)} \preceq LS_{BI}^{(1)}$ may also be satisfied, which is in accordance with the visual inspection of Fig. 2. Furthermore, because of [**Hyp-2**] (Sect. 3.1), $W_{PC}^{(1)} \preceq W_{BI}^{(1)}$ is true. It is consistent with the situation shown in Fig. 5 in that activated neurons in $W_{BI}^{(1)*}$ are fewer than those in $W_{PC}^{(1)*}$.

Figure 3 can be understood from a viewpoint of the neuron coverage. The empirical distribution of MNIST testing dataset TS is the same as that of MNIST training dataset LS. Because of the distortion relationships on training datasets, the distribution of TS is different from those of $LS_{MD}^{(1)}$ ($LS_{PC}^{(1)}$ or $LS_{BI}^{(1)}$). Moreover, Fig. 3 shows that $|Accuracy(W_{PC}^{(1)*}, TS) - Accuracy(W_{PC}^{(0)*}, TS)|$ is smaller than $|Accuracy(W_{BI}^{(1)*}, TS) - Accuracy(W_{BI}^{(0)*}, TS)|$. Therefore, we see that the relationship $LS_{PC}^{(1)} \preceq LS_{BI}^{(1)}$ is satisfied. Because of [**Hyp-2**], it implies $W_{PC}^{(1)*} \preceq W_{BI}^{(1)*}$. Therefore, the difference seen in Fig. 3 is consistent with the situation shown in Fig. 5.

In summary, the neuron coverage would be a good candidate as the metrics to quantitatively define the distortion degrees of trained machine learning models. However, because this view is based on the MNIST dataset experiments only, further studies are needed.

5.2   Test Input Generation

We will see how the dataset or data generation method in Sect. 3.2 is used in software testing. Because the program is categorized as untestable [13], Metamorphic Testing (MT) [1] is now a standard practice for testing of machine learning programs. We here indicate that generating an appropriate data is desirable to conduct effective testing. In the MT framework, given an initial test data x, a translation function T generates a new follow-up test data $T(x)$ automatically.

For testing machine learning software, either $\mathcal{L}_f$ (whether a training program is a faithful implementation of machine learning algorithms) [7,17] or $\mathcal{I}_f$ (whether an inference program shows acceptable prediction performance against incoming data), generating a variety of data to show *Dataset Diversity* [9] is a key issue. The function T_A introduced in Sect. 3.2 can be used to generate such a follow-up *dataset* used in the MT framework [10]. In particular, corner-case testing would be possible by carefully chosen such a group of biased datasets.

DeepTest [15] employs Data Augmentation methods [5] to generate test data. Zhou and Sun [19] adopts generating fuzz to satisfy application-specific properties. Both works are centered around generating test data for negative testing, but do not consider statistical distribution of data in datasets.

DeepRoad [18] adopts an approach with Generative Adversarial Networks (GAN) [2,16] to synthesize various weather conditions as driving scenes. GAN is formulated as a two-player zero-sum game. Given a dataset whose empirical distribution is ρ^{DS}, its Nash equilibrium, solved with Mixed Integer Linear Programing (MILP), results in a DNN-based generative model to emit new data to satisfy the relation $\boldsymbol{x} \sim_{i.i.d.} \rho^{DS}$. Thus, such new data preserve characteristics of the original machine learning problem. Consequently, we regard the GAN-based approach as a method to enlarge coverage of test scenes within what is anticipated at the training time because of $\boldsymbol{x} \sim_{i.i.d.} \rho^{DS}$.

Machine Teaching [20] is an inverse problem of machine learning, and is a methodology to generate a dataset to optimally derive a *given* trained machine learning model. The method is formalized as a two-level optimization problem, which is generally difficult to solve. We regard the machine teaching as a method to generate unanticipated dataset. Obtained datasets can be used in negative testing.

Our method uses an optimization problem with one objective function for generating datasets that are not far from what is anticipated, but probably are biased because of the semantic noises, and build up the dataset diversity.

6   Concluding Remarks

We introduced a notion of distortion degrees which would manifest themselves as faults and failures in machine learning programs, and presented initial studies to employ neuron coverages for quantitative measures of the distortion degrees. Because our views are solely based on experiments using the MNIST dataset, further studies are mandatory. These include whether the neuron coverages particularly measured for the penultimate layer are effective for general DNN, and how the data with semantic noises are effective for software testing of DNN programs. We conjecture that studying the relationship between the distortion degrees and the faults might open a new research area for assuring the quality of machine learning software.

Acknowledgment. The work is supported partially by JSPS KAKENHI Grant Number JP18H03224, and is partially based on results obtained from a project commissioned by the NEDO.

References

1. Chen, T.Y., et al.: Metamorphic testing: a review of challenges and opportunities. ACM Comput. Surv. **51**(1), 1–27 (2018). Article no. 4
2. Goodfellow, I., et al.: Generative adversarial nets. In: Advances in Neural Information Processing Systems (NIPS 2014), pp. 2672–2680 (2014)
3. Goodfellow, I., Bengio, Y., Courville, A.: Deep Learning. The MIT Press, Cambridge (2016)
4. Haykin, S.: Neural Networks and Learning Machines. Pearson India, Delhi (2016)
5. Krizhevsky, A., Sutskever, I., Hinton, G.E.: Imagenet classification with deep convolutional neural networks. In: Advances in Neural Information Processing Systems (NIPS 2012), pp. 1097–1105 (2012)
6. LeCun, Y., Bottou, L., Bengio, Y., Haffner, P.: Gradient-based learning applied to document recognition. Proc. IEEE **86**(11), 2278–2324 (1998)
7. Nakajima, S., Bui, H.N.: Dataset coverage for testing machine learning computer programs. In: Proceedings of the 23rd APSEC, pp. 297–304 (2016)
8. Nakajima, S.: Quality assurance of machine learning software. In: Proceedings of the IEEE (GCCE 2018), pp. 601–604 (2018)
9. Nakajima, S.: Dataset diversity for metamorphic testing of machine learning software. In: Duan, Z., Liu, S., Tian, C., Nagoya, F. (eds.) SOFL+MSVL 2018. LNCS, vol. 11392, pp. 21–38. Springer, Cham (2019). https://doi.org/10.1007/978-3-030-13651-2_2
10. Nakajima, S., Chen, T.Y.: Generating biased dataset for metamorphic testing of machine learning programs. In: Gaston, C., Kosmatov, N., Le Gall, P. (eds.) ICTSS 2019. LNCS, vol. 11812, pp. 56–64. Springer, Cham (2019). https://doi.org/10.1007/978-3-030-31280-0_4
11. Pei, K., Cao, Y., Yang, J., Jana, S.: DeepXplore: automated whitebox testing of deep learning systems. In: Proceedings of the 26th SOSP, pp. 1–18 (2017)
12. Quinonero-Candela, J., Sugiyama, M., Schwaighofer, A., Lawrence, N.D. (eds.): Dataset Shift in Machine Learning. The MIT Press, Cambridge (2009)
13. Segura, S., Towey, D., Zhou, Z.Q., Chen, T.Y.: Metamorphic testing: testing the untestable. IEEE Software (in press)
14. Szegedy, C., et al.: Intriguing properties of neural networks. In: Proceedings of the ICLR (2014)
15. Tian, Y., Pei, K., Jana, S., Ray, B.: DeepTest: automated testing of deep-neural-network-driven autonomous cars. In: Proceedings of the 40th ICSE, pp. 303–314 (2018)
16. Warde-Farley, D., Goodfellow, I.: Adversarial Perturbations of Deep Neural Networks, in Perturbation, Optimization and Statistics. The MIT Press, Cambridge (2016)
17. Xie, X., Ho, J.W.K., Murphy, C., Kaiser, G., Xu, B., Chen, T.Y.: Testing and validating machine learning classifiers by metamorphic testing. J. Syst. Softw. **84**, 544–558 (2011)
18. Zhang, M., Zhang, Y., Zhang, L., Liu, C., Khurshid, S.: DeepRoad: GAN-based metamorphic testing and input validation framework for autonomous driving systems. In: Proceedings of the 33rd ASE, pp. 132–142 (2018)
19. Zhou, Z.Q., Sun, L.: Metamorphic testing of driverless cars. Commun. ACM **62**(3), 61–67 (2019)
20. Zhu, X.: Machine teaching: an inverse problem to machine learning and an approach toward optimal education. In: Proceedings of the 29th AAAI, pp. 4083–4087 (2015)

A Divide & Conquer Approach to Testing Concurrent Java Programs with JPF and Maude

Canh Minh Do$^{(\boxtimes)}$ and Kazuhiro Ogata

Japan Advanced Institute of Science and Technology,
1-1 Asahidai, Nomi, Ishikawa 923-1292, Japan
{canhdominh,ogata}@jaist.ac.jp

Abstract. The paper proposes a new testing technique for concurrent programs. The technique is basically a specification-based testing one. For a formal specification S and a concurrent program P, state sequences are generated from P and checked to be accepted by S. We suppose that S is specified in Maude and P is implemented in Java. Java Pathfinder (JPF) and Maude are then used to generate state sequences from P and to check if such state sequences are accepted by S, respectively. Even without checking any property violations with JPF, JPF often encounters the notorious state space explosion while only generating state sequences. Thus, we propose a technique to generate state sequences from P and check if such state sequences are accepted by S in a stratified way. Some experiments demonstrate that the proposed technique mitigates the state space explosion instances from which otherwise only one JPF instance cannot suffice.

Keywords: Concurrent program · Divide & conquer · Java · JPF · Maude · Simulation · Specification-based testing

1 Introduction

Studies on testing concurrent programs [1] have been conducted for nearly 40 years or even more. Compared to testing techniques for sequential programs, however, any testing techniques for concurrent programs do not seem matured enough. Moreover, many important software systems, such as operating systems, are in the form of concurrent programs. Therefore, testing techniques for concurrent programs must be worth studying so that they can be matured enough.

For a formal specification S and a (concurrent) program P, to test P based on S, we can basically take each of the following two approaches: (1) P is tested with test cases generated from S and (2) it is checked that state sequences generated from P can be accepted by S. The two approaches would be complementary to each other. Approach (1) checks if P implements the functionalities

This work was supported in part by JSPS KAKENHI Grant Number JP19H04082.

© Springer Nature Switzerland AG 2020
H. Miao et al. (Eds.): SOFL+MSVL 2019 Workshop, LNCS 12028, pp. 42–58, 2020.
https://doi.org/10.1007/978-3-030-41418-4_4

specified in S, while approach (2) checks if P never implements what is not specified in S. In terms of simulation, approach (1) checks if P can simulate S, while approach (2) checks if S can simulate P. Approaches (1) and (2) are often used in the program testing community and the refinement-based formal methods community, respectively, while both (1) and (2), namely bi-simulation, are often used in process calculi. The present paper proposes a testing technique for concurrent programs based on approach (2) mainly because P is a concurrent program and then could produce many different executions due to the inherent nondeterminacy of P.

We suppose that S is specified in Maude [3] and P is implemented in Java. Java Pathfinder (JPF) [10] and Maude are then used to generate state sequences from P and to check if such state sequences are accepted by S, respectively. Even without checking any property violations with JPF, JPF often encounters the notorious state space explosion while only generating state sequences because there could be a huge number of different states reachable from the initial states, there could be a huge number of different state sequences generated due to the inherent nondeterminacy of concurrent programs and a whole big heap mainly constitutes one state in a program under test by JPF. Thus, we propose a technique to generate state sequences from P and check if such state sequences are accepted by S in a stratified way. The state space reachable from each initial state is divided into multiple layers. Let us suppose that each layer l has depth d_l. Let d_0 be 0. For each layer l, state sequences $s_0^l, \ldots, s_{d_l}^l$ whose depth is d_l are generated from each state at depth $d_0 + \ldots + d_{l-1}$ from P. Each s_i^l is converted into the state representation $f(s_i^l)$ used in S, where f is a simulation relation candidate from P to S. We conjecture that if S is refined enough, f would be an identity function. There may be adjacent states $f(s_i^l)$ and $f(s_{i+1}^l)$ such that $f(s_i^l)$ is the same as $f(s_{i+1}^l)$. If so, one of them is deleted. We then have state sequences $f(s_0^l), \ldots, f(s_N^l)$, where the number $N+1$ of the states in the sequence is usually much smaller than $d_l + 1$ because execution units in P are much finer than those in S. We check if each $f(s_0^l), \ldots, f(s_N^l)$ is accepted by S with Maude [4]. The proposed technique is called a divide & conquer approach to testing concurrent programs, which could be naturally parallelized. We have implemented a tool supporting the proposed technique in Java. Some experiments demonstrate that the proposed technique mitigates the state space explosion instances from which otherwise only one JPF instance cannot suffice.

The rest of the paper is organized as follows: Sect. 2 Preliminaries, Sect. 3 Specification-based Concurrent Program Testing with a Simulation Relation, Sect. 4 State Sequence Generation from Concurrent Programs, Sect. 5 A Divide & Conquer Approach to Generating State Sequences, Sect. 6 A Divide & Conquer Approach to Testing Concurrent Programs, Sect. 7 A Case Study: Alternating Bit Protocol (ABP), Sect. 8 Related Work and Sect. 9 Conclusion.

2   Preliminaries

A state machine $M \triangleq \langle S, I, T \rangle$ consists of a set S of states, the set $I \subseteq S$ of initial states and a binary relation $T \subseteq S \times S$ over states. $(s, s') \in T$ is called

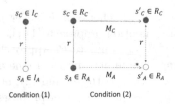

Fig. 1. A simulation relation from M_C to M_A

a state transition and may be written as $s \to_M s'$. Let $\to_M^*$ be the reflexive and transitive closure of $\to_M$. The set $R_M \subseteq S$ of reachable states w.r.t. M is inductively defined as follows: (1) for each $s \in I$, $s \in R$ and (2) if $s \in R$ and $(s, s') \in T$, then $s' \in R$. A state predicate p is called invariant w.r.t. M iff $p(s)$ holds for all $s \in R_M$. A finite sequence $s_0, \ldots, s_i, s_{i+1}, \ldots, s_n$ of states is called a finite semi-computation of M if $s_0 \in I$ and $s_i \to_M^* s_{i+1}$ for each $i = 0, \ldots, n-1$. If that is the case, it is called that M can accept $s_0, \ldots, s_i, s_{i+1}, \ldots, s_n$.

Given two state machines M_C and M_A, a relation r over R_C and R_A is called a simulation relation from M_C to M_A if r satisfies the following two conditions: (1) for each $s_C \in I_C$, there exists $s_A \in I_A$ such that $r(s_C, s_A)$ and (2) for each $s_C, s'_C \in R_C$ and $s_A \in R_A$ such that $r(s_C, s_A)$ and $s_C \to_{M_C} s'_C$, there exists $s'_A \in R_A$ such that $r(s'_C, s'_A)$ and $s_A \to_{M_A}^* s'_A$ [9] (see Fig. 1). If that is the case, we may write that M_A simulates M_C with r. There is a theorem on simulation relations from M_C to M_A and invariants w.r.t M_C and M_A: for any state machines M_C and M_A such that there exists a simulation relation r from M_C to M_A, any state predicates p_C for M_C and p_A for M_A such that $p_A(s_A) \Rightarrow p_C(s_C)$ for any reachable states $s_A \in R_{M_A}$ and $s_C \in R_{M_C}$ with $r(s_C, s_A)$, if $p_A(s_A)$ holds for all $s_A \in R_{M_A}$, then $p_C(s_C)$ holds for all $s_C \in R_{M_C}$ [9]. The theorem makes it possible to verify that p_C is invariant w.r.t. M_C by proving that p_A is invariant w.r.t. M_A, M_A simulates M_C with r and $p_A(s_A)$ implies $p_C(s_C)$ for all $s_A \in R_{M_A}$ and $s_C \in R_{M_C}$ with $r(s_C, s_A)$.

States are expressed as braced soups of observable components, where soups are associative-commutative collections and observable components are name-value pairs in this paper. The state that consists of observable components oc_1, oc_2 and oc_3 is expressed as $\{oc_1\ oc_2\ oc_3\}$, which equals $\{oc_3\ oc_1\ oc_2\}$ and some others because of associativity and commutativity. We use Maude [3], a rewriting logic-based computer language, as a specification language because Maude makes it possible to use associative-commutative collections. State transitions are specified in Maude rewrite rules.

Let us consider as an example a mutual exclusion protocol (the test&set protocol) in which the atomic instruction test&set is used. The protocol written in an Algol-like pseudo-code is as follows:

Loop : "RemainderSection(RS)"
    rs : **repeat while** test&set($lock$) = true;
      "CriticalSection(CS)"
    cs : $lock$:= false;

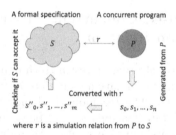

Fig. 2. Specification-based concurrent program testing with a simulation relation

lock is a Boolean variable shared by all processes (or threads) participating in the protocol. test&set(*lock*) does the following atomically: it sets *lock* false and returns the old value stored in *lock*. Each process is located at either rs (remainder section) or cs (critical section). Initially each process is located at rs and *lock* is false. When a process is located at rs, it does something (which is abstracted away in the pseudo-code) that never requires any shared resources; if it wants to use some shared resources that must be used in the critical section, then it performs the **repeat while** loop. It waits there while test&set(*lock*) returns true. When test&set(*lock*) returns false, the process is allowed to enter the critical section. The process then does something (which is also abstracted away in the pseudo-code) that requires to use some shared resources in the critical section. When the process finishes its task in the critical section, it leaves there, sets *lock* false and goes back to the remainder section.

When there are three processes p1, p2 and p3, each state of the protocol is formalized as a term $\{(\text{lock} : b) \ (\text{pc}[\text{p1}] : l_1) \ (\text{pc}[\text{p2}] : l_2) \ (\text{pc}[\text{p3}] : l_3)\}$, where b is a Boolean value and each l_i is either rs or cs. Initially b is false and each l_i is rs. The state transitions are formalized as two rewrite rules. One rewrite rule says that if b is false and l_i is rs, then b becomes true, l_i becomes cs and any other l_j (such that $j \neq i$) does not change. The other rewrite rule says that if l_i is cs, then b becomes false, l_i becomes rs and any other l_j (such that $j \neq i$) does not change. The two rules are specified in Maude as follows:

```
rl [enter] : {(lock: false) (pc[I]: rs) OCs}
  => {(lock: true) (pc[I]: cs) OCs} .
rl [leave] : {(lock: B) (pc[I]: cs) OCs}
  => {(lock: false) (pc[I]: rs) OCs} .
```

where **enter** and **leave** are the labels (or names) given to the two rewrite rules, I is a Maude variable of process IDs, B is a Maude variable of Boolean values and OCs is a Maude variable of observable component soups. OCs represents the remaining part (the other processes but process I) of the system. Both rules never change OCs. Let $S_{\text{t\&s}}$ refer to the specification of the test&set protocol in Maude.

3   Specification-Based Concurrent Program Testing with a Simulation Relation

We have proposed a concurrent program testing technique that is a specification-based one and uses a simulation relation candidate from a concurrent program to a formal specification [4]. The technique is depicted in Fig. 2. Let S be a formal specification of a state machine and P be a concurrent program. Let us suppose that we know a simulation relation candidate r from P to S. The proposed technique does the following: (1) finite state sequences $s_1, s_2, \ldots, s_n$ are generated from P, (2) each s_i of P is converted to a state s_i' of S with r, (3) one of each two consecutive states s_i' and s_{i+1}' such that $s_i' = s_{i+1}'$ is deleted, (4) finite state sequences $s_1'', s_2'', \ldots, s_m''$ are then obtained, where $s_i'' \neq s_{i+1}''$ for each $i = 1, \ldots, m-1$ and (5) it is checked that $s_1'', s_2'', \ldots, s_m''$ can be accepted by S.

We suppose that programmers write concurrent programs based on formal specifications, although it may be possible to generate concurrent programs (semi-)automatically from formal specifications in some cases. The FeliCa team has demonstrated that programmers can write programs based on formal specifications and moreover use of formal specifications can make programs high-quality [6]. Therefore, our assumption is meaningful as well as feasible. If so, programmers must have profound enough understandings of both formal specifications and concurrent programs so that they can come up with simulation relation candidates from the latter to the former. Even though consecutive equal states except for one are deleted, generating $s_1'', s_2'', \ldots, s_m''$ such that $s_i'' \neq s_{i+1}''$ for each $i = 1, \ldots, m-1$, there may not be exactly one transition step but zero or more transition steps so that s_i'' can reach s_{i+1}'' w.r.t. P. Therefore, we need to know the maximum number of such transition steps. We suppose that programmers can guess the maximum number. If programmers cannot, we can start with 1 as the maximum number b and gradually increment b as we find consecutive states s_i'' and s_{i+1}'' such that s_i'' cannot reach s_{i+1}'' in b transition steps unless the unreachability is caused by some flaws lurking in P.

Our previous work [4] focuses on the left part of Fig. 2 but does not describe the right part of Fig. 2, namely how to generate state sequences from P. The present paper describes how to generate state sequences from P as well, where P is a concurrent program written in Java and Java Pathfinder (JPF) is mainly used to generate state sequences from P.

4   State Sequence Generation from Concurrent Programs

4.1   Java Pathfinder (JPF)

JPF is an extensible software model checking framework for Java bytecode programs that are generated by a standard Java compiler from programs written in Java. JPF has a special Virtual Machine (VM) in it to support model checking of concurrent Java programs, being able to detect some flaws lurking in Java concurrent programs, such as race conditions and deadlocks, when it reports a whole execution leading to the flaw. JPF explores all potential executions of a program under test in a systematic way in theory, while an ordinary Java VM executes the code in only one possible way. JPF is basically able to identify points that represent execution choices in a program under test from which the execution could proceed differently.

Although JPF is a powerful model checker for concurrent Java programs, its straightforward use does not scale well and often encounters the notorious state space explosion. We anticipated previously [4] that we might mitigate the state space explosion if we do not check anything while JPF explores a program under test to generate state sequences. It is, however, revealed that we could not escape the state space explosion just without checking anything during the exploration conducted by JPF. This is because a whole big heap mainly constitutes one state in a program under test by JPF, while one state is typically expressed as a small term in formal specifications. The present paper then proposes a divide & conquer approach to state sequence generation from a concurrent program, which generates state sequences in a stratified way.

4.2 Generating State Sequences by JPF

Two main components of JPF are (1) a VM and (2) a search component. The VM is a state generator. It generates state representations by interpreting byte-code instructions. A state is mainly constituted of a heap and threads plus an execution history (or path) that leads to the state. Each state is given a unique ID number. The VM implements a state management that makes it possible to do state matching, state storing and execution backtracking that are useful to explore a state space. Three key methods of the VM are employed by the search component:

- **forward** - it generates the next state and reports if the generated state has a successor; if so, it stores the successor on a backtrack stack for efficient restoration;
- **backtrack** - it restores the last state on the backtrack stack;
- **restoreState** - it restores an arbitrary state.

At any state, the search component is responsible for selecting the next state from which the VM should proceed, either by directing the VM to generate the next state (forward) or by telling it to backtrack to a previously generated one (backtrack). The search component works as a driver for the VM. We have some strategies used to traverse the state space. By default, the search component uses depth-first search, we can configure to use different strategies, such as breadth-first search.

The most important extension mechanism of JPF is listeners. They provide a way to observe, interact with and extend JPF execution. We can configure JPF with many of our own listener classes that extend the ListenerAdapter class. The ListenerAdapter class consists of all event notifications from the VMListener and SearchListener classes. It allows us to subscribe to VMListener and SearchListener event notifications by overriding some methods, such as:

- **searchStarted** - it is invoked when JPF has just entered the search loop but before the first forward;
- **stateAdvanced** - it is invoked when JPF has just got the next state;
- **stateBacktracked** - it is invoked when JPF has just backtracked one step;
- **searchFinished** - it is invoked when JPF is just done.

A class SequenceState that extends class ListenerAdapter is made to observe and interact with JPF execution. In class SequenceState, we override the two important methods stateAdvanced and stateBacktracked. As described above, the stateAdvanced method is invoked when JPF has just got the next state. We need to retrieve all necessary information about the next state at this step. We use an instance Path of class ArrayList to keep up with the path on which we are staying. Each element of Path corresponds to a state in JPF and is encapsulated as an instance of a class Configuration we prepare. Each element of Path only stores the information for our testing purpose, which is mainly the values of observable components. For example, the information for the test&set mutual exclusion protocol is as follows:

- **stateId** - the unique id of state;
- **depth** - the current depth of search path;
- **lock** - a Lock object that contains the lock observable component value that is true or false;
- **threads** - an ArrayList object of threads, each of which consists of the current location information that is rs or cs.

We need to keep up with the change of observer components in each state stored in Path. Observer components are implemented as object data in JPF. So we need to look inside the heap of JPF. The heap contains a dynamic array of ElementInfo objects where the array indices are used as object reference values. An ElementInfo object contains a Fields object that actually stores the values we need. Hereby we can gather the values of observer components and create a new Configuration object and append it to Path as the stateAdvanced method is invoked.

Whenever JPF hits an end state, a state that has been already visited or a depth bound, we write the current path to a file, when we delete consecutive same states except for one. We also check if the current path has already been stored in some file. If so, we do not write the path into any files. When writing the current path into a file, we make the formats of each state and the path (state sequence) conform to those used in rewrite-theory specifications written in Maude so that Maude can check if the path can be accepted by such a rewrite-theory specification.

Because the state space could be huge even if it is bounded, we manage two bound parameters in order to prevent JPF from diverging. The two bound parameters are as follows:

- **DEPTH** - the maximum depth from the initial state; once JPF reaches any state whose depth from the initial state is DEPTH, we send a backtrack message to the search component for backtracking;

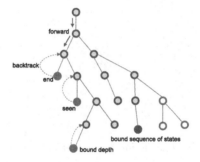

Fig. 3. A way to generate state sequences with JPF (Color figure online)

- **BOUND** - the maximum number of paths (or state sequences); we count the number of paths generated; when the number reaches to BOUND, we send a terminate message to the search component for stopping JPF.

Each of DEPTH and BOUND could be set unbounded, meaning that we ask JPF to generate as deep state sequences as possible and/or as many state sequences as possible. Every time JPF performs backtracking, we delete the last state from Path in the stateBacktracked method to keep up with the change if the last state does not have any more successor states.

The way to generate state sequences from concurrent programs with JPF is depicted in Fig. 3. Yellow nodes with a thick border in red are those that have been visited by JPF. So are blue ones but they cause backtracking because the node (or state) does not have any more successor states, the node has been seen (or visited) before or the depth of the node reaches DEPTH. The red node means that when JPF arrives at the node, it has just generated the BOUND number of state sequences and then it does not need to explore the remaining part of the state space composed of the white nodes with a thick border in blue.

5   A Divide & Conquer Approach to Generating State Sequences

JPF often encounters the notorious state space explosion even without checking any property violation while searching. When you do not set each of DEPTH and BOUND to a moderately small number and ask JPF to exhaustively (or almost exhaustively) explore all (or a huge number of) possible states, JPF may not finish the exploration and may lead to out of memory. To mitigate the situation, the present paper proposes a technique to generate state sequences from concurrent programs in a stratified way, which is called a divide & conquer approach to generating state sequences. We first generate state sequences from each initial state, where DEPTH is D1 (see Fig. 4). Note that BOUND may be set unbounded. If D1 is small enough, it is possible to do so. We then generate state sequences from each of the states at depth D1, where DEPTH is D2 (see

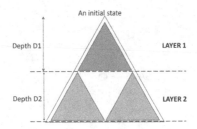

Fig. 4. A divide & conquer approach

Fig. 4). If D2 is small enough, it is also possible to do so. Given one initial state, there is one sub-state space in the first layer explored by JPF, while there are as many sub-state spaces in the second layer as the states at depth D1 (see Fig. 4). Combining each state sequence seq_1 in layer 1 and each state sequence seq_2 in layer 2 such that the last state of seq_1 equals the first state of seq_2, we are to generate state sequences, where DEPTH is D1 + D2 (see Fig. 4), which can be done even though D1 + D2 is too large. Although we have described the divide & conquer approach to generating state sequences such that there are two layers, the technique could be generalized such that the number of layers is $N \geq 2$. For example, we could generate state sequences from each of the states at depth D1 + D2, where DEPTH is D3; Combining each state sequence seq_1 in layer 1, each state sequence seq_2 in layer 2 and each state sequence seq_2 in layer 3 such that the last state of seq_1 equals the first state of seq_2 and the last state of seq_2 equals the first state of seq_3, we are to generate state sequences, where DEPTH is D1 + D2 + D3.

Generating state sequences for each sub-state space is independent from that for any other sub-state space. Especially for sub-state spaces in one layer, generating state sequences for each sub-state space is totally independent from that for each other. This characteristic of the proposed technique makes it possible to generate state sequences from concurrent programs in parallel. For example, once we have generated state sequences in layer 1, we can generate state sequences for all sub-state spaces in layer 2 simultaneously. This is another advantage of the divide & conquer approach to generating state sequences from concurrent programs.

Let us consider the test&set protocol and suppose that we write a concurrent program (denoted $P_{t\&s}$) in Java based on the specification $S_{t\&s}$ of the protocol. We suppose that there are three processes participating in the protocol. $S_{t\&s}$ has one initial state and so does $P_{t\&s}$. Let each of D1 and D2 be 50 and use the proposed technique to generate state sequences from $P_{t\&s}$. One of the state sequences (denoted seq_1) generated in layer 1 is as follows:

```
{(pc[p1]: rs) (pc[p2]: rs) (pc[p3]: rs) (lock: false)} |
{(pc[p1]: rs) (pc[p2]: cs) (pc[p3]: rs) (lock: true)} |
{(pc[p1]: rs) (pc[p2]: rs) (pc[p3]: rs) (lock: false)} | nil
```

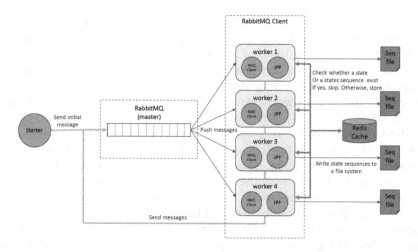

Fig. 5. Architecture of a tool supporting the proposed technique

where $\_|\_$ is the constructor for non-empty state sequences and nil denotes the empty state sequence. Note that atomic execution units used in $P_{t\&s}$ are totally different from those used in $S_{t\&s}$. Therefore, the depth of layer 1 is 50 but the length of the state sequence generated is 3. One of the state sequences (denoted seq_2) generated in layer 2 is as follows:

```
{(pc[p1]: rs) (pc[p2]: rs) (pc[p3]: rs) (lock: false)} |
{(pc[p1]: cs) (pc[p2]: rs) (pc[p3]: rs) (lock: true)} |
{(pc[p1]: rs) (pc[p2]: rs) (pc[p3]: rs) (lock: false)} | nil
```

Note that the last state in the first state sequence is the same as the first state in the second state sequence. Combining them the two state sequences, we get the following state sequence (denoted seq_3):

```
{(pc[p1]: rs) (pc[p2]: rs) (pc[p3]: rs) (lock: false)} |
{(pc[p1]: rs) (pc[p2]: cs) (pc[p3]: rs) (lock: true)} |
{(pc[p1]: rs) (pc[p2]: rs) (pc[p3]: rs) (lock: false)} |
{(pc[p1]: cs) (pc[p2]: rs) (pc[p3]: rs) (lock: true)} |
{(pc[p1]: rs) (pc[p2]: rs) (pc[p3]: rs) (lock: false)} | nil
```

This is one state sequence generated from $P_{t\&s}$, where DEPTH is 100.

6 A Divide & Conquer Approach to Testing Concurrent Programs

Once state sequences are generated from a concurrent program P, we check if a formal specification S can accept the state sequences with Maude. For example, we can check if seq_3 can be accepted by $P_{t\&s}$ with Maude. Instead of checking if *seq*₃ can be accepted by $P_{t\&s}$, however, it suffices to check if each of *seq*₁ and *seq*₂ can be accepted by $P_{t\&s}$. Besides, a tool component [4] previously implemented in Maude that can check the conformance of state sequences to specifications regardless of starting from any arbitrary state. So we can check if such state sequences are accepted by S in a stratified way.

For each layer l, we generate state sequences starting from each state located at depth $D1 + \ldots + D(l-1)$ from a concurrent program P with JPF and check if each state sequence generated in layer l can be accepted by a formal specification S with Maude. We could first generate all (sub-)state sequences from P in the stratified way and then could check if each state sequence can be accepted by S. But, we do not combine multiple (sub-)state sequences to generate a whole state sequence of P because we do not need to do so and it suffices to check if each (sub-)state sequence can be accepted by S in order to check if a whole state sequence can be accepted by S. This way to generate (sub-)state sequences from P and to check if each (sub-)state sequence is accepted by S is called a divide & conquer approach to testing concurrent programs.

A tool that supports the divide & conquer approach to testing concurrent programs has been implemented in Java. The tool architecture is depicted in Fig. 5. As shown in Fig. 5, the architecture is a master-worker model (or pattern), where there is one master and four workers. We use Redis (https://redis.io/) and RabbitMQ (https://www.rabbitmq.com/). Redis is an advanced key-value store. It holds its database entirely in memory. We can imagine it as a big hash table in memory. Redis is used as an effective cache to avoid duplicating states and state sequences when generating state sequences. RabbitMQ is used as a message broker. The RabbitMQ master maintains a message queue to dispatch messages to RabbitMQ (RMQ) clients. Each worker consists of a RabbitMQ client and JPF.

Initially, we run a starter program to send an initial message to the RabbitMQ master for kicking off the tool. Whenever a worker receives a message from the master, the worker internally starts JPF with a configuration that is built from the message. JPF traverses the (sub-)state space designated in the message. Whenever JPF reaches the designated depth or finds the current state have no more successor states, our listener class does the following:

1. Removing all consecutive same states but one from the state sequence;
2. Converting the state sequence to a string representation and using the SHA256 algorithm to generate an almost unique signature for the string;
3. Asking the Redis cache whether the state sequence exists; If yes, skipping what follows; Otherwise, saving the signature as the key and the string as the value into the Redis cache and writing the string into the file maintained by the worker;
4. Obtaining the last state from the state sequence, converting it to a string representation and using the SHA256 algorithm to hash the string to a unique signature;
5. Asking the Redis cache whether the state exists; If yes, skipping what follows; Otherwise, saving the signature as the key and the string as the value into the

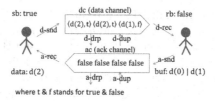

Fig. 6. A state of ABP

Redis cache and sending a message that contains the last state's information to the RabbitMQ master, which then prepares a message that asks a worker to generate state sequences from the state.

The current tool has not yet been integrated to Maude. The current tool requires human users to feed state sequences generated into Maude. Because each file maintained by a worker could be huge, however, it is necessary to split the file into multiple smaller ones, each of which is fed into Maude, because it would take much time to feed a huge file into Maude. The tool will be integrated to Maude, including split of a huge file into multiple smaller files.

7   A Case Study: Alternating Bit Protocol (ABP)

We report on a case study in which ABP has been used. ABP is a communication protocol and can be regarded as a simplified version of TCP. ABP makes it possible to reliably deliver data from a sender to a receiver even though two channels between the sender and receiver are unreliable in that elements in the channels may be dropped and/or duplicated. The sender maintains two pieces of information: sb that stores a Boolean value and $data$ that stores the data to be delivered next. The receiver maintains two pieces of information: rb that stores a Boolean value and buf that stores the data received. One channel dc from the sender to the receiver carries pairs of data and Boolean values, while the other one ac from the receiver to the sender carries Boolean values. There are two actions done by the sender: (sa1) the sender puts the pair $(data, sb)$ into dc and (sa2) if ac is not empty, the sender extracts the top Boolean value b from ac and compares b with sb; if $b \neq sb$, $data$ becomes the next data and sb is complemented; otherwise nothing changes. Actions (sa1) and (sa2) done by the sender are denoted d-snd and a-rec, respectively. There are two actions done by the receiver: (ra1) the receiver puts rb into ac and (ra2) if dc is not empty, the sender extracts the top pair (d, b) from dc and compares b with rb; if $b = sb$, d is stored in buf and rb is complemented; otherwise nothing changes. Actions (ra1) and (ra2) done by the receiver are denoted a-snd and d-rec, respectively. There are four more actions to dc and ac because the channels are unreliable. If dc is not empty, the top element is dropped (d-drp) or duplicated (d-dup), and if ac is not empty, the top element is dropped (a-drp) or duplicated (a-dup). Figure 6 shows a graphical representation of a state of ABP.

Each state of ABP is formalized as a term $\{(\text{sb} : b_1)\ (\text{data} : d(n))\ (\text{rb} : b_2)$ $(\text{buf} : dl)\ (\text{dc} : q_1)\ (\text{ac} : q_2)\}$, where b_1 and b_2 are Boolean values, n is a natural number, dl is a data list, q_1 is a queue of pairs of data and Boolean values and q_2 is a queue of Boolean values. $d(n)$ denotes data to be delivered from the sender to the receiver. Initially, b_1 is true, b_2 is true, n is 0, dl is the empty list, q_1 is the empty queue and q_2 is the empty queue. The state transitions that formalize the actions are specified in rewrite rules as follows:

```
rl [d-snd] : {(sb: B)(data: D)(dc: Ps) OCs}
=> {(sb: B)(data: D)(dc:(Ps | < D,B >)) OCs} .
crl [a-rec1] : {(sb: B)(data: d(N))(ac: (B' | Bs)) OCs}
=> {(sb:(not B))(data: d(N + 1))(ac: Bs) OCs} if B =/= B' .
crl [a-rec2] : {(sb: B)(data: D)(ac: (B' | Bs)) OCs}
=> {(sb: B)(data: D)(ac: Bs) OCs} if B = B' .
rl [a-snd] : {(rb: B)(ac: Bs) OCs} => {(rb: B) (ac: (Bs | B)) OCs} .
crl [d-rec1] : {(rb: B)(buf: Ds)(dc: (< D,B' > | Ps)) OCs}
=> {(rb: (not B))(buf: (Ds | D))(dc: Ps) OCs} if B = B' .
crl [d-rec2] : {(rb: B)(buf: Ds)(dc: (< D,B' > | Ps)) OCs}
=> {(rb: B)(buf: Ds)(dc: Ps) OCs} if B =/= B' .
rl [d-drp] : {(dc: (Ps1 | P | Ps2)) OCs} => {(dc: (Ps1 | Ps2)) OCs} .
rl [d-dup] : {(dc: (Ps1 | P | Ps2)) OCs}
=> {(dc: (Ps1 | P | P | Ps2)) OCs} .
rl [a-drp] : {(ac: (Bs1 | B | Bs2)) OCs} => {(ac: (Bs1 | Bs2)) OCs} .
rl [a-dup] : {(ac: (Bs1 | B | Bs2)) OCs}
=> {(ac: (Bs1 | B | B | Bs2)) OCs} .
```

Words that start with a capital letter, such as B, D, Ps and OCs, are Maude variables. B, D, Ps and OCs are variables of Boolean values, data, queues of (Data, Bool)-pairs and observable component soups, respectively. The types (or sorts) of the other variables can be understood from what have been described. The two rewrite rules a-rec1 and a-rec2 formalize action a-rec. What rewrite rules formalize what actions can be understood from what have been described. Let S_{ABP} refer to the specification of ABP in Maude. A concurrent program P'_{ABP} is written in Java based on S_{ABP}, where one thread performs two actions d-snd and a-rec, one thread performs two actions a-snd and d-rec, one thread performs two actions d-drp and a-drp and one thread performs two actions d-dup and a-dup. We intentionally insert one flaw in P'_{ABP} such that when the receiver gets the third data, it does not put the third data into buf but puts the fourth data into buf.

We suppose that the sender is to deliver four data to the receiver, the maximum state transition bound is 2, DEPTH is 100 for each layer and BOUND is unbounded for each layer. The simulation relation candidate from P'_{ABP} to S_{ABP} is essentially the identify function. We change each channel size as follows: 1, 2 and 3. We do not need to fix the number of layers in advance, but the number of layers can be determined by the tool on the fly. For each experiment, however, the number of layers is larger than 2. The experiments were carried out by an Apple iMac Late 2015 that had Processor 4 GHz Intel Core i7 and

Table 1. Experimental data

Channel size	Worker	Time1 (d:h:m)	#seqs	#small files	Total size (MB)	Time2 (s)
1	Worker 1	1:0:57	1,381	2	0.5	13
	Worker 2	1:0:57				
	Worker 3	1:0:57				
	Worker 4	0:18:43				
2	Worker 1	2:17:51	8,879	9	4.3	118
	Worker 2	2:11:45				
	Worker 3	2:10:52				
	Worker 4	2:11:51				
3	Worker 1	3:23:53	24,416	25	13.5	355
	Worker 2	3:20:27				
	Worker 3	3:20:37				
	Worker 4	3:17:41				

– Time1 – time taken to generate state sequences with JPF
– Time2 – time taken to check if state sequences are accepted by the formal specification with Maude
– Total size – the total size of all state sequences generated

Memory 32 GB 1867 MHz DDR3. The experimental data are shown in Table 1. Each small file contains at most 1,000 state sequences.

When each channel size is 1, it takes about 1 day to generate all state sequences with four workers. The number of the state sequences generated is 1,381, which is split into two groups (files): one file has 1,000 state sequences and the other file has 381 sequences. Each file is fed into Maude to check if each state sequence is accepted by S_{ABP} with Maude. It takes 13 s to do all checks. Maude detects that some state sequences have adjacent states s and s' such that s cannot reach s' by S_{ABP} in two state transitions. If that is the case, a tool component [4] implemented in Maude shows us some information as follows:

```
Result4Driver?: {seq: 31,msg: "Failure",
from: {sb: true data: d(2) rb: true buf: (d(0) | d(1))
      dc: < d(2),true > ac: nil},
to:{sb: true data: d(2) rb: false buf: (d(0) | d(1) | d(3))
      dc: nil ac: nil},index: 3,bound: 2}
```

This is because although the receiver must put the third data d(2) into *buf* when d(2) is delivered to the receiver, the receiver instead puts the fourth data d(3) into *buf*, which is the flaw intentionally inserted into P'_{ABP}. This demonstrates that our tool can detect the flaw.

When each channel size is 2, it takes about 2.75 days to generate all state sequences with four workers. The number of the state sequences generated is 8,879, which is split into nine groups (files): eight files have 1,000 state sequences and one file has 879 sequences. Each file is fed into Maude to check if each state sequence is accepted by S_{ABP} with Maude. It takes 118 s to do all checks. As is the case in which each channel is 1, Maude detects that some state sequences have an adjacent states s and s' such that s cannot reach s' by S_{ABP} in two state transitions due to the flaw intentionally inserted in P'_{ABP}.

When each channel size is 3, it takes about 4 days to generate all state sequences with four workers. The number of the state sequences generated is 24,416, which is split into 25 groups (files): 24 files have 1,000 state sequences and one file has 416 sequences. Each file is fed into Maude to check if each state sequence is accepted by S_{ABP} with Maude. It takes 355s to do all checks. As is the case in which each channel is 1, Maude detects that some state sequences have an adjacent states s and s' such that s cannot reach s' by S_{ABP} in two state transitions due to the flaw intentionally inserted in P'_{ABP}.

Note that without our approach and exactly using the same computer as above. The only use of JPF cannot terminate programs and reach to out of memory after that, even each channel size is 1. On other hands, when each channel is 3, the straightforward use of JPF did not complete the model checking but caused out of memory after it spent about 4 days to try exploring the reachable state space with almost the same computer as the one used in the experiments reported in the present paper [8]. Therefore, the proposed technique can alleviate the out-of-memory situation due to the state space explosion.

The experimental results say that it takes a few days to generate state sequences from a concurrent Java program with our tool in which JPF plays the main role, while it only takes several minutes to check if state sequences are accepted by a formal specification with Maude. It is one piece of our future work to accelerate generation of state sequences from concurrent programs. For example, instead of use of file system (disk) storage, it would be better to only use in-memory storage, which we anticipate would be feasible. Another piece of our future work is to integrate the current tool implemented in Java to the tool component [4] implemented in Maude.

8   Related Work

CovCon [2] is a coverage-guided approach to generating concurrent tests that can detect arbitrary kinds of concurrency bugs. The new idea they use is concurrent method pairs that represent the set of interleaving events. They measure how often method pairs have been executed concurrently and use that coverage information to generate tests on method pairs that have not been covered or have been covered less frequently than others.

Maximal causality reduction (MCR) [5] is a new technique for stateless model checking to efficiently reduce state spaces. MCR takes a trace as input and generates a set of new interleaving events. It exploits the events of thread execution in a trace to drive new execution that reaches a new distinct state. Thereby, MCR minimizes redundant interleaving events better than classical techniques. By using existing MCR with dynamic symbolic execution, a new technique called Maximal Path Causality is proposed to explore both the input space and the schedule space at the same time [11].

Model checking can exhaustively traverse all possible behaviors of concurrent programs, while it would take much time to complete verification due to their large state spaces. Metzler et al. [7] propose a novel iterative relaxed scheduling (IRS) approach to verification of concurrent programs that reduces that time. IRS introduces a set of admissible schedules and a suitable execution environment. It iteratively verifies each trace that is generated by the scheduling. As soon as a single trace is verified, it will be added to the set of admissible schedules. IRS execution environment does not need to wait until the program is fully verified. It may execute selected schedules from the set of admissible schedules that make the program be able to be safely used.

Those techniques seem orthogonal to the proposed technique in the present paper. So, some of them could be incorporated into our tool.

9 Conclusion

We have proposed a new testing technique for concurrent programs in a stratified way. The proposed technique could be naturally parallelized, which has been utilized by the tool supporting the technique. The experiments reported in the paper demonstrate that the proposed technique can mitigate the state space explosion instances from which otherwise only one JPF instance cannot suffice. In addition to some pieces of our future above mentioned, another piece of our future work is to conduct more case studies so that we can make sure that the proposed technique and the tool supporting it can mitigate the state space explosion reasonably well.

References

1. Arora, V., Bhatia, R.K., Singh, M.: A systematic review of approaches for testing concurrent programs. Concurr. Comput.: Pract. Exp. **28**(5), 1572–1611 (2016). https://doi.org/10.1002/cpe.3711
2. Choudhary, A., Lu, S., Pradel, M.: Efficient detection of thread safety violations via coverage-guided generation of concurrent tests. In: 39th ICSE, pp. 266–277 (2017). https://doi.org/10.1109/ICSE.2017.32
3. Clavel, M., et al.: Some tools. All About Maude - A High-Performance Logical Framework. LNCS, vol. 4350, pp. 667–693. Springer, Heidelberg (2007). https://doi.org/10.1007/978-3-540-71999-1_21
4. Do, C.M., Ogata, K.: Specification-based testing with simulation relations. In: 31st SEKE. KSI Research Inc. (2019, to appear)
5. Huang, J.: Stateless model checking concurrent programs with maximal causality reduction. In: 36th PLDI, pp. 165–174 (2015). https://doi.org/10.1145/2737924.2737975
6. Kurita, T., Chiba, M., Nakatsugawa, Y.: Application of a formal specification language in the development of the "Mobile FeliCa" IC chip firmware for embedding in mobile phone. In: Cuellar, J., Maibaum, T., Sere, K. (eds.) FM 2008. LNCS, vol. 5014, pp. 425–429. Springer, Heidelberg (2008). https://doi.org/10.1007/978-3-540-68237-0_31
7. Metzler, P., Saissi, H., Bokor, P., Suri, N.: Quick verification of concurrent programs by iteratively relaxed scheduling. In: 32nd ASE, pp. 776–781 (2017). https://doi.org/10.1109/ASE.2017.8115688

8. Ogata, K.: Model checking designs with CafeOBJ - a contrast with a software model checker. Workshop on Formal Method and Internet of Mobile Things, ECNU, Shanghai, China (2014)

9. Ogata, K., Futatsugi, K.: Simulation-based verification for invariant properties in the OTS/CafeOBJ method. ENTCS **201**, 127–154 (2007). Refine 2007

10. Visser, W., Havelund, K., Brat, G.P., Park, S., Lerda, F.: Model checking programs. Autom. Softw. Eng. **10**(2), 203–232 (2003). https://doi.org/10.1023/A: 1022920129859

11. Yi, Q., Huang, J.: Concurrency verification with maximal path causality. In: 26th FSE/17th ESEC, pp. 366–376 (2018). https://doi.org/10.1145/3236024.3236048

Formal Verification

An Approach to Modeling and Verifying Multi-level Interrupt Systems with TMSVL

Jin Cui[1(✉)], Xu Lu[2(✉)], and Buwen Liang[3]

[1] Xi'an Shiyou University, Xi'an 710071, People's Republic of China
cuijin_xd@126.com
[2] ICTT and ISN Laboratory, Xidian University, Xi'an 710071,
People's Republic of China
xlu@xidian.edu.cn
[3] The Second Oil Production Plant of PetroChina Changqing Oilfield Company,
Qingyang 745100, People's Republic of China

Abstract. In embedded systems and operating systems, the interrupt mechanism is an important way to ensure real-time response to kinds of asynchronous events. While the interrupt mechanism changes the execution traces of the main program, it makes modeling and verification of systems with interrupt difficulty. Therefore, we propose an approach to modeling and verifying multi-level interrupt systems. Firstly, the model of multi-level interrupt systems based on Time Projection Temporal Logic (TPTL) is proposed. On this basis, the model can be used to extend the TMSVL language and the TMSVL interpreter so that multi-level interrupt systems can be modeled, simulated and verified automatically. Finally, a case study is given to show the correctness and practicability of the proposed approach.

Keywords: Multi-level interrupt systems · Timed Projection Temporal Logic · TMSVL · Formal verification · Model checking

1 Introduction

The interrupt mechanism is an effective way to ensure real-time response to various asynchronous events in embedded systems and operating systems. Since the interrupt mechanism improves the timeliness of handling asynchronous events without occupying too much processor time in systems [1]. However, the use of interrupt mechanisms increases the difficulty to test systems. The triggering of the interrupt is random and has a lot of uncertainty. Thus, it is difficult to check interrupt errors only through dynamic execution or static code analysis. This

This research is supported by the NSFC Grant Nos. 61806158, 413619001, China Postdoctoral Science Foundation Nos. 2019T120881 and 2018M643585, and PhD research funding No. 134010012.

© Springer Nature Switzerland AG 2020
H. Miao et al. (Eds.): SOFL+MSVL 2019 Workshop, LNCS 12028, pp. 61–72, 2020.
https://doi.org/10.1007/978-3-030-41418-4_5

makes it difficult to guarantee the reliability of embedded systems or operating systems with multi-level interrupts, which we call multi-level interrupt systems.

Formal verification techniques [2] is a good complementation to guarantee the reliability of interrupt systems. With formal verification technique, the system to be verified is modeled with a formal formalism or language such as timed automata [3], Stateful Timed Communication Sequential Process (STCSP) [4], etc, the properties to be verified is specified with a property specification language such as LTL, CTL and their variations [5,6], and a verification algorithm as well as a supporting tool is developed to verify systems in a semi-automatical (for theorem proving approach [7,8]) or automatical manner (for model checking approach [9–11]).

In recent years, many studies have focused on formal modeling and verification of interrupt systems. In [12], semantics theories for programs with nested interrupts are defined for timing analysis. While it lacks a brief structure to model programs with multi-level interrupts. In [13], the authors proposed a verification framework for preemptive operating systems kernels with multi-level interrupts. In the verification framework, the specification language for defining the high-level abstract model of OS kernels, the program logic for refinement verification of concurrent kernel code with multi-level hardware interrupts, and automated tactics for developing mechanized proofs are provided. Since the correctness of API implementations in OS kernels is modeled as contextual refinement of their abstract specifications. The verification framework is developed mainly for verification of function correctness, while verification of temporal properties as well as timing properties is not considered. There are also some other work focusing on modeling and verification of interrupt systems. In [14], Timed Petri net models are defined for multi-level interrupt systems, which are transformed into timed automata to carry out the model checking process. In [15], the models based on iDola language for multi-level interrupt systems are defined, they are also transformed into timed automata to borrow the tools of timed automata to verify automatically. In the model checking process with time automata, properties to be verified is specified by LTL, CTL or their variations, which are difficult to express periodicity and interval properties [16]. In [17], the sequence diagram (SD) is extended to interrupt sequence diagram (ISD) to supports modeling of interrupt systems. The verification process is carried out by transforming ISD to interrupt automata (IA) to borrow the tools of IA to verify properties automatically. While the internal behavior of each participating entity cannot be presented, thus properties of participating entities is difficult to be verified. STCSP contains the interrupt statement $P\ interrupt[d]\ Q$ to describe the interrupt mechanism in real-time systems. This statement indicates that if process P ends execution before d time units, then Q will not be executed. Otherwise, after d time units, Q starts execute, while the execution of P is not resumed after the execution ends.

In this paper, we propose an efficient modeling and verification approach for multi-level interrupt systems. A general model $INP()$ for multi-level interrupt systems is defined. With $INP()$, a multi-level interrupt system with any number of interrupts can be easily modeled. The formal semantics for $INP()$ is defined using Timed Projection Temporal Logic (TPTL) [18]. Then, the TMSVL language [18] is extended with the new interrupt structure $INP()$. Thus, with multi-level interrupt systems be modeled by TMSVL language, properties to be verified with Propositional Projection Temporal Logic (PPTL), the unified model checking approach [19–21] can be adopted to verify whether properties are valid or not for multi-level interrupt systems.

The remainder of the paper is organized as follows. The next section gives an introduction to preliminaries for modeling multi-level interrupt systems, including TPTL and TMSVL language. In Sect. 3, we show how to formalize multi-level interrupt systems for verification. In Sect. 4, we show how a design instance with two level of interrupts is modeled and verified using the proposed approach. Finally, conclusions and future work are drawn in Sect. 5.

2   Preliminaries

2.1   TPTL

TPTL is extended from Projection Temporal Logic (PTL) [22] to model real-time systems. Its syntax is inductively defined as follows:

$$e ::= c \mid v \mid T \mid Ts \mid \bigcirc e \mid \ominus e \mid f(e_1,\ldots,e_m)$$
$$\phi ::= p \mid e_1 = e_2 \mid P(e_1,\ldots,e_m) \mid \phi_1 \wedge \phi_2 \mid \neg\phi \mid$$
$$\exists v : \phi \mid \bigcirc \phi \mid (\phi_1,\ldots,\phi_m) \text{ prj } \phi \mid \phi_1 \,!\, \phi_2 \mid$$
$$\{e_1, e_2\}\phi$$

Term e can be a constant c, variable v, time variable T, time interval variable Ts, e at the next state $(\bigcirc e)$, e at the previous state $(\ominus e)$, and function f. A TPTL formula ϕ can be a proposition p, an equality $e_1 = e_2$, a predict $P(e_1,\ldots,e_m)$, the conjunction of formulas ϕ_1 and ϕ_2, the negation of formula ϕ, quantifier formula $\exists v : \phi$, ϕ at the next state, the projection formula $(\phi_1,\ldots,\phi_m)$ prj ϕ, the cut formula $\phi_1 \,!\, \phi_2$, delay constrains formula $\{e_1, e_2\}\phi$. In TPTL, the newly introduced terms are time variable T, time interval variable Ts, the newly introduced formulas are $\{e_1, e_2\}\phi$ and $\phi_1 \,!\, \phi_2$, the other terms and formulas are the same as that of PTL.

An interval $\sigma = \langle s_0, s_1, \ldots\rangle$ is a non-empty (finite or infinite) sequence of states, the length of σ, denoted by $|\sigma|$, is ω if σ is infinite, and the number of states minus 1 otherwise. Usually, s_0 is called the first state and $s_{|\sigma|}$ the final state if σ is finite, $s_{|\sigma|}$ is undefined otherwise.

Projection formula $(\phi_1,\ldots,\phi_m)$ prj ϕ can be used to define kinds of interrupt mechanisms. Thus we focus on showing the semantics and derived formulas of the projection formula.

Intuitively, $(\phi_1,\ldots,\phi_m)$ prj ϕ means that formulas $\phi_1,\ldots,\phi_m$ are interpreted in a sequential manner over interval σ as shown in Fig. 1, where we take $m = 3$ as an example. The end points $(s_0, s_3, s_8, \text{ and } s_{15})$ of the intervals over which $\phi_1,\ldots,\phi_3$ are interpreted constructs the projection interval σ'. Assume ϕ is

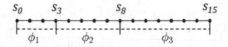

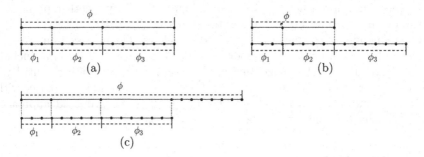

Fig. 1. The interpretation (semantics) of $\phi_1, \ldots, \phi_3$ in the sequential manner

Fig. 2. The interpretation (semantics) of the projection formula $(\phi_1, \ldots, \phi_3)$ prj ϕ

interpreted over interval σ_1, then σ_1 and σ' have the three possible relations: (1) σ_1 and σ' are the same (as shown in Fig. 2(a)); (2) σ_1 is a prefix subinterval of σ' (as shown in Fig. 2(b)); (3) σ' is a prefix subinterval of σ_1 (as shown in Fig. 2(c)).

Based on the projection operation (prj), we define the projection-plus operation (Definition A_1) and projection-star operation (prj⊛, Definition A_2). In Definition A_1, n represents any positive integer or infinity.

$A_1.\ (\phi_1, \ldots, (\phi_i, \ldots, \phi_l)^\oplus, \ldots, \phi_m)$ prj $\phi \overset{\text{def}}{=} (\phi_1, \ldots, (\phi_i, \ldots, \phi_l)^n, \ldots, \phi_m)$ prj ϕ

$A_2.\ (\phi_1, \ldots, (\phi_i, \ldots, \phi_l)^\circledast, \ldots, \phi_m)$ prj $\phi \overset{\text{def}}{=} (\phi_1, \ldots, \varepsilon, \ldots, \phi_m)$ prj $\phi \vee$
$\qquad\qquad\qquad\qquad\qquad\qquad\quad (\phi_1, \ldots, (\phi_i, \ldots, \phi_l)^\oplus, \ldots, \phi_m)$ prj ϕ

2.2 TMSVL

TMSVL is an executable subset of TPTL, it consists of arithmetic expressions e, boolean expressions b, and basic statements s, e and b are defined by the following grammar:

$$e ::= c \mid v \mid \bigcirc e \mid \ominus e \mid f(e_1, \ldots, e_m)$$
$$b ::= true \mid false \mid e_0 = e_1 \mid e_0 < e_1 \mid \neg b \mid b_0 \wedge b_1$$

where c is a constant, v a variable; $\bigcirc e$ and $\ominus e$ denote e at the next state and previous state over an interval, and f a function.

Statements s is listed in Table 1. Statements 1–4 are for the definition and assignment of variables. Statements 5–11 are for the structure controlling while statements 12–13 the state controlling; statement $len(n)$ specifies an interval of length n; statements 15–16 indicate where an interval ends. These statements are also defined in MSVL and the rest statements (17–21) are only defined in

Table 1. TMSVL statements

	Statements	Syntax		Statements	Syntax
1	State frame	$lbf(v)$	12	Next	$next\ \phi$
2	Frame	$frame(v)$	13	Always	$alw(\phi)$
3	Assignment	$v <== e$	14	Length	$len(n)$
4	Unit assignment	$v := e$	15	Synchronization	$await(b)$
5	Projection	$(\phi_1, \ldots, \phi_m)$ prj ϕ	16	Termination	$empty$
6	Sequential	$\phi_1 ; \phi_2$	17	Clock	$clock(e)$
7	Conditional	$if\ (b)\ then\ \{\phi_1\}\ else\ \phi_2$	18	Cut	$\phi_1\ !\ \phi_2$
8	While	$while(b)\{\phi\}$	19	Delay	$\{e_1, e_2\}\phi$
9	Selection	ϕ_1 or ϕ_2	20	Timeout	$\{e\}\phi$
10	Parallel	$\phi_1 \| \phi_2$	21	Interrupt	$\phi_1\ when(p, b)\ do\ \phi_2$
11	Conjunction	ϕ_1 and ϕ_2			

TMSVL. Their meanings are as follows: $clock(e)$ initializes global time variable T with e and increases T with time increment Ts; $\phi_1\ !\ \phi_2$ means that statements ϕ_1 and ϕ_2 are executed concurrently while ϕ_2 is terminated naturally or forcibly when ϕ_1 terminates; delay statement $\{e_1, e_2\}\phi$ indicates that the execution time of ϕ falls into the time duration $[e_1, e_2]$; $\{e\}\phi$ tells us that ϕ is terminated naturally or forcibly when the execution time reaches e; the interrupt statement $\phi_1\ when(p, b)\ do\ \phi_2$ means that when ϕ_1 is executing, if condition b becomes $true$, ϕ_1 is interrupted by ϕ_2 and is resumed when ϕ_2 terminates, here proposition p is used to mark the termination of ϕ_1.

3   Modeling of Multi-level Interrupt Systems

The interrupt mechanism provides an efficient way for a system to interact with and react to their operating environment. Most processors supports interrupts and most real-time operating systems provides the interrupt manage mechanism. Processors generally allow interrupts to be nested, that is, while serving an interrupt, the processor can suspend the current interrupt handler and respond other high priority interrupt requests. The interrupt mechanism changes the execution traces of the main program, it makes modeling and verification of a system difficult. Thus, we propose the model $INP()$ to easily modeling and verifying multi-level interrupt systems. In this section, first, we briefly present the syntax of $INP()$. Then we show how $INP()$ is defined using TPTL. Lastly, we introduce how to use $INP()$ to model interrupt systems with the number of interrupts being variable.

An interrupt system usually composes of the main program (denoted as Q), n external events $(a[0], \ldots, a[n-1])$ which trigger interrupt requests $(re[0], \ldots, re[n-1])$, and interrupt handlers (denoted as $H[0], \ldots, H[n-1]$) for responding the n interrupt requests. Thus, we use $INP(Q, fp(re, n), p)$ to denote the structure of the above interrupt systems, and $INP(Q, fp(re, n), p)$ is defined by the following TPTL formula with the projection star operator:

$$INP(Q, fp(re, n), p) \overset{\text{def}}{=}$$
$$((fp(re, n)^\circledast, p \wedge \varepsilon) \; \mathsf{prj} \; (Q; p \wedge \varepsilon)) \wedge halt(p)$$

where $fp(re, n)$ indicates how interrupt requests $re[0], \ldots, re[n-1]$ are responded in interrupt systems, p is a proposition used to ensure that the response to interrupts ends when the execution of main program Q terminates.

In the following, we show how to use $INP()$ to model multi-level interrupt systems when n takes different values. We assume that the smaller the subscript, the higher the priority of the interrupt request. Obviously, for the exceptive case where $n = 1$, the model is $INP(Q, fp(re, 1), p)$ and $fp(r, 1)$ can be defined as follows:

$$fp(re, 1) \overset{\text{def}}{=} if(re)then\{H\}else\{skip\}$$

When $n = 2$, the model is $INP(Q, fp(re, 2), p)$ and $fp(r, 2)$ is defined below:

$$fp(re, 2) \overset{\text{def}}{=} if(\neg re[0] \wedge re[1])then\{INP(H[1], fp(re, 1), p_1)\} \; and$$
$$\qquad if(re[0])then\{H[0]\} \; and$$
$$\qquad if(\neg re[0] \wedge \neg re[1])then\{skip\}$$
$$fp(re, 1) \overset{\text{def}}{=} if(re[0])then\{H[0]\}else \; skip$$

When $n = 3$, the model is $INP(Q, fp(re, 3), p)$, denoted as $INP(Q, fp (re, 3), p)$ for simplicity, and the definition of $fp(re, 3)$ is as follows:

$$fp(re, 3) \overset{\text{def}}{=} if(\neg re[0] \wedge \neg re[1] \wedge re[2]) \; then \; \{INP(H[2], fp(re, 2), p_1)\} \; and$$
$$\qquad if(\neg re[0] \wedge re[1])then\{INP(H[1], fp(re, 1), p_2)\}and$$
$$\qquad if(re[0])then\{H[0]\} \; and$$
$$\qquad if(\neg re[0] \wedge \neg re[1] \wedge \neg re[2]) \; then\{skip\}$$
$$fp(re, 2) \overset{\text{def}}{=} if(\neg re[0] \wedge re[1]) \; then \; \{INP(H[1], fp(re, 1), p_2)\} \; and$$
$$\qquad if(re[0]) \; then\{H[0]\} \; and$$
$$\qquad if(\neg re[0] \wedge \neg re[1]) \; then \; \{skip\}$$
$$fp(re, 1) \overset{\text{def}}{=} if(re[0])then\{H[0]\}else\{skip\}$$

From the above examples, we can see that to define the interrupt model $INP(Q, fp(re, n), p)$ when there are n interrupts, we only need to define $fp(re, n)$, $fp(re, n-1)$, $\ldots$, $fp(re, 1)$, namely, $fp(re, i)$ for $i = n, n-1, \ldots, 1$. Since $re[0], \ldots, re[n-1]$ are in different priorities, and the highest priority interrupt requests always be responded first. Thus $fp(re, i)$ for $i = 1, 2, \ldots, n$ can be easily defined as follows:

$$fp(re, i) \overset{\text{def}}{=} if(\neg re[0] \wedge \ldots \wedge \neg re[i-2] \wedge re[i-1])$$
$$\qquad then \; \{INP(H[i-1], f(r, i-1), p_1)\} \; and$$
$$\qquad if(\neg re[0] \wedge \ldots \wedge \neg re[i-3] \wedge re[i-2])$$
$$\qquad then \; \{INP(H[i-2], f(re, i-2), p_2)\} \; and$$
$$\qquad \cdots$$
$$\qquad if(re[0]) \; then \; H[0] \; and$$
$$\qquad if(\neg re[0] \wedge \ldots \wedge \neg re[i-1]) \; then \; skip$$

■ The main program Q is executing

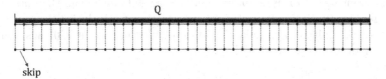

Fig. 3. No interrupt request when Q executes

▨ H[0] is executing
▨ H[1] is executing
▬ H[2] is executing
■ The main program is executing

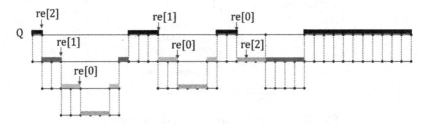

Fig. 4. An example of $INP()$ with $n = 3$

In $INP(Q, fp, p)$, if there is no interrupt request occurs when Q is executing, the model of $INP(Q, fp, p)$ can be expressed by Fig. 3 for n being arbitrary positive integers. While for n taking different values, and the interrupt request order being different, the model of $INP(Q, fp, p)$ will be different. For example, $n = 3$, when Q is executing, interrupt requests $re[1], re[2]$ and $re[3]$ occur at different time, a model (interpretation) of this case is shown in Fig. 4. This figure includes the cases of 3 levels, 2 levels of nested interrupts, and the case where one interrupt handler starts executing after the execution of the other interrupt handler completes.

In the above, we just show how to use $INP(Q, fp, p)$ to model the case where the priority of interrupt requests is fixed. In fact, the case where the priority of interrupt requests changes can also be modeled using $INP(Q, fp, p)$ just by redefining fp.

4   A Case Study

ARM CortexTM-M3 is a 32-bit micro-controller, it is widely used in fields such as industrial automation, intelligent control, etc. Figure 5 shows a design instance based on the processor platform. The design instance contains a main function and two interrupt service routines ISR1 and ISR2. The main function has a local variable sum. The value of sum is kept increasing with 1 in the while loop until it equals to 100 or the global variable *timerCount* becomes 0. ISR1 is triggered by external event $a[0]$. In ISR1, *timerCount* is counted down from the initial value until it reaches 0. ISR2 is triggered by external event $b[1]$. In ISR2, *timerCount* is reset to the initial value 20. In addition, interrupt event $a[0]$ has a higher priority than interrupt event $a[1]$.

The main function	The interrupt service routines

int timerCount=20;
 	
int main()
 	
{ int sum=0;
 	
while(!(timerCount= =0|| sum= =0))
 	
{sum=sum+1;}
 	
return sum;
 	
}
	void ISR1()
	{ //... disable interrupt
	  if(timerCount!=0)
	  {timerCount--;}
	  display();
	  //...enable interrupt
	}
	
	void ISR2()
	{ //... disable interrupt
	  timerCount=20;
	  display();
	  //...enable interrupt
	}

Fig. 5. A design instance of interrupt systems

Interrupt service routines can change the execution traces of programs. However, to ensure the data safety of the main program, it should not change values of local variables in the main function. As an example, we verify whether data are safe in the main program. Thus, we can use the multi-level interrupt structure $INP()$ and TMSVL language to model the design instance, PPTL to describe the property to be verified. Further, we utilize the TMSVL interpreter to verify whether the properties are valid or not in the design instance automatically.

Suppose that the TMSVL model of the design instance is M, the main function is Q, ISR1 is $H[0]$, ISR2 is $H[1]$. Additionally, we use Dc to denote the global variable definition module, boolean variables $re[0]$ and $re[1]$ denote whether interrupt events $a[0]$ and $a[1]$ occur or not, respectively. Thus, M can be defined in TMSVL as follows:

$$M \stackrel{\text{def}}{=} Dc; INP(Q, fp(re, 2), p)$$

$$fp(re, 2) \stackrel{\text{def}}{=} if \ \neg re[0] \wedge re[1] \ then \ INP(H[1], fp(re, 1), p_1) \ and$$
$$if \ re[0] \ then \ H[0] \ and$$
$$if \ \neg re[0] \wedge \neg re[1] \ then \ skip$$

$$fp(re, 1) \stackrel{\text{def}}{=} if \ re[0] \ then \ H[0] \ else \ skip$$

where Dc, Q, $H[0]$, and $H[1]$ are defined in Fig. 6. Specifically, the global variables in M consists of system variables *sum* and *timerCount* as well as the

Dc	Q
frame(sum,timerCount,ie, isr,iEv,inv1,inv2) and int sum<= =0 and int timerCount<= =20 and int iEv[2]<= ={0,0} and int isr[2]<= ={0,0} and int ie<= =1 and int inv1,inv2 and skip	while(timerCount!=0) { if(ie=0 or (iEv[0]=0 and iEv[1]=0)) then{sum:=sum+1 } else{skip} }
H[0]	H[1]
inv1:=sum and inv2:=timerCount and isr[0]:=1 ; ie:=0; timerCount:=timerCount-1; ie:=1; iEv[0]:=0 and isr[0]:=0	inv1:=sum and inv2:=timerCount and isr[1]:=1 ; ie:=0; timerCount:=20; ie:=1; iEv[1]:=0 and isr[1]:=0

Fig. 6. The TMSVL programs of the modules $Dc, Q, H[0]$ and $H[1]$ in M

introduced variables for modeling which include ie, isr, iEv, $inv1$ and $inv2$. Variable ie is a boolean variable indicating whether interrupt is enabled or not. isr and iEv are boolean arrays of size 2, isr indicates whether an interrupt event is being served. iEv represents that whether interrupt events occur, when the execution of interrupt handlers completes, the corresponding element in iEv and isr is set to 0. Variables $inv1$ and $inv2$ record values of system variables sum and $timerCount$ before the interrupt handler executes.

The main program is data safe means that values of variables in M before interrupt handlers execute and after interrupt handlers execute should always be the same. To express the properties in PPTL, we define the following propositions:

$$define \ p_1 : isr[0] = 1; \quad p_2 : isr[1] = 1;$$
$$q_1 : sum = inv1; q_2 : timerCount = inv2$$

where p_1 denotes that the interrupt handler of event $a[0]$ (ISR1) is executing, p_2 represents that the interrupt handler of event $a[1]$ (ISR2) is executing; q_1 means that the value of sum equals to that of $inv1$, q_2 means that the value of $timerCount$ equals to that of $inv2$. With these propositions, the safety of sum and $timerCount$ in the main function can be expressed by PPTL formulas ϕ_1 and ϕ_2, respectively which are defined as follows:

$$\phi_1 \stackrel{def}{=} \Box((p_1 \vee p_2) \to q_1)$$
$$\phi_2 \stackrel{def}{=} \Box((p_1 \vee p_2) \to q_2)$$

Table 2 lists the TMSVL models of three input instances as well as the corresponding verification results for ϕ_1 and ϕ_2. Input 1 shows that at the second time unit, interrupt event $a[0]$ occurs, followed by interrupt event $a[1]$ a time unit later. Input 2 represents that interrupt events $a[0]$ and $a[1]$ occur simultaneously at the fourth time unit. Input 3 describes that interrupt events $a[0]$ and $a[1]$ occur simultaneously at the fourth time unit, and after 25 time units, interrupt event $a[1]$ occurs, followed by interrupt event $a[1]$ a time unit later.

Table 2. The input instances and verification results

	Inputs	Verification result	
		ϕ_1	ϕ_2
Input 1	iEv[0]:=1;iEv[1]:=1;true	Valid	Violated
Input 2	len(4);iEv[0]<===1 and iEv[1]<===1	Valid	Violated
Input 3	len(4);iEv[0]<===1 and iEv[1]<===1 and empty; len(25);iEv[0]<===1 and skip; iEv[1]<===1	Valid	Violated

The verification results indicate that for the three cases, property ϕ_1 is valid while ϕ_2 is violated. In other words, in the three cases, variable *sum* always does not modified by interrupt handlers and it is safe in the main function; variable *timerCount* is modified by interrupt handlers and it is not safe in the main function. This is consistent with the fact since variable *sum* is a local variable in main function, while *timerCount* is a global variable, it is modified as long as interrupt events occur.

5   Conclusion

In this paper, we propose an efficient approach to modeling and verifying multi-level interrupt systems with TMSVL. The formal semantics of multi-level interrupt systems is given based on TPTL. Thus, the unified model checking process can be employed to verify and improve the safety and reliability of multi-level interrupt systems. Furthermore, our approach is general enough to model systems with the priority of interrupt requests being fixed as well as being variable. As for the future work, on the one hand, we will extend the MSVL compiler to execute TMSVL programs in a compile manner such that the efficiency of verification can be improved [23]; on the other hand, we need to consider how to cover more input instances for property verification.

References

1. Labrosse, J.J.: uC/OS-III: The Real-Time Kernel. Micrium Press, Weston (2009)
2. Wing, J.M.: A specifier's introduction to formal methods. Computer **23**(9), 8–22 (1990)
3. Alur, R., Dill, D.L.: A theory of timed automata. Theor. Comput. Sci. **126**(2), 183–235 (1994)
4. Sun, J., Liu, Y., Dong, J.S., Liu, Y., Shi, L., André, É.: Modeling and verifying hierarchical real-time systems using stateful timed CSP. ACM Trans. Softw. Eng. Methodol. **22**(1), 1–29 (2013)
5. Bouyer, P., Chevalier, F., Markey, N.: On the expressiveness of TPTL and MTL. Inf. Comput. **208**(2), 97–116 (2010)
6. Katoen, J.P.: Principles of Model Checking. The MIT Press, Cambridge (2008)
7. Gallier, J.H.: Logic for Computer Science: Foundations of Automatic Theorem Proving. Courier Dover Publications, Mineola (2015)
8. Duan, Z., Zhang, N., Koutny, M.: A complete proof system for propositional projection temporal logic. Theor. Comput. Sci. **497**, 84–107 (2013)
9. Wang, H., Duan, Z., Tian, C.: Model checking multi-agent systems with APTL. Adhoc Sens. Wirel. Netw. **37**, 35–52 (2017)
10. Clarke, E.M., Henzinger, T.A., Veith, H., Bloem, R.: Handbook of Model Checking, vol. 10. Springer, Heidelberg (2018). https://doi.org/10.1007/978-3-319-10575-8
11. Cui, J., Duan, Z., Tian, C., Zhang, N.: Modeling and analysis of nested interrupt systems. J. Softw. **29**, 1670–1680 (2018)
12. Huang, Y., He, J., Zhu, H., Zhao, Y., Shi, J., Qin, S.: Semantic theories of programs with nested interrupts. Front. Comput. Sci. **9**(3), 331–345 (2015)
13. Xu, F., Fu, M., Feng, X., Zhang, X., Zhang, H., Li, Z.: A practical verification framework for preemptive OS kernels. In: Chaudhuri, S., Farzan, A. (eds.) CAV 2016. LNCS, vol. 9780, pp. 59–79. Springer, Cham (2016). https://doi.org/10.1007/978-3-319-41540-6_4
14. Hou, G., Zhou, K., Chang, J., Li, R., Li, M.: Interrupt modeling and verification for embedded systems based on time petri nets. In: Wu, C., Cohen, A. (eds.) APPT 2013. LNCS, vol. 8299, pp. 62–76. Springer, Heidelberg (2013). https://doi.org/10.1007/978-3-642-45293-2_5
15. Liu, H., Zhang, H., Jiang, Y., Song, X., Gu, M., Sun, J.: iDola: bridge modeling to verification and implementation of interrupt-driven systems. In: Theoretical Aspects of Software Engineering Conference, pp. 193–200. IEEE (2014)
16. Zhang, N., Duan, Z., Tian, C.: Model checking concurrent systems with MSVL. Sci. China Inf. Sci. **59**(11), 118101 (2016)
17. Pan, M., Chen, S., Pei, Y., Zhang, T., Li, X.: Easy modelling and verification of unpredictable and preemptive interrupt-driven systems. In: Proceedings of the 41st International Conference on Software Engineering, pp. 212–222. IEEE Press (2019)
18. Cui, J., Duan, Z., Tian, C., Du, H., Zhang, N.: A novel approach to modeling and verifying real-time systems for high reliability. IEEE Trans. Reliab. **67**(2), 481–493 (2018)
19. Duan, Z., Tian, C.: A unified model checking approach with projection temporal logic. In: Liu, S., Maibaum, T., Araki, K. (eds.) ICFEM 2008. LNCS, vol. 5256, pp. 167–186. Springer, Heidelberg (2008). https://doi.org/10.1007/978-3-540-88194-0_12

20. Wang, M., Tian, C., Zhang, N., Duan, Z.: Verifying full regular temporal properties of programs via dynamic program execution. IEEE Trans. Reliab. **68**, 1101–1116 (2018)
21. Yu, B., Duan, Z., Tian, C., Zhang, N.: Verifying temporal properties of programs: a parallel approach. J. Parallel Distrib. Comput. **118**, 89–99 (2018)
22. Duan, Z.: Temporal Logic and Temporal Logic Programming. Science Press, Beijing (2005)
23. Yang, K., Duan, Z., Tian, C., Zhang, N.: A compiler for MSVL and its applications. Theor. Comput. Sci. **749**, 2–16 (2018)

Towards Formal Verification of Neural Networks: A Temporal Logic Based Framework

Xiaobing Wang[1], Kun Yang[1], Yanmei Wang[1], Liang Zhao[1(✉)],
and Xinfeng Shu[2(✉)]

[1] Institute of Computing Theory and Technology and ISN Laboratory,
Xidian University, Xi'an 710071, People's Republic of China
xbwang@foxmail.com, hengyk@qq.com, lvchu_wang@sina.com, lzhao@xidian.edu.cn
[2] School of Computer Science and Technology,
Xi'an University of Posts and Telecommunications,
Xi'an 710061, People's Republic of China
shuxf@xupt.edu.cn

Abstract. Due to extensive applications of deep learning and neural networks, their security has attracted more and more attentions from academic and industrial circles. Under the guidance of the theory of formal verification, this paper summarizes three basic problems which indicate the common features of different neural networks, and proposes three typical properties covering the correctness of a model, the correctness of a sample and the robustness of a model for neural network systems. The method is driven by these properties, the model is constructed using the MSVL language and the properties are characterized by the logic PPTL. On this basis, the modeling and verification process is done in the MC compiler.

Keywords: Neural network · Formal verification · MSVL · PPTL

1   Introduction

In recent years, deep learning and neural networks have become hotspots in scientific research, and have been widely used in computer vision [1], speech recognition [2] and other fields because of their good universality. However, there are still many problems in neural network systems. First, since the depth models are non-convex functions, it is very difficult to make theoretical research on neural networks. For any linear and nonlinear function, both a shallow network and a deep network can be found to represent them, and the depth model has better performance than the shallow model. But the expressibility of the deep

This research is supported by the NSFC Grant Nos. 61672403, 61272118, 61972301, 61420106004, and the Industrial Research Project of Shaanxi Province No. 2017GY-076.

© Springer Nature Switzerland AG 2020
H. Miao et al. (Eds.): SOFL+MSVL 2019 Workshop, LNCS 12028, pp. 73–87, 2020.
https://doi.org/10.1007/978-3-030-41418-4_6

network does not represent learnability and interpretability [3]. Second, whether a neural network system is safe has an important impact on the development of the industry. The neural network system itself may have serious defects and vulnerabilities, and may also be subject to different types of malicious attacks. Especially in the scenario of security [4], very small errors can lead to serious consequences. Because neural network models may have natural flaws, researchers have successfully used gradient-based or iterative-based attacks method to break through various excellent neural network models [5]. Therefore, it is necessary to check the security of neural network systems and to deepen the theoretical research of the neural network models.

Studies have shown that, the current majority of neural network systems use testing-based [6] methods for safety check and the high-probability test results determine whether a system is efficient and reliable. However, when neural networks are generalized into more general scenarios, the nature of confrontation [7] may appear, although the probability of confrontation is extremely low. Therefore, the test method does not prove that there is no error in a system, and it is not safe enough to use the tested system in some security-critical scenarios. Moreover, frequent large-scale tests often have long operating cycles, consume a lot of resources, have limited test scenarios, and fail to obtain error feedback information in a timely manner.

In the formalization field, the formal verification of concurrent systems [8] and internet security [9] has received extensive attentions due to its rigorousness. Formal verification [10] uses mathematical models and logics to describe software and hardware systems at the abstract level, and techniques such as model checking [11] and theorem proving [12] to infer whether a system meets certain properties. In this way, whether systems meet relevant design specifications or requirements is strictly verified. For the above reasons, it is crucial to use formal verification to study the properties of neural network models.

Well-known neural network systems include face recognition systems, autopilot systems, recommendation systems, translation systems, etc. These systems often have large amounts of data, large amounts of code, and complex implementation logics. Therefore, how to abstract these different neural network systems, how to reduce the state space after the abstraction to build a reasonable system model, and how to simulate existing relatively mature attack techniques are the most tricky question of formal modeling. Of course, how to find out the abnormity of a well-established neural network system model and how to generalize these potential abnormal states are very challenging problems in the formal verification process. In this paper, the combination of modeling of a neural network system and verification of its important and common properties is tried and explored.

The rest of the paper is organized as follows. Section 2 briefly describes the theoretical and instrumental basis of the method. Section 2.1 explains the general idea of neural network system modeling, common property analysis and verification. Section 2.2 elaborates the practicality and effectiveness of the method with a specific case. Finally, Sect. 2.3 discusses the current related work and Sect. 5 gives the conclusion and future work.

2   Background

This section gives a brief introduction of the MSVL language, the PPTL logic and the MC compiler.

2.1   MSVL

MSVL is a temporal logic programming language for modeling, simulation, and verification [13]. It is an executable subset of projection temporal logic (PTL) [14].

The syntax of arithmetic expressions e and boolean expressions b of MSVL is given as follows, where d is a constant, x is a variable, $\bigcirc$ (next) and $\ominus$ (previous) are temporal operators.

$$e ::= d \mid x \mid \bigcirc x \mid \ominus x \mid e_1 + e_2 \mid e_1 - e_2 \mid e_1 * e_2 \mid e_1/e_2 \mid e_1 \, mod \, e_2$$
$$b ::= true \mid false \mid \neg b \mid b_1 \wedge b_2 \mid e_1 = e_2$$

The basic statements of MSVL, generally represented by p and q, are given as follows.

(1)Termination *empty*	(2)Assignment $x \Leftarrow e$
(3)Unit Assignment $x := e$	(4)Conjunction p *and* q
(5)Selection p *or* q	(6)Next *next* p
(7)Always *alw*(p)	(8)Sequence p ; q
(9)Parallel $p \parallel q$	(10)Skip *skip*
(11)Await *await(b)*	(12)Len *len(n)*
(13)Interval *Frame* *frame(x)*	(14)Local *Variable* *local x:p*
(15)Conditional *if b then p else q*	(16)While *while b do p*
(17)Projection $h(p_1, ..., p_m)prj\, q$	(18)Function Call $f(e_1, ..., e_n)$
(19)External Function Call *extf*$(e_1, ..., e_n)$	

Readers may refer to [15] for the semantics and details of the statements.

2.2   PPTL

PPTL is the propositional version of PTL [16], which abstracts away variables, quantifiers and predicates. It is suitable to characterize properties of computer programs and systems.

The syntax of basic formulas of PPTL is provided as follows. Generally, we use a capital letter P, possibly with subscripts, to represent PPTL formulas, where p is an atomic proposition, $\bigcirc$ (next) and prj (projection) are temporal operators.

$$P ::= p \mid \neg\, P \mid P_1 \wedge P_2 \mid \bigcirc P \mid (P_1, \, ..., \, P_m) \, prj \, P$$

A commonly used set of derived formulas for PPTL is shown in Fig. 1.

$$\varepsilon \overset{\text{def}}{=} \neg \bigcirc true \qquad more \overset{\text{def}}{=} \neg \varepsilon$$

$$P; Q \overset{\text{def}}{=} (P, Q)\, prj\, \varepsilon \qquad \Diamond P \overset{\text{def}}{=} true; P$$

$$len(0) \overset{\text{def}}{=} \varepsilon \qquad len(n) \overset{\text{def}}{=} \bigcirc len(n-1)(n > 0)$$

$$\Box P \overset{\text{def}}{=} \neg \Diamond \neg P \qquad fin(P) \overset{\text{def}}{=} \Box(\varepsilon \to P)$$

Fig. 1. Derived formulas of PPTL

2.3   MC

MC is a compiler based on LLVM for the MSVL language, with modeling and verification functionalities [15]. Figure 2 shows the workflow of internal execution process of MC. The compiler accepts a well-formed MSVL program as its input, and through the analysis and process of the vocabulary, grammar, semantics, etc., generates an executable binary object code.

The main functionalities of the MC compiler are introduced as follows.

(1) Modeling. MC builds the model by constructing the program's normal form graph (NFG), which contains the state sequence of all state nodes and state transition edges of the program execution process. Instead of simply executing a program, the modeling process generates all possible paths of the program.

(2) Verification. The model is implemented in the MSVL language and each property is formalized as a PPTL formula. Figure 3 shows the verification principle of the compiler. Since an MSVL program is also a temporal logic formula [17], the compiler combines the MSVL program M with the negation of the PPTL formula P to obtain a special "violation" program to be executed. If such a program executes successfully, the execution path is exactly a counter-example path which indicates the program M violates the property P. Otherwise, the program satisfies the property as there is no counter-example path.

3   A Practical Verification Method for Neural Networks Based on MSVL

Common structures of neural networks include deep neural networks (DNN), convolutional neural networks (CNN), and recurrent neural networks (RNN). At present, the research on neural networks mainly focuses on three problems. First, how to define the correctness of the model. Second, how to use the correct model for anomaly detection. Third, how to make a correct model show obvious mistake.

Generally, in the field of formal verification, we need to summarize the research process of neural networks. Here, we briefly describe the process for solving the above three problems as the verification of the correctness of the model, the correctness of the sample, and the robustness of the model. The overall research process is shown in Fig. 4.

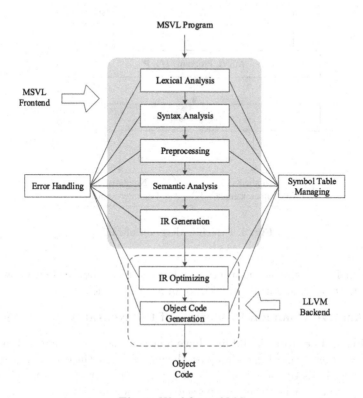

Fig. 2. Workflow of MC

Step 1 Prepare the Data Set

There are many ways to obtain data. Traditional neural network research often uses public datasets, such as Minist datasets and CIFAR-10 datasets. Social network researchers prefer to dynamically retrieve real-time user data through data crawlers, for example crawling Sina Weibo data. Of course, sometimes for research needs, custom data sets based on actual production and life are also a good choice. The data sets may be customized according to actual needs in order to adapt to the research purpose.

Step 2 Construct a Neural Network Model Using MSVL

The neural network has a variety of model structures, for example, CNN, including AlexNet, VGGNet, GoogleNet, ResNet and DenseNet. After the structure is selected, the model begins to build around the research purpose. Existing research tools allow either direct construction, which is manually coding the

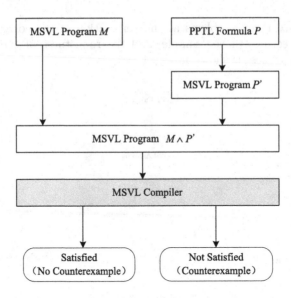

Fig. 3. Principle diagram of MC

MSVL model, or indirect construction, which is using the C2MSVL conversion tool to convert a C-language model into an MSVL model.

Step 3 Analyze Common Properties of the Neural Network Model

A typical neural network should first have a clear classification effect. If a model can correctly classify most data samples, the model meets the correctness requirement. On the basis of the correctness of the model, correct classification of all samples is detected when they are passed to the neural network model. At this point, the samples satisfy the correctness requirement. Notice that the correctness of the model does not mean that the model is totally robust. Nevertheless, if an attacker fails to lead a clearly erroneous sample to the correct category in a limited iteration, or the disturbed sample can still be correctly classified after being passed to the model, the model satisfies the robustness requirement.

Step 4 Formalize Common Properties of the Neural Network Model Using PPTL

Based on the research and analysis of the correctness of the model, the correctness of the sample and the robustness of the model in the previous step, properties of neural network models are characterized as PPTL formulas. Especially, every detail can be represented as an atomic proposition and the composition of atomic propositions obtains a PPTL formula. For example, in the verification of the correctness of the model, "correct classification of most samples" means that 90% of the samples successfully pass the neural network model, and "obvious classification effect" means that the model classification effect is TRUE. They can be formalized as composable propositions.

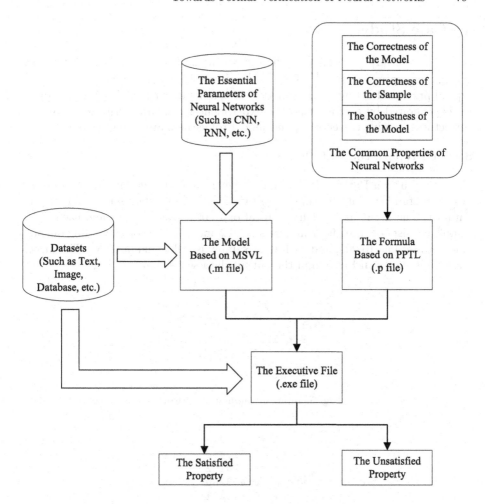

Fig. 4. Overall design of modeling and verification

Step 5 Verify Common Properties of the Neural Network Model with MC

Based on the above steps, it is dynamically verified whether the model meets the requirements of the properties or not. If a property is satisfied, the verification result is valid, which indicates that the model meets the actual requirements under the constraint of this property. Otherwise, the verification result is invalid, which indicates that either the model or the property is flawed, or an unpredictable anomaly occurs during the running of the model.

4   Case Study

In this case study, we illustrate the effectiveness of our method by fitting an arithmetic expression $Rs = \frac{(Va + Vb + Vc)}{3}$ using a BP neural network. This is a typical process of fitting a linear model using a nonlinear model, where the data set is generated by a script, and the experimental validation criteria for model correctness, sample correctness, and model robustness are given below.

Step 1 Prepare the Data Set

This study uses a Python data script to generate a custom dataset. A training or test or standard data set consists of two files, an input data set and an output data set. The input data set has a total of 10,000 data samples and each data sample consists of three float numbers V_a, V_b and V_c. The corresponding output data set also has 10,000, and each data sample is a float number R_s. The input data set is shown in Fig. 5, and the output data set is shown in Fig. 6.

```
1   0.789592,0.603599,0.447134
2   0.111393,0.653905,0.345247
3   0.896718,0.512995,0.009887
4   0.255888,0.413704,0.246280
5   0.532924,0.299292,0.430609
```

Fig. 5. Input of the neural network

```
1   0.613442
2   0.370182
3   0.473200
4   0.305291
5   0.420942
```

Fig. 6. Output of the neural network

As is shown in these figures, the first input data sample is $[V_a = 0.789592, V_b = 0.603599, V_c = 0.447134]$, and the first output data sample is $[R_s = 0.613442]$.

Step 2 Construct a Neural Network Model Using MSVL

We adopt BP neural networks to illustrate our method. A BP neural network is trained to construct the system model of arithmetic expression system. Through the comparison and analysis of the results of the arithmetic expression and the output of the neural network model, the neural network model is continuously optimized, and the key common properties are explored.

Specifically, a three-layer BP neural network is constructed, in which the input layer contains two nodes, the hidden layer contains five nodes, and the output layer contains one node. For the activation function, we select the sigmoid function $f(x) = \frac{1}{1+e^{-x}}$. And for the loss function, we use the square loss function $l(y_i, \hat{y}_i) = \frac{(y_i - \hat{y}_i)^2}{2}, y_i, \hat{y}_i \in R$.

Step 3 Analyze Common Properties of the Neural Network Model

Once the model is built, we begin to solve the three basic problems of the neural network model.

(1) The correctness of the model. Whether the neural network model is correct and effective depends on whether the model can correctly classify all or most of given data samples in a specific production and living environment. If the model meets our classification requirements, we consider the model to be correct. In this experiment, if most of the data samples in the test data set pass through the model and the square error between the simulated output and the actual calculation results is kept within a certain range, the arithmetic expression system model can be considered to be correct. The square error is called prediction error in the following and the range is specified according to actual needs which may be either an empirical value summarized in the past or an evaluation value of the standard data set.

(2) The correctness of the sample. After selecting the correct neural network model, we focus on how to detect abnormal samples. Traditional neural network researchers believe that when a data sample is correctly classified, the sample can be located as a normal sample. Formal methods require us to quantify normal indicators. That is, when a data sample passes through the neural network model, if its simulation output satisfies certain conditions, the data sample can be considered normal. We use the average of the square error between the simulated output of the standard data set and the actual calculated result as a measure, which is called average error. If a sample passes the selected neural network model and its prediction error is lower than the average error, the sample satisfies the normal criteria.

For example, consider the average error $aveE_k$ [0.000002] and one data sample O_a [$V_a = 0.991998, V_b = 0.919734, V_c = 0.859287$] with the calculation result R_s [0.923673]. If its simulation result is R'_s [0.911534], the prediction error is E_k [0.000074]. Since the prediction error is larger than the average error, the data sample is in an abnormal state and does not satisfy sample correctness.

(3) The robustness of the model. Neural networks are very fragile in that even a sample that suffers from small disturbances may fool a neural network model. When a certain attack method is applied to the sample, how robust the model is a very interesting question. We can use a formal approach to make this problem clear by studying the magnitude of the disturbance of the sample or the number of iterations of the attack. If the input sample is able to lead a clearly erroneous sample to the correct result after a finite number

of perturbations, the model is successfully attacked, that is, the model may have significant defects.

We use the classic fast gradient sign method (FGSM) to illustrate this process. The magnitude of the disturbance of the adversarial sample relative to the original sample is measured by the L_2 distance $||x||_2 = sqrt\left(\sum (\nabla x)^2\right)$. First, the gradients of back propagation is calculated. Second, using the sign function

$$sgn(x) = \begin{cases} -1 : x < 0 \\ 0 : x = 0 \\ 1 : x > 0 \end{cases}$$, the eigenvalues of the sample based on the gradients are

manipulated. If the two steps are iterated, the robustness that neural network model trying to maintain would be destroyed.

In this experiment, the original sample is the data sample O_a in (2). After the original sample is disturbed by 14488 iterations of FGSM, an adversarial sample is generated as O'_a [$V'_a = 1.008701, V'_b = 0.936437, V'_c = 0.875990$], of which the corresponding simulation result is R'_s [0.922130]. From the comparison of the current simulation results R'_s and the actual result R'_s in (2), the prediction error has been reduced to $E'_k = 0.000001$, which satisfies the sample correctness. However, from the comparison of the original simulation result R'_s and the actual result R_s, a clearly erroneous sample completes a perfect targeted attack and the robustness of the model is compromised.

Step 4 Formalize Common Properties of the Neural Network Model Using PPTL

(1) The correctness of the model. If more than 90% of the samples in the test set are correctly classified by the neural network model and the prediction error is controlled within a certain range, the model is correct and effective. Two propositions and a PPTL formula are defined as follows.

$$p \stackrel{\text{def}}{=} bpnn\_sim\_percent > 0.9;$$
$$q \stackrel{\text{def}}{=} check\_model = 1;$$
$$P_1 \stackrel{\text{def}}{=} fin(p \wedge q)$$

Here, the proposition p indicates that more that 90% of the data samples in the test set pass the neural network model, q indicates that the prediction error of the sample is within an acceptable range, and the property formula P_1 indicates that both p and q hold at the final state of model execution.

(2) The correctness of the sample. A sample is considered to be normally reliable if it can successfully pass a neural network model that satisfies the correctness, i.e., the prediction error of the sample is less than the average error of the standard data set. Three propositions and a PPTL formula are defined as follows.

$$p_0 \overset{\text{def}}{=} E_k! = 0;$$
$$p_1 \overset{\text{def}}{=} aveE_k! = 0;$$
$$q \overset{\text{def}}{=} E_k < aveE_k;$$
$$P_2 \overset{\text{def}}{=} fin(p_0 \wedge p_1 \rightarrow q)$$

Here, the proposition p_0 indicates that the prediction error of the sample is not zero, p_1 indicates that the average error of the standard data set is not zero, q indicates that the prediction error is less than the average error, and the property formula P_2 indicates that p_0 and p_1 imply q at the final state of model execution.

(3) The robustness of the model. If a correct neural network model can withstand 1000 iteration attacks of FSGM, and the prediction error of the sample is always greater than the average error in this process, it is reasonable to consider the model to be robust. Three propositions and a PPTL formula are defined as follows.

$$p \overset{\text{def}}{=} bpnn\_sim\_single <= 1000;$$
$$q \overset{\text{def}}{=} bpnn\_sim\_single\_Ek\_v > aveE_k;$$
$$r \overset{\text{def}}{=} bpnn\_sim\_single\_Ek\_out > aveE_k;$$
$$P_3 \overset{\text{def}}{=} \Box(p \wedge q \wedge r)$$

Here, the proposition p indicates that the number of iterative attacks is limited to 1000 times, q indicates that the initial prediction error is greater than the average error, r indicates that the prediction error is greater than the average error during the running of the program, and the property formula P_3 indicates that at every state of the model execution p, q, r hold simultaneously.

Alternatively, we can consider another notion of robustness where the number of FGSM iterations is not limited. When a neural network model is attacked, if the L_2 distance between the adversarial sample and the original sample is higher than 0.025000, the model can be considered to be robust enough.

$$p \overset{\text{def}}{=} l_2 > 0.025000;$$
$$q \overset{\text{def}}{=} bpnn\_sim\_single\_Ek\_v > aveE_k;$$
$$r \overset{\text{def}}{=} bpnn\_sim\_single\_Ek\_out <= aveE_k;$$
$$P_4 \overset{\text{def}}{=} fin(p \wedge q \wedge r)$$

Here, the proposition p indicates that the L_2 distance is greater than 0.025000, q indicates that the initial prediction error is greater than the average error, r indicates that the prediction error is less than the average error when the attack is successful, and the property formula P_4 indicates that at the final state of model execution p, q, r hold simultaneously.

```
Verification Result: Valid!!!
release ThreadPool success!!!
The run time is: 957565ms
```

Fig. 7. Verification result of satisfaction

```
Verification Result: Invalid!!!
release ThreadPool success!!!
The run time is: 15444ms
```

Fig. 8. Verification result of unsatisfaction

Step 5 Verify Common Properties of the Neural Network Model with MC

The MSVL program first reads, analyzes, and processes the data set, and then it is compiled and executed by the MC compiler. This process is basically similar to the compilation and execution process of C programs. If the program is executed smoothly, PPTL formulas can be used in the MC compiler to verify properties of the model. When the verification is completed, we analyze whether each property of the model is satisfied according to the verification results.

If a property is satisfied, the result is shown as in Fig. 7. While if a property is not satisfied, the result is shown as in Fig. 8.

The verification results of our experiment are shown in Table 1. The first property indicates that the neural network model is correct and valid under certain constraints. The second property indicates that the input data sample is in an abnormal state, i.e., the sample itself does not meet the requirements of the system model. The third property indicates that in a finite number of iterative attacks, the model may not be successfully attacked, i.e., the model is robust enough to resist a certain number of attacks. The forth property indicates that although the model is attacked, the distance between the adversarial sample and the original sample is too large when the attack is successful. This indicates that the adversarial sample does not adapt to the needs of the model, and in turn the model meets the robustness requirement.

Table 1. Verification results

Property	Property described	Verification result	Time
P_1	The correctness of model	Valid	957.565 s
P_2	The correctness of sample	Invalid	15.444 s
P_3	The robustness of model	Valid	43,709.561 s
P_4	The robustness of model	Valid	567,866.743 s

5   Related Work

The research on formal verification methods of neural network systems aim to ensure the reliability of the systems when they are applied to more critical-safety missions. Formal verification is an automated process that relies on rigorous mathematical reasoning to ensure that part or all of a system's specifications are realized. These specifications are able to meet the security requirements of neural network systems to some extent.

Regarding the research on the security of neural network systems, many achievements in academic are worthy of further discussion. By studying linear and nonlinear properties of neural networks, Goodfellow et al. propose a simple and fast method FGSM to generate adversarial samples [18]. The method is generalized to different neural network structures and then applied to specific physical scenes, and the classification effect is significantly affected by adversarial samples. Scholars from University of Georgia, University of Liverpool and University of Oxford collaborate to propose a typical black box attack method that requires minimal cost without any structural features of the neural network [19]. Besides, Huang et al. propose an automated verification framework for multi-layer feed-forward neural networks based on satisfiable module theory (SMT) [20]. The framework aims to evaluate the security of neural network models by systematically searching and analyzing the domains around the data points. Then, the analysis is propagated to a deeper network to determine which sets of operations can direct the data samples to the specified category.

In the field of formal verification, Wang et al. use the interval operation to solve the strict output limit of DNN, and propose a new direction to formalize the security properties of DNN [21]. The paper minimizes the output boundary by symbol interval analysis and corresponding optimization scheme. Their design is implemented and evaluated in the system ReluVal, and the results show that its performance is far superior to the prior method Reluplex. Scholars from University of California attempt to propose a formal specification of deep neural networks from the perspective of semantic property classification and trace theory classification [22]. The classification of semantic property aims to study the potential meaning and relevance of neural network system verification. The classification of trace theory aims to study what kind of domain is represented by the trace sets. In order to make neural network systems no longer be confined to consulting systems, Zeshan Kurd and Tim Kelly define a series of safety standards for neural network systems [23]. To further explain the rationality of ANN in security applications, the authors develop a security case and verify the security of the neural network, while considering the adaptability of performance and the versatility of the program.

6 Conclusions

The verification method of neural network systems focuses on three basic common problems. For these problems, we summarize three common properties including the correctness of the model, the correctness of the sample and the robustness of the model. The neural network system model is driven by properties, modeled and verified in the MC compiler.

First, the data set is prepared. Second, the neural network model is constructed using the MSVL language. Furthermore, common properties of the neural network model are acquired and analyzed. Then, these properties are formalized as PPTL formulas. Finally, using the MC compiler, it is dynamically verified whether the neural network model satisfies these properties.

For future work, we will increase the complexity of the model and apply it to more ubiquitous scenarios. In addition, we will gradually deepen the discussion and research on potential common properties of neural network systems.

References

1. Lu, H., Li, Y.: Artificial Intelligence and Computer Vision. Springer, Heidelberg (2017). https://doi.org/10.1007/978-3-319-46245-5
2. Hinton, G., et al.: Deep neural networks for acoustic modeling in speech recognition: the shared views of four research groups. IEEE Signal Process. Mag. **29**, 82–97 (2012)
3. Zhang, Q., Zhu, S.: Visual interpretability for deep learning: a survey. Front. Inf. Technol. Electron. Eng. **19**, 27–39 (2018)
4. Cheng, C., et al.: Neural networks for safety-critical applications - challenges, experiments and perspectives. In: Design, Automation and Test in Europe, pp. 1005–1006. IEEE Press (2018)
5. Akhtar, N., Mian, A.: Threat of adversarial attacks on deep learning in computer vision: a survey. IEEE Access **6**, 14410–14430 (2018)
6. Taylor, B., Darrah, M., Moats, C.: Verification and validation of neural networks: a sampling of research in progress. In: Intelligent Computing: Theory and Applications, pp. 8–16. SPIE (2003)
7. Szegedy, C., et al.: Intriguing properties of neural networks. arXiv 1312/6199 (2014)
8. Zhang, N., Duan, Z., Tian, C.: Model checking concurrent systems with MSVL. Sci. China Inf. Sci. **59**, 101–118 (2016)
9. Tian, C., Chen, C., Duan, Z.: Differential testing of certificate validation in SSL/TLS implementations: an RFC-guided approach. ACM Trans. Softw. Eng. Methodol. **28**, 24:1–24:37 (2019)
10. Cui, J., Duan, Z., Tian, C., Du, H.: A novel approach to modeling and verifying real-time systems for high reliability. IEEE Trans. Reliab. **67**, 481–493 (2018)
11. Duan, Z., Tian, C., Zhang, N.: A canonical form based decision procedure and model checking approach for propositional projection temporal logic. Theor. Comput. Sci. **609**, 544–560 (2016)
12. Duan, Z., Zhang, N., Maciej, K.: A complete proof system for propositional projection temporal logic. Theor. Comput. Sci. **497**, 84–107 (2013)
13. Duan, Z., Maciej, K.: A framed temporal logic programming language. J. Comput. Sci. Technol. **19**, 341–351 (2004)
14. Zhang, N., Duan, Z., Tian, C., Du, D.: A formal proof of the deadline driven scheduler in PPTL axiomatic system. Theor. Comput. Sci. **554**, 229–253 (2014)
15. Yang, K., Duan, Z., Tian, C., Zhang, N.: A compiler for MSVL and its applications. Theor. Comput. Sci. **749**, 2–16 (2017)
16. Duan, Z., Tian, C., Zhang, L.: A decision procedure for propositional projection temporal logic with infinite models. Acta Informatica **45**, 43–78 (2008)
17. Wang, M., Tian, C., Zhang, N., Duan, Z.: Verifying full regular temporal properties of programs via dynamic program execution. IEEE Trans. Reliab. **68**, 1101–1116 (2019)

18. Goodfellow, I., Shlens, J., Szegedy, C.: Explaining and harnessing adversarial examples. ArXiv:1412.6572 (2014)
19. Wicker, M., Huang, X., Kwiatkowska, M.: Feature-guided black-box safety testing of deep neural networks. In: Beyer, D., Huisman, M. (eds.) TACAS 2018. LNCS, vol. 10805, pp. 408–426. Springer, Cham (2018). https://doi.org/10.1007/978-3-319-89960-2_22
20. Huang, X., Kwiatkowska, M., Wang, S., Wu, M.: Safety verification of deep neural networks. In: Majumdar, R., Kunčak, V. (eds.) CAV 2017. LNCS, vol. 10426, pp. 3–29. Springer, Cham (2017). https://doi.org/10.1007/978-3-319-63387-9_1
21. Wang, S., Pei, K., Whitehouse, J., Yang, J., Jana, S.: Formal security analysis of neural networks using symbolic intervals. In: USENIX Conference on Security Symposium, pp. 1599–1614. USENIX Association (2018)
22. Seshia, S.A., et al.: Formal specification for deep neural networks. In: Lahiri, S.K., Wang, C. (eds.) ATVA 2018. LNCS, vol. 11138, pp. 20–34. Springer, Cham (2018). https://doi.org/10.1007/978-3-030-01090-4_2
23. Kurd, Z., Kelly, T.: Establishing safety criteria for artificial neural networks. In: Palade, V., Howlett, R.J., Jain, L. (eds.) KES 2003. LNCS (LNAI), vol. 2773, pp. 163–169. Springer, Heidelberg (2003). https://doi.org/10.1007/978-3-540-45224-9_24

UMC4M: A Verification Tool via Program Execution

Meng Wang, Junfeng Tian$^{(\boxtimes)}$, and Hong Zhang

Cyberspace Security and Computer College,
Hebei University, Baoding 071000, China
`tjf@hbu.edu.cn`

Abstract. Most of the software model checkers available for code level verification can only verify safety properties since desired properties are specified by assertions. However, other temporal properties such as liveness cannot be verified with these tools. To tackle this problem, we develop a verification tool called *UMC4M* to verify full regular temporal properties of programs. *UMC4M* takes a modeling, simulation and verification language (MSVL) program M and a desired property specified by a propositional projection temporal logic (PPTL) formula P as its input. $\neg P$ is then translated to an MSVL program M. Thus, the property can be verified by checking whether there is an acceptable execution of "M and M'", which can be solved with MSVL compiler *MC*. Further, *UMC4M* is used to verify the dining cryptographers protocol.

Keywords: Software model checking · Runtime verification · Temporal property · Program execution

1 Introduction

Software model checkers in early years limit to verification of safety properties. Tools like SLAM [2], BLAST [3] and CPAchecker [4] adopt Counterexample-Guided Abstraction Refinement (CEGAR) [8, 22, 23] for checking whether desired properties of programs are valid or not. With this approach, an initial predicate abstraction of the program to be verified is constructed, and then reachability of error labels is checked. If a spurious counterexample is found, the abstraction is refined using a refinement algorithm. Afterwards the property continues to be verified until a counterexample is found or it is ensured that the property is valid. Whereas tools like CBMC [19], SMT-CBMC [1] and LLBMC [20] are based on bounded model checking. In this way, loops in programs are unwound within a given bound and a backend solver is used to find reachable error states. All these tools can only verify safety properties, however, other temporal properties such as liveness are not supported.

Nowadays, more tools have been developed for the verification of various temporal properties. Terminator [9] converts the liveness property verification

This research is supported by School Funds of Hebei University (No. 299) and Advanced Talents Incubation Program of the Hebei University (No. 521000981346).

© Springer Nature Switzerland AG 2020
H. Miao et al. (Eds.): SOFL+MSVL 2019 Workshop, LNCS 12028, pp. 88–98, 2020.
https://doi.org/10.1007/978-3-030-41418-4_7

of programs to termination checking. As an improvement of Terminator, T2 [5] replaces the SLAM-based C interface with LLVM and verifies CTL, Fair-CTL, and CTL* properties via a reduction technique. For improving the verification efficiency of Terminator, Ultimate LTLAutomizer [10] removes paths with infeasible finite prefixes, thus avoids many termination checks. However, these tools are hard to verify programs in large scale. In addition, execution details are difficult to acquire without executing programs, which may lead to false positives.

Runtime verification tools verify a single execution path each time, which alleviates the state-explosion problem and decreases false positives. RiTHM [21] verifies LTL properties of programs by constructing a time-triggered monitor. Java PathExplorer (JPax) [18] rewrites a property formula to current and future parts. Then it is checked whether the current state satisfies the current part of the formula during execution of a program. If so, the program continues to execute until the formula reduces to true, otherwise, the program violates the property. However, programs and properties are specified using different logics. Thus, programs to be verified need to be instrumented, and related information requires to be extracted from the executing path and then sent to the monitor. These lead to a large time cost. A better solution is to describe programs and properties using a same logic framework.

We develop a verification tool called $UMC4M$, which uses modeling, simulation and verification language (MSVL) [11,12,29,30] to write program M and propositional projection temporal logic (PPTL) [14,15,24,31] to specify a desired property P. Both MSVL and PPTL are subsets of projection temporal logic (PTL). In this way, programs and properties are specified using a same logic framework. The working principle [25] of $UMC4M$ is briefly described as follows:

(1) $UMC4M$ takes an MSVL program M and a property specified by a PPTL formula P as input.
(2) $\neg P$ can be translated to an MSVL program M'. Then a new program "M and M'" containing the program and property is acquired.
(3) "M and M'" is compiled into a binary code $MM'.exe$ by MSVL compiler MC [26].
(4) Input values of variables namely verification cases are generated by means of dynamic symbolic execution (DSE) tool $Cloud9$ [6].
(5) With a verification case as input, $UMC4M$ executes $MM'.exe$ to generate a path. If the path is acceptable, a counterexample is found, otherwise, the program continues to be verified using other verification cases as inputs.

Further, $UMC4M$ is used to verify security protocols. In this paper, we take the verification of the dining cryptographers protocol [7] as a case study.

The remainder of the paper is organized as follows. In Sect. 2, MSVL and PPTL are introduced. The design and implementation of $UMC4M$ is presented in Sect. 3. Section 4 shows an application of $UMC4M$. Section 5 concludes the paper.

2   Preliminaries

This section briefly introduces MSVL and PPTL, which are borrowed from [11, 13, 14, 16, 17, 27, 28].

2.1   MSVL

With MSVL, expressions can be treated as terms and statements as formulas in PTL. The arithmetic and boolean expressions of MSVL can inductively be defined as follows:

$$e ::= c \mid x \mid g(e_1, \ldots, e_m) \mid ext\ f(e_1, \ldots, e_n) \mid \bigcirc e \mid \ominus e$$
$$b ::= true \mid false \mid \varepsilon \mid \ni \mid \neg b \mid b_0 \wedge b_1 \mid e_0 = e_1 \mid e_0 < e_1$$

where c is a constant, m and n integers, x a variable, $g(e_1, \ldots, e_m)$ a state function, and f a function. A state function is a function with no temporal operators. Note that usual arithmetic operations such as $+$, $-$, $*$ and $\%$ can be viewed as two-arity state functions $g(e_1, e_2)$. $ext\ f(e_1, \ldots, e_n)$ is an external call of f. It means that we concern only the return value of f but not the interval over which f is executed. $\bigcirc e$ means the value of e at the next state while $\ominus e$ the value of e at the previous state. In the boolean expressions, we have $\ni \overset{def}{=} \bigcirc true$ and $\varepsilon \overset{def}{=} \neg \ni$. The following are the elementary statements in MSVL:

1. Termination	`empty`	2. Assignment	`x<==e`
3. Unit Assignment	`x:=e`	4. Interval Frame	`frame(x)`
5. Conjunction	`p and q`	6. Selection	`p or q`
7. Next	`next p`	8. Always	`alw(p)`
9. Sequence	`p;q`	10. Local variable	`local x:p`
11. Parallel	`p ‖ q`	12. While	`while(b){p}`
13. Await	`await(b)`	14. Function call	`f(e₁,...,eₙ)`
15. External function call	`ext f(e₁,...,eₙ)`		
16. Projection	`{p₁,...,pₘ} prj q`		
17. Conditional	`if(b)then{p}else{q}`		

MSVL supports basic flow control statements in structured programming language such as sequential, conditional and while-loop statements. Moreover, MSVL also supports selection, conjunction and parallel statements for non-determinism and concurrent programming. Note that all the above statements are defined by PTL formulas. In addition, rich data types including integer, float, string, char, pointer, array and struct have been defined in MSVL.

2.2   PPTL

The syntax and semantics of PPTL are briefly introduced in this subsection.

Syntax. The syntax of a PPTL formula P over the countable set *Prop* of atomic propositions is given as follows:

$$P ::= p \mid \bigcirc P \mid \neg P \mid P \vee Q \mid (P_1, \cdots, P_m) \; prj \; P \mid P^+$$

where $p \in Prop$ is an atomic proposition; $P_1, \cdots, P_m$, P and Q are all well-formed PPTL formulas. For semantics of PPTL formulas, please refer to [14].

LNFGs of PPTL Formulas. Normal form and Labeled Normal Form Graph (LNFG) of a PPTL formula are defined as follows, which are borrowed from [16].

Definition 1. *A PPTL formula P is in its normal form if*

$$P \equiv \bigvee_{i=1}^{l} P_{ei} \wedge \varepsilon \vee \bigvee_{j=1}^{t} P_{cj} \wedge \bigcirc P_{fj}$$

where $l \geq 0$, $t \geq 0$ and $l + t \geq 1$. For $1 \leq j \leq t$, P_{fj} is a PPTL formula without "$\vee$" being the main operator; P_{ei} and P_{cj} are true or state formulas of the form: $\bigwedge_{k=1}^{m} \dot{p}_k$. Here, $\dot{p}_k$ means p_k or $\neg p_k$ for each $p_k \in Pr$.

An LNFG of a PPTL formula can be constructed based on its normal form.

Definition 2. *Given a PPTL formula P, an LNFG of P is a tuple $LNFG = (CL, EL, V_0, \mathbb{L} = \{\mathbb{L}_{l_1}, \ldots, \mathbb{L}_{l_k}\})$ where*

- $CL = \{n_1, \ldots, n_s\}$ *is a set of nodes, where n_i $(1 \leq i \leq s)$ is a PPTL formula.*
- $EL = \{el_1, \ldots, el_m\}$ *is the set of directed edges connecting nodes in CL. Edge el_k $(1 \leq k \leq m)$ is a triple $\langle n_i, p_{i,j}, n_j \rangle$, where $p_{i,j}$ is the state formula labeled on el_k.*
- V_0 *is the set of initial nodes.*
- $\mathbb{L}_{l_i} \subseteq CL$, $1 \leq i \leq k$, *is the set of nodes with l_i being the fin label.*

Note that fin labels are used to check whether a path is acceptable. For more details, please refer to [16].

3   Design and Implementation of *UMC4M*

Based on unified model checking, we develop a temporal property verification tool *UMC4M* to verify programs at code level. The architecture of *UMC4M* is shown as Fig. 1. It contains 3 stages: translation, compiling and execution. Specifically, 6 modules are called during verification of a program: *PPTL2LNFG*, *LNFG2MSVL*, *MC*, *Cloud9*, *Execute* and *PathCheck*. The white rectangles are existing tools invoked by *UMC4M*; the yellow rectangles stand for the modules implemented in this paper and the grey rectangles are files generated by these tools and modules. *UMC4M* takes an MSVL program M and a PPTL formula P as its input and the working process is briefly given as follows:

(1) At the translation stage, *PPTL2LNFG* constructs an LNFG G_P of P and checks whether P is satisfiable. If not, the property is invalid, otherwise, *PPTL2LNFG* constructs an LNFG $G_{\neg P}$ of $\neg P$ and checks the satisfiability of $\neg P$. If $\neg P$ is unsatisfiable, the property is valid, otherwise, *LNFG2MSVL* translates $G_{\neg P}$ to an MSVL program.

(2) At the compiling stage, MSVL compiler *MC* and *Multi-thread* scheduler compile MSVL program "M and M'" to binary codes $MM'.exe$ and LLVM IR MM'_{IR}.

(3) At the execution stage, *Cloud9* takes MM'_{IR} as input and generates verification cases VC for program "M and M'". Further, module *Execute* runs $MM'.exe$ with a verification case in VC to generate execution paths. Afterwards, *PathCheck* checks whether there is an acceptable path. If so, a counterexample is found, otherwise, *Execute* runs $MM'.exe$ with other verification cases. Repeat above process until a counterexample is found or all verification cases in VC are checked.

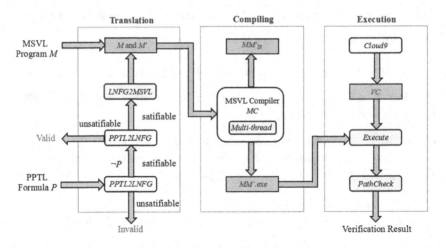

Fig. 1. Architecture of *UMC4M* (Color figure online)

3.1   *LNFG2MSVL*

LNFG2MSVL takes an LNFG $G = (CL, EL, V_0, \mathbb{L} = \{\mathbb{L}_{l_1}, ..., \mathbb{L}_{l_k}\})$ as input and outputs an MSVL program M', where $CL = \{n_1, ..., n_s\}$ and $EL = \{el_1, ..., el_m\}$. For convenience, we call an edge pointing to ε (resp. other nodes) a terminal (non-terminal) edge. To do the translation, some notations are defined as follows. *CuNode* represents the current node being explored. *Init* stands for the initial program initializing *CuNode*. N, E and *Case* are three global variables. N and E stand for MSVL programs translated from non-terminal and terminal edges, respectively. $Case = 1$, 2 or 3 is used to show whether there are terminal, non-terminal edges or both in G. Figure 2 shows the flow chart of $LNFG2MSVL$. If there is only a true node in V_0, the program is true, otherwise, initialization program $Init$ of $CuNode$ is obtained. Further $NE2M(G)$ is called to generate N and E. In parallel, the value of $Case$ is set. Finally, according the value of $Case$, we can obtain the program w.r.t. N and E.

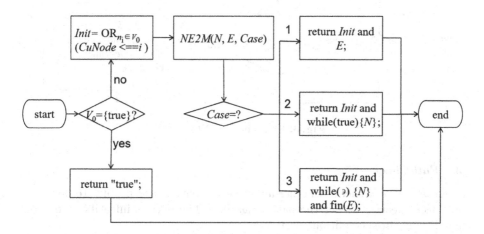

Fig. 2. Flow chart of $LNFG2MSVL$

Let $L_{n_i} = \{l_x | n_i \in \mathbb{L}_{l_x}\}$ ($1 \leq x \leq k$) denote a set of fin labels appearing at node n_i. L is used to store fin labels at current node. S_i and P_i stand for MSVL programs translated from non-terminal and terminal edges starting from n_i, respectively. Figure 3 shows the flow chart of $NE2M$.

3.2 Multi-thread and Execute

To verify multiple paths generated by executing undetermined statements "p or q" in MSVL program efficiently, thread pool mechanism is adopted to handle the paths in parallel. To do that, module $Multi\text{-}thread$ imports a global array $flag$ to represent paths to be verified and a task queue $queue$ to store those paths. Further, module $Execute$ creates a thread pool with m threads to execute multiple paths in parallel, where m is tuned to the computing resources available to the program, such as parallel processors, cores and memory. $flag[i][j] = 0$ (resp., $flag[i][j] = 1$) indicates that the left (resp., right) branch of the jth selection statement is chosen to be executed by the ith thread in the thread pool.

However, if all these threads change global variables in an MSVL program at the same time, which makes the values of these variables changed illogically, the verification will be meaningless. Thus, $Multi\text{-}thread$ copies these global variables into m copies and the ith thread can only visit the ith copy of these variables. In this way, multiple paths can be verified in a parallel way.

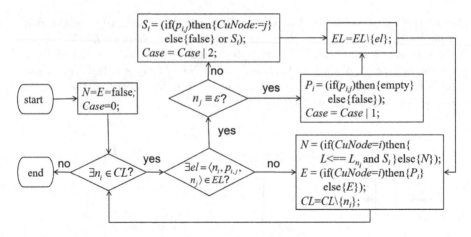

Fig. 3. Flow chart of *NE2M*

3.3 *PathCheck*

Module *PathCheck* checks whether an execution path is acceptable. To do that, *PathCheck* checks whether the path is feasible. The path is infeasible if one of the following three conditions occurs:

(1) A "false" statement is executed.
(2) A variable is assigned different values at a state.
(3) Conjunction statement p *and* q is executed, however, the length of the interval over which p is executed is different with that of q.

For a feasible path, *PathCheck* further checks whether it is acceptable. A finite feasible path is always acceptable, while an infinite feasible path is acceptable only if the nodes that the path explores for infinite times share no same fin labels. If there is an acceptable path, a counterexample is found.

4 Case Study

Security protocols run in complex and insecure environment and it is difficult to find errors in protocols with the method of artificial cognition. Therefore, in order to analyze the security of security protocols, formal analysis tools are necessary. In this section, the dining cryptographers protocol presented by Chaum [7] is verified using *UMC4M*.

4.1 Description of the Dining Cryptographers Protocol

Three cryptographers are sitting around table for dinner. The organization of the dinner, National Security Agency (NSA), might pay for the dinner, or one of the cryptographers pays for it. These cryptographers respect each other's right to make an anonymous payment. However, they want to know whether NSA is paying. Thus, they solve this problem using the following protocol:

(1) Each cryptographer flips a coin between him and the cryptographer on his right and only the two cryptographers can see the outcome.
(2) Each cryptographer checks the two coins on his left-hand and right-hand to see whether the two coins fell on the same side. If he is the payer, he says out the opposite of what he sees, otherwise, he tells others the actual outcome he sees.
(3) They count up the number of cryptographers stating difference. If the number is odd, it indicates that a cryptographer pays for it, otherwise, NSA pays.

According to the protocol, if a cryptographer pays for dinner, the other two know a cryptographer pays, however, neither of them knows who pays for it. This satisfies the anonymity property.

4.2   Protocol Modeling and Specification Description

In this subsection, we use an MSVL program to model the protocol and a PPTL formula to specify the desired property.

We assume cryptographer 1 sits on the right of cryptographer 0 and cryptographer 2 sits on the right of cryptographer 1. Thus, cryptographer 0 sits on the right of cryptographer 2. To model this protocol in MSVL, some notations are defined as follows:

(1) An array $coin[3]$ stores the side of the coin that each cryptographer flips. $coin[i] = 1$ ($i = 0, 1, 2$) means that the coin which cryptographer i flips is head up. $coin[i] = 0$ represents that the coin lands on tails. When cryptographer i flips a coin, the value of $coin[i]$ is undetermined. Thus, we can obtain the following MSVL program:

$$COIN \stackrel{\text{def}}{=} AND_{i=0}^{2}(coin[i] <== 0 \text{ or } coin[i] <== 1)$$

where $AND_{i=0}^{n} \ p_i \stackrel{\text{def}}{=} p_0 \text{ and } p_1 \text{ and } ... \text{ and } p_n$.
(2) An array $payer[3]$ stores whether a cryptographer is the payer. The value of $payer[i]$ ($i = 1, 2, 3$) is 1, if cryptographer i pays for the bill, and 0 otherwise. Each cryptographer may be the payer or not. Thus, we have the following program:

$PAY \stackrel{\text{def}}{=}$
$(payer[0] <== 0 \text{ and } payer[1] <== 0 \text{ and } payer[2] <== 0) \text{ or}$
$(payer[0] <== 1 \text{ and } payer[1] <== 0 \text{ and } payer[2] <== 0) \text{ or}$
$(payer[0] <== 0 \text{ and } payer[1] <== 1 \text{ and } payer[2] <== 0) \text{ or}$
$(payer[0] <== 0 \text{ and } payer[1] <== 0 \text{ and } payer[2] <== 1)$

(3) An array $saydif[3]$ stores results which cryptographers say out. $saydif[i] = 0$ represents cryptographer i says that the two outcomes of coins he sees are the same. $saydif[i] = 1$ means cryptographer i says that the outcomes are different. According to the protocol, we can obtain the following program:

$$SAY \stackrel{\text{def}}{=}$$

```
i := 0;
while(i < 3){
    if(coin[i] = coin[(i + 2)%3] and payer[i] = 0 or
    coin[i]! = coin[(i + 2)%3] and  payer[i] = 1)
    then{saydif₁ := 0}else{saydif₁ := 1};
    i := i + 1}
```

where SAY, $i := 0$, the $while(i < 3)$ block with $if(coin[i] = coin[(i+2)\%3]$ and $payer[i] = 0$ or $coin[i]! = coin[(i+2)\%3]$ and $payer[i] = 1)$ then $\{saydif_1 := 0\}$ else $\{saydif_1 := 1\}$; $i := i + 1$.

(4) *count* denotes the number of cryptographers stating difference. It can be obtained using the following program:

$$count := saydif[0] + saydif[1] + saydif[2]$$

In order to verify the property that if the number of cryptographers stating difference is odd, a cryptographer pays for it, otherwise, NSA pays, we define the following propositions:

$$\text{define } p : count\%2 = 0;$$
$$\text{define } q_i : payer[i] = 0;$$

where p represents the number of cryptographers stating difference is even and q_i ($i = 0, 1, 2$) denotes cryptographer i is not the payer. Moreover, the property can be specified by the following PPTL formula:

$fin(p \rightarrow q_0$ and q_1 and $q_2)$ and
$fin(\neg p \rightarrow \neg q_0$ and q_1 and q_2 or q_0 and $\neg q_1$ and q_2 or q_0 and q_1 and $\neg q_2)$

We further use $UMC4M$ to verify this property of the protocol and obtain the result: the property is valid.

5   Conclusion

We develop a novel runtime temporal property verification tool called $UMC4M$, which reduces the temporal property verification issue into a program execution task. With this tool, a system to be verified is written in MSVL and a desired property is specified by a PPTL formula. By translating $\neg P$ to an MSVL program M', the verification can be done by executing new MSVL program "M and M'" to see whether there exists an acceptable execution. Further, $UMC4M$ is used to verify the dining cryptographers protocol. In the near future, we plan to perform more experiments to further optimize our approach.

References

1. Armando, A., Mantovani, J., Platania, L.: Bounded model checking of software using SMT solvers instead of SAT solvers. Int. J. Softw. Tools Technol. Transfer **11**(1), 69–83 (2009)
2. Ball, T., Rajamani, S.K.: Automatically validating temporal safety properties of interfaces. In: Dwyer, M. (ed.) SPIN 2001. LNCS, vol. 2057, pp. 102–122. Springer, Heidelberg (2001). https://doi.org/10.1007/3-540-45139-0_7
3. Beyer, D., Henzinger, T.A., Jhala, R., Majumdar, R.: The software model checker BLAST: applications to software engineering. Int. J. Softw. Tools Technol. Transfer **9**(5), 505–525 (2007)
4. Beyer, D., Keremoglu, M.E.: CPACHECKER: a tool for configurable software verification. In: Gopalakrishnan, G., Qadeer, S. (eds.) CAV 2011. LNCS, vol. 6806, pp. 184–190. Springer, Heidelberg (2011). https://doi.org/10.1007/978-3-642-22110-1_16
5. Brockschmidt, M., Cook, B., Ishtiaq, S., Khlaaf, H., Piterman, N.: T2: temporal property verification. In: Chechik, M., Raskin, J.-F. (eds.) TACAS 2016. LNCS, vol. 9636, pp. 387–393. Springer, Heidelberg (2016). https://doi.org/10.1007/978-3-662-49674-9_22
6. Bucur, S., Ureche, V., Zamfir, C., Candea, G.: Parallel symbolic execution for automated real-world software testing. In: Proceedings of the Sixth Conference on Computer Systems (EuroSys 2011), pp. 183–198. ACM, New York (2011). https://doi.org/10.1145/1966445.1966463
7. Chaum, D.: The dining cryptographers problem: unconditional sender and recipient untraceability. J. Cryptol. **1**(1), 65–75 (1988)
8. Clarke, E., Grumberg, O., Jha, S., Lu, Y., Veith, H.: Counterexample-guided abstraction refinement. In: Emerson, E.A., Sistla, A.P. (eds.) CAV 2000. LNCS, vol. 1855, pp. 154–169. Springer, Heidelberg (2000). https://doi.org/10.1007/10722167_15
9. Cook, B., Podelski, A., Rybalchenko, A.: Termination proofs for systems code. In: Proceedings of the 27th ACM SIGPLAN Conference on Programming Language Design and Implementation (PLDI), pp. 415–426. ACM, New York (2006)
10. Dietsch, D., Heizmann, M., Langenfeld, V., Podelski, A.: Fairness modulo theory: a new approach to LTL software model checking. In: Kroening, D., Păsăreanu, C.S. (eds.) CAV 2015. LNCS, vol. 9206, pp. 49–66. Springer, Cham (2015). https://doi.org/10.1007/978-3-319-21690-4_4
11. Duan, Z.: An extended interval temporal logic and a framing technique for temporal logic programming. Ph.D. thesis, Department of Computer Science, Newcastle University, Newcastle upon Tyne, UK (1996)
12. Duan, Z.: Temporal Logic and Temporal Logic Programming. Science Press, Beijing (2005)
13. Duan, Z., Koutny, M.: A framed temporal logic programming language. J. Comput. Sci. Technol. **19**(3), 341–351 (2004)
14. Duan, Z., Tian, C.: A practical decision procedure for propositional projection temporal logic with infinite models. Theor. Comput. Sci. **554**, 169–190 (2014)
15. Duan, Z., Tian, C., Zhang, L.: A decision procedure for propositional projection temporal logic with infinite models. Acta Informatica **45**(1), 43–78 (2008)
16. Duan, Z., Tian, C., Zhang, N.: A canonical form based decision procedure and model checking approach for propositional projection temporal logic. Theor. Comput. Sci. **609**, 544–560 (2016)

17. Duan, Z., Yang, X., Koutny, M.: Framed temporal logic programming. Sci. Comput. Prog. **70**(1), 31–61 (2008)
18. Havelund, K., Rosu, G.: Monitoring java programs with java pathexplorer. Electron. Notes Theor. Comput. Sci. **55**(2), 200–217 (2001)
19. Kroening, D., Tautschnig, M.: CBMC–C bounded model checker. In: Ábrahám, E., Havelund, K. (eds.) TACAS 2014. LNCS, vol. 8413, pp. 389–391. Springer, Heidelberg (2014). https://doi.org/10.1007/978-3-642-54862-8_26
20. Merz, F., Falke, S., Sinz, C.: LLBMC: bounded model checking of C and C++ programs using a compiler IR. In: Joshi, R., Müller, P., Podelski, A. (eds.) VSTTE 2012. LNCS, vol. 7152, pp. 146–161. Springer, Heidelberg (2012). https://doi.org/10.1007/978-3-642-27705-4_12
21. Navabpour, S., et al.: RiTHM: a tool for enabling time-triggered runtime verification for c programs. In: Proceedings of the 2013 9th Joint Meeting on Foundations of Software Engineering, pp. 603–606. ACM, New York (2013)
22. Tian, C., Duan, Z., Duan, Z., Ong, C.H.L.: More effective interpolations in software model checking. In: Proceedings of the 32nd IEEE/ACM International Conference on Automated Software Engineering, pp. 183–193. IEEE Press (2017)
23. Tian, C., Duan, Z., Duan, Z.: Making cegar more efficient in software model checking. IEEE Trans. Softw. Eng. **40**(12), 1206–1223 (2014)
24. Wang, H., Duan, Z., Tian, C.: Model checking multi-agent systems with APTL. Adhoc Sens. Wireless Netw. **37**, 35–52 (2017)
25. Wang, M., Tian, C., Zhang, N., Duan, Z.: Verifying full regular temporal properties of programs via dynamic program execution. IEEE Trans. Reliab. **68**, 1–16 (2018)
26. Yang, K., Duan, Z., Tian, C., Zhang, N.: A compiler for MSVL and its applications. Theor. Comput. Sci. **749**, 2–16 (2018)
27. Yang, X., Duan, Z.: Operational semantics of framed tempura. J. Logic Algebraic Program. **78**(1), 22–51 (2008)
28. Yu, B., Duan, Z., Tian, C., Zhang, N.: Verifying temporal properties of programs: a parallel approach. J. Parallel Distrib. Comput. **118**, 89–99 (2018)
29. Zhang, N., Duan, Z., Tian, C.: A mechanism of function calls in MSVL. Theor. Comput. Sci. **654**, 11–25 (2016)
30. Zhang, N., Duan, Z., Tian, C.: Model checking concurrent systems with MSVL. Sci. China Inf. Sci. **59**(11), 118101 (2016)
31. Zhang, N., Yang, M., Gu, B., Duan, Z., Tian, C.: Verifying safety critical task scheduling systems in PPTL axiom system. J. Comb. Optim. **31**(2), 577–603 (2016)

Parallel Runtime Verification Approach for Alternate Execution of Multiple Threads

Bin Yu[1], Jinhui Liu[1], Ming Lei[1(✉)], Yong Yu[1(✉)], and Hao Chen[2]

[1] School of Computer Science, Shaanxi Normal University, Xi'an 710062, China
{binyu,jh.liu,leiming,yuyong}@snnu.edu.cn
[2] Beijing Edutainment World Education Technology Co., Ltd., Beijing 100000, China
chenhao@stemedu.cn

Abstract. Since resources are shared by threads created in a multi-threaded program, these threads are not completely independent of each other. The execution of these threads usually needs to satisfy a certain order restriction. In this paper, we employ a multi-core machine based parallel runtime verification approach to efficiently monitor the alternate execution of multiple threads. First, the problem is described in Modeling, Simulation and Verification Language (MSVL). Second, the desired periodically repeated property is specified by a Propositional Projection Temporal Logic (PPTL) formula. Third, the state sequence generated by the execution of the MSVL program is divided into several segments which are verified in parallel. Finally, verification results for different segments are merged. Experimental results show that the alternate execution of multiple threads implemented through invoking Windows Application Programming Interface (API) functions *SuspendThread* and *ResumeThread* will lead to these threads out of sequence.

Keywords: Multiple threads · Alternate execution · Parallel · Runtime verification · Multi-core system

1 Introduction

In order to effectively utilize the increasingly common multi-core computing resources, programmers need to write multi-threaded programs to improve software performance. However, many factors can affect the execution of a multi-threaded program, such as the scheduling policy for multiple threads employed by the operating system, time slice allocation strategy used by the Central Processing Unit (CPU) and the dynamic load at machine runtime. Therefore, a

This work is supported by National Key R&D Program of China (2017YFB0802000), National Natural Science Foundation of China (61872229, 61802239), Natural Science Basic Research Plan in Shaanxi Province of China (Program No. 2019JQ-667) and China Postdoctoral Science Foundation (2018M631121).

© Springer Nature Switzerland AG 2020
H. Miao et al. (Eds.): SOFL+MSVL 2019 Workshop, LNCS 12028, pp. 99–109, 2020.
https://doi.org/10.1007/978-3-030-41418-4_8

multi-threaded program often does not perform as expected [1]. In breakpoint debugging during the early testing, the suspension of a program often affects the status of the above uncertainties. The change of these uncertainties may lead to many unpredictable results. All of these make the debugging of a multi-threaded program extremely complicated, which leads to the result that even if a program executes correctly during the testing phase, errors may occur in a practical running environment.

As a new lightweight formal verification technique, runtime verification combines the traditional formal verification with program execution [2,3]. By monitoring actual behaviors, runtime verification can take action in time once the desired property is found to be violated. Runtime verification has been widely used in many familiar areas, including the monitor of Java programs [4] or malware attacks [5], verification of temporal properties for data flows [6].

In runtime verification, logic languages are usually employed to express the desired properties. Linear Time Temporal Logic (LTL) [7] and Computation Tree Logic (CTL) [8] are the two most commonly used languages in available tools. However, the expressiveness of LTL and CTL is not powerful enough, actually, not full regular. There are at least two types of properties in practice which cannot (or with difficulty) be specified by LTL and CTL: (1) some time duration related properties, such as a property P holds after 100th time unit and before 200th time unit; (2) some periodically repeated properties, such as a property P always holds at even states.

In addition, most existing runtime verification approaches simply take a sequential method to validate the state sequence produced by program execution [2,9]. In these approaches, the very common multi-core computing resources can not be taken full advantage of, which makes that the problem finding is much later that its occurrence.

In a multi-threaded program, multiple threads share computing resources and can communicate with each other. Therefore, threads are often not completely independent, and there will be certain dependencies during the program execution. For example, two threads are created for document processing and printing respectively. Only when the document processing is completed, can the printing thread execute the task. After the printing is finished, the document processing thread decides whether to continue processing new documents or reprint the last one based on the result of the printing thread. At this time, their execution must satisfy a certain order restriction.

For this kind of problem, this paper present a runtime verification approach to monitor whether several threads can execute alternately in a predefined order. To achieve this, we first model the problem in a Modeling, Simulation and Verification Language (MSVL) program [10–13]. Then, we specify the desired property in a Propositional Projection Temporal Logic (PPTL) formula [14–18]. The reason why PPTL is adopted is that it has the expressiveness of full regular expressions and can easily describe the alternating order feature which can be regarded as a periodically repeated property. At last, the program is verified during its execution. In this process, we employ the parallel approach proposed in

[19] so as to increase the verification efficiency. A number of experimental results show that the invoking of API functions *SuspendThread* and *ResumeThread* supplied by Windows to solve the problem will result in the out-of-order threads. Besides, the parallel verification approach can increase the efficiency and detect the property violation in time.

This paper is organized as follows. The following section briefly presents the language MSVL used for the implementation of the model and PPTL used for the description of the property. Section 3 introduces the problem of alternate execution of multiple threads in detail. The runtime verification process is presented in Sect. 4. Section 5 shows the experimental results of our approach. Finally, the conclusion is drawn in Sect. 6.

2 Preliminaries

In this section, we will introduce programming language MSVL and property language PPTL, both of which are subsets of Projection Temporal Logic (PTL) [20]. The contents in this section are borrowed from [10,13,14].

2.1 MSVL

The arithmetic expression e and boolean expression b are inductively defined as follows:

$$e ::= c \mid x \mid g(e_1, \ldots, e_m) \mid ext\ f(e_1, \ldots, e_n) \mid \ominus e \mid \bigcirc e$$
$$b ::= true \mid false \mid \varepsilon \mid \ni \mid \neg b \mid b_0 \wedge b_1 \mid e_0 = e_1 \mid e_0 < e_1$$

In the arithmetic expression, c is a constant, x a variable, m and n integers, g a state function, and f a function. A state function $g(e_1, \ldots, e_m)$ contains no temporal operators. $ext\ f(e_1, \ldots, e_n)$ is an external call of function f meaning that we only concern the return value of function f rather than the interval over which the function is executed. $\ominus e$ and $\bigcirc e$ respectively stand for the value of e at the previous state and the next state. In the boolean expressions, $\ni \overset{\text{def}}{=} \bigcirc true$ and $\varepsilon \overset{\text{def}}{=} \neg \ni$.

The following are the elementary statements in MSVL:

1. Termination	`empty`	2. Assignment	`x<==e`
3. Unit Assignment	`x:=e`	4. Interval Frame	`frame(x)`
5. Selection	`p or q`	6. Conjunction	`p and q`
8. Always	`alw(p)`	7. Next	`next p`
9. Sequence	`p;q`	10. Local variable	`local x:p`
11. Projection	`{p₁,…,pₘ} prj q`	12. Parallel	`p ∥ q`
13. Conditional	`if(b)then{p}else{q}`	14. While	`while(b){p}`
15. Await	`await(b)`	16. Function call	`g(e₁,…,eₘ)`
17. External function call `ext f(e₁,…,eₙ)`			

where x is a variable, e and b denote an arithmetic expression or a boolean expression, respectively. p_1, ..., p_m, p and q are programs of MSVL. The meaning of each statement is given in [10] and omitted here.

2.2 PPTL

Syntax: Over a countable set *Prop* of atomic propositions, the syntax of a PPTL formula P is inductively defined as follows:

$$P ::= p \mid \bigcirc P \mid \neg P \mid P_1 \vee P_2 \mid (P_1, \ldots, P_m) \; prj \; P \mid P^+$$

where $p \in Prop$ is an atomic proposition; $P_1, \ldots, P_m$ and P are all well-formed PPTL formulas.

Semantics: The boolean domain $\mathcal{B} = \{true, false\}$. A state s is a mapping from *Prop* to $\mathcal{B}$. $s[p]$ represents the value of the atomic proposition p at state s. A non-empty sequence of states $\sigma = \langle s_0, s_1, \ldots \rangle$ is called an interval. $|\sigma|$ denotes the length of σ. If σ is finite, $|\sigma|$ equals the number of states minus 1. Otherwise, $|\sigma|$ equals ω. In order to consider both finite and infinite intervals in a unified way, the integers is extended as $N_\omega = N_0 \cup \{\omega\}$, where N_0 denotes the set of non-negative integers. Besides, the comparison operators $=, <, \leq$ to N_ω is also extended by considering $\omega = \omega$ and $i < \omega$ for all $i \in N_0$. Further, $\preceq$ is defined as $\leq -\{(\omega, \omega)\}$. A sub-interval $\langle s_i, \ldots, s_j \rangle$ can be denoted as $\sigma_{(i..j)}$ for simplicity. For an interval σ and integers $r_1, \ldots, r_h$ such that $0 \leq r_1 \leq r_2 \leq \ldots \leq r_h$, the operation $\downarrow$ can be utilized to obtain the projected interval, $\sigma \downarrow (r_1, \ldots, r_h) = \langle s_{t_1}, s_{t_2}, \ldots, s_{t_l} \rangle$, where $t_1, \ldots, t_l$ are obtained from $r_1, \ldots, r_h$ by deleting the duplicates. $\sigma_1 \cdot \sigma_2 = \langle s_0, \ldots, s_n, s_0', \ldots \rangle$ denotes the concatenation of a finite interval $\sigma_1 = \langle s_0, \ldots, s_n \rangle$ with another interval $\sigma_2 = \langle s_0', \ldots \rangle$.

For an interval σ, $i \in N_0$, $j \in N_\omega$, and $i \preceq j \leq |\sigma|$, an interpretation of a PPTL formula is $\mathcal{I} = (\sigma, i, j)$. The satisfaction relation $\models$ is inductively defined as follows:

$\mathcal{I} \models p$ iff $s_i[p] = true$, and $p \in Prop$ is an atomic proposition.

$\mathcal{I} \models \bigcirc P$ iff $i < j$ and $(\sigma, i+1, j) \models P$.

$\mathcal{I} \models \neg P$ iff $\mathcal{I} \not\models P$.

$\mathcal{I} \models P \wedge Q$ iff $\mathcal{I} \models P$ and $\mathcal{I} \models Q$.

$\mathcal{I} \models (P_1, \ldots, P_m) \; prj \; P$ iff there exist integers $r_0, \ldots, r_m$, and $i = r_0 \leq \ldots \leq r_{m-1} \preceq r_m \leq j$ such that $(\sigma, r_{l-1}, r_l) \models P_l$, $1 \leq l \leq m$, and $(\sigma', 0, |\sigma'|) \models P$ for one of the following σ' :

    (a) $r_m < j$ and $\sigma' = \sigma \downarrow (r_0, \ldots, r_m) \cdot \sigma_{(r_m+1..j)}$,

    (b) $r_m = j$ and $\sigma' = \sigma \downarrow (r_0, \ldots, r_h)$ for some $0 \leq h \leq m$.

$\mathcal{I} \models P^+$ iff there exist finitely many integers $r_0, \ldots, r_n$ and $i = r_0 \leq \ldots \leq r_{n-1} \preceq r_n = j$ $(n \geq 1)$ such that $(\sigma, r_{l-1}, r_l) \models P$, $1 \leq l \leq n$; or $j = \omega$ and there are infinitely many integers $k = r_0 \leq r_1 \leq \ldots$ such that $\lim_{i \to \infty} r_i = \omega$ and $(\sigma, r_{l-1}, r_l) \models P$, $l \geq 1$.

In order to explicitly illustrate the model of a PPTL formula P, we can construct its corresponding LNFG. An LNFG is defined as a tuple $G = (CL(P), EL(P), V_0, \mathbb{L} = \{\mathbb{L}_1, \cdots, \mathbb{L}_k\})$, where $CL(P)$ denotes the set of nodes and $EL(P)$ denotes the set of directed edges among $CL(P)$, V_0 is the set of initial nodes, and each $\mathbb{L}_i \subseteq CL(P)$, $1 \le i \le k$, is the set of nodes with l_i being the label. Each node is specified by a PPTL formula; each edge is labeled with a state formula; and the extra propositions l_k labeled on some nodes are used to identify an infinite acceptable path. In an LNFG, a finite path, $\pi = \langle n_0, p_0, \cdots, \varepsilon \rangle$, is an alternating sequence of nodes and edges from an initial node to the ε node, while an infinite path, $\pi = \langle n_0, p_0, \cdots, (n_i, p_i, \cdots, n_j, p_j)^\omega \rangle$, is an infinite alternate sequence of nodes and edges emanating from an initial node. In an infinite path, the set of nodes which infinitely often occur is denoted by $Inf(\pi)$. If a path π is finite or infinite with all the nodes in $Inf(\pi)$ not sharing a same label, it is called acceptable. Theories relative to LNFGs can be referred to [21,22]. In order to show how an LNFG looks like, Fig. 1 illustrates the LNFG of PPTL formula $\Diamond(p \wedge \Box(\neg q))$ as an example. In this LNFG, $\pi = \langle 1, p \wedge \neg q, 3, \neg q, 4 \rangle$ is a finite path, while $\pi = \langle 1, true, (2, true)^\omega \rangle$ is an infinite path. In this infinite path, we have $Inf(\pi) = \{2\} \subseteq \mathbb{L}_1 = \{2\}$, which means that the nodes occurring infinitely often have the same label l_1. Hence, this path is unacceptable.

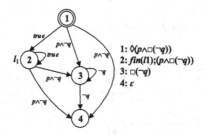

Fig. 1. LNFG of formula $\Diamond(p \wedge \Box(\neg q))$

3   The Problem of Alternate Execution of Multiple Threads

In general, after several threads are created by a process, these threads are executed simultaneously at the macro level. However, at the micro level, they are executed alternately on a CPU kernel with a time slice circular scheduling algorithm or simultaneously on multiple CPU kernels at the same time. At this time, these threads are executed in a random order. In real life, there exist many scenarios that rigorously require the alternate execution of multiple threads. For example, a shared resource is alternately accessed by multiple threads or each thread in a loop execution depends on the results generated by others.

In this section, we will model the alternate execution of two threads. The model of multiple threads can be obtained in a similar way. To achieve this, we create a manager thread to schedule these two child threads. In the manager thread, a shared variable *turn* is used to control the execution of threads.

When $turn = 0$, the manager thread is executed, meanwhile child threads are suspended. On the contrary, when $turn = 1$, child threads are executed, meanwhile the manager thread is suspended. The corresponding Unified Modeling Language (UML) sequence diagram is presented in Fig. 2.

The frameworks of C programs for the manager thread and a child thread are shown in Fig. 3. In the manager thread given in Fig. 3(a), a specified file is first opened for later write operations. Then a `while-true` loop is invoked to continually execute two alternate threads. The procedure of each loop iteration can be summarized as follows:

(1) The shared variable $turn$ is first assigned to 1, representing that the manager thread gives priority to the child threads for program execution.
(2) The function $ResumeThread$ is invoked to resume child thread 1 which is suspended before. When child thread 1 is executed, the manager thread suspends itself with function $SwitchToThread$.
(3) After child thread 1 is executed, the variable $turn$ is assigned to 0 in the child thread, which makes the manager thread stop suspending. At this time, child thread 1 is suspended by function $SuspendThread$ and wait to be executed next time.
(4) Child thread 2 is operated in the same way.

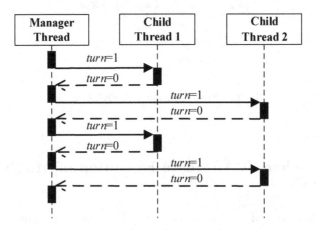

Fig. 2. The UML sequence diagram for alternate execution of threads

In the child thread given in Fig. 3(b), there is also a `while-true` loop invoked to accomplish some specific task. The procedure of each loop iteration can be summarized as follows:

(1) The task is performed. In this example, the task is inserting a character into the file pointed by variable $fp1$.
(2) The shared variable $turn$ is assigned to 0, representing that the child thread gives priority to the manager thread for program execution.

(3) This child thread suspends itself with function *SwitchToThread*. Only when the manager thread assigns variable *turn* to 1 and invokes function *ResumeThread* to resume this child thread, does this thread stop suspending and start the next round of execution.

4 Runtime Verification for the Alternating Property

4.1 MSVL Program for the Problem

An MSVL program is implemented for the above model. In the program, APIs supplied by the Windows system are invoked as external functions. Hence, from the manager thread perspective, each execution of one child thread is regarded as one state in an interval. To mark that one child thread is executed successfully, a global variable *threadNum* is introduced to represent the number of the thread being currently executed. The initial value of *threadNum* is 0. When child thread 1 or child thread 2 is executed, *threadNum* is assigned to 1 or 2, respectively. Therefore, the value of variable *threadNum* will alternate between 1 and 2 when two child threads are executed alternately.

```
unsigned int ManagerThread(LPVOID para)
{
    fp1 = fopen("result.txt", "w+");
    while (true){
        turn = 1; childHandle1->ResumeThread();
        while (turn != 0){ SwitchToThread();
        }
        childHandle1->SuspendThread();
        turn = 1; childHandle2->ResumeThread();
        while (turn != 0){ SwitchToThread();
        }
        childHandle2->SuspendThread();
    }
    fclose(fp1); return 1;
}
```

```
unsigned int ChildThread1(LPVOID para){
    while (true){ fprintf(fp1, "a"); turn = 0;
        while (turn != 1){
            SwitchToThread();
        }
    }
}
```

(a) Framework of the manager thread   (b) Framework of a child thread

Fig. 3. Frameworks of the manager thread and a child thread

4.2 Property Description

Since the property specifying that two threads are executed alternately is a periodically repeated property, it can not be formalized by an LTL or CTL formula directly. With the full regular expressiveness, PPTL can easily express the property, which is shown as follows:

$$P \triangleq \bigcirc^2((\bigcirc(p \wedge \varepsilon); \bigcirc(q \wedge \varepsilon))^*)$$

where the atomic propositions p and q respectively represent $threadNum = 1$ and $threadNum = 2$. The value of p is $true$ when child thread 1 is executed while the value of q is $true$ when child thread 2 is executed. The formula P means that from the fourth state of the program, child thread 1 and child thread 2 are executed alternately. The reason why we do not consider the first three states is that these states are used to initialize the program and child threads have not yet been executed.

4.3   Runtime Verification

With the traditional runtime verification approach, finding counterexamples amounts to sequentially exploring acceptable paths in the automaton constructed for the negation of a desired property. In order to take full advantage of hardware resources supplied by a multi-core machine, a parallel approach has been proposed in [19] to verify full regular temporal properties for real-world programs.

In this approach, the produced trace (possibly incomplete) is first divided into several segments which can be verified in parallel. Then, a thread pool is created for each segment. The thread pool provides an opportunity for each thread to track nondeterministic branches in the LNFG of the negation of the property concurrently. When some of the segments have been verified, the obtained results are merged to show whether the trace satisfies or violates the desired property. If we know that the property is valid or invalid with the already verified segments, it is unnecessary to keep on executing the program and verifying more segments. Otherwise, the verification module continues working until a conclusive result is given or all the segments are verified.

This verification approach is particularly suitable for the problem presented in this paper from the following two aspects:

(1) The creation of the manager thread and child threads indicates that the machine has the computing power to support several threads for verification to increase efficiency.
(2) The execution of the established model will not stop with the `while-true` loop, which leads to the result that we can not perform the verification after the program finishes. With the verification approach given in this section, the execution of the program is terminated once the property is found to be violated.

5   Experiments

The tool *PPTLCheck* presented in [19] is employed to accomplish the verification task. The verification experiments are carried out on one 64-bit Windows 7 PC. The CPU is Intel(R) Core(TM) i5-2410M at 2.3 GHz and the memory is 8 GB. These experiments are carried out to answer the following two questions:

(1) Can two threads be executed alternately through invoking Windows API functions *SuspendThread* and *ResumeThread*?

(2) Can the parallel verification approach based on a multi-core system improve the verification efficiency?

To achieve the above purposes, in the condition that each segment contains 1000 states, we continuously adjust the number of segments (from 1 to 6) verified in parallel and branches (from 1 to 4) explored at the same time in the LNFG. We repeat the verification ten times for each case. When the verification module finds that the property is violated, it will terminate the program execution and record the current state index and consumed time. Since the thread scheduling is random, the recorded state index is different in each verification. To show the impact of our parallel verification mechanism on the verification efficiency, we calculate the average time spent to verify each 1000 states in each case. Due to limited space, Table 1 shows partial experimental results. In the table, "m segments, n branches" means m segments are verified in parallel, and in the verification for each segment, n branches in the LNFG are explored at the same time.

Table 1. Verification results for the alternate execution of two threads

1 segment, 1 branch		3 segments, 2 branches		5 segments, 3 branches		6 segments, 3 branches	
State index	Time (ms)	State index	Time (ms)	State index	Time (ms)	State index	Time (ms)
12292	134	24666	192	15061	92	26572	194
6001	64	28753	234	23162	140	15529	114
23315	248	20983	171	9623	62	17490	121
13087	152	8324	67	27885	164	16732	116
10689	109	13054	110	9953	64	23667	176
25099	284	22875	174	11361	69	16237	124
19110	204	7769	65	16693	104	14188	102
16670	182	15190	127	13176	82	22247	167
14345	157	17103	132	16688	94	7027	51
17043	184	23843	151	25798	152	27546	207
Average	10.9	Average	7.8	Average	6.1	Average	7.3

From Table 1, we can see that each program execution will violate the property, with the maximum state index being 28753. Since the aim of this program is to alternately write the characters "a" and "b" into a specific text file, we can also view the file contents to check the verification results. Figure 4 shows the partial output in one program execution, where the character string "aaa" should be "aba". The result indicates that the sequence of threads will be disordered when we invoke the API functions *SuspendThread* and *ResumeThread* to accomplish the alternating execution of two threads.

In addition, we can see from Table 1 that the verification efficiency varies in different configurations. When no parallel mechanism is adopted, the consumed time for verifying each 1000 states is 10.9 ms, which is shown in the first column. When five segments are verified in parallel and three threads are created

bababababababababababa

ababababaaabababababab

bababababababababababa

Fig. 4. Partial output in one program execution

for each segment, the verification time can be reduced to 6.1 ms, making the verification efficiency increase by 44%. We find that the CPU utility ratio can reach over 90% at the optimized configuration. If more threads are created for parallel segments or branches, it will increase the workload of threads scheduling, which further decreases the verification efficiency, as shown in the last column in Table 1. Hence, we can get the conclusion that the parallel approach can make the verification more efficient when a suitable number of threads are created.

6   Conclusion

This paper aims to employ a parallel approach to verify whether two threads can executed alternately. To achieve this, the problem is first modeled in an MSVL program; then the desired periodically repeated property is specified as a PPTL formula; finally the state sequence generated by the program execution is divided into several segment and verified by different threads in parallel. The experimental results show that the invoking of functions *SuspendThread* and *ResumeThread* to solve the problem will result in the out-of-order threads. Moreover, the parallel approach can terminate the `while-true` loop once the property is found to be violated and increase the verification efficiency.

Since there is an upper boundary to the computing power of one single CPU, which supports a limited number of threads to perform the verification in cooperation. In the near future, the proposed approach will be extended to a distributed system for accomplishing the verification tasks by different computers in parallel, so as to further improve the verification efficiency.

References

1. Tzannes, A., Heumann, S.T., Eloussi, L., Vakilian, M., Adve, V.S., Han, M.: Region and effect inference for safe parallelism. Autom. Softw. Eng. **26**(2), 463–509 (2019). https://doi.org/10.1007/s10515-019-00257-3
2. Leucker, M., Schallhart, C.: A brief account of runtime verification. J. Log. Algebraic Program. **78**(5), 293–303 (2009)
3. Bartocci, E., Falcone, Y., Francalanza, A., Reger, G.: Introduction to runtime verification. In: Bartocci, E., Falcone, Y. (eds.) Lectures on Runtime Verification. LNCS, vol. 10457, pp. 1–33. Springer, Cham (2018). https://doi.org/10.1007/978-3-319-75632-5_1

4. Meredith, P.O., Jin, D., Griffith, D., Chen, F., Roşu, G.: An overview of the mop runtime verification framework. Int. J. Softw. Tools Technol. Transf. **14**(3), 249–289 (2012). https://doi.org/10.1007/s10009-011-0198-6

5. Beaucamps, P., Gnaedig, I., Marion, J.-Y.: Behavior abstraction in malware analysis. In: Barringer, H., et al. (eds.) RV 2010. LNCS, vol. 6418, pp. 168–182. Springer, Heidelberg (2010). https://doi.org/10.1007/978-3-642-16612-9_14

6. Basin, D., Klaedtke, F., Zălinescu, E.: Runtime verification of temporal properties over out-of-order data streams. In: Majumdar, R., Kunčak, V. (eds.) CAV 2017. LNCS, vol. 10426, pp. 356–376. Springer, Cham (2017). https://doi.org/10.1007/978-3-319-63387-9_18

7. Pnueli, A.: The temporal logic of programs. In: 18th Annual Symposium on Foundations of Computer Science, pp. 46–57. IEEE (1977)

8. Clarke, E.M., Emerson, E.A.: Design and synthesis of synchronization skeletons using branching time temporal logic. In: Kozen, D. (ed.) Logic of Programs 1981. LNCS, vol. 131, pp. 52–71. Springer, Heidelberg (1982). https://doi.org/10.1007/BFb0025774

9. Falcone, Y., Havelund, K., Reger, G.: A tutorial on runtime verification. Eng. Dependable Softw. Syst. **34**, 141–175 (2013)

10. Duan, Z., Yang, X., Koutny, M.: Framed temporal logic programming. Sci. Comput. Program. **70**(1), 31–61 (2008)

11. Zhang, N., Duan, Z., Tian, C.: Model checking concurrent systems with MSVL. Sci. Chin. Inf. Sci. **59**(11), 118101 (2016)

12. Wang, M., Tian, C., Duan, Z.: Full regular temporal property verification as dynamic program execution. In: Proceedings of the 39th International Conference on Software Engineering Companion, pp. 226–228. IEEE Press (2017)

13. Duan, Z., Koutny, M.: A framed temporal logic programming language. J. Comput. Sci. Technol. **19**(3), 341–351 (2004). https://doi.org/10.1007/BF02944904

14. Duan, Z.: An extended interval temporal logic and a framing technique for temporal logic programming. PhD thesis, University of Newcastle upon Tyne (1996)

15. Tian, C., Duan, Z.: Propositional projection temporal logic, büchi automata and ω-regular expressions. In: Agrawal, M., Du, D., Duan, Z., Li, A. (eds.) TAMC 2008. LNCS, vol. 4978, pp. 47–58. Springer, Heidelberg (2008). https://doi.org/10.1007/978-3-540-79228-4_4

16. Duan, Z., Zhang, N., Koutny, M.: A complete proof system for propositional projection temporal logic. Theor. Comput. Sci. **497**, 84–107 (2013)

17. Tian, C., Duan, Z.: Expressiveness of propositional projection temporal logic with star. Theor. Comput. Sci. **412**(18), 1729–1744 (2011)

18. Duan, Z., Tian, C., Zhang, L.: A decision procedure for propositional projection temporal logic with infinite models. Acta Informatica **45**(1), 43–78 (2008). https://doi.org/10.1007/s00236-007-0062-z

19. Yu, B., Duan, Z., Tian, C., Zhang, N.: Verifying temporal properties of programs: a parallel approach. J. Parallel and Distrib. Comput. **118**, 89–99 (2018)

20. Duan, Z.: Temporal Logic and Temporal Logic Programming. Science Press, Berlin (2005)

21. Duan, Z., Tian, C.: A practical decision procedure for propositional projection temporal logic with infinite models. Theor. Comput. Sci. **554**, 169–190 (2014)

22. Duan, Z., Tian, C., Zhang, N.: A canonical form based decision procedure and model checking approach for propositional projection temporal logic. Theor. Comput. Sci. **609**, 544–560 (2016)

Problem Solving

A Planning Approach Based on APTL

Haiyang Wang[1(✉)] and Yao Liu[2]

[1] Xi'an University of Technology, Xi'an, China
`hywang@xaut.edu.cn`
[2] Beijing Institute of Control and Electronics Technology,
Beijing 100038, People's Republic of China

Abstract. This paper proposes a path planning approach for multi-agent systems (MASs) with Alternating Projection Temporal Logic (APTL). Our approach aims to calculate a path efficiently which satisfies specific properties in a MAS. The MAS is formalized in an interpreted system, then symbolically represented, and properties of paths are expressed by APTL formulas. We implement a robotic soccer game in order to illustrate the availability of this approach, actions and strategies of each robot are described in detail in interpreted system. The toolkit MCMAS_APTL2 has been developed, where we just enter an APTL formula of specific properties and the model of the robotic soccer game into the toolkit, then a path satisfies the formula is calculated and provided.

Keywords: Multi-agent system · Alternating projection temporal logic · Planning · Interpreted system

1 Introduction

Intelligent machines have become a fairly matured research area of technology and the research on mobile robotics has been advancing tremendously. Over the past decade, a significant shift of focus has occurred in the field of mobile robotics as researchers have begun to investigate problems involving multi robots. In particular, the research on MASs [1,2] has also attracted great attention. A MAS is a group of robots that coexist in an environment and can interact with each other in several different ways in order to complete a specific task. Generally, a MAS do have the ability to solve complex problems easily while an individual cannot. However, path planning [3]of a MAS is one of the crucial issues.

Soccer robot system is a tremendously promising intelligent system. It is developed to imitate human soccer game, based on the multi-discipline research: robotics, intelligent control, game theory. Soccer robot system consists of multi robots and it is a competitive and dynamic system in which each robot has to make a decision for fulfilling their specific goals. From the standpoint of MASs, the soccer game is a good example of the problems in real world. Robotic soccer game is associated with cooperation, decision making, planning, modeling,

This research is supported by the NSFC Grant No. 413619001.

© Springer Nature Switzerland AG 2020

H. Miao et al. (Eds.): SOFL+MSVL 2019 Workshop, LNCS 12028, pp. 113–122, 2020.
https://doi.org/10.1007/978-3-030-41418-4_9

learning, robot architecture, vision tracking algorithm, sensing, communication. A basic problem is to determine what action an agent should take in a given situation in a robotic soccer game. For soccer robot system, robot path planning strategy is a very important subject concerning to performance and intelligence degree of the system.

The path planning problem of MASs is interesting, robots in the same group are cooperative and share a common goal, while robots in different groups are competitive. The problem of coordination is the process that ensures that the individual decisions of the robots result in global optimal decisions for the group. Game theoretic techniques can be applied to solve the problem of competition.

Our Contribution. In this paper, we propose a path planning approach for MASs, which is based on the APTL [4,5]. APTL is a logic based on game theory and its theoretical research has been detailed introduced in [4]. A MAS is modeled as an interpreted system [6,7], the rules and game strategies of the MAS are specified in the interpreted system. We intend to plan paths that satisfy specific properties, which are formalized by APTL formulas. Then, we enter the APTL formula and the model into the toolkit MCMAS_APTL2, a path satisfying the specific property will be obtained. To illustrate the efficiency of our approach and toolkit, a robotic soccer game as a case study is provided in this paper.

Paper Structure. Section *Planning with APTL* introduces APTL simply, and the planning approach with APTL. Section *Strategy Model for Multi-agent Systems in Robotic Soccer* presents the method to design and describe the model of robotic soccer game formally. Section *Conclusions and Future Work* summarises our works and points to new research area.

2 Planning with APTL

In this section, the logic APTL and interpreted system are introduced simply, and the planning approach is presented.

2.1 Alternating Projection Temporal Logic

APTL is the extension of Propositional Projection Temporal Logic [8,9]. Alternating properties of MRSs can be expressed with APTL formulas, expediently. In APTL, projection and chop operators are also useful for expressing iterative and sequential properties [10–12], respectively.

Let $\mathcal{P}$ be a finite set of atomic propositions and $\mathcal{A}$ a finite set of agents. The formulas of APTL are given by the following grammar:

$$P ::= p \mid \neg P \mid P \vee Q \mid \bigcirc_{\ll A \gg} P \mid (P_1, \cdots, P_m) prj_{\ll A \gg} Q \qquad (1)$$

where $p \in \mathcal{P}$, $A \subseteq \mathcal{A}$, $P_1, \cdots, P_m$, P and Q are all well-formed APTL formulas. $\bigcirc_{\ll A \gg}$ (next) and $prj_{\ll A \gg}$ (projection) are basic temporal operators with a set of agents.

For more details on the semantics of APTL, refer to [4]. The semantics of APTL formulas are given in terms of Concurrent Game Structures (CGSs) [13]. A CGS is a tuple $C = (\mathcal{P}, \mathcal{A}, S, S_0, l, \Delta, \tau)$ where

- $\mathcal{P}$ is a finite nonempty set of atomic propositions;
- $\mathcal{A}$ is a finite set of agents;
- S is a finite nonempty set of states;
- S_0 is a finite nonempty set of initial states;
- $l : S \rightarrow 2^{\mathcal{P}}$ is a labeling function that decorates each state with a subset of the atomic propositions;
- $\Delta^a(s)$ is a nonempty set of possible decisions for an agent $a \in \mathcal{A}$ at state s; $\Delta^A(s) = \Delta^{a_1}(s) \times \ldots \times \Delta^{a_k}(s)$ is a nonempty set of decision vectors for the set of agents $A = \{a_1, \ldots, a_k\} \in 2^{\mathcal{A}}$ at state s; accordingly, $\Delta^{\mathcal{A}}(s)$ is simplified as $\Delta(s)$ and denotes the decisions of all agents in $\mathcal{A}$; and for a decision $d \in \Delta(s)$, d_a denotes the decision of agent a within the decision d, and d_A denotes the decision of the set of agents $A \subseteq \mathcal{A}$ within d;
- For each state $s \in S$, $d \in \Delta(s)$, $\tau(s, d)$ maps s and a decision d of the agents in $\mathcal{A}$ to a new state in S. Note that in a CGS, for a state s , each transition is made by a decision $d \in \Delta(s)$ of all agents in $\mathcal{A}$. In some cases, if we just concern with the decisions of $A \subseteq \mathcal{A}$ without caring about the ones of other agents, notation d_A is used. Particularly, if A is a singleton, d_a is adopted.

The alternating transition relationship of a CGS is actually can be represented as $T : S \times \mathcal{P} \times 2^{\mathcal{A}} \rightarrow \mathbb{B}^+(S)$, where $\mathbb{B}^+(S)$ is a positive boolean formula. For a given set S of states, the positive boolean formula $\mathbb{B}^+(S)$ is boolean formula built from elements in S using $\wedge$ and $\vee$. We say that $S_1 \subseteq S$ satisfies a formula $\theta \in \mathbb{B}^+(S)$ if the truth assignment that assigns $true$ to the members of S_1 and $false$ to the members of $S \backslash S_1$ satisfies θ. For example, suppose $S = \{s_0, s_1, s_2\}$, the set $\{s_0\}$ and $\{s_1, s_2\}$ both satisfy the formula $s_0 \vee s_1 \wedge s_2$, where the set $\{s_1\}$ does not.

A path $\lambda = s_0, s_1, \ldots$ is a nonempty sequence of states, which can be finite or infinite. Let $r_1, \ldots, r_k$ be integers ($h \geq 1$) such that $0 = r_1 \leq \ldots \leq r_h \preceq |\lambda|$. The projection of λ onto $r_1, \ldots, r_h$ is the path, $\lambda \downarrow (r_1, \ldots, r_h) = s_{t_1}, s_{t_2}, \ldots, s_{t_l}$ where $t_1, \ldots, t_l$ are obtained from $r_1, \ldots, r_h$ by deleting all duplicates. $t_1, \ldots, t_l$ is the longest strictly increasing subsequence of $r_1, \ldots, r_h$. For example, $s_0, s_1, s_2, s_3, s_4 \downarrow (0, 0, 2, 2, 2, 3) = s_0, s_2, s_3$.

Following the definition of CGS, we define a state s over $\mathcal{P}$ to be a mapping from $\mathcal{P}$ to $B = \{true, false\}$, $s : \mathcal{P} \rightarrow B$. A path $\lambda(s)$ starting from a state s in a CGS satisfies the APTL formula P, denoted by $\lambda(s) \models P$. A CGS C satisfies an APTL formula P iff all of the paths starting from initial states of the CGS satisfy the APTL formula P, denoted by $C \models P$.

The satisfaction relation ($\models$) is inductively defined as follows.

- $\lambda(s) \models p$ for atomic propositions $p \in \mathcal{P}$, iff $p \in l(s)$.
- $\lambda(s) \models \neg P$, iff $\lambda(s) \not\models P$.
- $\lambda(s) \models P \vee Q$, iff $\lambda(s) \models P$ or $\lambda(s) \models Q$.

- $\lambda(s) \models \bigcirc_{\ll A \gg} P$ iff $|\lambda(s)| \geq 2$, and there exists a strategy f_A for the agents in A, such that $\lambda(s) \in out(s, f_A)$, and $\lambda(s)[1, |\lambda|] \models P$.
- $\lambda(s) \models (P_1, \ldots, P_m) prj_{\ll A \gg} Q$ iff there exists a strategy f_A for the agents in A, and $\lambda(s) \in out(s, f_A)$, and integers $0 = r_0 \leq r_1 \leq \ldots \leq r_m \leq |\lambda(s)|$ such that $\lambda(s)[r_{i-1}, r_i] \models P_i$, $0 < i \leq m$ and $\lambda \models Q$ for one of the following λ:
  (a) $r_m < |\lambda(s)|$ and $\lambda = \lambda(s) \downarrow (r_0, \ldots, r_m) \cdot \lambda(s)[r_m + 1, \ldots, |\lambda(s)|]$ or
  (b) $r_m = |\lambda(s)|$ and $\lambda = \lambda(s) \downarrow (r_0, \ldots, r_m)$ for some $0 \leq h \leq m$.

Any APTL formula can be transformed into normal form [14], which is a requisite for interpreting of an APTL formula. Let Q_P be the set of atomic propositions appearing in the APTL formula Q. Normal form of Q can be defined as $Q \equiv Q_e \wedge \varepsilon \vee \bigvee_{i=0}^{n} (Q_{ci} \wedge Q_i)$ where $Q_i \equiv \bigwedge_{j=1}^{r} \bigcirc_{\ll A_{ij} \gg} Q_{ij}$, Q_e is a state formula, $Q_{ci} \equiv \bigwedge_{k=1}^{l} \dot{q}_k$, $q_k \in Q_p$, $\dot{q}_k$ denotes q_k or $\neg q_k$, and $Q_{ci} \neq Q_{cj}$ if $i \neq j$; each Q_{ij} is an arbitrary APTL formula.

The algorithms for transforming APTL formulas into normal forms are represented and also implemented. For example, the normal form of $\square_{\ll A \gg} p$ is $p \wedge \varepsilon \vee p \wedge \bigcirc_{\ll A \gg} \square_{\ll A \gg} p$.

2.2   Interpreted System and ISPL

Interpreted system IS [6] is a formal representation of multi-agent systems, IS can be formally described as a tuple $IS =< (L_i, Act_i, P_i, t_i)_{i \in \Sigma \cup \{E\}}, S_0, h >$, and the Interpreted System Programming Language (ISPL) [6] is used to specify interpreted systems. $\Sigma = \{1, \ldots, n\}$ is a set of agents, L_i is a finite set of local states of agent i, Act_i is a finite set of local actions of agent i, and $P_i : L_i \to 2^{Act_i \setminus \emptyset}$ is a local protocol function of agent i, specifying which actions may be performed at a given state. $t_i : L_i \times L_E \times Act_1 \times \ldots \times Act_n \times Act_E \to L_i$ is a local transition function. The environment is modeled by means of an agent E, a set of local states L_E, a set of actions Act_E, and a protocol P_E. The evolution of its local states is described by a function $t_E : L_E \times Act_1 \times \ldots \times Act_n \times Act_E \to L_E$. $S_0 \subseteq L_0 \times \cdots \times L_n \times L_E$ is the set of initial global states. $h \subseteq L_0 \times \cdots \times L_n \times L_E \times AP$ is a labeling function that decorates each global state with a subset of the atomic propositions.

Let $G \subseteq (L_0 \times \cdots \times L_n \times L_E)$ is the set of reachable global states and $ACT = Act_0 \times \cdots \times Act_n \times Act_E$ is the set of possible joint actions for the system. A tuple $g = (l_0, \ldots, l_n, l_E) \in G$, where $l_i \in L_i$ for each agent $i \in \Sigma \cup \{E\}$, is called a global state and gives a description of the system at a particular instant of time. The evolution of the global states of the system can be described by a function $t : G \times ACT \to G$. Function t is the composition of all the functions t_i, and it is defined by $t(g, a) = g'$ iff $\forall i, t_i(l_i(g), l_E(g), a) = l_i(g')$, where $l_i(g)$ denotes the local state of agent i in global state g and $a \in ACT$.

Interpreted systems and CGSs are closely related. And interpreted systems have been proven a suitable formalism for reasoning about temporal properties of multiple agents.

2.3   The Planning Approach

We present a path planning approach for MASs, which is based on APTL. With our approach, the MAS is formalized as an interpreted system IS, a property of paths is specified by an APTL formula. To plan a path which satisfies APTL ϕ on the IS, we just need to enter the APTL formula ϕ and the system model M_{IS} of IS into the toolkit. If ϕ is a well formed APTL formula, then ϕ is translated into normal form [4,15], and M_{IS} is symbolically represented. Then we calculate whether there exists a path satisfying the APTL formula ϕ. If there exists some paths that satisfy the formula ϕ, a path is shown. Otherwise, there exists no path satisfies the APTL formula ϕ.

In Algorithm 1, we present the algorithm CALAPATH for calculating a path which satisfies the formula φ. Where the set $Sat(\phi) \subseteq G$ includes all the states departing from which there exists at least one computation satisfying ϕ: $Sat(\phi) = \{g \in G | \exists \lambda \in Computations(G) \models \phi$ and $\lambda[0] = g\}$. $Sat_{\bar{v}}(\phi)$ is the characteristic function of $Sat(\phi)$. The function PRE is defined as: $\text{PRE}(A, G_1, t') = \{g \in G_1 | \exists g' \in G_1.t'(g, P_A) = g'\}$.

Algorithm 1. CALAPATH$(S'_{0\bar{v}}, \varphi, R_{t(\bar{v}, \bar{v}')})$

Require: $S'_{0\bar{v}}$ is a boolean function of a set of states, φ is an APTL formula,
    $R_{t(\bar{v}, \bar{v}')}$ is the temporal transition of a multi-agent system;
Ensure: A path satisfies φ;

1: $mark[\varphi] = 0$;
2: $NF_{\varphi} = \text{NF}(\varphi) = \bigvee_{i=1}^{n} \varphi_i$; $\{\varphi_i \equiv \varphi_e \wedge \varepsilon$ or $\varphi_i \equiv \varphi_{i'} \wedge \bigwedge_{j=1}^{m} \bigcirc \ll A_{i'j} \gg \varphi_{i'j}\}$
3: $mark[\varphi_{i'j}] = 0$;
4: i=0;
5: **while** i!=n **do**
6:   i++;
7:   **if** $\varphi_i \equiv \varphi_e \wedge \varepsilon$ **then**
8:     $ss = S'_{0\bar{v}} \cdot Sat_{\bar{v}}(\varphi_e) \cdot Sat_{\bar{v}}(\varepsilon)$;
9:     **if** ss!=0 **then**
10:       Pick ss in P[i] and break;
11:     **else**
12:       continue;
13:     **end if**
14:   **else if** $\varphi_i \equiv \varphi_{i'} \wedge \bigwedge_{j=1}^{m} \bigcirc \ll A_{i'j} \gg \varphi_{i'j}$ and for some formula $\varphi_{i'k}$, $1 \leq k \leq m, mark[\varphi_{i'k}] == 0$ and for some formula $\varphi_{i'r}$, $1 \leq r \leq m, mark[\varphi_{i'r}] == 1$ **then**
15:     for all $\varphi_{i'k}$ make $mark[\varphi_{i'k}] = 1$;
    $ss = S'_{0\bar{v}} \cdot Sat_{\bar{v}}(\varphi_{i'}) \cdot$
    $\prod_k(\text{PRE}(A_{ik}, \text{CALAPATH}(\phi_{i'k}, R_{t(\bar{v}, \bar{v}')}),$
    $R_{t(\bar{v}, \bar{v}')})) \cdot \prod_r(\text{PRE}(A_{i'r}, \text{FIXPOINT}(\mathfrak{c}(Sat_{\bar{v}}(\phi_{i'r_e}),$
    $R_{t(\bar{v}, \bar{v}')})), R_{t(\bar{v}, \bar{v}')}))$;
    where $\varphi_{i'r} \equiv \varphi_{i'r_e} \wedge \bigwedge_{x=1}^{y} \bigcirc_{<<A_{i'r_{ex}}>>} \varphi_{i'r_{ex}}$,
    $\mathfrak{c}(X, R)$ is computed with the update value of X.

$$\{\varphi_{i'r} \equiv \varphi_{i'r_e} \wedge \bigwedge_{x=1}^{y} \bigcirc \ll A_{i'r_{ex}} \gg \varphi_{i'r_{ex}}\};$$

```
16:    if ss!=0 then
17:        Pick ss in P[i];
18:    else
19:        continue;
20:    end if
21:    end if
22:    break;
23: end while
24: if P[i] is a path then
25:    return  P[i];
26: else
27:    There exists no path satisfies φ.
28: end if
```

The MCMAS_APTL2 Toolkit. The planning toolkit MCMAS_APTL2 has been developed, the system is modeled by ISPL and properties of paths are specified by APTL formulas. In order to calculate whether a system exist a path satisfies an APTL formula ϕ, we just entering ϕ and the model of the system into MCMAS_APTL2. The planning process is divided into three phases: The first phase is lexical analysis of the model and then syntax analysis. After that, the symbolical representation of the model employs the corresponding part of MCMAS. The second phase is lexical analysis of the formula ϕ and is followed by the syntax analysis. Then, the formula ϕ is translated into normal form. In the last phase, the characteristic function $\mathcal{C}(Sat(\phi))$ of $Sat(\phi)$ is calculated, $Sat(\phi)$ contains all the states departing from which there exists at least one computation satisfying ϕ. And then compute $\mathcal{C}(Sat(\phi)) \cdot \mathcal{C}(S_0)$, if $\mathcal{C}(Sat(\phi)) \cdot \mathcal{C}(S_0) = 0$, it means that the intersection of $Sat(\phi)$ and S_0 is empty and there exists no path that satisfies ϕ. Furthermore, if $\mathcal{C}(Sat(\phi)) \cdot \mathcal{C}(S_0) \neq 0$, it means that we can find a path λ from state $Sat(\phi) \cap S_0$ such that $\lambda \models \phi$.

3   Strategy Model for Multi-agent Systems in Robotic Soccer

Robotic soccer games [16] are typical applications of MASs, which involving collaboration and competition among the robots. In this section, we particular describe a model of robotic soccer games using our approach, and the soccer field model and strategy model are illustrated respectively.

3.1   Soccer Field Model

The field of robotic soccer game must be rectangular, in normal size of $9000\,mm \times 6000\,mm$. It is divided into three fields: offensive-field, mid-field and back-field. The three fields are marked with lines. The field is quantified as 30 units × 20 units, per unit length represents 300 mm. (x, y) is the coordinate of a position in the field. The coordinate of the center point is (15,10), and the radius of the center circle is three units. The width of the goal is 4 units. The endpoints of the goal-lines are (0,8), (0,12) and (30,8), (30,12) respectively. The penalty areas size are 4 units × 8 units.

3.2   Strategy Model

Robotic soccer path planning is more complex than conventional robot system, because it has a time-vary workspace and it is a MAS with stringent realtime demand. At the same time, the path planning must also consider the affect from opposite team robots and the game regulation. Therefore, there are several possible and optimal path choices for each robot in a specific scenario.

The regulation of soccer robot game is much similar to human soccer game. In general, the actions can be taken by a robot are shown in the following:

- Kick off: At the beginning of the game, a robot kicks the ball.
- Go to defend: A robot goes to defend opposing player.
- Go to the ball: A robot goes to the ball.
- Intercept the ball: A robot attempts to intercept the ball when the ball is kicked by opposite players.
- Pass the ball to its teammate: A robot sends the ball to its teammate when the opponent goal is blocked by opposite player.
- Shoot the ball into the goal: A robot shoots the ball to the opponent goal.
- Go forward with the ball: A robot carries the ball to the position near the opponent goal.

At any moment in the game, each robot is aware of the ball, both goals position, its own position and other robots' approximate position on the field.

According to different situations, new roles are assigned for the team players, including striker, midfielder, defender. Goalkeeper is different from the other players, and the goalkeeper role does not change in the game. The goalkeeper software is very simple and consists of looking and observing the ball all the time. When the ball approaches, the goalkeeper kicks the ball in order to prevent the opponent from scoring. The kick not only avoids a goal but also kicks the ball far away from its goal.

For a robotic soccer game, one team employs an attack tactic which possess the ball, while the other team employs a defensive tactic. Below we describe strategies for a soccer game which contains team A and team B.

3.3   Robotic Soccer Games

In order to demonstrate the process of our approach, we implement a robotic soccer game using the toolkit MCMAS_APTL2. The two team of the game are the red team and the yellow team, both of them have three players. The three players are goalkeeper, striker and midfielder. The goalkeeper's activity area is restricted in the penalty area.

The actions can be taken by goalkeepers including *act_none*, *run*, *intercept* and *kick the ball*. Expressly, the action *act_none* means the goalkeeper does not take any action; *intercept* means that the goalkeeper to intercept the goal of opposing players. The actions can be taken by strikers and midfielders including *act_none*, *kick off*, *kick the ball*, *run*, *intercept*, *shoot*, *pass the ball*, *take a pass* and *dribbling*, where *pass the ball* means that a robot pass the ball to its teammate and *take a pass* means that a robot get a pass from its teammate; *dribbling* indicates that robot run with the ball.

The strategy of robots is described in the section *Strategy Model for Multiagent Systems in Robotic Soccer*. The model of the robotic soccer game is specified as an interpreted system, and written in ISPL. The red team contains three agents: r_gk, r_1 and r_2, whose roles are goalkeeper, striker and midfielder, respectively. The yellow team also contains three agents: y_gk, y_1 and y_2. The agent *environment* contains some observed variables which represent the evolution of the game process.

The set of atomic properties is $AP = \{redscore, yellowscore\}$. *redscore* represents that the red team scored a goal and *yellowscore* means the yellow team scored a goal. The system has two groups $g_1 = \{r\_gk, r\_1, r\_2\}$, $g_2 = \{y\_gk, y\_1, y\_2\}$. We want to get a path that sometimes the yellow team scored a goal. Then we give the APTL formula $\Diamond_{\ll g_2 \gg} yellowscore$, if the yellow team can score a goal, and the toolkit will present a path satisfying the formula $\Diamond_{\ll g_2 \gg} yellowscore$. Finally, a corresponding track of the soccer is shown in Fig. 1.

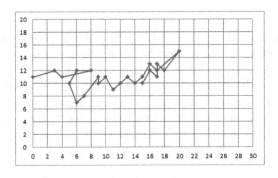

Fig. 1. A path satisfies $\Diamond_{\ll g_2 \gg} yellowscore$.

We also implement a 2×2 robotic soccer game, whose strategy model is similar to the 3×3 one. The set of atomic properties is $AP = \{redscore, yellowscore\}$. *redscore* represents that the red team scored a goal and *yellowscore* means the yellow team scored a goal. The system has two groups $g_1 = \{red\_gk, red\_f\}$, $g_2 = \{yellow\_gk, yellow\_f\}$. The agent *red_f* kicks the ball off at the beginning of the game. We want to get a path that sometimes the red team scored a goal. Then we give the APTL formula $\Diamond_{\ll g_1 \gg} redscore$, if the red team can score a goal, and the toolkit will present a path satisfying the formula $\Diamond_{\ll g_1 \gg} redscore$. The experimental result of the game is shown that the formula is satisfied on some paths. Finally, a corresponding track of the soccer is shown in Fig. 2.

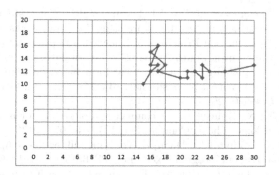

Fig. 2. A path satisfies $\Diamond_{\ll g_1 \gg} redscore$.

4 Conclusions and Future Work

In this paper, a path planning approach for MASs is proposed, which is based on APTL. With this approach, a MAS is modeled as an interpreted system and written in ISPL. To plan paths satisfying a property which is specified as an APTL formula, we just enter the model and the APTL formula into toolkit MCMAS_APTL2, then a path satisfying the APTL formula is obtained. We have implemented a robotic soccer game to illustrate our approach, and the obtained results show that our method is feasible. In the future, we will further study more efficient path planning method for MASs, and improve the efficiency of the toolkit MCMAS_APTL2.

References

1. Iocchi, L., Nardi, D., Salerno, M.: Reactivity and deliberation: a survey on multi-robot systems. BRSDMAS 2000. LNCS (LNAI), vol. 2103, pp. 9–32. Springer, Heidelberg (2001). https://doi.org/10.1007/3-540-44568-4_2
2. Kim, D.H., Kim, Y.J., Kim, K.C., Kim, J.H., Vadakkepat, P.: Vector field based path planning and petri-net based role selection mechanism with Q-learning for the soccer robot system. Intell. Autom. Soft Comput. **6**(1), 75–87 (2000)
3. Xu, L., Tian, C., Duan, Z., Hongwei, D.: Planning with spatio-temporal search control knowledge. IEEE Trans. Knowl. Data Eng. **30**(10), 1915–1928 (2018)
4. Wang, H., Duan, Z., Tian, C.: Model checking multi-agent systems with APTL. Ad Hoc Sens. Wirel. Netw. **37**(1–4), 35–52 (2017)

5. Wang, H.Y., Duan, Z.H., Tian, C., Ruan, J., Xue, B.: Tool for checking satisfiability of APTL formulas. J. Softw. **29**(6), 1635–1646 (2018). (in Chinese). http://www.jos.org.cn/1000-9825/5459.htm
6. Lomuscio Alessio, Q., Hongyang, R.F.: MCMAS: an open-source model checker for the verification of multi-agent systems. Int. J. Softw. Tools Technol. Transf. **173**(9–10), 1–22 (2015)
7. Lomuscio, A., Michaliszyn, J.: Model checking multi-agent systems against epistemic HS specifications with regular expressions. In: Proceedings of the Fifteenth International Conference on Principles of Knowledge Representation and Reasoning, KR 2016, Cape Town, South Africa, 25–29 April 2016, pp. 298–308 (2016)
8. Duan, Z., Tian, C., Zhang, N.: A canonical form based decision procedure and model checking approach for propositional projection temporal logic. Theor. Comput. Sci. **609**, 544–560 (2016)
9. Duan, Z., Zhang, N., Koutny, M.: A complete proof system for propositional projection temporal logic. Theor. Comput. Sci. **497**, 84–107 (2013)
10. Wang, M., Tian, C., Zhang, N., Duan, Z.: Verifying full regular temporal properties of programs via dynamic program execution. TR **68**(3), 1101–1116 (2019)
11. Cui, J., Duan, Z., Tian, C., Hongwei, D.: A novel approach to modeling and verifying real-time systems for high reliability. IEEE Trans. Reliab. **67**(2), 481–493 (2018)
12. Bin, Y., Duan, Z., Tian, C., Zhang, N.: Verifying temporal properties of programs: a parallel approach. J. Parallel Distrib. Comput. **118**, 89–99 (2018)
13. Alur, R., Henzinger, T.A., Kupferman, O.: Alternating-time temporal logic. J. ACM **49**(5), 672–713 (2002)
14. Tian, C., Duan, Z.: Alternating interval based temporal logics. In: Dong, J.S., Zhu, H. (eds.) ICFEM 2010. LNCS, vol. 6447, pp. 694–709. Springer, Heidelberg (2010). https://doi.org/10.1007/978-3-642-16901-4_45
15. Tian, C., Duan, Z.: Detecting spurious counterexamples efficiently in abstract model checking. In: ICSE, pp. 202–211 (2013)
16. Guarnizo, J.G., Mellado, M., Low, C.Y., Aziz, N.: Strategy model for multi-robot coordination in robotic soccer. Appl. Mech. Mater. **393**, 592–597 (2013)

Solving Constraint Optimization Problems Based on Mathematica and Abstraction

Guoteng Pan, Mengjun Li$^{(\boxtimes)}$, and Guodong Ou

National University of Defense Technology, Changsha, China
gtpan@163.com, mengjun.li@163.com, ouguodong@nudt.edu.cn

Abstract. Solving constraint optimization problems is widely applicable in computer science. The computer algebra system Mathematica provides MaxValue, MinValue and other functions to solve constraint optimization problems. However many cases of constraint optimization problems cannot be solved by these functions directly. In this paper, based on these Mathematica functions and abstraction, a practical approach is presented for computing the upper bounds and the lower bounds of the optimization values of constraint optimization problems. The optimization values of many constraint optimization problems, which cannot be solved by Mathematica functions directly, can be computed automatically by using the approach presented in this paper. The experimental results demonstrate the practicality of this approach.

Keywords: Constraint optimization problems · Upper and lower bounds · Mathematica · Abstraction

1 Introduction

Solving constraint optimization problems is widely applicable in computer science. The IMT (Integer Linear Programming Modulo Theories) approach has been applied to industrial synthesis and design problems with real-time constraints arising in the development of the Boeing 787, many other problems ranging from operations research to software verification routinely involve linear constraints and optimization [1].

Computing the minimum and the maximum of constraint optimization problems is an alternative for verifying the universal-quantifier formulae. For example, for the formulae like $\forall x_1, \cdots, x_n.f(t_1, \cdots, t_m) \geq c$, where f is a function, c is a constant and $t_1, \cdots, t_m$ are expressions over the variables $x_1, \cdots, x_n$ and constants, if min can be computed automatically, which is the minimum or a lower bound of the minimum of $f(t_1, \cdots, t_m)$ under the constraint

---

This work was supported by the National Natural Science Foundation of China (Grant No. 61672525).

© Springer Nature Switzerland AG 2020
H. Miao et al. (Eds.): SOFL+MSVL 2019 Workshop, LNCS 12028, pp. 123–140, 2020.
https://doi.org/10.1007/978-3-030-41418-4_10

$x_1, \cdots, x_n \in dom(f)$, then the formula $min \geq c$ will be an alternative for verifying the above formula since $min \geq c$ implies $\forall x_1, \cdots, x_n.f(t_1, \cdots, t_m) \geq c$. In the similar way, for the formulae like $\forall x_1, \cdots, x_n.f(t_1, \cdots, t_m) \leq c$, if max can be computed automatically, which is the maximum or an upper bound of the maximum of $f(t_1, \cdots, t_m)$ under the constraint $x_1, \cdots, x_n \in dom(f)$, then the formula $max \leq c$ will be an alternative for verifying the above formula $\forall x_1, \cdots, x_n.f(t_1, \cdots, t_m) \leq c$.

In [2,3], in the Event-B [4] model for the aircraft collision avoidance system example, the invariant $\forall t.t \in dom(rhoc) \Rightarrow 2 * rhoc(t) * sin(phi/2) \geq p$ need to be preserved. If min can be computed automatically, which is the minimum or a lower bound of the minimum of $2 * rhoc(t) * sin(phi/2)$ under the constraint $t \in dom(rhoc)$, then the formula $min \geq p$ will be an alternative for verifying the above invariant since $min \geq p$ implies $\forall t.t \in dom(rhoc) \Rightarrow 2 * rhoc(t) * sin(phi/2) \geq p$.

The computer algebra system Mathematica is developed by Wolfram Research, a full range of state-of-the-art optimization techniques have been integrated into the Wolfram language. These optimization techniques include constrained nonlinear optimization, interior point methods, and integer programming as well as original symbolic methods. The wolfram language's symbolic architecture provides seamless access to industrial-strength system and model optimization, efficiently handling million-variable linear programming and multi-thousand-variable nonlinear problems.

Mathematica provides **MaxValue**, **MinValue** and other functions to solve constraint optimization problems. **MaxValue**$[\{expr, \Phi\}, \{\eta\}]$(**MinValue** $[\{expr, \Phi\}, \{\eta\}]$) gives the maximum (the minimum) of the objective expression $expr$ subject to the constraint Φ with the variable list $\{\eta\}$. When the objective expressions and the constraints are both polynomials, these functions can compute the maximum and the minimum of constraint optimization problems automatically.

However, when the objective expressions are not polynomials, many cases of constraint optimization problems cannot be solved by the above Mathematica functions. Consider the simple optimization problem **MinValue** $[\{\textbf{Cos}[x+y], x+y \leq 3\}, \{x,y\}]$, Mathematica outputs **MinValue**$[\{\textbf{Cos}[x+y], x+y \leq 3\}, \{x,y\}]$ as answer, which means Mathematica cannot solve this constraint optimization problem. Furthermore, consider the more complex optimization problem

MinValue$[\{r*\textbf{Sqrt}[5-4\textbf{Cos}[\textbf{Pi}/3-v*(t-(rhoi-\textbf{Sqrt}[3]r)/v)/r]],$
$(rhoi-\textbf{Sqrt}[3]r)/v \leq t \&\& t \leq (rhoi-\textbf{Sqrt}[3]r)/v+\textbf{Pi}*r/(3*v)\&\& r > 0\&\& v > 0\}, \{t\}]$

this constraint optimization problem is induced by the aircraft collision avoidance system example in [3], Mathematica outputs the constraint optimization problem itself as answer, which also means Mathematica cannot solve this optimization problem.

The optimization values of many constraint optimization problems cannot be solved automatically when the objective expressions are not polynomials, computing the upper bounds and the lower bounds of the optimization values may be a choice. Computing the upper bounds and the lower bounds, which are the conservative approximations of the maximums or the minimums of the constraint optimization problems, will make more valuable information be output automatically, and will make more universal-quantified formulae be verified with their alternatives.

For the above reasons, a practical approach that computing the upper bounds and the lower bounds of constraint optimization problems based on Mathematica and abstraction is presented. The contributions of this paper include:

(1) A practical approach for computing the upper bounds and the lower bounds of constraint optimization problems based on Mathematica and abstraction is presented. Combining the symbolic analysis of Mathematica and the abstraction, the maximums and the minimums of many constraint optimization problems can be computed automatically by using this approach, which cannot be solved by Mathematica.

(2) Based on the approach presented in this paper, the algorithms are developed, which are written in Mathematica language and runs in the Mathematica environment. And the experiments results demonstrate the practicality of the approach for computing upper bounds and lower bounds of constraint optimization problems.

This paper is structured as follows: the motivation examples are given in Sects. 2, 3 presents the preliminary, the algorithms for computing the upper bounds and the lower bounds of constraint optimization problems based on Mathematica and abstraction are shown in Sect. 4, the experimental results are shown in Sects. 5, 6 discusses the related work, and Sect. 7 concludes this paper.

2 Motivation

Consider the simple optimization problem **MinValue**[{**Cos**[x+y],x+y≤3}, {x,y}], Mathematica cannot solve this optimization problem. The expression **Cos**[x+y] has the sub-expression x+y, replace x+y with a new variable z, the optimization problem **MinValue**[{**Cos**[x+y], x+y≤3}, {x,y}] is transformed equivalently into the constraint optimization problem **MinValue**[{**Cos**[z], -∞≤z&&z≤3&&z=x+y&&x+y≤3}, {x,y,z}], where −∞ and 3 are the minimum and the maximum of x+y. By ignoring the irrelevant constraints z=x+y and x+y≤3, the constraint optimization problem will be **MinValue**[{**Cos**[z], -∞≤z&&z≤3}, {x,y,z}], for this obtained constraint optimization problem, Mathematica outputs the result −1, which means the obtained optimization problem has the optimization value −1. It is obvious that −1 is the minimum of the original constraint optimization problem **MinValue**[{**Cos**[x+y], x+y≤3}, {x,y}].

Note that the optimization problem **MinValue**[{**Cos**[x+y], x+y≤3}, {x,y}] is equivalent to the optimization problem **MinValue**[{**Cos**[z], -∞≤z&&z≤3&&

z=x+y&&x+y≤3}, {x,y,z}], since the irrelevant constraints z=x+y and x+y≤3 are ignored in the obtained optimization problem **MinValue**[{**Cos** [z], -∞≤z&&z≤3}, {x,y,z}], the set satisfying the constraint -∞≤z&&z≤3&& z=x+y&&x+y≤3 is the subset of the set satisfying the constraint -∞≤z &&z≤3, so the minimum of **MinValue**[{**Cos**[z], -∞≤z&&z≤3}, {x,y,z}] is an lower bound of the minimum of **MinValue**[{**Cos**[x+y], x+y≤3}, {x,y}], in this sense, the constraint optimization problem **MinValue**[{**Cos**[z], -∞≤ z&&z≤3}, {x,y,z}] is an abstraction of the constraint optimization problem **Min-Value**[{**Cos**[x+y], x+y≤3}, {x,y}].

Although   Mathematica cannot solve the optimization problem **MinValue**[{**Cos**[x+y], x+y≤3}, {x,y}], after abstracting the constraint optimization problem, Mathematica can compute automatically the optimization value −1 of the abstracted optimization problem **MinValue**[{**Cos**[z], -∞≤z&&z≤3}, {x,y,z}].

Furthermore, consider the more complex optimization problem

$$\textbf{MaxValue}[\{r*\textbf{Sqrt}[5\text{-}4\textbf{Cos}[\textbf{Pi}/3\text{-}v*(t\text{-}(rhoi\text{-}\textbf{Sqrt}[3]r)/v)/r]],$$
$$(rhoi\text{-}\textbf{Sqrt}[3]r)/v \le t\&\&t \le (rhoi\text{-}\textbf{Sqrt}[3]r)/v\text{+}\textbf{Pi}*r/(3*v)\&\&r > 0\&\&v > 0\}, \{t\}],$$

Mathematica cannot solve this optimization problem. The expression r*Sqrt[5-4**Cos**[**Pi**/3-v*(t-(rhoi-**Sqrt**[3]r)/v)/r]] has the sub-expression **Pi**/3-v*(t-(rhoi-**Sqrt**[3]r)/v)/r, the following optimization problems will compute its minimum and its maximum:

$$\textbf{MinValue}[\{\textbf{Pi}/3\text{-}v*(t\text{-}(rhoi\text{-}\textbf{Sqrt}[3]r)/v)/r,$$
$$(rhoi\text{-}\textbf{Sqrt}[3]r)/v \le t\&\&t \le (rhoi\text{-}\textbf{Sqrt}[3]r)/v\text{+}\textbf{Pi}*r/(3*v)\&\&r > 0\&\&v > 0\}, \{t\}]$$

$$\textbf{MaxValue}[\{\textbf{Pi}/3\text{-}v*(t\text{-}(rhoi\text{-}\textbf{Sqrt}[3]r)/v)/r,$$
$$(rhoi\text{-}\textbf{Sqrt}[3]r)/v \le t\&\&t \le (rhoi\text{-}\textbf{Sqrt}[3]r)/v\text{+}\textbf{Pi}*r/(3*v)\&\&r > 0\&\&v > 0\}, \{t\}]$$

The computed minimum and the maximum are 0 and **Pi**/3 respectively. Replace **Pi**/3-v*(t-(rhoi-**Sqrt**[3]r)/v)/r with a new variable z1 and constrain z1 with the minimum 0 and the maximum **Pi**/3, the above optimization problem is transformed into the following constraint optimization problem:

$$\textbf{MaxValue}[\{r*\textbf{Sqrt}[5\text{-}4\textbf{Cos}[z1]], (rhoi\text{-}\textbf{Sqrt}[3]r)/v \le t\&\&t \le (rhoi\text{-}$$
$$\textbf{Sqrt}[3]r)/v\text{+}\textbf{Pi}*r/(3*v)\&\&r > 0\&\&0 \le z1\&\&z1 \le \textbf{Pi}/3\}, \{t,z1\}]$$

Note that the following constraint optimization problem

$$\textbf{MaxValue}[\{r*\textbf{Sqrt}[5\text{-}4\textbf{Cos}[\textbf{Pi}/3\text{-}v*(t\text{-}(rhoi\text{-}\textbf{Sqrt}[3]r)/v)/r]],$$
$$(rhoi\text{-}\textbf{Sqrt}[3]r)/v \le t\&\&t \le (rhoi\text{-}\textbf{Sqrt}[3]r)/v\text{+}\textbf{Pi}*r/(3*v)\&\&r > 0\&\&v > 0\}, \{t\}]$$

is equivalent to the constraint optimization problem

$$\textbf{MaxValue}[\{r*\textbf{Sqrt}[5\text{-}4\textbf{Cos}[z1]], z1\text{=}\textbf{Pi}/3\text{-}v*(t\text{-}(rhoi\text{-}\textbf{Sqrt}[3]r)/v)/r\&\&$$
$$0 \le z1\&\&z1 \le \textbf{Pi}/3\&\&(rhoi\text{-}\textbf{Sqrt}[3]r)/v \le t\&\&$$
$$t \le (rhoi\text{-}\textbf{Sqrt}[3]r)/v\text{+}\textbf{Pi}*r/(3*v)\&\&r > 0\&\&v > 0\}, \{t,z1\}],$$

since the irrelevant constraints z1=**Pi**/3-v*(t-(rhoi-**Sqrt**[3]r)/v)/r and v>0 are ignored in the obtained optimization problem **MaxValue**[{r***Sqrt**[5-4**Cos**[z1]], (rhoi-**Sqrt**[3]r)/v≤t&&t≤(rhoi-**Sqrt**[3]r)/v+**Pi***r/(3*v)&&0≤z1&&z1≤**Pi**/3&& r>0},{t,z1}], and the set satisfying the constraint 0≤z1&&z1≤**Pi**/3&&z1 = **Pi**/3- v*(t-(rhoi-**Sqrt**[3]r)/v)/r&&(rhoi-**Sqrt**[3]r)/v≤t&&t≤(rhoi-**Sqrt**[3]r)/ v+**Pi***r /(3*v)&&r>0&&v>0 is the subset of the set satisfying the constraint (rhoi-**Sqrt**[3]r)/v≤ t&&t≤(rhoi-**Sqrt**[3]r)/v+**Pi***r/(3*v)&&r>0&&0≤z1&&z1 ≤**Pi**/3, then the maximum of

$$\textbf{MaxValue}[\{r\text{*}\textbf{Sqrt}[5\text{-}4\textbf{Cos}[z1]], (\text{rhoi-}\textbf{Sqrt}[3]r)/v \leq t\&\&t \leq (\text{rhoi-}\textbf{Sqrt}[3]r)/v\text{+}\textbf{Pi}\text{*}r/(3\text{*}v)\&\&r > 0\&\&0 \leq z1\&\&z1 \leq \textbf{Pi}/3\}, \{t,z1\}]$$

is an upper bound of the maximum of

$$\textbf{MaxValue}[\{r\text{*}\textbf{Sqrt}[5\text{-}4\textbf{Cos}[\textbf{Pi}/3\text{-}v\text{*}(t\text{-}(\text{rhoi-}\textbf{Sqrt}[3]r)/v)/r]], (\text{rhoi-}\textbf{Sqrt}[3]r)/v \leq t\&\&t \leq (\text{rhoi-}\textbf{Sqrt}[3]r)/v\text{+}\textbf{Pi}\text{*}r/(3\text{*}v)\&\&r > 0\&\&v > 0\}, \{t\}],$$

in this sense, the constraint optimization problem **MaxValue**[{r***Sqrt**[5-4 **Cos**[z1]], (rhoi-**Sqrt**[3]r)/v≤t&&t≤(rhoi-**Sqrt**[3]r)/v+**Pi***r/(3*v)&&r>0&&0≤ z1&& z1≤**Pi**/3},{t,z1}] is an abstraction of the constraint optimization problem

$$\textbf{MaxValue}[\{r\text{*}\textbf{Sqrt}[5\text{-}4\textbf{Cos}[\textbf{Pi}/3\text{-}v\text{*}(t\text{-}(\text{rhoi-}\textbf{Sqrt}[3]r)/v)/r]], (\text{rhoi-}\textbf{Sqrt}[3]r)/v \leq t\&\&t \leq (\text{rhoi-}\textbf{Sqrt}[3]r)/v\text{+}\textbf{Pi}\text{*}r/(3\text{*}v)\&\&r > 0\&\&v > 0\}, \{t\}].$$

Further, the expression r***Sqrt**[5-4**Cos**[z1]] has the sub-expression **Cos**[z1], and the following optimization problems will compute the minimalum and the maximum of **Cos**[z1]:

$$\textbf{MinValue}[\{\textbf{Cos}[z1], 0 \leq z1\&\&z1 \leq \textbf{Pi}/3\}, \{z1\}]$$

$$\textbf{MaxValue}[\{\textbf{Cos}[z1], 0 \leq z1\&\&z1 \leq \textbf{Pi}/3\}, \{z1\}].$$

The obtained minimum and the maximum of **Cos**[z1] are 1/2 and 1 respectively. Replace the sub-expression **Cos**[z1] with a new variable z2, the above optimization problem is transformed into the following optimization problem:

$$\textbf{MaxValue}[\{r\text{*}\textbf{Sqrt}[5\text{-}4\text{*}z2], (\text{rhoi-}\textbf{Sqrt}[3]r)/v \leq t\&\&t \leq (\text{rhoi-}\textbf{Sqrt}[3]r)/v\text{+} \textbf{Pi}\text{*}r/(3\text{*}v) \&\&r > 0\&\&1/2 \leq z2\&\&z2 \leq 1\}, \{t,z1,z2\}].$$

Note that the following constraint optimization problem

$$\textbf{MaxValue}[\{r\text{*}\textbf{Sqrt}[5\text{-}4\textbf{Cos}[z1]], (\text{rhoi-}\textbf{Sqrt}[3]r)/v \leq t\&\&t \leq (\text{rhoi-}\textbf{Sqrt}[3]r)/v\text{+} \textbf{Pi}\text{*}r/(3\text{*}v) \&\&0 \leq z1\&\&z1 \leq \textbf{Pi}/3\&\&r > 0\}, \{t,z1\}]$$

is equivalent to the constraint optimization problem

$$\textbf{MaxValue}[\{r\text{*}\textbf{Sqrt}[5\text{-}4z2], z2=\textbf{Cos}[z1]\&\&(\text{rhoi-}\textbf{Sqrt}[3]r)/v \leq t \&\&t \leq (\text{rhoi-}\textbf{Sqrt}[3]r)/v\text{+}\textbf{Pi}\text{*}r/(3\text{*}v) \&\&r > 0\&\&0 \leq z1\&\&z1 \leq \textbf{Pi}/3 \&\&1/2 \leq z2\&\&z2 \leq 1\}, \{t,z1,z2\}],$$

since the irrelevant constraints z2=Cos[z1]&&0≤z1&&z1≤**Pi**/3 are ignored in the obtained optimization problem, and the set satisfying the constraint z2=Cos[z1]&&(rhoi-**Sqrt**[3]r)/v≤t&&t≤(rhoi-**Sqrt**[3]r)/v+**Pi***r/(3*v) &&0≤z1 &&z1≤**Pi**/3 &&r>0&&1/2≤z2&&z2≤1 is the subset of the set satisfying the constraint   (rhoi-**Sqrt**[3]r)/v≤t&&t≤(rhoi-**Sqrt**[3]r)/v+**Pi***r/(3*v)&&r>0&& 1/2≤z2&&z2≤1, then the maximum of

$$\textbf{MaxValue}[\{r^*\textbf{Sqrt}[5\text{-}4^*z2], (rhoi\text{-}\textbf{Sqrt}[3]r)/v \leq t \&\&t \leq (rhoi\text{-}\textbf{Sqrt}[3]r)/v+$$
$$\textbf{Pi}^*r/(3^*v) \&\&1/2 \leq z2\&\&z2 \leq 1\&\&r > 0\}, \{t,z1,z2\}]$$

is an upper bound of the maximum of

$$\textbf{MaxValue}[\{r^*\textbf{Sqrt}[5\text{-}4\textbf{Cos}[z1]], (rhoi\text{-}\textbf{Sqrt}[3]r)/v \leq t\&\&t \leq (rhoi\text{-}\textbf{Sqrt}[3]r)/v+$$
$$\textbf{Pi}^*r/(3^*v) \&\&0 \leq z1\&\&z1 \leq \textbf{Pi}/3\&\&r > 0\}, \{t,z1\}],$$

in this sense, the constraint optimization problem **MaxValue**[{r***Sqrt**[5-4*z2], (rhoi-**Sqrt**[3]r)/v≤t&&t≤(rhoi-**Sqrt**[3]r)/v+**Pi***r/(3*v)&&1/2≤z2&&z2≤1&& r>0} ,{t,z1,z2}] is an abstraction of the optimization problem

$$\textbf{MaxValue}[\{r^*\textbf{Sqrt}[5\text{-}4\textbf{Cos}[z1]], (rhoi\text{-}\textbf{Sqrt}[3]r)/v \leq t\&\&t \leq (rhoi\text{-}\textbf{Sqrt}[3]r)/v+$$
$$\textbf{Pi}^*r/(3^*v) \&\&0 \leq z1\&\&z1 \leq \textbf{Pi}/3\&\&r > 0\}, \{t,z1\}].$$

For the above abstracted constraint optimization problem **MaxValue**[{r***Sqrt** [5- 4*z2],(rhoi-**Sqrt**[3]r)/v≤t&&t≤(rhoi-**Sqrt**[3]r)/v+**Pi***r/(3*v)&&r>0&&1/2 ≤z2 &&z2≤1},{t,z1,z2}], Mathematica outputs the following results:

$$\begin{cases} \textbf{Sqrt}[3]\textbf{Sqrt}[r^2] & r > 0 \\ -\infty & \text{True.} \end{cases}$$

Simplify the above computed result with the Mathematica function **Full-Simplify** under the constraint (rhoi-**Sqrt**[3]r)/v≤t&&t≤(rhoi-**Sqrt**[3]r)/v+ **Pi***r/(3*v) &&r>0&&v>0&&0≤z1&&z1≤**Pi**/3 &&1/2≤z2&&z2≤1, the simplified result **Sqrt**[3]r is obtained. It is easy to check that **Sqrt**[3]r is the maximum of the original constraint optimization problem **MaxValue**[{r***Sqrt**[5-4**Cos** [**Pi**/3-v*(t-(rhoi-**Sqrt**[3]r)/v)/r]], (rhoi-**Sqrt**[3]r)/v≤t&&t≤(rhoi-**Sqrt**[3]r)/v+ **Pi***r/(3*v)&&r>0 &&v>0},{t}].

Although Mathematica cannot solve automatically the optimization problem

$$\textbf{MaxValue}[\{r^*\textbf{Sqrt}[5\text{-}4\textbf{Cos}[\textbf{Pi}/3\text{-}v^*(t\text{-}(rhoi\text{-}\textbf{Sqrt}[3]r)/v)/r]],$$
$$(rhoi\text{-}\textbf{Sqrt}[3]r)/v \leq t\&\&t \leq (rhoi\text{-}\textbf{Sqrt}[3]r)/v+\textbf{Pi}^*r/(3^*v) \&\&r > 0\&\&v > 0\}, \{t\}],$$

after abstracting the constraint optimization problem two times, Mathematica can compute automatically the optimization value **Sqrt**[3]r of the abstracted optimization   problem   **MaxValue**[{r***Sqrt**[5-4*z2],(rhoi-**Sqrt**[3]r)/v≤t&&t ≤(rhoi-**Sqrt**[3]r)/v+**Pi***r/(3*v)&&r>0&&1/2≤z2&&z2≤1 t,z1,z2}].

The above two examples demonstrate that constraint optimization problems, which cannot be solved by Mathematica directly, can be abstracted by replacing sub-expressions with new variables, constraining these new variables with the minimum and the maximum of corresponding sub-expressions, ignoring the irrelevant constraints, and finally the abstracted constrained optimization problems can be solved automatically by Mathematica.

3   Preliminary

In this section, some preliminary definitions will be given.

Definition 1 *(Expression Set). Let $\mathcal{V}$ be the set of variables, $\mathcal{C}$ be the set of constants, and $\mathcal{F}$ be the set of functions, the expression set $\mathcal{E}$ generated based on $\mathcal{V}$, $\mathcal{C}$ and $\mathcal{F}$ is defined inductively as follows:*

(1) Each variable $x \in \mathcal{V}$ is an expression in $\mathcal{E}$.
(2) Each constant $c \in \mathcal{C}$ is an expression in $\mathcal{E}$.
(3) Let $f \in \mathcal{F}$ be an n-ary function, then $f(e_1, \cdots, e_n)$ is an expression in $\mathcal{E}$, where $e_1, \cdots, e_n$ are expressions in $\mathcal{E}$.

Definition 2 *(n-Part of Expression). Let e be an expression, if e is a variable or a constant, then the length of e is 0; if e is $f(e_1, \cdots, e_n)$, then the length of $f(e_1, \cdots, e_n)$ is n, and the i-part$(1 \leq i \leq n)$ of $f(e_1, \cdots, e_n)$ is e_i.*

For example, the length of the expression x is 0, the length of the expression 2 is 0. The length of the expression $x + y$ is 2, the 1-part of the expression $x + y$ is x, and the 2-part of the expression $x + y$ is y.

Definition 3 *(n-level of Expression). The n-level of an expression e is inductively defined as follows:*

(1) The 0-level of e is the set $\{e\}$.
(2) If $f(e_1, \cdots, e_n)$ is in the n-level of e, then $e_1, \cdots, e_n$ will be in the (n+1)-level of e, otherwise the (n+1)-level of e is $\emptyset$.

For example, the 0-level of the expression x is $\{x\}$, the 1-level of the expression x is $\emptyset$. The 0-level of the expression $x + y$ is $\{x+y\}$, the 1-level of the expression $x + y$ is $\{x, y\}$, and the 2-level of the expression $x + y$ is $\emptyset$.

Definition 4 *(Depth of Expression). The depth of an expression e is inductively defined as follows:*

(1) For a variable x and a constant c, their depths are both 1.
(2) If the maximum of the depths of $e_1, \cdots, e_n$ is m, then the depth of $f(e_1, \cdots, e_n)$ is $m + 1$.

For example, the depth of the expression x is 1, the depth of the expression $x+y$ is 2.

Definition 5 *(Constraint optimization Problem). Constraint optimization problems are the problems described as follows:*

$$\{exp, \Phi, \{x, y, \cdots\}\}$$

where an expression exp is to be minimized and maximized subject to Φ, exp is called the objective expression, and Φ is a boolean-valued formula and called the constraint, $\{x, y, \cdots\}$ is the list of variables occurring in the objective expression exp and the constraint Φ.

In the wolfram language, the constraint Φ can be an arbitrary boolean combination of equations $e = 0$, weak inequalities $e \geq 0$, strict inequalities $e > 0$, and $x \in Z$ statements where Z is a set such as integers or reals, and e is assumed an polynomial in this paper.

Definition 6 *(Abstraction Position). Let $\{exp, \Phi, \{x, y, \cdots\}\}$ be a constraint optimization problem and m be the depth of exp, $f(e_1, \cdots, e_n)$ be in the n-level of exp$(0 \leq n \leq m-1)$, if the maximum or the minimum of $f(e_1, \cdots, e_n)$ under the constraint Φ cannot be computed by **MaxValue** and **MinValue**, but both the maximum and the minimum of all $e_1, \cdots, e_n$ under the constraint Φ can be computed successfully by **MaxValue** and **MinValue**, then $f(e_1, \cdots, e_n)$ is called an abstraction position of exp.*

For example, in the constraint optimization problem $\{\mathbf{Cos}[x+y], x+y \leq 3, \{x, y\}\}$, $\mathbf{Cos}[x+y]$ is an abstraction position of the objective expression $\mathbf{Cos}[x+y]$, since the maximum and the minimum of $\mathbf{Cos}[x+y]$ under the constraint $x+y \leq 3$ cannot be computed, but the maximum and the minimum of $x+y$ under the constraint $x+y \leq 3$ can be computed successfully.

In the constraint optimization problem

$$\{r*\mathbf{Sqrt}[5\text{-}4\mathbf{Cos}[\mathbf{Pi}/3\text{-}v*(t\text{-}(rhoi\text{-}\mathbf{Sqrt}[3]r)/v)/r]],$$
$$(rhoi\text{-}\mathbf{Sqrt}[3]r)/v \leq t \&\& t \leq (rhoi\text{-}\mathbf{Sqrt}[3]r)/v + \mathbf{Pi}*r/(3*v) \&\& r > 0 \&\& v > 0, \{t\}\},$$

$\mathbf{Cos}[\mathbf{Pi}/3\text{-}v*(t\text{-}(rhoi\text{-}\mathbf{Sqrt}[3]r)/v)/r]$ is an abstraction position of the objective expression $r*\mathbf{Sqrt}[5\text{-}4\mathbf{Cos}[\mathbf{Pi}/3\text{-}v*(t\text{-}(rhoi\text{-}\mathbf{Sqrt}[3]r)/v)/r]]$, since the maximum and the minimum of $\mathbf{Cos}[\mathbf{Pi}/3\text{-}v*(t\text{-}(rhoi\text{-}\mathbf{Sqrt}[3]r)/v)/r]$ cannot be computed, but the maximum and the minimum of $\mathbf{Pi}/3\text{-}v*(t\text{-}(rhoi\text{-}\mathbf{Sqrt}[3]r)/v)/r$ can be computed successfully.

Definition 7 *(Expression-Relevant Constraint). Let $\{exp, \Phi, \{x, y, \cdots\}\}$ be a constraint optimization problem and $\Phi = \Phi_1 \&\& \cdots \&\& \Phi_n$, then $\Phi' = \Phi_{k_1} \&\& \cdots \&\& \Phi_{k_m}$ is called the expression-relevant constraint of Φ with respect to exp, where $\Phi_{k_i} \in \{\Phi_1, \cdots, \Phi_n\}(i = 1, \cdots, m)$ such that there exists at least one variable or one constant occurs both in exp and Φ_{k_i}.*

For example, for the constraint optimization problem $\{\mathbf{Cos}[z_1], (\text{rhoi-}\mathbf{Sqrt}[3]r)/v \leq t\ \&\&t \leq (\text{rhoi-}\mathbf{Sqrt}[3]r)/v + \mathbf{Pi}*r/(3*v)\&\&r > 0\&\&v > 0\&\&z_1 \geq 0\&\&z_1 \leq \mathbf{Pi}/3, \{t, z_1\}\}$, the expression-relevant constraint is $z_1 \geq 0\&\&z_1 \leq \mathbf{Pi}/3$ since only the variable z_1 occurs in the expression $\mathbf{Cos}[z_1]$.

Definition 8 *(Constraint optimization Problem Abstraction).* *Let* $\{exp, \Phi, \{x, y, \cdots\}\}$ *be a constraint optimization problem and* $f(e_1, \cdots, e_k)$ *be an abstraction position of exp,* m_i *and* n_i *be the maximum and the minimum of* $e_i (i = 1, \cdots, k)$ *under the constraint* Φ, $z_1, \cdots, z_k$ *be new variables, exp' be the expression obtained by replacing* $f(e_1, \cdots, e_k)$ *in exp with* $f(z_1, \cdots, z_k)$, *and* $\Phi' = \Phi''\&\& n_1 \leq z_1\&\&z_1 \leq m_1 \cdots n_k \leq z_k\&\&z_k \leq m_k$, *then* $\{exp', \Phi', \{z_1, \cdots, z_k, x, y, \cdots\}\}$ *is called the abstraction of the constraint optimization problem* $\{exp, \Phi, \{x, y, \cdots\}\}$, *where* Φ'' *is the expression-relevant constraint of* Φ *with respect to exp.*

For example, the abstraction of the constraint optimization problem $\{\mathbf{Cos}[x+y], x+y \leq 3, \{x, y\}\}$ is $\{\mathbf{Cos}[z_1], -\infty \leq z_1\&\&z_1 \leq 3, \{x, y, z_1\}\}$, and the abstraction of the constraint optimization problem

$$\{r*\mathbf{Sqrt}[5-4\mathbf{Cos}[\mathbf{Pi}/3-v*(t-(\text{rhoi-}\mathbf{Sqrt}[3]r)/v)/r]],$$
$$(\text{rhoi-}\mathbf{Sqrt}[3]r)/v \leq t\&\&t \leq (\text{rhoi-}\mathbf{Sqrt}[3]r)/v + \mathbf{Pi}*r/(3*v)\ \&\&r > 0\&\&v > 0, \{t\}\}$$

is

$$\{r*\mathbf{Sqrt}[5-4\mathbf{Cos}[z_1]], (\text{rhoi-}\mathbf{Sqrt}[3]r)/v \leq t\&\&t \leq (\text{rhoi-}$$
$$\mathbf{Sqrt}[3]r)/v + \mathbf{Pi}*r/(3*v)\ \&\&z_1 \geq 0\&\&z_1 \leq \mathbf{Pi}/3\&\&r > 0, \{t, z_1\}\}$$

4 Solving Constraint Optimization Problems Based on Mathematica and Abstraction

Intuitively, to compute the upper bounds and the lower bounds of constraint optimization problems, the upper bounds and the lower bounds of each sub-expressions in the objective expressions need to be computed firstly, for simplicity, **MaxValue** and **MinValue** will be used to compute them automatically. If there exist abstraction positions, each abstraction position will be abstracted by replacing sub-expressions with new variables, constraining these new variables with the minimum and the maximum of corresponding sub-expressions, computing the expression-relevant constraints, and generating a new abstracted constraint optimization problem. After tackling all abstraction positions, the maximum and the minimum of the abstracted constraint optimization problem will be computed and simplified.

4.1 The Algorithms for Solving Constraint Optimization Problems

The algorithm for computing the expression-relevant constraint is presented in Fig. 1, and the algorithm for solving constraint optimization problems based on Mathematica and abstraction is presented in Fig. 2.

$newPhi[\Phi_-, subexp_-] := \mathbf{Module}[\{phi1, subexp1\},$
Where
    $subexp:$ a sub-expression
    $\Phi:$ a constraint
    $relPhi:$ the expression relevant constraint of Φ with respect to $subexp$
begin
    $phi1 = \Phi;$
    $subexp1 = subexp;$
    $phiList = \mathbf{StringSplit}[\mathbf{ToString}[phi1], "\&\&"];$
    $len = \mathbf{Length}[phiList];$
    $varList = \{\};$
    $\mathbf{For}[ii = 0, ii \leq \mathbf{Depth}[subexp1], ii + +,$
        $subexpList = \mathbf{Level}[subexp1, \{ii\}]$
        $len1 = \mathbf{Length}[subexpList];$
        $\mathbf{For}[jj = 1, jj \leq len1, jj + +,$
            $elem = \mathbf{Extract}[subexpList, \{jj\}];$
            $\mathbf{If}[\mathbf{Length}[elem] == 0\&\&\mathbf{NumberQ}[elem] == \mathbf{False},$
                $varList=\mathbf{Append}[varList,elem];,];];];$
    $rrelPhi = \{\};$
    $\mathbf{For}[kk = 1, kk \leq \mathbf{Length}[varList], kk + +,$
        $var = \mathbf{Extract}[varList, \{kk\}];$
        $\mathbf{For}[ll = 1, ll \leq \mathbf{Length}[phiList], ll + +,$
            $phi = \mathbf{Extract}[varList, \{ll\}]$
            $\mathbf{If}[\mathbf{Length}[\mathbf{Position}[\mathbf{ToExpression}[phi], \mathbf{ToExpression}[var]]] > 0,$
                $rrelPhi = Append[rrelPhi, phi];,];,];];];$
    $rrelPhi = \mathbf{DeleteDuplicates}[rrelPhi];$
    $relPhi = \mathbf{ToExpression}[\mathbf{Extract}[rrelPhi, \{1\}]];$
    $\mathbf{For}[ss = 2, ss \leq \mathbf{Length}[rrelPhi], ss + +,$
        $relPhi = relPhi\&\&\mathbf{ToExpression}[\mathbf{Extract}[rrelPhi, \{ss\}];$
    $\mathbf{Return}[relPhi];$
end

Fig. 1. Algorithm for computing the expression-relevant constraint

In Figs. 1 and 2, the Mathematica function **Depth**$[exp]$ returns the depth of exp, **Level**$[exp, \{i\}]$ returns the list of sub-expressions of exp in the level i, **Length**$[exp]$ returns the length of exp, **Extract**$[expr, \{i\}]$ returns the part of expr at the position specified by the list $\{i\}$, **Part**$[expr, i]$ returns the i-part of expr, **FullSimplify**$[expr, assum]$ tries a wide range of transformations on $expr$ by using assumption $assum$ and returns the simplest form it finds, and **Position**$[expr, pattern]$ gives a list of the positions at which objects matching $pattern$ appear in $expr$.

In Fig. 1, to compute the expression-relevant constraint $relPhi$ of Φ with respect to $subexp$, the algorithm firstly divides the constraint Φ into sub-constraints list $phiList$ by using Mathematica function **StringSplit** with $\&\&$ as delimiter, and computes the list $varList$ of variables and constants occur in the expression $subexp$. If a sub-expression sub of $subexp$ satisfying the condition **Length**[*sub*] == 0 and **NumberQ**[*sub*]! = **True**, then *sub* is a variable or a constant and *sub* is appended into the list *varList*, where **Length**[*sub*] == 0 means *sub* is a variable or a constant, **NumberQ**[*sub*]! = **True** means *sub* is not a number. For each variable or constant *var* and for each sub-constraint *phi*, **Position**[**ToExpression**[phi], **ToExpression** [var]] gives a list of the positions at which var appear in phi, **Length** [**Position**[**ToExpression**[phi], **ToExpression** [var]]] >0 means the position list is not empty, var occurs in the sub-constraint phi, then phi will be a sub-constraint of relPhi, and the duplicates in relPhi are deleted by using **DeleteDuplicates**.

In Fig. 2, to compute the upper bound and the lower bound of the constraint optimization problem $\{exp, \Phi, \{\eta\}\}$, each sub-expression *subexp* of *exp* from $(d-1)$-depth down to 0-depth will be checked whether they are abstraction positions or not, where $d =$ **Depth**[*exp*] is the depth of the objective expression *exp*, **Level**[*exp*, $\{i\}$] returns a list *subexpList* of all sub-expressions on the level i, **Length**[*subexpList*] returns the length of *subexpList*, **Extract**[*subexpList*, $\{j\}$] returns the j-th sub-expression *subexp* in *subexpList*, and for the sub-expression *subexp* in *subexpList*, **MaxValue**[$\{subexp, phi\}, \{\eta\}$] will compute the maximum max of *subexp* under the constraint *phi*, **MinValue**[$\{subexp, phi\}, \{\eta\}$] will compute the minimum min of *subexp* under the constraint *phi*, **FullForm**[*max*] and **FullForm**[*min*] give the full form of the *max* and *min* respectively, if the string of the full form of *min* or *max* is with the **MinValue** or **MaxValue** as the first word, then *subexp* is an abstraction position since the optimization problem cannot be solved by Mathematica.

If *subexp* is an abstraction position, all its sub-expressions will be replaced with new variables and these new variables will be constrained with the maximum and the minimum of the corresponding sub-expression. **Part**[*subexp*, k] gives the k-th sub-expression of *subexp*, **AtomQ**[*subsubexp*] == **False** denotes that the sub-expression *subsubexp* is neither a variable nor a constant, then *subsubexp* will be replaced with new variable Z_{new} and Z_{new} will be constrained with the maximum and the minimum of *subsubexp*. **Position**[*exp*, *subsubexp*] gives the position at which *subsubexp* appears in *exp*, and **ReplacePart**[*exp*, *pos* $- > Z_{new}$] yields an expression in which the *pos* part of *exp* is replaced by the new variable Z_{new}. And the objective expression *exp* is refreshed by replacing the sub-expression *subsubexp* with the new variable Z_{new}, the constraint Φ is refreshed by adding new constraints $Z_{new} \geq min0$ and $Z_{new} \leq max0$, the variable list η is refreshed by appending the new variable Z_{new}. With the refreshed objective expression, constraint and variable list, the abstracted constraint optimization problem $\{exp, \Phi, \{\eta\}\}$ is generated.

After tackling all abstraction positions, the maximum and the minimum of the final abstracted constraint optimization problem will be computed and simplified with **FullSimplify**. Finally, the list $\{upBound, lowBound\}$ will be returned as the output of the algorithm.

input
  exp : an objective expression
  Φ : constraints
  η : variables list
output
  upBound : the upper bound
  lowBound : the lower bound
begin
  $d = \mathbf{Depth}[exp]$;
  $\mathbf{For}[i = d - 1, i \geq 0, i - -,$
    $subexpList = \mathbf{Level}[exp, \{i\}]$
    $lengthList = \mathbf{Length}[subexpList]$
    $\mathbf{For}[j = 1, j \leq lengthList, j + +,$
      $subexp = \mathbf{Extract}[subexpList, \{j\}]$;
      $phi = newPhi[\Phi, subexp]$;
      $min = \mathbf{MinValue}[\{subexp, phi\}, \{\eta\}]$;
      $max = \mathbf{MaxValue}[\{subexp, phi\}, \{\eta\}]$;
      $\mathbf{If}[\mathbf{StringMatchQ}[\mathbf{ToString}[\mathbf{FullForm}[min]], "\mathrm{MinValue}[" \sim\sim \_\_\!]] == \mathbf{True}\vee$
        $\mathbf{StringMatchQ}[\mathbf{ToString}[\mathbf{FullForm}[max]], "\mathrm{MaxValue}[" \sim\sim \_\_\!]] == \mathbf{True},$
      $length = \mathbf{Length}[subexp]$;
      $\mathbf{For}[k = 1, k \leq lengthexp, k + +,$
        $subsubexp = \mathbf{Part}[subexp, k]$;
        $\mathbf{If}[\mathbf{AtomQ}[subsubexp] == \mathbf{False},$
          $phi = newPhi[\Phi, subsubexp]$;
          $min0 = \mathbf{MinValue}[\{subsubexp, phi\}, \{\eta\}]$;
          $min0 = \mathbf{FullSimplify}[min0, \Phi]$;
          $max0 = \mathbf{MaxValue}[\{subsubexp, phi\}, \{\eta\}]$;
          $max0 = \mathbf{FullSimplify}[max0, \Phi]$;
          $pos = \mathbf{Position}[exp, subsubexp]$;
          $exp = \mathbf{ReplacePart}[exp, pos- > Z_{new}]$;
          $\Phi = \Phi \wedge Z_{new} \leq max0 \wedge Z_{new} \geq min0$;
          $\eta = \mathbf{Append}[\eta, Z_{new}]$;
          ,];];,];];];
  $phi = newPhi[\Phi, exp]$;
  $upBound = \mathbf{MaxValue}[\{exp, phi\}, \{\eta\}]$;
  $upBound = \mathbf{FullSimplify}[upBound, \Phi]$;
  $lowBound = \mathbf{MinValue}[\{exp, phi\}, \{\eta\}]$;
  $lowBound = \mathbf{FullSimplify}[lowBound, \Phi]$;
Return $[\{upBound, lowBound\}]$;
end

Fig. 2. Algorithm for computing the upper bounds and the lower bounds of constrained optimization problems

4.2   The Correctness Theorem

The following theorem proves that the computed upper bound is an upper bound of the maximum of the original constraint optimization problem, and the computed lower bound is a lower bound of the minimum of the original constrained optimization problem.

Theorem 1. Let $\{exp', \Phi', \{z_1, \cdots, z_n, \cdots, x, y, \cdots\}\}$ be the abstraction of $\{exp, \Phi, \{x, y, \cdots\}\}$, let the computed upper bound and the lower bound of $\{exp', \Phi', \{z_1, \cdots, z_n, \cdots, x, y, \cdots\}\}$ be α' and β', let the maximum and the minimum of $\{exp, \Phi, \{x, y, \cdots\}\}$ be α and β, then $\beta' \leq \beta$ and $\alpha \leq \alpha'$.

Proof. The proof is by induction on n, which is the number of abstraction positions in $\{exp, \Phi, \{x, y, \cdots\}\}$.

When $n = 0$, there exists no abstraction position, $\{exp', \Phi', \{z_1, \cdots, z_n, x, y, \cdots\}\}$ is $\{exp, \Phi, \{x, y, \cdots\}\}$, so $\beta' \leq \beta$ and $\alpha \leq \alpha'$ hold.

When $n = k (k \geq 0)$, we assume that $\beta' \leq \beta$ and $\alpha \leq \alpha'$ hold.

When $n = k + 1 (k \geq 0)$, we assume that the abstracted constraint optimization problem will be $\{exp'', \Phi'', \{z_{k1}^k, \cdots, z_{kn}^k, \cdots, x, y \cdots\}\}$ after tackling k abstraction positions, and the conclusion $\beta'' \leq \beta$ and $\alpha \leq \alpha''$ holds, where α'' and β'' are the computed upper bound and the lower bound of the abstracted constraint optimization problem $\{exp'', \Phi'', \{z_{k1}^k, \cdots, z_{kn}^k, \cdots, x, y \cdots\}\}$ respectively.

Let $f(e_1, \cdots, e_s)$ be the abstraction position in exp'', m_i and n_i be the maximum and the minimum of $e_i (i = 1, \cdots, s)$ under the constraint Φ'', $z_1, \cdots, z_s$ be new variables, exp' be the expression obtained by replacing $f(e_1, \cdots, e_s)$ in exp'' with $f(z_1, \cdots, z_s)$, and $\Phi' = \Phi''' \&\& n_1 \leq z_1 \&\& z_1 \leq m_1 \&\& \cdots \&\& n_s \leq z_s \&\& z_s \leq m_s$, where Φ''' is the expression-relevant constraint of Φ'' with respect to exp', and the variable list will be $\{z_1, \cdots, z_s, z_{k1}^k, \cdots, z_{kn}^k, \cdots, x, y \cdots\}$.

The abstracted constraint optimization problem $\{exp'', \Phi'', \{z_{k1}^k, \cdots, z_{kn}^k, \cdots, x, y \cdots\}\}$ is equivalent to the following constraint optimization problem

$$\{exp', \Phi'' \&\& z_1 = e_1 \&\& \cdots \&\& z_s = e_s, \{z_1, \cdots, z_s, z_{k1}^k, \cdots, z_{kn}^k, \cdots, x, y \cdots\}\},$$

since the expression e_i is replaced by the new variable z_i and the constraint $z_i = e_i$ is appended into Φ''.

It is obvious that the constraint $\Phi'' \&\& z_1 = e_1 \&\& \cdots \&\& z_s = e_s$ implies $\Phi'' \&\& z_1 = e_1 \&\& \cdots \&\& z_s = e_s \&\& n_1 \leq z_1 \&\& z_1 \leq m_1 \&\& \cdots \&\& n_s \leq z_s \&\& z_s \leq m_s$, and $\Phi'' \&\& z_1 = e_1 \&\& \cdots \&\& z_s = e_s \&\& n_1 \leq z_1 \&\& z_1 \leq m_1 \&\& \cdots \&\& n_s \leq z_s \&\& z_s \leq m_s$ implies $\Phi'' \&\& n_1 \leq z_1 \&\& z_1 \leq m_1 \&\& \cdots \&\& n_s \leq z_s \&\& z_s \leq m_s$ since the constraint $z_1 = e_1 \&\& \cdots \&\& z_s = e_s$ are taken away, $\Phi'' \&\& n_1 \leq z_1 \&\& z_1 \leq m_1 \&\& \cdots \&\& n_s \leq z_s \&\& z_s \leq m_s$ also implies $\Phi''' \&\& n_1 \leq z_1 \&\& z_1 \leq m_1 \&\& \cdots \&\& n_s \leq z_s \&\& z_s \leq m_s$, by the transitive property of the implies, the constraint $\Phi'' \&\& z_1 = e_1 \&\& \cdots \&\& z_s = e_s$ implies $\Phi''' \&\& n_1 \leq z_1 \&\& z_1 \leq m_1 \&\& \cdots \&\& n_s \leq z_s \&\& z_s \leq m_s$, which means the set satisfying the constraint $\Phi'' \&\& z_1 = e_1 \&\& \cdots \&\& z_s = e_s$ is a subset of the set satisfying the constraint $\Phi''' \&\& n_1 \leq z_1 \&\& z_1 \leq m_1 \&\& \cdots \&\& n_s \leq z_s \&\& z_s \leq m_s$.

Let the computed upper bound and the lower bound of $\{\exp', \Phi', \{z_1, \cdots, z_n, \cdots, x, y, \cdots\}\}$ be α' and β', since the set satisfying the constraint $\Phi''\&\&z_1 = e_1\&\&\cdots\&\&z_s = e_s$ is a subset of the set satisfying the constraint $\Phi'''\&\&n_1 \leq z_1\&\&z_1 \leq m_1\&\&\cdots\&\&n_s \leq z_s\&\&z_s \leq m_s$, then $\beta' \leq \beta''$ and $\alpha'' \leq \alpha'$. Since $\beta'' \leq \beta$ and $\alpha \leq \alpha''$, we have the conclusion $\beta' \leq \beta$ and $\alpha \leq \alpha'$ holds.   □

By Theorem 1, the computed upper bound and the lower bound of the abstracted constraint optimization problem are conservative approximations of the maximum and the minimum of the original constraint optimization problem.

5   Experimental Results

The experiment is implemented on a laptop having Intel Core i5 2.7 GHz CPU and 8G memory. The experimental results are listed in Table 1. In Table 1, since all objective expressions are not polynomial, all the tested constraint optimization problems cannot be solved directly by **MaxValue** and **MinValue**, Mathematica outputs these constraint optimization problems themselves as answers. Although these objective expressions in Table 1 are simple, they may act as sub-expressions to construct many more complex objective expressions, thus there exist many constraint optimization problems cannot be solved directly by **MaxValue** and **MinValue**.

Using the algorithms presented in this paper, upper bounds and lower bounds of these tested constraint optimization problems are all computed automatically. Furthermore, it is easy to check that all the computed upper bounds and lower bounds are their maximums and minimums of the tested constraint optimization problems.

In the sixth constraint optimization problem, though x+y is monotonic-increasing and **Cos**[x+y] is monotonic-decreasing under the constraint x+y≥2 &&x+y≤3, the algorithms compute the optimization values 2**Cos**[2] and 3**Cos**[3] automatically. In the fifteenth and the sixteenth constraint optimization problems, the algorithms compute the optimization values **Sqrt**[3]r and r automatically by abstracting abstraction positions two times, it is demonstrated that complex constraint optimization problems can be solved automatically by abstracting abstraction positions more times.

Combining the symbolic analysis of Mathematica and abstraction, the experimental results demonstrate that the practicality of the algorithms presented in this paper.

Table 1. Experimental results.

Objective expressions	Constraints	Variables	Upper bound	Lower bound	Time
Sin[x+y]	2≤x+y&&x+y≤8	x,y	1	−1	0.07 s
Cos[x+y]	2≤x+y&&x+y≤8	x,y	1	−1	0.06 s
Tan[x+y]	2≤x+y&&x+y≤3	x,y	**Tan**[3]	**Tan**[2]	0.13 s
Cot[x+y]	2≤x+y&&x+y≤3	x,y	**Cot**[2]	**Cot**[3]	0.12 s
x+2**Sin**[y]	x^2≤1&&y^2≤1	x,y	1+2**Sin**[1]	-1-2**Sin**[1]	0.14 s
(x+y)**Cos**[x+y]	x+y ≥ 2&&x+y≤3	x,y	2**Cos**[2]	3**Cos**[3]	0.06 s
Tan[Power[x,5]+y]	0 ≤ **Power**[x,5] + y&& **Power**[x,5] + y ≤ 1	x,y	**Tan**[1]	0	0.16 s
Tan[Tan[x]]	0 ≤ x&&x ≤ Pi/4	x	**Tan**[1]	0	2.1 s
Cot[Cot[x]]	Pi/4 ≤ x&&x ≤ Pi/2	x	∞	**Cot**[1]	2.3 s
Sin[Sqrt[x+y]]	x+y ≤ 3&&x+y ≤ 4	x,y	**Sin[Sqrt**[3]]	**Sin**[2]	0.08 s
Sqrt[Exp[x+y]]	0 ≤ x+y&&x+y ≤ Pi/3	x,y	**Sqrt[Exp**[Pi/3]]	1	0.9 s
Sqrt[Log[x+y]]	1 ≤ x+y&&x+y ≤ 9	x,y	**Sqrt[Log**[9]]	0	0.04 s
Log[Log[x+y]]	10 ≤ x+y&&x+y ≤ 12	x,y	**Log[Log**[12]]	**Log[Log**[10]]	0.03 s
Log[Power[10,x+y]]	10 ≤ x+y&&x+y ≤ 12	x,y	12	10	0.04 s
r***Sqrt**[5-4**Cos[Pi**/3-v*(t-(rhoi-**Sqrt**[3]r)/v)/r]]	(rhoi-**Sqrt**[3]r)/v≤t&& t≤(rhoi-**Sqrt**[3]r)/v+ Pi*r/(3*v)&& r>0&&v>0	t	**Sqrt**[3]r	r	0.39 s
r***Sqrt**[5-4**Cos**[v*(t-(rhoi-**Sqrt**[3]r)/v-Pi*r/v)/r]]	(rhoi-**Sqrt**[3]r)/v+ Pi*r/(3*v)≤t&& t≤(rhoi-**Sqrt**[3]r)/v+ 4Pi*r/(3*v)&& r>0&&v>0	t	**Sqrt**[3]r	r	0.38 s

6   Related Work

In [2,3], in the Event-B model for the aircraft collision avoidance system example, in order to prove automatically the invariant $\forall t.t \in dom(rhoc) \Rightarrow 2 * rhoc(t) * sin(phi/2) \geq p$ is preserved, besides the axiom $2rhoi * sin(phi/2) \geq \sqrt{3}p$, several extra axioms are given in the Axioms component of the context f_c1 [5] such as $\forall t.t \in 0..t1 \Rightarrow 2 * (rhoi - v * t) * sin(phi\_d\_2) \geq p$, $\forall t.t \in t1..t1 + t2 \Rightarrow 2 * r * sqrt(5 - 4 * cos(pi/3 - v * (t - t1)/r)) * sin(phi\_d\_2) \geq p$ and $\forall t.t \in t1 + t2 + t3..t1 + t2 + t3 + t2 \Rightarrow 2 * r * sqrt(5 - 4 * cos(v * (t - (t1 + t2 + t3))/r)) * sin(phi\_d\_2) \geq p$. By using the alternative $min \geq p$(where min is the minimum or a lower bound of the minimum of $2 * rhoc(t) * sin(phi/2)$ under the constraint $t \in dom(rhoc)$) and the algorithms presented in this paper, all minimums of the constraint optimization problems are computed automatically, and all proof obligations on preserving the invariant $min \geq p$ are proved automatically under the assumption $2rhoi * sin(phi/2) \geq \sqrt{3}p$ and the invariants $\sqrt{3}r \leq rhoi$ and $2r * sin(phi/2) \geq p$.

In [6], a novel framework is presented for the symbolic bounds analysis of pointers, array indices, and accessed memory regions. The framework formulates each analysis problem as a system of inequality constraints between symbolic bound polynomials. It then reduces the constraint system to a linear program. The solution to the linear program provides symbolic lower and upper bounds for the values of pointer and array index variables and for the regions of memory that each statement and procedure accesses.

In [7], a precise numerical abstract domain for use in timing analysis is presented. The numerical abstract domain is parameterized by a linear abstract domain and is constructed by means of two domain lifting operations. One domain lifting operation is based on the principle of expression abstraction (which involves defining a set of expressions and specifying their semantics using a collection of directed inference rules) and has a more general applicability. It lifts any given abstract domain to include reasoning about a given set of expressions whose semantics is abstracted using a set of axioms. The other domain lifting operation incorporates disjunctive reasoning into a given linear relational abstract domain via introduction of max expressions.

RealPaver [8] is an interval software for modeling and solving nonlinear systems. Reliable approximations of continuous or discrete solution sets are computed, using Cartesian product of intervals. Systems are given by sets of equations or inequality constraints over integer and real variables.

The open-source tool dReal [9] is an SMT solver for nonlinear formulas over the reals. The tool can handle various nonlinear real functions such as polynomials, trigonometric functions, exponential functions, etc. dReal implements the framework of δ-complete decision procedures: It returns either unsat or δ-sat on input formulas, where δ is a numerical error bound specified by the user. dReal also produces certificates of correctness for both δ-sat(a solution) and unsat answers(a proof of unsatisfiability).

In [10], an efficient SMT-based optimization algorithm SYMBA is presented for objective functions in the theory of linear real arithmetic (LRA). Given a formula ϕ and an objective function t, SYMBA finds a satisfying assignment of ϕ that maximizes the value of t. SYMBA utilizes efficient SMT solvers as black boxes. As a result, it is easy to implement and it directly benefits from future advances in SMT solvers. Moreover, SYMBA can optimize a set of objective functions, reusing information between them to speed up the analysis. SYMBA is implemented and evaluated on a large number of optimization benchmarks drawn from program analysis tasks. The results indicate the power and efficiency of SYMBA in comparison with competing approaches, and highlight the importance of its multi-objective-function feature.

Based on random testing, constraint solving and verification, a practical approach is presented in [11] for generating equality loop invariants. More importantly, a practical verification approach of loop invariant based on the finite difference technique is presented also. This approach is efficient since the constraint system is linear equational system. The effectiveness of the approach is demonstrated on examples. In [12], based on finite difference techniques, a formal characterization for equality loop invariants is presented. Integrating the formal characterization with the automatic verification approach in [11], the algorithm for automatic proving or disproving equality loop invariants is presented. The effectiveness of the algorithm is demonstrated with the experimental results.

Both the approach in [11] and the algorithm in [12] are all implemented with Mathematica.

Compared with the above work, by combining the symbolic analysis of Mathematica and abstraction, this paper provides a practical approach for computing the upper bounds and the lower bounds of constraint optimization problems with the objective expressions may be polynomials or non-polynomials such as trigonometric functions.

7   Conclusions and Future Works

In this paper, based on Mathematica functions and abstraction, a practical approach is presented for computing the upper bounds and the lower bounds of constraint optimization problems. And the experimental results demonstrate the practicality of this approach. Many constraint optimization problems cannot be solved automatically by Mathematica functions, but their optimization values can be computed automatically by using the algorithms presented in this paper.

In the future, the algorithms in this paper will be utilized to proving the generated proof obligations automatically of Event-B models.

References

1. Manolios, P., Papavasileiou, V.: ILP modulo theories. In: Sharygina, N., Veith, H. (eds.) CAV 2013. LNCS, vol. 8044, pp. 662–677. Springer, Heidelberg (2013). https://doi.org/10.1007/978-3-642-39799-8_44

2. Abrial, J.-R., Su, W., Zhu, H.: Formalizing hybrid systems with Event-B. In: Derrick, J. (ed.) ABZ 2012. LNCS, vol. 7316, pp. 178–193. Springer, Heidelberg (2012). https://doi.org/10.1007/978-3-642-30885-7_13

3. Su, W., Abrial, J.-R., Zhu, H.: Formalizing hybrid systems with Event-B and the Rodin platform. Sci. Comput. Program **94**, 164–202 (2014)

4. Abrial, J.-R: Modeling in Event-B: System and Software Engineering, 1st edn. Cambridge University Press, United Kingdom (2010)

5. http://www.lab205.org/home/download/hybrid/Examples.pdf

6. Rugina, R., Rinard, M.: Symbolic bounds analysis of pointers, array indices, and accessed memory regions. In: Proceedings of the 2000 ACM SIGPLAN Conference on Programming Language Design and Implementations, pp. 182–195. ACM, NewYork (2000)

7. Gulavani, B.S., Gulwani, S.: A numerical abstract domain based on *Expression Abstraction* and *Max Operator* with application in timing analysis. In: Gupta, A., Malik, S. (eds.) CAV 2008. LNCS, vol. 5123, pp. 370–384. Springer, Heidelberg (2008). https://doi.org/10.1007/978-3-540-70545-1_35

8. Granvilliers, L., Benhamou, F.: Algorithm 852: RealPaver: an interval solver using constraint satisfaction techniques. ACM Trans. Math. Softw. **32**(1), 138–156 (2006)

9. Gao, S., Kong, S., Clarke, E.M.: dReal: an SMT solver for nonlinear theories over the reals. In: Bonacina, M.P. (ed.) CADE 2013. LNCS (LNAI), vol. 7898, pp. 208–214. Springer, Heidelberg (2013). https://doi.org/10.1007/978-3-642-38574-2_14

10. Li, Y., Albarghouthi, A., Kincaid, Z., Gurfinkel, A., Chechik, M.: Symbolic optimization with SMT solvers. In: The 41st Annual ACM SIGPLAN-SIGACT Symposium on Principles of Programming Languages, pp. 607–618. ACM, NewYork (2014)
11. Li, M.: A practical loop invariant generation approach based on random testing, constraint solving and verification. In: Aoki, T., Taguchi, K. (eds.) ICFEM 2012. LNCS, vol. 7635, pp. 447–461. Springer, Heidelberg (2012). https://doi.org/10.1007/978-3-642-34281-3_31
12. Li, M.: Automatic proving or disproving equality loop invariants based on finite difference techniques. Inf. Process. Lett. 115(4), 468–474 (2015)

A Forward Chaining Heuristic Search with Spatio-Temporal Control Knowledge

Xu Lu[1], Jin Cui[2(✉)], Yansong Dong[1], Wensheng Wang[1], Runzhe Ma[1], Yifeng Li[3], and Qing Feng[1]

[1] ICTT and ISN Lab, Xidian University,
Xi'an 710071, People's Republic of China
[2] Xi'an Shiyou University, Xi'an 710065, People's Republic of China
cuijin_xd@126.com
[3] Xi'an University of Posts and Communications,
Xi'an 710121, People's Republic of China

Abstract. Planning systems use a variety of heuristic search or control knowledge in order to enhance the performance. Control knowledge is often described in a specific formalism, e.g. temporal logic, automata, or HTN (Hierarchical Task Network) etc. Heuristic search exploits heuristic functions to evaluate potential feasible moves. Control knowledge constraints the search space by pruning the states which violate the knowledge. In this paper, we propose a general heuristic algorithm that combines control knowledge specified by a spatio-temporal logic named PPTL^{SL}. Both heuristic search and control knowledge are handled in a forward chaining manner. Our approach involves the evaluation of PPTL^{SL} formulas using a variant of the traditional progression technique during heuristic search. Consequently, we are enabled to take advantage of the two methods together to further reduce the search space.

Keywords: Planning · Control knowledge · Heuristic search · Forward chaining

1 Introduction

The planning problem in Artificial Intelligence is about the decision making performed by intelligent creatures like robots, humans, or computer programs when trying to achieve some goal. In particular, the most basic form of classical planning tries to find a sequence of actions leading from the initial state to a state which includes all goal constraints. Since the search space usually grows exponentially when the number of actions increases [8], search algorithms should be enhanced in order to guide the search appropriately. One of the best known method is using heuristic functions which estimate the distance from a given

This research is supported by the National Natural Science Foundation of China Grant Nos. 61806158, China Postdoctoral Science Foundation Nos. 2019T120881 and 2018M643585.

© Springer Nature Switzerland AG 2020
H. Miao et al. (Eds.): SOFL+MSVL 2019 Workshop, LNCS 12028, pp. 141–154, 2020.
https://doi.org/10.1007/978-3-030-41418-4_11

state to the nearest (or optimum) goal state. Another one is adopting control knowledge which describes additional information of a specific planning problem to constrain the search space.

On one hand, although a number of heuristic search algorithms are proposed for the last two decades, these algorithms are limited in that they are only suitable for certain kinds of planning problems. On the other hand, it is proved practically that even with rather basic search strategy and proper control knowledge, planners can achieve surprising effectiveness. We believe that control knowledge can be benefit in improving the performance of heuristic search. In this paper we will show how to combine heuristic search and control knowledge in the same framework.

A promising way of specifying control knowledge is to use temporal logic. For example, the "next" operator from LTL (Linear Temporal Logic) allows one to specify what can and cannot be held at the next time step, while the "always" operator can assert the invariants holding in any state reachable from the initial state. Bacchus et al. develop a planner TLPlan [1], where domain-dependent control knowledge encoded in bounded first-order LTL to prune the search space via standard forward-chaining search. Kvarnström introduces a complex logic, called TAL (Temporal Action Logic), which encodes actions into logical formulas, and also employs this kind of domain-dependent control knowledge in the forward-chaining planner named TALplanner [11]. TLPlan can only generate sequential plans, while TALplanner is capable of producing parallel plans (actions executed concurrently). Baier and McIlraith convert LTL formulas into automata with infinite loops which can be added to a planning task, where additional variable for each state of the automata is introduced in the search space [2]. In their work, LTL is used for expressing the temporally extended goals, not for pruning the search space. Wang et al. present a method to describe landmarks and their associated orderings in LTL [20]. They translate LTL formulas into automata and augment the famous FF heuristic [10] by including the automata variables in the relaxed planning graph, and show such "landmarks" are effective in computing high-quality plans quickly. HTN (Hierarchical Task Network) [6] based planning planners, e.g., SHOP2 [14], in which the dependency among actions is given in advance by hierarchically structured networks. The network represents a hierarchy of tasks each of which can be executed. The task is either primitive, or can be decomposed into refined subtasks. The planning process starts by decomposing the initial task network and continues until all compound tasks are decomposed into primitive ones.

We find the above mentioned work are encountered a challenge in common: it is difficult to solve the planning problem with spatial and temporal constraints, e.g., the CityCar domain in IPC 2014[1], or the DataNetwork domain in IPC 2018[2]. Since the control knowledge formalism is mainly temporal logic or task networks which can only express temporal constraints. Additionally, the current dominant heuristic approaches also solve such problems inefficiently due to

---

[1] https://helios.hud.ac.uk/scommv/IPC-14/domains_sequential.html.

[2] https://ipc2018-classical.bitbucket.io/#domains.

the lack of useful guiding information. In this paper, in order to enhance the performance of planning systems, we propose an approach based on a forward-chaining heuristic search framework, in which we combine a spatio-temporal logic PPTL^{SL} for the sake of describing the control knowledge. PPTL^{SL} uses separation logic [15] as the spatial dimension and PPTL (Propositional Projection Temporal Logic) [4,5,23] as the temporal dimension. Separation logic is a spatial logic for reasoning about heap-manipulating programs. PPTL, an expressive temporal logic [17,18], has already been successfully applied to planning [21], real-time system verification [3], efficient temporal properties verification [22] etc. We illustrate how PPTL^{SL} formulas can be integrated into the heuristic search in the sequel. In words, this can be done by a progression technique specialized on PPTL^{SL} formulas.

This paper is organized in the following way: Sect. 2 gives some background about the relevant formalism used in this paper. We explain the novel algorithm combing heuristic search and PPTL^{SL} in Sect. 3. In Sect. 4, experiments and evaluations are illustrated and analyzed. Finally, we give conclusions and list future work in Sect. 5.

2 Preliminaries

In this section we give the definitions of planning and PPTL^{SL} formalisms used in this paper.

2.1 Planning Representation

We consider classical planning tasks or planning problems as the following standard definition:

Definition 1 (Planning Task). *A planning task is a tuple* $\mathcal{P} = (\Pi, A, I, G)$, *where*

- Π *is a finite set of propositional variables.*
- A *is a finite set of actions, and for each action* $a \in A$, $a = (pre(a), add(a), del(a), cost(a))$, *where* $pre(a) \subseteq \Pi$, $add(a) \subseteq \Pi$, $del(a) \subseteq \Pi$ *and* $cost(a) \in \mathbb{N}_0$.
- $I \subseteq \Pi$ *is the initial state.*
- $G \subseteq \Pi$ *is the set of goal constraints.*

A state s is defined as a set of propositional variables, i.e., the set of facts, the variables which do not appear in s are assumed to be false (closed world assumption). An action a is applicable to a state s if $pre(a) \subseteq s$. When a is applied to s, the successor state is defined as: $succ_a(s) = (s \backslash del(a)) \cup add(a)$. A sequence of actions $\rho = \langle a_0, a_1, \ldots, a_n \rangle$ is applicable to s_0 if a_0 is applicable to s_0, and a_i is applicable to $succ_{a_{i-1}}(s_{i-1})$, $1 \leq i \leq n$. We abbreviate the notation $succ_{a_n}(\ldots(succ_{a_0}(s))\ldots)$ as $succ_{\langle a_0,\ldots,a_n \rangle}(s)$. When applying a sequence of actions ρ to a state s, a sequence of states from s to $succ_\rho(s)$ is obtained. If $s = I$ and $G \subseteq succ_\rho(s)$, ρ is called a plan. The cost of a plan is obtained as the sum of the cost of each action in the plan, i.e., $\overset{n}{\underset{i=0}{\Sigma}} cost(a_i)$.

2.2   Spatio-Temporal Logic PPTL^{SL}

Since there are many planning tasks involving spatial and temporal constraints, we choose to use the spatio-temporal logic PPTL^{SL} as the control knowledge. Let Var and Loc be the set of spatial variables and spatial locations respectively. nil is employed to represent the inactive location. The syntax of PPTL^{SL} is defined by the following grammar:

$$e ::= nil \mid l \mid x$$
$$\phi ::= p \mid GOAL(p) \mid e_1 = e_2 \mid e_0 \mapsto \{e_1, \ldots, e_n\} \mid \neg\phi \mid \phi_1 \vee \phi_2 \mid \phi_1 \# \phi_2 \mid \exists x : \phi$$
$$P ::= \phi \mid \neg P \mid P_1 \vee P_2 \mid \bigcirc P \mid (P_1, \ldots, P_m)\, prj\, P_0 \mid P^*$$

where $p \in \Pi$ is a propositional variable, $x \in Var$ a spatial variable, and $l \in Loc$ a location, ϕ denotes separation logic formulas and P PPTL^{SL} formulas.

Let $\mathsf{Val} = Loc \cup \{nil\}$ be the spatial values, and $\mathbb{B} = \{true, false\}$ the boolean domain. A state s is a triple (I_p, I_v, I_l), where $I_p : \Pi \to \mathbb{B}$, $I_v : Var \to \mathsf{Val}$ and $I_l : Loc \rightharpoonup \bigcup_{i=1}^{n} \mathsf{Val}^i$. Intuitively, in our spatial model, $I_l(l) = (l_1, l_2)$ denotes a spatial cell labeled by l and with (l_1, l_2) stored in. We will refer to the domain of I_l by $dom(I_l)$. We say I_{l_1} and I_{l_2} are disjoint, written as $I_{l_1} \perp I_{l_2}$, if $dom(I_{l_1}) \cap dom(I_{l_2}) = \emptyset$. The operation $I_{l_1} \bullet I_{l_2}$ is defined for the union of I_{l_1} and I_{l_2}. The notation $s[e]$ indicates the evaluation of e with respect to s. Given G as the goal constraints of a planning task, semantics of separation logic formulas is defined by the satisfaction relation $\models_{\mathrm{SL}}$ below.

$s \models_{\mathrm{SL}} p$ iff $p = true$.

$s \models_{\mathrm{SL}} e_1 = e_2$ iff $s[e_1] = s[e_2]$.

$s \models_{\mathrm{SL}} e_0 \mapsto \{e_1, \ldots, e_n\}$ iff $dom(I_l) = \{s[e_0]\}$ and $I_l(s[e_0]) = (s[e_1], \ldots, s[e_n])$.

$s \models_{\mathrm{SL}} \neg\phi$ iff $s \not\models_{\mathrm{SL}} \phi$.

$s \models_{\mathrm{SL}} \phi_1 \vee \phi_2$ iff $s \models_{\mathrm{SL}} \phi_1$ or $s \models_{\mathrm{SL}} \phi_2$.

$s \models_{\mathrm{SL}} \phi_1 \# \phi_2$ iff $\exists I_{l_1}, I_{l_2} : I_{l_1} \perp I_{l_2}, I_l = I_{l_1} \bullet I_{l_2}, (I_p, I_v, I_{l_1}) \models_{\mathrm{SL}} \phi_1$, and $(I_p, I_v, I_{l_2}) \models_{\mathrm{SL}} \phi_2$.

$s \models_{\mathrm{SL}} \exists x : \phi$ iff $\exists l \in \mathsf{Val} : (I_p, I_v(x/l), I_l) \models_{\mathrm{SL}} \phi$.

$s \models_{\mathrm{SL}} GOAL(p)$ iff $\forall s :$ if G is true in s, then $s \models_{\mathrm{SL}} p$.

The following shows some useful derived formulas. Formula $e \mapsto e_i$ denotes there is a link between e and e_i. $ls^n(e_1, e_2)$ precisely describes a path from e_1 to e_2 of length n without any other locations (e_2 is also excluded). $e_1 \to^+ e_2$ and $e_1 \to^* e_2$ indicate that e_2 is reachable from e_1.

$$e \mapsto e_i \stackrel{\text{def}}{=} e \mapsto \{e_1, \ldots, e_i, \ldots, e_n\}$$
$$ls^1(e_1, e_2) \stackrel{\text{def}}{=} e_1 \mapsto e_2 \quad ls^{n+1}(e_1, e_2) \stackrel{\text{def}}{=} \exists x : e_1 \mapsto x \# ls^n(x, e_2)$$
$$e_1 \to^+ e_2 \stackrel{\text{def}}{=} \bigvee_{i=1}^{n} ls^i(e_1, e_2) \# true \quad e_1 \to^* e_2 \stackrel{\text{def}}{=} e_1 = e_2 \vee e_1 \to^+ e_2$$

An interval $\sigma = \langle s_0, s_1, \ldots \rangle$ is a nonempty sequence of states, possibly finite or infinite. The length of σ, denoted by $|\sigma|$, is ω if σ is infinite, otherwise it is the number of states minus one. We consider the set N_0 of non-negative integers, define $N_\omega = N_0 \cup \{\omega\}$ and $\preceq$ as $\leq \setminus \{(\omega, \omega)\}$. $\sigma_{(i \ldots j)} (0 \leq i \preceq j \leq |\sigma|)$ denotes the sub-interval $\langle s_i, \ldots, s_j \rangle$. The concatenation of σ with another interval σ' is denoted by $\sigma \cdot \sigma'$. Let $\sigma = \langle s_k, \ldots, s_{|\sigma|} \rangle$ be an interval and $r_1, \ldots, r_n$ be integers such that $0 \leq r_1 \leq \cdots \leq r_n \preceq |\sigma|$. The projection of σ onto $r_1, \ldots, r_n$ is the interval, $\sigma \downarrow (r_1, \ldots, r_n) = \langle s_{t_1}, \ldots, s_{t_m} \rangle$, where $t_1, \ldots, t_m$ are obtained from $r_1, \ldots, r_n$ by deleting all duplicates.

An interpretation of a PPTL^{SL} formula is a triple $\mathcal{I} = (\sigma, k, j)$ where $\sigma = \langle s_0, s_1, \ldots \rangle$ is an interval, k a non-negative integer and j an integer or ω such that $0 \leq k \preceq j \leq |\sigma|$. We write $(\sigma, k, j) \models P$ to mean that a formula P is interpreted over a sub-interval $\sigma_{(k \ldots j)}$ of σ with the current state being s_k. The precise semantics of PPTL^{SL} built upon σ is given below.

$\mathcal{I} \models \phi$ iff $s_k \models_{\text{SL}} \phi$.

$\mathcal{I} \models P_1 \vee P_2$ iff $\mathcal{I} \models P_1$ or $\mathcal{I} \models P_2$.

$\mathcal{I} \models \neg P$ iff $\mathcal{I} \not\models P$.

$\mathcal{I} \models \bigcirc P$ iff $k < j$ and $(\sigma, k+1, j) \models P$.

$\mathcal{I} \models (P_1, \ldots, P_m) \, prj \, P$ iff $\exists r_0, \ldots, r_m$ and $k = r_0 \leq r_1 \leq \cdots \leq r_m \preceq j$ such that $(\sigma, r_{i-1}, r_i) \models P_i$ for all $1 \leq i \leq m$ and $(\sigma', 0, |\sigma'|) \models P$ for one of the following σ' :

(a) $r_m < j$ and $\sigma' = \sigma \downarrow (r_0, \ldots, r_m) \cdot \sigma_{(r_m+1 \ldots j)}$.

(b) $r_m = j$ and $\sigma' = \sigma \downarrow (r_0, \ldots, r_{i'})$ for some $0 \leq i' \leq m$.

$\mathcal{I} \models P^*$ iff $\exists r_0, \ldots, r_n$ and $k = r_0 \leq r_1 \leq \cdots \leq r_{n-1} \preceq r_n = j (n \geq 0)$ such that $(\sigma, r_{i-1}, r_i) \models P$ for all $1 \leq i \leq n$; or $\exists r_0, \ldots,$ and $k = r_0 \leq r_1 \leq r_2 \leq \cdots$ such that $\lim_{i \to \infty} r_i = \omega$ and $(\sigma, r_{i-1}, r_i) \models P$ for all $i \geq 1$.

A formula P is satisfied over an interval σ, written as $\sigma \models P$, if $(\sigma, 0, |\sigma|) \models P$ holds. We also have some derived temporal formulas:

$$\varepsilon \stackrel{\text{def}}{=} \neg \bigcirc true \qquad\qquad P_1; P_2 \stackrel{\text{def}}{=} (P_1, P_2) \, prj \, \varepsilon$$

$$\Diamond P \stackrel{\text{def}}{=} true; P \qquad\qquad \Box P \stackrel{\text{def}}{=} \neg \Diamond \neg P$$

Here, ε denotes an interval with zero length, $\Box$ and $\Diamond$ have the standard meanings as in LTL. Formula $P_1; P_2$ asserts that P_1 holds from now on until some point in the future, and from that point on, P_2 holds.

Example 1 (Example of Control Knowledge). *The CityCar domain simulates the impact of road building/demolition in traffic networks. Some cars need to move to their destinations, while roads may be built and removed dynamically (the most costly actions). CityCar domain is the second hardest problem in the 8th IPC for the reason that the roads can shape in a variety of ways (most of which are infeasible). Consider the following control knowledge which is useful for the CityCar domain:*

$\Box(\forall j_1, j_2, j_3, j_4 : (\exists r_1, r_2 : road\_connect(r_1, j_1, j_3) \wedge road\_connect(r_2, j_1, j_4)) \rightarrow$
$\neg(j_3 \rightarrow^* j_2 \# j_4 \rightarrow^* j_2))$

The above formula can be read as "for any locations j_1, j_2, j_3, j_4, if there exist two road r_1 and r_2 sharing the same starting location j_1, any two paths between j_1 and j_2 should not be disjoint". $road\_connect(r, j_1, j_2)$ denotes that there is a road r from j_1 to j_2. $\#$ is able to express the disjointness of two paths. Since all variables are bounded, we can use quantifiers to obtain concise formulas. Note that all predicates can be replaced by propositional variables.

Since roads are limited resource, we should keep at most one path from a location to another to reduce the usage of roads. This knowledge provides valuable information for reducing the cost a plan, as well as the search space.

3   Combining PPTL^{SL} with Heuristic Search

Our aim is to exploit PPTL^{SL} style control knowledge in heuristic search. We assume control knowledge is given at the beginning of the search in terms of a "global" PPTL^{SL} formula. We will show how control knowledge can be added into the search process in this section.

3.1   Progression of PPTL^{SL}

We can rewrite PPTL^{SL} formulas in a special form of what has to be held in the current state and the following states. This can be accomplished by Theorems 1 and 2 [12,13].

Theorem 1 (Equisatisfiable Translation). *For any PPTL^{SL} formula P, there exists an equisatisfiable RPPTL^{SL} formula R which is defined as,*

$$R ::= p \mid GOAL(p) \mid e_1 = e_2 \mid \neg R \mid R_1 \vee R_2 \mid \bigcirc R \mid (R_1, \dots, R_m) \, prj \, R \mid R^*$$

RPPTL^{SL} has no formulas describing spatial states. The translation process from PPTL^{SL} to RPPTL^{SL} is omitted here for reasons of brevity, please refer to [12,13] for more detail.

Theorem 2 (Normal Form Translation). *Any RPPTL^{SL} formula R can be rewritten into its normal form which is defined as,*

$$R \equiv \bigvee_{j=1}^{m} (\phi_j \wedge \varepsilon) \vee \bigvee_{i=1}^{n} (\phi_i' \wedge \bigcirc R_i)$$

where ϕ_j and ϕ_i' are separation logic formulas, and R_i is a general RPPTL^{SL} formula.

We borrow the basic idea of progression technique from [1]. A RPPTL^{SL} formula R can be evaluated progressively over a sequence of states $\langle s_0, s_1, \dots \rangle$. Intuitively, progressing R with $\langle s_0, s_1, \dots \rangle$ means that we obtain a new formula R' which is satisfied by $\langle s_1, \dots \rangle$, where the original sequence of states satisfies R. The following definition includes all progression rules required by RPPTL^{SL}.

Definition 2 (Progression Rules). *Let P be a $PPTL^{SL}$ formula, we can first translate P to a $RPPTL^{SL}$ formula R, then rewrite R in its normal form $\bigvee_{j=1}^{m} (\phi_j \wedge \varepsilon) \vee \bigvee_{i=1}^{n} (\phi'_i \wedge \bigcirc R_i)$. R is evaluated over a sequence of states starting with state s. $progress(R, s)$ is recursively defined as follows:*

- $progress(\varepsilon, s) = \varepsilon$
- $progress(\phi, s) = true$ *if* $s \models_{SL} \phi, false$ *otherwise*
- $progress(R_1 \vee R_2, s) = progress(R_1, s) \vee progress(R_2, s)$
- $progress(R_1 \wedge R_2, s) = progress(R_1, s) \wedge progress(R_2, s)$
- $progress(\bigcirc R_1, s) = R_1$

Theorem 3 (Progression). *Given an interval $\sigma = \langle s_0, s_1, \ldots \rangle$, for any $RPPTL^{SL}$ formula R, $progress(R, s_i) \neq \varepsilon$, the following condition must hold:*

$$(\sigma, i+1, |\sigma|) \models progress(R, s_i) \qquad \textit{iff} \qquad (\sigma, i, |\sigma|) \models R$$

Proof. The proof proceeds by induction on R. Since we can translate R into its normal form, there exists the following cases:

- $R \equiv \phi$. If R is a state formula ϕ, $(\sigma, i, |\sigma|) \models R$ if and only if $s_i \models_{SL} \phi$. By Definition 2, $progress(\phi, s_i) = true$ or $false$ dependents on whether s_i satisfies ϕ. Any state satisfies $true$, falsifies $false$. Hence, this case holds.
- $R \equiv \varepsilon$. If R is ε, $progress(R, s_i) = \varepsilon$ which violates the precondition. Hence, this case holds.
- $R \equiv R_1 \vee R_2$. $(\sigma, i, |\sigma|) \models R$ if and only if $(\sigma, i, |\sigma|) \models R_1$ or $(\sigma, i, |\sigma|) \models R_2$. By inductive hypothesis, $(\sigma, i, |\sigma|) \models R_1$ if and only if $(\sigma, i+1, |\sigma|) \models progress(R_1, s_i)$, and $(\sigma, i, |\sigma|) \models R_2$ if and only if $(\sigma, i+1, |\sigma|) \models progress(R_2, s_i)$. Hence, $(\sigma, i, |\sigma|) \models R$ if and only if $(\sigma, i+1, |\sigma|) \models progress(R_1, s_i) \vee progress(R_2, s_i)$. By Definition 2, $progress(R_1, s_i) \vee progress(R_2, s_i) = progress(R_1 \vee R_2, s_i)$.
- $R \equiv R_1 \wedge R_2$. Similar to the proof of the case $R \equiv R_1 \vee R_2$.
- $R \equiv \bigcirc R_1$. Based on the semantics of $\bigcirc$, $(\sigma, i, |\sigma|) \models R$ if and only if $(\sigma, i+1, |\sigma|) \models R_1$. By Definition 2, $(\sigma, i+1, |\sigma|) \models progress(R, s_i)$. $\square$

As we will see later, the progression technique is the essential when using $PPTL^{SL}$ in heuristic planning process.

3.2 Incorporation of Heuristic Search Framework with $PPTL^{SL}$

In fact the planning search space is a tree with the root be the initial state. When exploring the space, heuristic algorithms mainly compute heuristic functions to choose which nodes to expand. The major difference or the key is the functions they use according to different applications. The algorithms usually maintain two queues to save nodes. One is a priority queue called open list in which saves

Algorithm 1. Planning algorithm with heuristic search and PPTL^{SL} control knowledge

Input: Initial state I, goal G, actions A, PPTL^{SL} formula P.
Output: *Plan.*

```
 1: g(I) = 0;
 2: h(I) = heuristic estimate for I;
 3: priority(I) = g(I) + h(I);
 4: open = { I };
 5: closed = ∅;
 6: Plan = ⟨⟩;
 7: Translate P_I to an equisatisfiable RPPTL^SL formulas R_I;
 8: R_I = progress(R, I);
 9: while open ≠ ∅ do
10:     select s ∈ open which has the highest priority;
11:     closed = closed ∪ { s };
12:     if G ⊆ s then
13:         return Plan;
14:     end if
15:     for action a ∈ A applicable to s do
16:         s' = succ_a(s);
17:         R_{s'} = progress(R_s, s');
18:         if R_{s'} is unsatisfiable then
19:             continue;
20:         end if
21:         Plan = Plan · a;
22:         g(s') = g(s) + cost(a);
23:         h(s') = heuristic estimate for s';
24:         if ∄s'' : s'' ∈ open ∪ closed and s'' = s' then
25:             open = open ∪ { s' };
26:             priority(s') = g(s') + h(s');
27:         else if ∃s'' : s'' ∈ open ∪ closed and s'' = s' and g(s') < g(s'') then
28:             priority(s') = g(s') + h(s');
29:             if s' ∈ closed then
30:                 closed = closed \ { s' };
31:                 open = open ∪ { s' };
32:             end if
33:         else
34:             remove tail a of Plan;
35:         end if
36:     end for
37: end while
38: return no solution;
```

unexpanded nodes, and the other is called closed list to record expanded ones. The node with the highest priority in the open list will be selected for the future expansion.

For example, the best-first search algorithm A* [7], examines which node n in the open list has the lowest value with respect to $f(n) = g(n) + h(n)$, which means n possesses the highest priorities. $g(n)$ represents the exact cost from the initial node to the current node n, and $h(n)$ represents the heuristic estimated cost from n to the goal. Specifically, $h(n)$ can be calculated in various ways for different purpose. Our algorithm employs A* as the underlying heuristic search framework, since A* is guaranteed to return an optimal plan if the heuristic function h used by A* is admissible. A heuristic function is said to be admissible if it never overestimates the cost of reaching the goal.

The corresponding pseudo code is shown in Algorithm 1. For simplicity, we just use states to represent nodes. The algorithm takes the planning problem and the control formula as input, and searches for a plan. At the beginning of the algorithm, several initializations are done in line 1–8. The exact cost of the initial state $g(I)$ is assigned to 0, the heuristic estimate $h(I)$ is also calculated (depends on implementation). The open list is initialized with a single element I with priority $g(I) + h(I)$, the closed list and the action sequence $Plan$ is empty. The global formula P (control knowledge) is translated into an equisatisfiable RPPTL^{SL} formula R. Then R with the initial state is progressed, resulting in R_I. For each iteration of the main loop, we first select an element s which has the highest priority from the open list and put it in the closed list. As long as s satisfies the goal, i.e., $G \subseteq s$, a plan ($Plan$) is found and returned (line 12–14). Otherwise we try to execute an action a which is applicable to s, and the successor state s' is obtained. Then the current control knowledge R_s is progressed with s'. If the progression result R'_s is unsatisfiable, node s' will be discarded by trying another applicable action (line 18–20). If not, from line 21 to 23, we add a to $Plan$, calculate the exact cost $g(s')$ for reaching s', and estimate the heuristic cost $h(s')$. After that, the algorithm checks if s' is in the open list or the closed list. There exists three different cases. First, if s' is a new state, it will be inserted into the open list with priority $g(s') + h(s')$. Second, if s' is not a new state, but $g(s')$ is lower than before, we simply updates the g value of s'. Note that we do not need to recalculate the heuristic estimate since it is only state dependent. Moreover, if s' is already in the closed list, we should take it from the closed list and insert it into the open list again. Third, if s' is not new and has a higher g value, we do nothing but only remove the tail of the $Plan$ since the existing g value is at least good or even better than the newly found one. Finally, if the main loop ends without finding a solution, the algorithm will report that the problem is unsolvable. In the algorithm, the progression technique will be helpful to prune more state space by giving additional restrictions together with heuristics.

We often hope to find a plan with the cost as low as possible. To this end, we can slightly modify the algorithm by providing a bound cost initially, thus any plan over cost will not be returned.

4   Experiment

The above mentioned framework has been implemented on top of *S-TSolver* [12,13], a domain-dependent planner using basic search (e.g., depth first search). Note that we do not specify any heuristic strategy in Algorithm 1. In the implementation, a traditional heuristic method is employed via relaxed planning task exploration.

Definition 3 (Relaxed Planning Task). *Given a planning task* $\mathcal{P} = (\Pi, A, I, G)$*, the relaxation* $\mathcal{P}'$ *of* $\mathcal{P}$ *is defined as* $\mathcal{P}' = (\Pi, A', I, G)$*, with*

$$A' = \{\, (pre(a), add(a), \emptyset, cost(a)) \mid (pre(a), add(a), del(a), cost(a)) \in A \,\}$$

In words, one obtains the relaxed planning task by ignoring the delete effects of all actions. The basic idea behind the relaxed planning task is that the number of facts in a state during search is guaranteed to be increased or stable compared with the previous state. Given a planning task $\mathcal{P} = (\Pi, A, I, G)$ and a state s, we estimates the cost of a relaxed plan that achieves the goals starting from s for the task $\mathcal{P}' = (\Pi, A', s, G)$. More concretely, the base heuristic estimates a rough approximation as the following cost values:

$$hcost_s(p) = \begin{cases} 0 & \text{if } p \in s \\ n + cost(a) & \text{if } min\{\, \Sigma_{q \in pre(a)} hcost_s(q)) \mid a \in A', p \in add(a) \,\} = n \\ \infty & \text{otherwise} \end{cases}$$

Given a set of facts, we assume they are achieved independently in the sense that the *hcost* of the facts is estimated as the sum of the individuals. The heuristic estimate for a state is:

$$h(s) = hcost_s(G) = \Sigma_{g \in G} hcost_s(g)$$

The assumptions that each fact is achieved independently ignores positive interactions of actions. In fact, two facts may be achieved exclusively. However, it can be proved that relaxed planing task is solvable in polynomial time.

Example 2 (An Example of Heuristic Estimate). *Consider the following example of a simple planning task, where* $G = \{\, g_1, g_2 \,\}$ *and three actions* $a_1 = (\{\, p \,\}, \{\, g_1 \,\}, \emptyset, 1), a_2 = (\{\, q \,\}, \{\, g_2 \,\}, \emptyset, 1), a_3 = (\{\, p \,\}, \{\, q \,\}, \emptyset, 1)$*. Given two states* $s_1 = \{\, p \,\}, s_2 = \{\, q \,\}$*, the heuristic estimate for* s_1 *and* s_2 *are:*

$$\begin{aligned} h(s_1) &= hcost_{s_1}(G) \\ &= hcost_{s_1}(g_1) + hcost_{s_1}(g_2) \\ &= hcost_{s_1}(p) + cost(a_1) + hcost_{s_1}(q) + cost(a_2) \\ &= 0 + 1 + hcost_{s_1}(p) + cost(a_1) + 1 \\ &= 1 + 2 = 3 \end{aligned}$$

$$h(s_2) = hcost_{s_2}(G)$$
$$= hcost_{s_2}(g_1) + hcost_{s_2}(g_2)$$
$$= \infty + hcost_{s_2}(q) + cost(a_2)$$
$$= \infty + 1 = \infty$$

Obviously, s_1 has better heuristic value than s_2.

We extend the planner, *S-TSolver*, by replacing the basic forward search with heuristic mechanism. Two standard input files (written in PDDL) namely the domain file and problem file are needed, the former gives the definitions of actions and the latter lists the initial state and the goal constraints. At each step, the heuristic value of every new reachable state (after applying an action) is calculated, while only the states satisfy the control knowledge are maintained.

Experiment has been carried out on *S-TSolver*. We compare *S-TSolver* of two modes, one with basic search and the other with heuristic search. We use a timeout of 10 min per run. To evaluate the plans found by the search, the search time and cost for each plan are considered as metrics. Table 1 shows the result of running *S-TSolver* for the CityCar domain. In the table, the column "cost" indicates the minimum plan cost found by the planner, "time" the search time and "len" the length of the plan. The column *S-TSolver* shows the result with basic search and control knowledge, and *S-TSolver*(heuristic) shows the result with both heuristic search and control knowledge. We do not compare the mode that *S-TSolver* uses only heuristic search without control knowledge. The reason is that the heuristic is so weak that only several solutions can be given for few instances. Even Fast Downward [9], one of the best heuristic planner so far, adopting complex and delicate heuristics only gives solutions for five simple instances[3].

The minimum cost and least time for each instance are in bold. In general, the higher the cost, the longer the length. Heuristic really helps the planner to improve the quality of a plan. In particular, all plans found by *S-TSolver*(heuristic) have better quality than those by *S-TSolver*. However, *S-TSolver* takes the advantage of search time, i.e., mostly the plans' search time is less since *S-TSolver*(heuristic) spends additional time to compute the heuristic estimates. But this is not all the cases, sometimes heuristic enables the search to move closer towards goals as soon as possible. Instead, the search time is not affected (increased) by computing heuristics, especially for some difficult instances (e.g., p17–p19).

---

[3] https://helios.hud.ac.uk/scommv/IPC-14/resDoc.html.

Table 1. Performance of *S-TSolver* with (without) heuristic: CityCar domain

Problem instance	*S-TSolver*			*S-TSolver*(heuristic)		
	cost	time	len	cost	time	len
p01	**70**	0.50	17	**70**	**0.08**	17
p02	126	**6.03**	27	**122**	57.18	33
p03	106	**0.79**	27	**100**	4.24	32
p04	**136**	**4.92**	41	**136**	11.10	41
p05	94	**1.60**	37	**86**	4.52	39
p06	154	**4.22**	23	**138**	4.34	28
p07	154	**3.69**	23	**134**	23.28	23
p08	**114**	1.98	22	**114**	**1.22**	22
p09	108	**5.77**	28	**102**	18.12	32
p10	176	16.01	38	**152**	**15.10**	34
p11	**184**	8.88	36	**184**	**3.46**	38
p12	202	**5.00**	36	**158**	31.88	40
p13	350	**26.31**	62	**206**	27.02	52
p14	164	**11.63**	48	**126**	13.64	38
p15	260	21.22	48	**239**	**21.12**	47
p16	150	**12.00**	44	**136**	22.24	39
p17	304	33.06	56	**230**	**19.74**	48
p18	180	19.43	56	**144**	**14.20**	49
p19	416	38.29	84	**240**	**1.18**	60
p20	280	**44.14**	82	**204**	110.54	62

5   Conclusion

This paper introduces an algorithm that combines control knowledge and heuristic search in the same framework. PPTL^{SL} formulas representing control knowledge are evaluated at each planning step by progression technique. Then we incorporate progression of PPTL^{SL} formulas with a general forward heuristic search. The experiment demonstrates that the effectiveness and efficiency of heuristic search can be further improved by exploiting domain specific knowledge. Generally speaking, our approach belongs to model checking framework. In the future, we will plan to exploit some existing efficient model checking techniques, e.g., abstract model checking [16,19], logic based model checking [24], in our work. We believe that one will obtain better results in this way.

References

1. Bacchus, F., Kabanza, F.: Using temporal logics to express search control knowledge for planning. Artif. Intell. **116**(1–2), 123–191 (2000). https://doi.org/10.1016/S0004-3702(99)00071-5
2. Baier, J.A., McIlraith, S.A.: Planning with first-order temporally extended goals using heuristic search. In: Proceedings of the Twenty-First National Conference on Artificial Intelligence and the Eighteenth Innovative Applications of Artificial Intelligence Conference, July 16–20, 2006, Boston, Massachusetts, USA, pp. 788–795 (2006). http://www.aaai.org/Library/AAAI/2006/aaai06-125.php
3. Cui, J., Duan, Z., Tian, C., Du, H.: A novel approach to modeling and verifying real-time systems for high reliability. IEEE Trans. Reliab. **67**(2), 481–493 (2018). https://doi.org/10.1109/TR.2018.2806349
4. Duan, Z., Tian, C.: A practical decision procedure for propositional projection temporal logic with infinite models. Theor. Comput. Sci. **554**, 169–190 (2014). https://doi.org/10.1016/j.tcs.2014.02.011
5. Duan, Z., Tian, C., Zhang, N.: A canonical form based decision procedure and model checking approach for propositional projection temporal logic. Theor. Comput. Sci. **609**, 544–560 (2016). https://doi.org/10.1016/j.tcs.2015.08.039
6. Erol, K., Hendler, J.A., Nau, D.S.: HTN planning: complexity and expressivity. In: Proceedings of the 12th National Conference on Artificial Intelligence, Seattle, WA, USA, July 31–August 4, 1994, vol. 2, pp. 1123–1128 (1994). http://www.aaai.org/Library/AAAI/1994/aaai94-173.php
7. Hart, P.E., Nilsson, N.J., Raphael, B.: A formal basis for the heuristic determination of minimum cost paths. IEEE Trans. Syst. Sci. Cybern. **4**(2), 100–107 (1968). https://doi.org/10.1109/TSSC.1968.300136
8. Helmert, M.: Complexity results for standard benchmark domains in planning. Artif. Intell. **143**(2), 219–262 (2003). https://doi.org/10.1016/S0004-3702(02)00364-8
9. Helmert, M.: The fast downward planning system. J. Artif. Intell. Res. **26**, 191–246 (2006). https://doi.org/10.1613/jair.1705
10. Hoffmann, J., Nebel, B.: The FF planning system: fast plan generation through heuristic search. J. Artif. Intell. Res. **14**, 253–302 (2001). https://doi.org/10.1613/jair.855
11. Kvarnström, J., Magnusson, M.: Talplanner in IPC-2002: extensions and control rules. CoRR. http://arxiv.org/abs/1106.5266 (2011)
12. Lu, X., Tian, C., Duan, Z.: Temporalising separation logic for planning with search control knowledge. In: Proceedings of the Twenty-Sixth International Joint Conference on Artificial Intelligence, IJCAI 2017, Melbourne, Australia, August 19–25, 2017, pp. 1167–1173 (2017). https://doi.org/10.24963/ijcai.2017/162
13. Lu, X., Tian, C., Duan, Z., Du, H.: Planning with spatio-temporal search control knowledge. IEEE Trans. Knowl. Data Eng. **30**(10), 1915–1928 (2018). https://doi.org/10.1109/TKDE.2018.2810144
14. Nau, D.S., et al.: SHOP2: an HTN planning system. J. Artif. Intell. Res. (JAIR) **20**, 379–404 (2003). https://doi.org/10.1613/jair.1141
15. Reynolds, J.C.: Separation logic: a logic for shared mutable data structures. In: Proceedings 17th IEEE Symposium on Logic in Computer Science (LICS 2002), July 22–25, 2002, Copenhagen, Denmark, pp. 55–74 (2002). https://doi.org/10.1109/LICS.2002.1029817

16. Tian, C., Duan, Z., Duan, Z., Ong, C.L.: More effective interpolations in software model checking. In: Proceedings of the 32nd IEEE/ACM International Conference on Automated Software Engineering, ASE 2017, Urbana, IL, USA, October 30–November 03, 2017, pp. 183–193 (2017). https://doi.org/10.1109/ASE.2017.8115631

17. Tian, C., Duan, Z.: Complexity of propositional projection temporal logic with star. Math. Struct. Comput. Sci. **19**(1), 73–100 (2009). https://doi.org/10.1017/S096012950800738X

18. Tian, C., Duan, Z.: Expressiveness of propositional projection temporal logic with star. Theor. Comput. Sci. **412**(18), 1729–1744 (2011). https://doi.org/10.1016/j.tcs.2010.12.047

19. Tian, C., Duan, Z., Duan, Z.: Making CEGAR more efficient in software model checking. IEEE Trans. Softw. Eng. **40**(12), 1206–1223 (2014). https://doi.org/10.1109/TSE.2014.2357442

20. Wang, L., Baier, J., McIlraith, S.: Viewing landmarks as temporally extended goals. In: ICAPS 2009 Workshop on Heuristics for Domain-Independent Planning, pp. 49–56 (2009)

21. Yang, K., Duan, Z., Tian, C., Zhang, N.: A compiler for MSVL and its applications. Theor. Comput. Sci. **749**, 2–16 (2018). https://doi.org/10.1016/j.tcs.2017.07.032

22. Yu, B., Duan, Z., Tian, C., Zhang, N.: Verifying temporal properties of programs: a parallel approach. J. Parallel Distrib. Comput. **118**(Part), 89–99 (2018). https://doi.org/10.1016/j.jpdc.2017.09.003

23. Zhang, N., Duan, Z., Tian, C.: A complete axiom system for propositional projection temporal logic with cylinder computation model. Theor. Comput. Sci. **609**, 639–657 (2016). https://doi.org/10.1016/j.tcs.2015.05.007

24. Zhang, N., Duan, Z., Tian, C.: Model checking concurrent systems with MSVL. Sci. China Inf. Sci. **59**(11), 118101 (2016). https://doi.org/10.1007/s11432-015-0882-6

Formal Development and Verification of Reusable Component in PAR Platform

Qimin Hu[1,2(✉)], Jinyun Xue[1,2], Zhen You[1,2], Zhuo Cheng[1,2], and Zhengkang Zuo[1,2]

[1] National Networked Supporting Software International S&T Cooperation Base of China, Jiangxi Normal University, Nanchang, Jiangxi, People's Republic of China
qiminhu@163.com, jinyun@vip.sina.com,
yucy0405@163.com, zhuo_cheng@126.com,
zhengkang2005@iscas.ac.cn
[2] Key Laboratory of High Performance Computing Technology, Jiangxi Normal University, Nanchang, Jiangxi, People's Republic of China

Abstract. Formal method is an important approach to develop high trust software systems. Coq is an interactive proof assistant for the development of mathematical theories and formally certified software. Set, Bag, List, Tree, Graph are important reusable components in PAR platform. This paper tries to formally develop 'Set' components which have linear structure and verify the correctness of this component mechanically with Coq. The formal development of this component involves formalization of specification, the recurrence relation of problem-solving sequence and loop invariant. Specification language Radl of PAR platform was used to describe the specification, recurrence relation and loop invariants; Software modelling language Apla was used to describe the abstract model of those components. The Dijkstra's Weakest Precondition method is used to verify abstract model by the interactive proof tool Coq. Finally, the abstract model denoted by Apla was transformed to concrete model written by executable language; such as C++, Java, VB and C#, etc., based on the program generating systems in PAR platform.

Keywords: Reusable component · Formal development · Loop invariant · PAR platform

1 Introduction

Component-based software engineering emerged as an approach to software systems development based on reusing software components. A software component can be deployed independently and is subject to composition by third parties [2]. Reusing software component has now become the dominant development paradigm for web-based information systems and enterprise systems. Formal methods are mathematically-based approaches to software development where you define a formal model of the software [11]. CBSE and formal methods are two important but largely independent approaches which have been visibly influential in recent years [6, 7].

© Springer Nature Switzerland AG 2020
H. Miao et al. (Eds.): SOFL+MSVL 2019 Workshop, LNCS 12028, pp. 155–166, 2020.
https://doi.org/10.1007/978-3-030-41418-4_12

PAR means PAR (Partition-and-Recur) method [14, 16–19] and its supporting platform, called PAR platform. PAR method and PAR platform consists of specification and algorithm describing language Radl, software modeling language Apla, a set of rules for specification transformation, a set of reusable components and a set of automatic generating tools such as Radl to Apla generating system, Apla to Java, C++, C# executable program generating systems.

Set, Bag, List, Tree, Graph are reusable components defined in PAR platform. Set and Bag (an element may occur many times) have unordered linear structure. List has ordered linear structure. Tree and Graph have non-linear structure. With the support of those reusable components, the programs written by Apla are very short and easy to prove their correctness.

The reusable components are important for PAR platform. It is a challenge and urgent work to develop them formally and guarantee the correctness of those components.

The Coq [23] proof assistant is based on the calculus of inductive constructions. This calculus is a higher-order typed λ-calculus. Theorems are types and their proofs are terms of the calculus. The Coq systems helps the user to build the proof terns and offers a language of tactics to do so.

In this paper, Set components was formally developed. Using formal specification language Radl to describe the specification of reusable components. Using the quantifier transformation rules to transform specification and construct the recurrence relation of problem. Using new strategies of developing loop invariants to develop loop invariants and construct the abstract programs written by Apla language. Using executable program generating system to generate the codes of reusable components.

The paper was organized as follows. The second section gave the related preliminary knowledge of PAR platform and verification steps with Coq; the third section gave the formal development and verification of Set component, the fourth section gave an example of constructing program by composing the reusable components; Finally, a short conclusion was presented.

2 Preliminary

2.1 PAR Method and PAR Platform

PAR is a long-term research projects supported by a series of nature science research foundations of China. According to the methodology of MDD, PAR has been used in developing software with high reliability and safety, such as non-trivial algorithm programs [15, 20–22], traffic scheduling system [13], bank account management system and electric control system.

2.1.1 Specification Language Radl

Radl (Recur-based Algorithm Design Language) used the idiomatic mathematical symbols and style to describe the algorithm specification, specification transformation rules and the recurrence relation. Radl is the front language of the Apla language, with mathematical referential transparency. Using the unified format(Q i: r(i): f(i)) given by

Dijkstra to denote quantifiers [4], where Q can be ∀ (all quantifier), ∃(exists quantifier), MIN (minimum quantifier), MAX (maximum quantifier), Σ (summation quantifier), etc, and i is a bounded variable, $r(i)$ is the variant range of i and $f(i)$ is a function.

2.1.2 Software Modelling Language Apla

Apla (Abstract Programming Language) is the software modelling language and the target language of Radl to Apla program generating system, and the source language of Apla to Java, C++, C#, Dephi executable program generating system.

2.1.3 The Formal Development Steps with PAR

The formal development steps with PAR can be 6 steps:

Step 1. Construct the formal specification of problem using Radl;

Step 2. Partition the problem into a couple of subproblems each of that has the same structure with the original problem;

Step 3. Formally derive the algorithm from the formal specification. The algorithm is described using Radl and represented by recurrence relation;

Step 4. Develop loop invariant directly based on new strategy;

Step 5. Transformed the Radl program to the Apla program;

Step 6. Transforms the Apla program to an executable language program.

2.2 Verification Steps with Coq

2.2.1 Introduction of Coq

Coq [24, 25] is an interactive theorem proving tool based on high-order logic developed by INRIA Institute in France. It uses Gallina to express the properties of programs, programs and their proofs.

Coq system consists of two parts: certification development system and certification checker. The proof development system is similar to the program development system, which has the declarative mode and the proof mode. In declarative mode, programmers can declare variables, assumptions and axioms just like programmers; in proof mode, programmers can construct lemmas or theorems by using declared objects and proof strategies provided by systems, just like programmers. The proof checker is used to verify formally expressed programs. The core of the proof checker is the type checking algorithm, which determines whether the proof is valid by checking whether the program meets the program specifications.

2.2.2 Verification Steps with Coq

The formal verification based on Coq is divided into the following five steps:

Step 1. Give the formal semantics of the program, that is, give the exact description of the pre-and post-assertion of the program.

Step 2. Starting from the pre-and post-assertion of the program, the recurrence relation of the program solution is derived formally, and construct the loop invariant P and the program.

Step 3. Using Gallina language and inductive type, recursive type and dependency product mechanism of Coq system, defining related data types, data structures, and related functions; describing the loop invariants obtained in step 2 with Gallina language.

Step 4. The theorem that the program should satisfy the relevant attributes is given and described in Gallina language. If the program statement is represented by S, the predicate formulas Q and R represent the pre-and post-assertions of the program, and the weakest pre-predicate WP ('S', R) is defined from S and R. The theorem that the program should satisfy is: Q→WP ('S', R).

Step 5. Using the proof rules provided by Coq system and the data type, data structure and correlation function defined in step 3, prove the theorems of step 4.

3   Formal Development and Verification of Set Component

3.1   Introduction of Set Reusable Component

A set is simply a collection of distinct (different) elements [5]. In PAR platform, the description of reusable component set's data and operations is given below:

```
Specify Set (sometype data, [size])
    //data denotes the data type of elements in set
    //size denotes the upper bound of set size
type set(sometype data, [size])
var
    n: integer;              //n  is the number of elements in set;
    A, B : set := {},{};     // A,B is empty set;
    e: data;                 //e is element in set;
Operator:
    # A      // the number of elements in set
    A∩B      // the intersection of set A and B
    A∪B      // the union of set A and B
    A - B    // the difference of set A and B
    x∈A      //  judge whether x is a member of set A
    A ⊂B     // judge whether set A is a proper subset of set B
    A = B    // judge whether set A is equal to set B
    A := B   // replace set A with set B
endspec;
```

3.2   Formal Development of Set Component

In order to guarantee the correctness of set component, we formally developed the body of operations of set component. Following is the formal development of the operation which can be used to judge whether set A is a proper subset of set B.

(1) **Problem and Its Specification**

Given a set A[1..m] containing m elements, a set B[1..n] containing n elements. Include(A[1..m], B[1..n]) means set A is a subset of set B.

The specification is following:

$$Q : \text{Given set } A[1..m] \text{ and set } B[1..n], \ m < n$$
$$R : \text{Include}(A[1..m], B[1..n]) \equiv (\forall i{:}1 \leqslant i \leqslant m : (\exists j{:}1 \leqslant j \leqslant n{:}A[i] = B[j]))$$

(2) **Partition**

We partition computing Include(A[1..m], B[1..n]) into computing Include(A[1..m − 1], B[1..n]) with A[m], then partition computing Include(A[1..m − 1], B[1..n]) into computing Include(A[1..m − 2], B[1..n]) with A[m − 1],..., until computing Include(A[1], B[1..n]). Let F be the partition function to be determined, we have

$$\text{Include}(A[1..m], B[1..n]) = F(\text{Include}(A[1..m − 1], B[1..n]), \ A[m]) \quad m < n$$

So, the key of constructing recurrence relation is to determine function F.

(3) **Constructing Recurrence Relation**

Suppose Include(A[1..m − 1], B[1..n]) has been solved. We can derive the function F by using the properties of quantifiers. We have

Include(A[1..m], B[1..n])
$\equiv (\forall i{:}1 \leqslant i \leqslant m{:}(\exists j{:}1 \leqslant j \leqslant n{:}A[i] = B[j]))$
{Range Splitting}
$\equiv (\forall i{:}1 \leqslant i \leqslant m − 1{:}(\exists j{:}1 \leqslant j \leqslant n{:}A[i] = B[j])) \wedge (\forall i{:}1 \leqslant i = m{:}(\exists j{:}1 \leqslant j \leqslant n{:}A[i] = B[j]))$
{Singleton Range with i = m}
$\equiv (\forall i{:}1 \leqslant i \leqslant m − 1{:}(\exists j{:}1 \leqslant j \leqslant n{:}A[i] = B[j])) \wedge (\exists j{:}1 \leqslant j \leqslant n{:}A[m] = B[j])$
{The definition of Include}
$\equiv \text{Include}(A[1..m − 1], B[1..n]) \wedge (\exists j{:}1 \leqslant j \leqslant n{:}A[m] = B[j])$

Let is_a_member(A[m], B[1..n]) = $(\exists j{:}1 \leq j \leq n{:}A[m] = B[j])$, which denotes whether A[m] is a member of set B[1..n], We have the following recurrence:

Recurrence 1.

$$\text{Include}(A[1..m], B[1..n]) = \begin{cases} \text{Include}(A[1..m − 1], B[1..n]) & \text{is\_a\_member}(A[m], B[1..n]) \text{ is true} \\ \text{False} & \text{is\_a\_member}(A[m], B[1..n]) \text{ is false} \end{cases}$$

To compute is_a_member(A[m], B[1..n]), we try to find the recurrence relation. Suppose is_a_member(A[m], B[1..n − 1]) has been computed, based on the properties of quantifiers, we have

is_a_member$(A[m], B[1..n])$
$\equiv (\exists j:1 \leqslant j \leqslant n:A[m] = B[j])$
{Range Splitting}
$\equiv (\exists j:1 \leqslant j < n:A[m] = B[j]) \vee (\exists j:1 \leqslant j = n:A[m] = B[j])$
{Singleton Range with $j = n$}
$\equiv (\exists j:1 \leqslant j < n:A[m] = B[j]) \vee (A[m] = B[n])$
{The definition of is_a_member}
$\equiv$ is_a_member$(A[m], B[1..n-1]) \vee (A[m] = B[n])$

Based on the above derivation, we have the following recurrence.
Recurrence 2.

$$\text{is\_a\_member}(A[m], B[1..n]) = \begin{cases} \text{is\_a\_member}(A[m], B[1..n-1]) & A[m]! = B[n] \\ \text{True} & A[m] == B[n] \end{cases}$$

(4) Developing Loop Invariant and Program

Based on the above recurrence relations, let variable *In* whose data type is boolean denotes the value of Include$(A[1..i], B[1..n])$, the loop invariant can be constructed mechanically as following:

$$\rho: \ In = \text{Include}(A[1..i], B[1..n]) \wedge 1 \leqslant i \leqslant m < n$$

Based on the recurrence relations and loop invariant, the abstract algorithmic program written by Apla language is following:

```
i:=m;
do i ≥ 1 →
    if ¬ is_a_member(A[i],B[1..n]) → In:=false; return;
        is_a_member(A[i],B[1..n]) → i:=i-1;
    fi
od
In:=true;
```

3.3   Verification of Set Component

Because we have developed loop invariant in Sect. 3.2, we can go directly to Step 3.
Step 3. Define relevant data types, data structures, and related functions.

Using the abstract mechanism of inductive type, recursion and dependency product provided by Coq, function is_a_member and Include is defined as follows:

Fixpoint is_a_member (x:z,S:set):bool:=Match S with
| nil => false
|cons y q => if x=y then true else is_a_member x q

Fixpoint Include(S:set,R:set):bool:=Match S with
| nil => true
|cons y q=>if Involve y R then Include q R else false

At the same time, the nth element of the set S and the subset of the first j elements of the set S are defined as follows:

Fixpoint nth (n: z, S: set) : z = match S with
| nil => default
| x::r => match n with
|0 => x
|S m =>nth m r default
end.
end.
Fixpoint upto (j: z, S: set) : set =match j with
|0 => match s with
| nil => nil
| a::l => a::nil end
| S n => match s with
| nil => nil
| a::l => a::(firstn n l) end
end.

Step 4. Give the theorems that the program should satisfy:

Using the inductive types and functions defined above, it is proved that the loop invariants are true before and after each loop execution as follows:

① Firstly, we give the theorem that the loop invariant is true for the first execution cycle.
Theorem wp1:

$$i = 0 \wedge \text{Include}(\text{upto}(0, S), R) \rightarrow \text{Include}(\text{upto}(i,\ S), R) \wedge 0 \leqslant i \wedge i < m$$

② Secondly, the theorem that the invariants of each cycle are true is given.
Theorem wp2.1:

$$\text{Include}(\text{upto}(i, S), R) \wedge 0 \leqslant i \wedge i < m \wedge \text{Involve}(\text{nth}(i, S), R) \rightarrow$$
$$\text{Include}(\text{upto}(\text{suc } i, \ S), R) \wedge 0 \leqslant \text{suc } i \wedge \text{suc } i \leqslant m$$

Theorem wp2.2:

$$\text{Include}(\text{upto}(i, S), R) \wedge 0 \leqslant i \wedge i < m \wedge \text{negb Involve}(\text{nth}(i, S), R) \rightarrow$$
$$\text{negb Include}(\text{upto}(\text{suc } i, \ S), R) \wedge 0 \leqslant i \wedge i < m$$

③ Thirdly, we give the theorem that the postposition assertion is true when the cycle terminates.
Theorem wp3:

$$\text{Include}(\text{upto}(i, \ S), R) \wedge 0 \leqslant i \wedge i < m \wedge m - 1 \leqslant i$$
$$\rightarrow \text{Include}(\text{upto}(m - 1, \ S), R)$$

The theorem of proof of loop termination is relatively simple, which is omitted here.

Step 5. Prove the Theorem

The above theorems can be verified by using the rules of "Induction" and "Apply auto" in the proving tool Coq.

4   Construct Program by Composing Reusable Components

4.1   Simple and Accurate Apla Program Based on Reusable Components

With the support of reusable components, the apla program is simple and accurate. It gave a simplified way to prove correctness.

We formally derive the Prim minimum spanning tree algorithm in [14] and the Dijkstra single-source shortest path algorithm in [16]. With the support of set and graph (graph component included edge and vertex component in it. We will give the formal development of graph component which has non-linear structure in future work) reusable components, we can write the apla program of Prim minimum spanning tree as following:

```
program  prim;
  type vertextype=vertex(char);
 edgetype=edge(char,integer);
var
g:digraph((char,maxnumv),(integer,maxnume));
rr:vertex(char);
other,S:set(vertextype,maxnumv);
i,j,numv,nume:integer;
e,e1:edge(char,integer);
tt:set(edgetype,maxnume);
source:vertex(char);
write("choose the source vertex:");read(source);
tt,S:={ },{source};
other:=g.V-{source};
i:=1;
do i≤#(g.V)-1→i:=i+1;choosemin(e,S,other);
           tt,S,other:=tt∪{e},S∪{e.t},other-{e.t};
od;
i:=0;
writeln("The sequence of choosing vertexes to minispantree:");
do i ≤ #(S)-1→write(S(i).d,",");i:=i+1;od;
writeln("The start vertex,end vertex,weight of all edges in minispantree");
i:=0;
do i≤#(tt)-1→writeln("start vertex:",tt(i).h.d,",end vertex:",tt(i).t.d,",weight:",tt(i).w);i:=i+1;od;
end.
```
   The core of the apla program is just 3 lines codes.

   The core of the apla program is just 3 lines codes.

4.2   Generate Executable Program by Program Generating System

The executable program can be generated automatically from the Apla to C++, JAVA, C#, Vb.net generating system in PAR platform.

   As shown in Fig. 1, we choose the "Apla to C++ program generating system" to generate executable C++ program.

- Firstly, we input the Apla program in 4.1. The algorithm is very short, in the left side of Fig. 1.
- Secondly, we click "Generate" button, the corresponding C++ program which has dozens of codes in the right side of Fig. 1 will be generated.
- Thirdly, we click "Run" button, the C++ program can run immediately and the result is correct.

Fig. 1. The Apla to C++ program generating system

5 Related Works

Abrial introduced the mechanism of abstract machine modelling and refinement in B-Method into structured program generation [9, 10]. Considering the generation of correct-by-construction programs, they suggested to integrate models, refinements and proofs into reusable proof-based patterns for alleviating the task of proof obligation and refinement checking. It was difficult for B-Method to derive formally logically intricate problems.

Smith implemented a number of algorithm design tactics in program generation systems such as KIDS and Designware developed by the Kestrel Institute [12]. The framework raises the level of automation, but the selection of appropriate algorithm design tactics is still difficult.

VDM [8], Z [1] could construct formal specification and proof. But they can't support the complete development steps from specification to executable programs.

Propositional Projection Temporal Logic (PPTL) is a useful logic in the specification and verification of concurrent systems [3, 26–28]. PPTL will be used to verify the concurrent component in our future work.

6 Conclusion

We formally develop and verify the set reusable components in PAR platform. Formal development gives us the formal specification, the recurrence relation of problem-solving sequence, accurate loop invariant. Based on the loop invariant, the correctness of reusable components is verified by proof assistant tool Coq. The merits of this research can be summarized as following:

- The formal development can greatly improve reliability of reusable components. The recurrence relation of problem-solving sequence and loop invariants were formally derived, the concrete executable codes of reusable components are generated with a series of program generating systems.
- Verification programs with Coq could be divided into five steps. It could overcome the error-prone of the traditional manual verification.
- With the support of formally developed and verified reusable components, the reliability of the abstract programs described by software modelling language Apla could be promoted.

We will do the research continuously and apply PAR method and PAR platform to develop more safety critical systems in industrial application.

Acknowledgments. This work was supported by the National Nature Science Foundation of China (Grant No. 61662036,No.61862033), the Natural Science Foundation of Jiangxi Province.

References

1. Abrial, J.R., Hayes, I.J., Hoare, T.: The Z Notation: A Reference Manual, 2nd edn. Oriel College, Oxford (1998)
2. Szyperski, C.: Component Software: Beyond Object-Oriented Programming, 2nd edn. Addison-Wesley, Boston (2002)
3. Tian, C., Duan, Z., Zhang, N.: An efficient approach for abstraction-refinement in model checking. Theoret. Comput. Sci. **461**, 76–85 (2012)
4. Dijkstra, E.W.: A Discipline of Programming. Springer, Heidelberg (1994)
5. Gries, D., Schneider, F.B.: A Logical Approach to Discrete Math. Springer, Heidelberg (1981)
6. He, J., Liu, Z., Li, X.: Component calculus. In: Workshop on Formal Aspects of Component Software (FACS 2003), Satellite Workshop of FME 2003, Pisa, Italy (2003)
7. Jifeng, H., Li, X., Liu, Z.: Component-based software engineering. In: Van hung, D., Wirsing, M. (eds.) ICTAC 2005. LNCS, vol. 3722, pp. 70–95. Springer, Heidelberg (2005). https://doi.org/10.1007/11560647_5
8. Jones, C.B.: Systematic Software Development Using VDM, 2nd edn. Prentice Hall, Upper Saddle River (1990)
9. Morgan, C.C.: Programming from Specification. Prentice Hall, Upper Saddle River (1994)
10. Schneider, S.: The B-Method: An Introduction. Palgrave, Addison Wesley (2001)
11. Sommerville, I.: Software Engineering, 9th edn. Pearson Education, London (2011)
12. Smith, D.R.: Designware: software development by refinement. In: Proceedings of the Eight International Conference on Category Theory and Computer Science, Edinburgh, September 1999
13. Wu, G., Xue, J.: PAR method and PAR platform used in development process of software outsourcing. Comput. Modernization **11**, 042 (2013)
14. Xue, J.: A unified approach for developing efficient algorithmic programs. J. Comput. Sci. Technol. **12**(4) (1997)
15. Xue, J.: Two new strategies for developing loop invariants and their applications. J. Comput. Sci. Technol. **8**(2), 147–154 (1993)
16. Xue, J.: Formal derivation of graph algorithmic programs using partition-and-recur. J. Comput. Sci. Technol. **13**(6), 553–561 (1998)

17. Xue, J.: Methods of Programming. Higher Education Press, Beijing (2002)
18. Xue, J.: New concept of loop invariant and its application. In: The 3rd Colloquium on Logic in Engineering Dependable Software, Nanchang, China (2013)
19. Xue, J.: PAR method and its supporting platform. In: Proceedings of AWCVS 2006, Macao, 29–31 October 2006
20. Xue, J., Davis, R.: A simple program whose derivation and proof is also. In: Proceedings of the First IEEE International Conference on Formal Engineering Method (ICFEM 1997). IEEE CS Press (1997)
21. Xue, J.: Implementation of model-driven development using PAR. In: Keynote Speech on the 6th International Workshop on Harnessing Theories for Tool Support in Software, Nanchang, China (2013)
22. Zuo, Z., You, Z., Xue, J.: Derivation and formal proof of non-recursive post-order binary tree traversal algorithm. Comput. Eng. Sci. **32**(3), 119–125 (2010)
23. The Coq proof assistant [EB /OL] (2014). http://coq.inria.fr/
24. Bertot, Y., Casteran, P.: Interactive Theorem Proving and Program Development-Coq'Art: The Calculus of Inductive Constructions. Springer, London (2004). https://doi.org/10.1007/978-3-662-07964-5
25. The Coq Development Team. The Coq proof assistant reference manual-version V81 0 (2004)
26. Duan, Z.: Temporal Logic and Temporal Logic Programming. Science Press, Beijing (2005)
27. Duan, Z., Tian, C., Zhang, L.: A decision procedure for propositional projection temporal logic with infinite models. Acta Informatica **45**(1), 43–78 (2008)
28. Duan, Z., Yang, X., Koutny, M.: Framed temporal logic programming. Sci. Comput. Program. **70**(1), 31–61 (2008)

A New Mutant Generation Algorithm Based on Basic Path Coverage for Mutant Reduction

Xu Qin[1,2(✉)], Shaoying Liu[1], and Zhang Tao[2]

[1] Faculty of Computer and Information Sciences, Hosei University, Tokyo, Japan
qin.xu.6d@stu.hosei.ac.jp
[2] School of Software Northwestern, Polytechnical University, Xi'an, China

Abstract. Mutation testing is a fault-based testing technique that can be used to measure the adequacy of a test set, but its application usually incurs a high cost due to the necessity of generating and executing a great number of mutants. How to reduce the cost still remains a challenge for research. In this paper, we present a new mutant generation algorithm based on a basic path coverage that can help reduce mutants. The algorithm is characterized by implementing a basic path segments identification criterion for determining appropriate program points at which faults are inserted and a mutant generation priority criterion for selecting proper mutant operators to make a fault for insertion. We discuss the algorithm by analysing how the two criteria are realized based on analysing the control flow graph of the program and applying effective mutation operators on the appropriate statements in the relevant path segments. We also present an automated mutation testing tool that supports the proposed approach, and a small experiment to evaluate our tool by comparing it with a traditional mutation testing method on six programs. The result of the experiment suggests that the proposed method can significantly reduce the number of mutants and improve the efficiency of mutation testing.

Keywords: Mutation testing · Path coverage · Mutant reduction

1 Introduction

Mutation testing [1] is a effectively white-box testing technique which can be used to evaluate and improve test suite's adequacy, and predict the possible faults present in our system. As a testing technique, mutation testing can truly reveal various flaws of software. But in industry the mutation testing technique has not been widely applied [2,3]. The main reason is that mutation testing is so time-consuming (a large number of mutants and long execution time).

In recent years, many researches have been carried out in order to apply mutation testing in practical application, including mutant random selection [10], high-order mutant [12], mutant clustering methods [13], selective mutation

© Springer Nature Switzerland AG 2020
H. Miao et al. (Eds.): SOFL+MSVL 2019 Workshop, LNCS 12028, pp. 167–186, 2020.
https://doi.org/10.1007/978-3-030-41418-4_13

operators [11], mutant detection optimization [18], mutant compilation optimization [19], and parallel execution of mutants [20].

Although the above mutant reduction methods have been used, there is little work on combining the mutation testing with the conventional path coverage testing. In our research, an algorithm for generating mutants based on the basic path coverage is proposed. We first introduce the criteria for identifying the path segments where faults need to be inserted and the mutant generation priority criteria for producing mutants. We then present a mutant generation algorithm under the constraint of these criteria. The main idea is to insert simple syntactic changes on each basic path of the given program to produce mutants. Combining the traditional path testing coverage with the mutation testing can not only assess the efficiency of the ability of test suite for detecting some possible faults, but also achieve basic path coverage which can effectively improve the effectiveness of given test case set.

It is difficult to do mutation testing without a software tool. So we present an a mutation testing tool that supports the proposed approach, which can generates and executes the mutants automatically. We design three components for our tool: the mutant generator, the mutant viewer, and the test executor. The mutant generator component generates mutants automatically by using the effective mutation operators. It takes Java files as input and a set of mutants as output. The mutant viewer lists the information of our generated mutants. And it also show the original code and the code of each mutant, which can help us to know which part was changed. The test executor run the test case set on generated mutants and shows the test result by analyzing the mutation score of our test case set. All this three components provide GUI for testers to use. We have carried out an experiment on the tool for validating the effectiveness of our proposed approach. From the result we can see that our method can significantly improve the efficiency of mutation testing by reducing mutants but also with high mutation score.

Here lists our contributions:

- Proposing a new mutant generation algorithm by combing the mutation testing and basic path coverage testing for reducing generated mutants.
- Designing and implementing a mutation testing tool to validate our proposed method.

The rest of the paper has the following organization. Section 2 introduces the related work on reducing the mutation testing cost. Section 3 gives some definitions and discuses the implementation process of our proposed mutant generation algorithm based on basic path coverage. Section 4 designs and implements a mutation testing tool to support the proposed approach. Section 5 presents an empirical research to evaluate the efficiency of our proposed method. The conclusion of this paper and the future direction of our research are shown in Sect. 6.

2   Background on Mutation Testing and Program Control Flow Graph

In this section, we introduce some basic concepts used in our discussions throughout this paper. They are known as mutation testing, program control flow graph, and independent path.

2.1   Mutation Testing

The mutation testing is a fault-based software testing technique with two steps. The first step is to use a specific mutation operator to simulate a particular type of error and implant the error into the source program. The second step is to explore the source program with a given test set, and assess the adequacy of the test set by the mutation score.

The traditional mutation testing process is described below, Fig. 1 graphically shows a traditional mutation process.

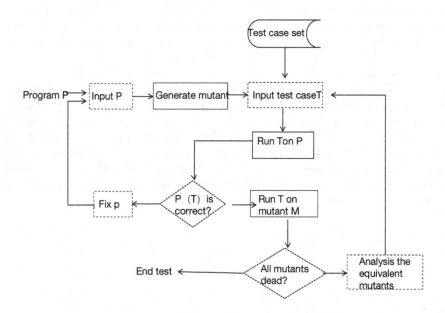

Fig. 1. Traditional mutation testing process

- Input the original program P and use the mutation operators to generate mutants M.
- Input the given test cases and then run the test case on P to get a expected result.

- Run the test case T on each generated mutant. And then compare the result with expected result. If the two is different, we can say the mutant is killed, else the mutant is marked as being alive.
- After running all test cases on mutants, we compute a mutation score. The mutation score is the ratio of killed mutants as a percentage of all mutants. The higher mutation score is, the more mutants are killed. So we need to improve the mutation score to 1.00, suggesting that we killed all the generated mutants. If the test case set can kill all the mutants, we can say it is enough for our testing.
- If the mutation score meets the requirements, the mutation testing ends. Otherwise, the tester need to add more test cases to kill the live mutants. Then we repeat adding new test cases, run the test case and compute a new mutation score until we get a high mutation score.

2.2 Program Control Flow Graph

Program control flow graph is an abstract representation of a process or program. In computer science, a control-flow graph lists all the control flows and shows all the possible path when we execute the program. It was first proposed by Frances. E. Allen in 1970 [5]. The program control flow graph is defined as follows:

A control flow graph, can be represented by $CFG = (B, E, nentry, nexit)$ where B is a node (represents some statements of program P) in the graph and E is edges in CFG [5]. If there is a directed edge goes from node b_i to node b_j, we can say the ordered pair (b_i, b_j) of nodes is an edge. Nentry and nexit are the entry and exit node of the program, respectively. It has a unique starting node START and a unique ending node STOP. There can be at most two direct successors for each node in the CFG. For a node with two direct successors, its outgoing edge has the attribute 'T' or 'F', for a node with only one direct successor, its outgoing edge has the default attribute 'T'. And any node N in the CFG has a path from START to N to STOP.

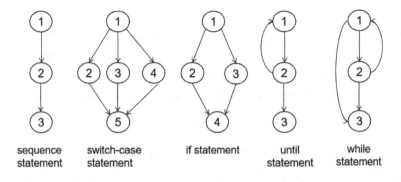

Fig. 2. The CFG of the basic program structures

A node is a linear sequence of program statements, which may have some predecessor nodes and many successor nodes. A START node doesn't have predecessor node and a STOP node doesnt have successor node.

The CFG of the basic program structures are shown in Fig. 2: each statements in our program under test is represented by a node in CFG. Then, we can get all the independent paths (basic paths) of our program by tracing the flow. An independent path or basic path means that at least one new processing statement or a newly determined program path is introduced compared to other independent paths. If we go thorough each basic path, we can say that we have executed all the statement in our program at least once and each basic path has been judged to 'TRUE' or 'FALSE'.

3 Our Proposed Mutant Generation Algorithm

In this part, we propose a new mutant generation algorithm, which aims to generate a less mutants that can simulate software defects. Based on the selective mutation technique, this algorithm uses mutation points as research objects and selects appropriate program path segments and target sentences for mutation on each basic path. The proposed algorithm combines mutation testing and basic path coverage testing.

3.1 Preliminary

In order to facilitate the description of the algorithm, we first give the following definitions:

Definition 1 (Immediate predecessor node and successor node). A immediate predecessor node n_h of a node n_i in is a node that satisfy $P_G(n_i) = n_h|(n_h, n_i) \in E$. ($P_G(n_i)$ means the immediate predecessor node of node n_i; E is a set of directed edges in G.)

A immediate successor node n_j of a node n_i in is a node that satisfy $S_G(n_i) = n_j|(n_i, n_j) \in E$. ($S_G(n_i)$ means the immediate successor node of node n_i.)

Definition 2 (Leaf node, sequence node and selection node). A leaf node n_i is a node that satisfy $S_G(n_i) = \emptyset$ and $\exists!P_G(n_i)$. It means a leaf node only have one input edge and no output edge.

A sequence node n_i is a node that satisfy $\exists!P_G(n_i)$ and $\exists!S_G(n_i)$. It means a sequence node only has one input edge and one output edge.

A selection node n_i is a node containing a condition. It means a selection node have more than one output edge. Note that compound Boolean expressions generate at least two predicate node in control flow graph.

Definition 3 (Sequence path-segment, Unique path-segment). A sequence path-segment $sp = (n_1, n_2, ...n_n)$ is a path segment that the first node is a selection node and the other nodes n_i of sp is either a sequence node or a leaf node.

A unique path-segment is a path-segment that satisfy $ups_i = (N_i, E_i)|E_i \notin \forall ups_j$. It means that any edges of a ups is unique from other unique path-segments.

3.2   Recognition of Target Path Segments to Be Mutated

In order to generate mutants, we need to find the target mutation path segments and then select the target mutation sentence in these segments to generate the mutant using the appropriate mutation operator. Here, we propose a identification criterion for path segments to be inserted into error. The purpose is to select the unique path segments in the basic path for error insertion, ensure the basic path coverage, and make the mutation of each path as independent as possible. And also a mutation sentence selection priority criteria is proposed to select the node with high importance as the target sentence, which choose the sentence that has a greater impact on the execution result of each path in the basic path. For each criterion, a simple example will be given.

Fault Insertion Path Segments Identification Rule 1 (R1)
If there exists a leaf node n_i in the control flow graph, then trace back to its immediate predecessor node n_h, if n_h is a sequence node, then continue to trace back to its immediate predecessor node until we meet a non sequence node n_a, and mark this sequence-path segment $sp = (n_a, ..., n_h, n_i)$ as a path segment to be inserted into fault.(a fault is a simple syntactic change).

The following figure Fig. 3 illustrates the application of R1: node 5 is a leaf node and trace back to its immediate predecessor node 4 and continue to trace back to the non sequence node 2. Then marks the sequence-path segment $sp = (n_2, n_4, n_5)$ as a path segment for fault insertion.

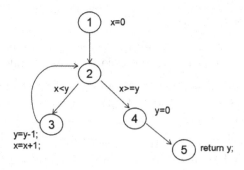

Fig. 3. A example for identification rule 1

Fault Insertion Path Segments Identification Rule 2 (R2)
Find all the unique path-segment ups $ups_i = (N_i, E_i)|E_i \notin \forall ups_j$ in each basic paths in the control flow graph CFG and mark this ups as a path segment. If

there is a loop structure in the program, the basic path only includes no loop and one loop.

Figure 4 illustrates the application of the rule R2: we can find all the basic paths, path1:1-7; path2:1-2-3-6-7; path3:1-2-4-6-7; path4:1-2-4-5-6-7, and then find the unique path-segment ups1:1-7; ups2:2-3-6; ups3:4-6; ups4:-4-5-6. These unique path-segments are path segments suitable for fault insertion.

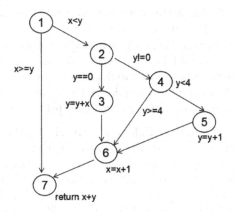

Fig. 4. A example for identification rule 2

3.3 Recognition of Target Path Segments to Be Mutated

The statements in a program are not purely independent, they have a certain relationship. Each statement has different effects on the execution of different paths. Using the relationship between them, selecting important sentences for mutation testing to generate mutants can reduce testing cost and improve testing efficiency.

This part proposes a criterion for selecting target sentences to be mutated based on our mutation sentence selection priority criteria. Different from the traditional mutation test method, we first analyze the sentence corresponding to each node in the basic path, and select the node with high importance as the target sentence. First establish the evaluation index, then set the sentence priority, and finally propose our mutation sentence selection priority criteria to generate mutants for the target mutation path segments in the previous section.

Evaluation Index: First, consider whether the node where the statement is located will cause a change in the execution path. Based on our previous definition of different nodes in the path. Different nodes have different effects on each path. Among them, the sequence node (expression statement) has the least impact on the execution path. It only affects the execution results of this path and has no effect on other paths. The second is the single node (return value statement), which mainly affects the return value. Finally, the selection node (loop statements, conditional statements) have the greatest impact on the program, it may cause the execution path to change.

Next consider the number of variables in the statement. In general, more variables have a greater impact on program execution. So it makes sense to consider how many variables the target statement contains.

Set the Statement Priority: Our goal is to select the statements that will affect the execution results of this path but have less impact on the execution results of other paths. Through the analysis of the above evaluation indicators, we can know that evaluation index 1 is negatively correlated with our goal, so our priority setting should be: sequence node >single node >select node. Evaluation index 2 is positively correlated with our goal, so the priority should be: statements include with more variables >statements with less variables.

Then propose our mutation sentence selection priority criteria:

Mutation Sentence Selection Priority Criteria 1 (P1)
For each path-segment of path-segments set $ps = (ps_1, ps_2, ..., ps_n)$, if there is a sequence node n_i at the ps_i, we insert the fault at the statement of n_i. And if $n_i = (s_1, s_2, ..., s_n)$ (s means statement), we insert a fault at the first statement.

As shown in Fig. 4: for the path segment ps1:2-3-6, using P1 we find a single node 3, and use the appropriate mutation operator AOM to generate the mutant ,the statement 'y = y + x' of the node3 will be mutated to 'y = y − x'.

Mutation Sentence Selection Priority Criteria 2 (P2)
For each path-segment of path-segments set $ps = (ps_1, ps_2, ..., ps_n)$, if there is no sequence node and there is a selection node (predicate operation) n_i at the ps_i, use the appropriate mutation operator to insert the simple syntactic change (fault) at the selection node n_i.

As shown in Fig. 4: for the path segment ps2:4-6, using P2 we find a selection node 4, and generate the mutant 'if$(y \leq 4)$' for the node 4 statement 'if$(y < 4)$' using the appropriate mutation operator CBM.

Mutation Sentence Selection Priority Criteria 3 (P3)
If there is no sequence node and no selection node in the ps_i, inserted fault in the first statement of remaining nodes which are suitable to be inserted fault.

3.4   The Mutant Generation Algorithm

Applying the Fault Insertion basic path segments Identification Criterion for deter- mining appropriate program segments at which faults are inserted and a Mutation Sentence Selection Priority Criterion for selecting proper statements to make a fault for insertion above, we propose an algorithm whose input is a program and the output is a mutant set.

The algorithm is shown as follows: first, draw the control flow graph CFG of the original program. Then, using the Fault Insertion basic path segments Identification Criterion to determine appropriate program points at which faults are

Algorithm 1. Basic Path Coverage based on Mutant Generation Algorithm

Input:
    Original program, P;
Output:
    Mutant set, M;
 1: Function mutant-generation(program p) {
 2:   Draw CFG for each functions in original program p;
 3:   Set FPS=∅;
 4: **for** each $CFG_i \in CFG$ **do**
 5:     initialize $FPS_i = \emptyset$;
 6:     **if** $\exists SPinCFG_i$ **then**
 7:       add sp into FPS_i, $FPS_i \rightarrow FPS_i + sp$;
 8:     **end if**
 9:     **for** each CFG_iinCFG **do**
10:       find all the unique path-segment ups;
11:       add ups into FPS_i, $FPS_i \rightarrow FPS_i + ups$;
12:     **end for**
13: **end for**
14: add FPS_i into FPS, $FPS = (FPS_1, FPS_2, ..., FPS_n)$;
15: **for** each ps in EPS **do**
16:     Set M=∅;
17:     **if** $\exists sequencenode$ **then**
18:       generate mutant m_i from the sequence node statement s_i for fault insertion;
19:       add m_i into M, $M \rightarrow M + m_i$;
20:     **else if** $\exists selectionnode$ **then**
21:       generate mutant m_j from the selection node statement s_j for fault insertion;
22:       add m_j into M, $M \rightarrow M + m_j$;
23:     **else'**
24:       generate mutant m_k from the selection node statement s_k for fault insertion;
25:       add m_k into M, $M \rightarrow M + m_k$;
26:     **end if**
27: **end for**
28: Return M;
29: }

inserted by analyzing the program control flow graph(CFG) and find the appropriate fault insertion path segments in the CFG. Finally, using the Mutation Sentence Selection Priority Criterion to generate a mutant at the appropriate statement of the path segments we marked above. The steps of this algorithm are shown as follows:

Step 1. For the original program p, we divide it into some program modules or functions $p = (f_1, f_2, ..., f_n)$ and draw a CFG for each module or function $CFG = (CFG_1, CFG_2, ..., CFG_n)$.

Step 2. Do analysis for CFG_i, find the appropriate fault insertion basic path-segments FPS_i in the CFG.

- First Initialize FPS_i to empty, if the CFG have leaf node, apply the Fault Insertion basic path segments Identification Rule 1 (R1) to find a sequence path-segment sp, add sp into FPS_i;
- Then apply the rule 2 to find unique path-segments *ups* on the CFG, add each *ups* into FPS_i;
- Then we can get a fault insertion path-segment set $FPS_i = (sp_1, ups_1, ups_2, ..., ups_n)$.

Step 3. Repeat step 2 for each CFG_i to get the total fault insertion path-segment set $FPS = (FPS_1, FPS_2, ..., FPS_n)$ for the original program.

Step 4. Do analysis for each path-segment ps_i in the fault insertion path-segment set FPS using the Mutation Sentence Selection Priority Criterion above and get a mutants set M_i.

- apply P1, generate mutant for a sequence node statement using appropriate mutation operator. For example, MAO, BOC, VMC;
- apply P2, generate mutant for a predicate node statement;
- apply P3, generate mutant for the first statement of remaining node that can be inserted into fault.

Step 5. For each path-segment ps_i in the fault insertion path-segments set FPS, Repeat the above step (4) to get the mutants set $M = M_1, M_2, ..., M_n$ of the original program P.

4   Tool Design and Implementation

Our proposed algorithm is aiming at reducing the cost of mutation testing by generating less but effectively mutants. In order to validate the efficiency and effectiveness (accuracy of mutation score), we implement an automated mutation testing tool to support our algorithm. It takes the program and test case set as input, does the mutation testing automatically, and finally produces a analysis report to show the test result.

The main functions of this automated mutation testing tool are using effective mutation operators to generate mutants (mutant generation), executing the given test case set on the mutants (mutant execution), showing the result and report of mutation testing (result analysis). Figure 5 shows the overall structure of our mutation testing tool. It is composed of 3 components.

The mutant generator generates mutants by using the effective mutation operators. It generate mutants for selected java files. The GUI for the mutant generator can help us to choose which project and which files under test. The mutant viewer component lists the detailed information for each generated mutant including operatorType, lineNumber, description and so on. And it also shows the code of original program and mutant which help us to know which statement of program under test is mutated and design test cases to kill the generated mutants. The test executor runs the test case set on generated mutants and reports the testing result by computing the mutation score of given test case set.

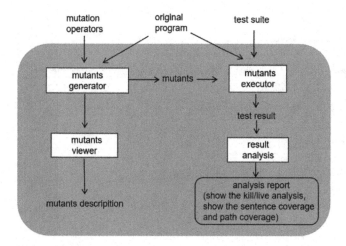

Fig. 5. The overall structure of the automated mutation testing tool.

4.1   Mutants Generator

According to the above design, we implement the tool using Java Swing and the user interface are shown as follows. Figure 6 shows how the Mutants Generator works. We can select the project and a set of Java files under test to create mutants, view the description of applied mutation operators, and press the Generate button to prompt the tool to generate mutants. The Mutants Viewer panel will show the information for each mutant after generation.

The specific steps are as follows:

- Step1, push the 'search' button to select the java project to be tested.
- Step2, view mutation operators description.
- Step3, select the Java files to test and the user can push the 'ALL' button to choose all the files listed.
- Step4, push the 'Generate' button to generate mutants for the selected java files.

4.2   Mutants Viewer

When generating a mutant, we produce a mutant description, including the operator type, className, description, lineNumber. This description details the alternate operations applied in each fault insertion statement we marked before. Using this, the tester can easily position the mutation statement and the mutation operator type which is beneficial to the later mutant viewing and result statistics.

The Mutants Viewer pane in Fig. 7 lists all the generated mutants and shows some detailed description of each mutant. It help us to analyze mutants by displaying the information of each mutant and which statement of given program

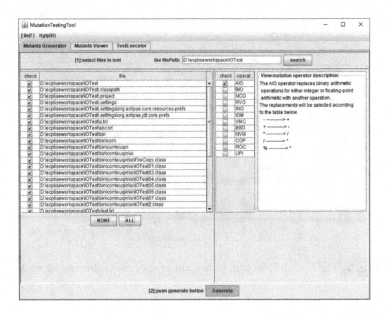

Fig. 6. The Mutants Generator GUI.

is changed by the mutant. It is divided into two parts. The upper part is a mutants list which shows a brief descriptions of the each mutant including a operatorType, className, description and lineNumber. The lower part shows the original code and the mutant. By choosing a mutant in the mutants list of the upper part, the lower part will show the original java file and the mutant, which helps testers to know which statement is mutated, design test cases to kill mutants which are difficult to kill.

4.3   Test Executor

Figure 8 shows the GUI of the Test Executor pane. It runs the test case set on mutants and reports the testing result by analysing the mutation score. Lower left part shows the number of mutants generated by each operator. The lower right part shows the results of mutation testing and the number of live mutants and dead mutants. The test case can be created or provided by testers. The specific step is as follow:

First, the testers need to select the class and the test case set and then push the 'Run' button to run the test cases on the mutants.

When the test is finished, the OP Number panel will show the mutants number of each operator and the mutants result panel will show the mutation testing result including the mutation score and the number of killed mutants, live mutants and the total mutants. Also, the tester can export the result into a

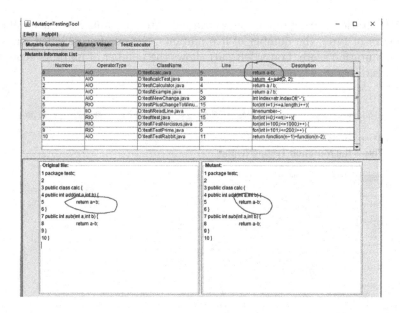

Fig. 7. The Mutants Viewer GUI.

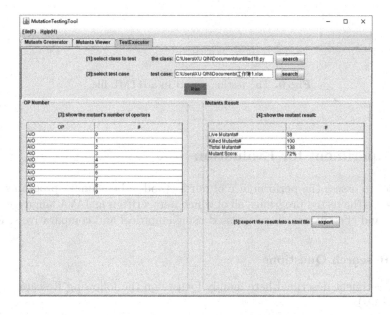

Fig. 8. The Test Executor GUI.

HTML file, which shows test results more clearly and can be saved as important test document. Push the 'export' button in the test executor panel, a test report will be generated. Figure 9 shows the report.

The mutation testing report shows the generated mutants list, the number of each operator type, the number of live mutants, the number of killed mutants, and the mutation score. Lower left part shows the number of mutants generated by different operator type.

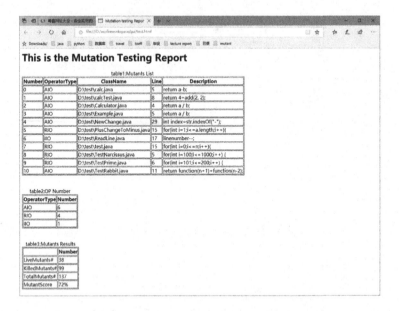

Fig. 9. The testing report in a HTML file.

5   Experiment for Evaluation

In order to assess the performance of our method, 6 benchmark programs were selected as the tested programs, all of which were written in JAVA language. Feasibility and effectiveness were assessed using empirical and comparative studies.

5.1   Research Questions

The experiment described here mainly focuses on the following Research Questions (RQs):

RQ 1. Can our algorithm proposed in this paper effectively reduce the number of mutants? (by calculating the reduction rate of mutants)

The effectiveness of this method in reducing mutants was evaluated by comparing the number of mutants in the proposed algorithm of the selected programs with the number of mutants in traditional method and selective mutation technique using the same mutation operators. We proposed a mutant reduction rate to assess the ability of the mutant reduction. The mutant reduction rate is:

$$MRR = \frac{M_t - M_p}{M_t} \tag{1}$$

M_t: mutant's number generated by traditional method, M_p: mutant's number generated by other methods. The MRR shows that the higher the reduction rate is, the better the effectiveness of this method in reducing mutants becomes.

RQ 2. Can a test case set that kills mutants generated by the proposed algorithm be able to kill mutants of traditional methods?

The set of traditional mutants was tested with the test cases that killed the mutants generated by this algorithm, and the results were expressed as mutation score:

$$MS = \frac{M_K}{M_a - M_e} * 100 \tag{2}$$

M_k: killed mutant's number, M_a: all generated mutant's number, M_e: all equivalent mutant's number.

The test case set used in this paper's experimental evaluation is constructed using traditional test case generation algorithms, such as boundary value analysis, statement coverage, and branch coverage.

5.2   Experiment Subjects

Table 1 shows the detailed description of each experiment subjects. We choose those programs which are popular used in other mutation testing researches. The 'ID' and 'Test Subject' show the names of each experiment subjects and the 'line of code' shows the line number of each code and 'function program' record the function of each program.

Table 1. The description of each experiment subject.

ID	Test subjects	Line of code	Program function description
J1	Trityp	36	Judge the triangle type
J2	Mid	26	Calculate the median of three integers
J3	Quadratic	25	Finding the root of a quadratic equation
J4	Bubble sort	19	Bubble Sorting
J5	Cal	46	Compute days between two days
J6	MyCalendar	50	Ask for a calendar of a certain month

5.3   Experiment Result Analysis

As shown in Table 2 below, by comparing the number of mutants generated by this algorithm and number of mutants generated by selective mutation (SM) with the number of mutants generated by traditional non-optimized methods, we clearly see that the both the number of mutants generated by our proposed method and the number of mutants generated by selective mutation were significantly reduced. For example, the J2 program is reduced from 63 to 35 and 18, and the J6 program is reduced from 66 to 31 and 19.

Table 2. The reduction rate of selective mutation and our algorithm.

ID	Number of mutants in traditional method	Number of mutants in SM	Reduction rate of SM	Number of mutants in our method	Reduction rate of our method
J1	39	23	43.6%	9	76.9%
J2	63	35	44.4%	18	71%
J3	67	34	49.3%	17	74.6%
J4	42	26	38.1%	9	78.6%
J5	40	25	37.5%	9	77.5%
J6	66	31	53.3%	19	71.2%
Average			44.4%		74.96%

In the selective mutation, J6 has the largest reduction rate of 53.3% in 6 programs, and the average reduction rate of 6 programs is 44.4%. In our algorithm, J4 has the largest reduction rate of 78.6% in 6 programs, and the average reduction rate of 6 programs is 74.96%. We can see that all the procedures using our proposed algorithm achieve higher reduction rates, and the reduction rates are higher than the reduction rate of selective mutation, which indicates that our proposed method is better than selective mutation in reducing the number of mutants.

The sufficient test case set for the algorithm proposed in this paper is applied to all the mutants generated in traditional mutation method and the mutation score is calculated. The calculated mutation score finally indicates the effectiveness of the proposed method. The following Table 3 shows the detection results of the test case set that can detect the mutants generated by the proposed method on the traditional mutants set. The mutation score is used as the evaluation index.

From Table 3, we can see that the mutation score of the test case set that is 100% sufficient for the proposed algorithm can reach 90.6% on average, and the lowest one is 87.5%. The J2 program has the highest mutation score of 93.7%, and the J5 program has the lowest mutation score of 87.5%. The experimental results show that for all test subjects, the average mutation score exceeds 90.6%, and we only use a small number of mutants (74.96%).

We also analyzed the number of mutants per mutation operator. From the result we can see that the number of MAO replacement mutants is relatively

Table 3. The reduction rate of each experimental subject.

ID	Number of mutants in traditional method	Number of mutants in proposed method	Reduction rate
J1	39	35	89.7%
J2	63	59	93.7%
J3	67	62	92.5%
J4	42	37	89%
J5	40	35	87.5%
J6	66	60	91%
Average			90.6%

large, while others are relatively small. For the program J1, the number of BOC, NCO is very large and number of the RVO, VMC is zero. Although some operators is used less but we can not say it is useful because those operators are designed to find specific faults which are not shown in our experiment subjects.

The proposed algorithm optimizes traditional mutation method by selecting the appropriate mutation point. Through the analysis of the above results, it can be seen that our algorithm can generate a less number of mutants with a high mutation score, which can significantly reduce the cost of mutation testing while maintaining the effectiveness.

5.4   Result Validity Analysis

As with other case studies, when discussing the validity of the experimental results in this paper, some restrictive factors in the experimental process must be considered, including the following three cases:

- In this experiment, only 6 tested instances were selected, and it is not certain that all the tested instances will have the same experimental results;
- The number of test cases for elections is less than 100. It is uncertain whether the reduction efficiency of test cases will increase for a larger number of test cases;
- All the mutation operators were not selected in the experiment, and there was no manual analysis of whether there were equivalent mutants in the unkilled mutant, so the calculated MS value may be too small.

6   Related Work

In recent years, in order to apply mutation testing in industry and improve the efficiency of mutation testing, many research have been carried out. Here, we briefly show the research progress of test optimization techniques about reducing mutant's number.

Acree [10] proposed a method called mutant sampling, which select a certain proportion of mutants randomly from all mutants generated for mutation testing. This way can effectively reduce the mutant but with lower mutation score.

Hussian [13] proposed a method called the method of Mutant Clustering which classify mutants with similar characteristics, and then randomly select a part of variants from each class for mutation testing. Experiment shows that the clustering method can achieve a good reduction of mutants without affecting the validity of the mutation testing.

Mathur [11] proposed a method which select partial mutation operators applied for mutation testing. This method of generating fewer mutants using a small number of mutation operators is called constraint mutation. Offutt et al. further proposed a method of "selective mutation".

Jia and Harman [12] introduced a Higher Order Mutation method. That is, a high-order mutation consists of multiple single-order mutations, and the use of higher-order mutants can effectively speed up mutation testing.

Delamaro et al. [16] studied the validity of a mutation testing using only one mutation operator. The experimental results show that the SDL operator is probably the most useful mutation operator among all the mutation operators.

Yao et al.'s [15] research shows that some mutation operators are very possible to create equivalent mutants, but the resulting stubborn mutants (which are difficult to detect, but not equivalent mutants) are rare; others are susceptible to stubborn mutants and the generated equivalent mutants are few, so when generating mutants, different selection priorities can be set for the mutation operators.

Although the above mutant reduction technology can reduce the number of mutants, it can not guarantee the path coverage of the program, which affects the sufficiency evaluation ability of the test case set. In our research, a mutant generation algorithm based on basic path coverage and control flow analysis is used to select the appropriate sentence segment to be inserted into error of the basic path, which reduce the number of mutants and realize the basic path coverage. It not only assess whether the test case set can kill the mutants, but also assess whether the test case set can achieve basic path coverage.

7   Conclusion

Mutation testing is widely used to evaluate test case sufficiency and evaluate the effectiveness of software testing techniques. However, a large number of mutants affect the efficiency of mutation testing and limit the application of mutation testing in software testing practice.

In this paper, a mutant generation method based on basic path coverage is proposed for reducing generated mutant's number in mutation testing. Different from the previous methods, by analyzing the control flow structure and basic path of the source program, an identification of path segments suitable for fault insertion and a priority criteria for generating mutants are proposed. By using these criteria to select some appropriate statements for mutation operation, the mutants needed to kill is reduced and the coverage of the basic path is achieved, which improves the effectiveness of the mutation testing. In order to evaluate the efficiency (mutant's number) and effectiveness (accuracy of mutation score) of our proposed method, we implement an automated mutation testing tool to support our algorithm. Our method was applied to 6 tested programs, and the results showed that using the method of this paper, the high mutation score can be maintained while reducing the number of mutants.

This work has opened up a research direction of mutation test optimization technology. The next steps include using more efficient mutation operators to generate mutants, using a larger industrial application sample program to evaluate the effectiveness of the method, and exploring other more efficient mutant reduction techniques.

References

1. Jia, Y., Harman, M.: An analysis and survey of the development of mutation testing. IEEE Trans. Softw. Eng. **37**(5), 649–678 (2011)
2. Offutt, A.J., Untch, R.H.: Mutation 2000: Uniting the Orthogonal. Mutation Testing for the New Century. Kluwer Academic Publishers, Berlin (2001)
3. Just, R., Ernst, M.D., Fraser, G.: Efficient mutation analysis by propagating and partitioning infected execution states (2014)
4. Namin, A.S., Andrews, J.H., Murdoch, D.J.: Sufficient mutation operators for measuring test effectiveness. In: ACM Press the 13th International Conference on Software Engineering - ICSE 2008 - Leipzig, Germany, 10–18 May 2008, p. 351 (2008)
5. Allen, F.E.: Control flow analysis. ACM Sigplan Not. **5**(7), 1–19 (1970)
6. Zapata, F., Akundi, A., Pineda, R., Smith, E.: Basis path analysis for testing complex system of systems. Procedia Comput. Sci. **20**(Complete), 256–261 (2013)
7. Papadakis, M., Malevris, N.: Automatically performing weak mutation with the aid of symbolic execution, concolic testing and search-based testing. Softw. Qual. J. **19**(4), 691–723 (2011)
8. Eason, G., Noble, B., Sneddon, I.N.: On certain integrals of Lipschitz-Hankel type involving products of Bessel functions. Phil. Trans. Roy. Soc. London **A247**, 529–551 (1955)
9. Fraser, G., Zeller, A.: Mutation-driven generation of unit tests and Oracles. IEEE Trans. Softw. Eng. **38**(2), 278–292 (2012)
10. Acree, A.T.: On mutation. Ph.D. Dissertation, Georgia Institute of Technology (1980)
11. Mathur, A.P.: Performance, effectiveness, and reliability issues in software testing. In: International Computer Software & Applications Conference. IEEE (1991)
12. Jia, Y., Harman, M.: Constructing Subtle Faults Using Higher Order Mutation Testing. In: 2008 Eighth IEEE International Working Conference on Source Code Analysis and Manipulation. IEEE (2008)
13. Hussain, S.: Mutation clustering. Ph.D. Dissertation, King's College, London, UK (2008)
14. Zhang, J.: Scalability studies on selective mutation testing. In: 2015 IEEE/ACM 37th IEEE International Conference on Software Engineering (ICSE), Florence, Italy, 5–24 May 2015, pp. 851–854 (2015)

15. Yao, X., Harman, M., Jia, Y.: A study of equivalent and stubborn mutation opera-tors using human analysis of equivalence. In: Proceedings of the 36th International Conference on Software Engineering - ICSE 2014, Hyderabad, India, 31 May–07 June 2014, pp. 919–930 (2014)

16. Delamaro, M.E., Li, N., Offutt, J., et al.: Experimental evaluation of SDL and one-op mutation for C. In: IEEE Seventh International Conference on Software Testing. IEEE (2014)

17. Hutchins, M., Foster, H., Goradia, T., et al.: Experiments on the effectiveness of dataflow- and control-flow-based test adequacy criteria. In: International Confer-ence on Software Engineering. IEEE (1994)

18. Harman, M., Jia, Y., Mateo, R.P., et al.: Angels and monsters: an empirical inves-tigation of potential test effectiveness and efficiency improvement from strongly subsuming higher order mutation. In: Proceedings of the 29th ACM/IEEE Inter-national Conference on Automated Software Engineering. ACM (2014)

19. Girgis, M.R., Woodward, M.R.: An integrated system for program testing using weak mutation and data flow analysis. In: International Conference on Software Engineering. IEEE Computer Society Press (1985)

20. Krauser, E.W., Mathur, A.P., Rego, V.J.: High performance software testing on SIMD machines. IEEE Trans. Softw. Eng. **17**(5), 403–423 (2002)

21. Allen, F.E., Cocke, J.: A program data flow analysis procedure. Commun. ACM **19**(3), 137 (1976)

Formal Specification and Model Checking of a Ride-sharing System in Maude

Eiichi Muramoto, Kazuhiro Ogata$^{(\boxtimes)}$, and Yoichi Shinoda

School of Information Science, JAIST, Nomi, Japan
{muramoto,ogata,shinoda}@jaist.ac.jp

Abstract. We report on a case study in which we have formally specified a ride-sharing system in Maude, a rewriting logic-based specification/programming language and model checked that the system enjoys desired liveness as well as safety properties with the Maude LTL model checker. In our approach to formal specification of the system, a map, a collection of cars and a collection of persons are treated as parameters. Thus, it suffices to write one formal systems specification from which the specification instance is generated for each fixed map, each fixed collection of cars and each fixed collection of persons. We often need fairness assumptions to model check liveness properties, which makes model checking performance slower or even infeasible. The case study also demonstrates that such a situation can be alleviated by a divide & conquer approach to liveness model checking under fairness.

Keywords: Divide & conquer · Fairness · Liveness property · LTL · Parameterized specification · Rewrite-theory specification

1 Introduction

Ride-sharing services have been on the market and have many customers. In addition, a new era would be around the corner [1], in which fully autonomous cars would be delivered to passengers and carry them to their destinations. These fully autonomous cars must be controlled by software, which would be a very complex fault-tolerant real-time distributed system. Such a system called a ride-sharing system in the present paper must be formally analyzed to make sure that the system enjoys desired properties.

Although some studies have been conducted on formal analysis of such systems, we need to conduct more studies on it because the quality of such systems would be most likely to heavily affect our future lives and then it is necessary to accumulate experiences and findings on it to make sure that such systems could be highly trustworthy. This paper then reports on a case study in which we have formally specified a simple ride-sharing system and model checked that the system enjoys some desired properties. We mean by "simple" that the system

This work was supported in part by JSPS KAKENHI Grant Number JP19H04082.

© Springer Nature Switzerland AG 2020

H. Miao et al. (Eds.): SOFL+MSVL 2019 Workshop, LNCS 12028, pp. 187–204, 2020.
https://doi.org/10.1007/978-3-030-41418-4_14

is neither fault-tolerant nor real-time. We only take into account small maps on which the service provided by the system is available. Because studies on formal analysis of such systems have not been saturated, it would be reasonable to start with a moderately simplified setting.

We use Maude [2] as a specification language and the Maude LTL model checker as a model checker. This is because Maude allows us to use rich data structures, such as inductively defined ones and associative and/or commutative ones, in systems specifications that can be model checked. The capabilities of Maude's are very convenient to deal with maps (or areas) on which the service provided by the system is available. For each map, we would like to avoid writing a new formal systems specification every time. Thus, we make the formal specification of the system generic such that maps can be treated as parameters of the specification. In our approach, a collection of cars and a collection of persons as well as a map are treated as parameters. This way to write formal systems specifications in which some important data are treated as parameters of the specifications is one of our contributions. We also demonstrate that Maude makes it possible to write such generic formal systems specifications.

Liveness as well as safety properties are model checked for the system. It is often necessary to use fairness assumptions to model check liveness properties, which drastically makes model checking performance slower or even infeasible. We demonstrate that a divide & conquer approach to liveness model checking under fairness [3] can mitigate such situations when model checking liveness properties under fairness assumptions for a ride-sharing system, which is another contribution of ours.

The rest of the paper is organized as follows. Section 2 describes some preliminaries. Section 3 describes a ride-sharing system concerned in the research. Section 4 describes how to formally specify the system as a rewrite theory specification in Maude. Section 5 describes how to model check some safety and liveness properties for the system based on the rewrite theory specification with the Maude LTL model checker. Section 6 describes how to mitigate a stagnating situation caused by fairness assumptions. Section 7 mentions some existing related work. Finally the paper is concluded in Sect. 8.

2   Preliminaries

A Kripke structure (KS) K is a 5 tuple $\langle S, I, P, L, T \rangle$, where S is a set of states, $I \subseteq S$ is the set of initial states, $P \subseteq U$ is a set of atomic state propositions, where U is the universal set of symbols, L is a labeling function whose type is $S \to 2^P$, and $T \subseteq S \times S$ is a total binary relation. An element $(s, s') \in T$ may be written as $s \to s'$ and referred as a transition. The syntax of a formula φ in LTL for K is: $\varphi ::= \top \mid p \mid \neg\varphi \mid \varphi \vee \varphi \mid \bigcirc \varphi \mid \varphi \mathcal{U} \varphi$, where $p \in P$. Let $\mathcal{F}$ be the set of all formulas in LTL for K. A path π is $s_0, \ldots, s_i, s_{i+1}, \ldots$ such that $s_i \in S$ and $(s_i, s_{i+1}) \in T$ for each i. Let π^i be $s_i, s_{i+1}, \ldots$ and $\pi(i)$ be s_i. Let P be the set of all paths. π is called a computation if $\pi(0) \in I$. Let C be the set of all computations. For $\pi \in \mathcal{P}$ of K and $\varphi \in \mathcal{F}$ of K, $K, \pi \models \varphi$ is inductively defined as follows:

- $K, \pi \models \top$;
- $K, \pi \models p$ if and only if (iff) $p \in L(\pi(0))$;
- $K, \pi \models \neg\varphi_1$ iff $K, \pi \not\models \varphi_1$;
- $K, \pi \models \varphi_1 \vee \varphi_2$ iff $K, \pi \models \varphi_1$ or $K, \pi \models \varphi_2$;
- $K, \pi \models \bigcirc\varphi_1$ iff $K, \pi^1 \models \varphi_1$;
- $K, \pi \models \varphi_1 \,\mathcal{U}\, \varphi_2$ iff there exists a natural number i such that $K, \pi^i \models \varphi_2$ and for all natural numbers $j < i$, $K, \pi^j \models \varphi_1$,

where φ_1 and φ_2 are LTL formulas. Then, $K \models \varphi$ iff $K, \pi \models \varphi$ for each computation $\pi \in \mathcal{C}$ of K. The temporal connectives $\bigcirc$ and $\mathcal{U}$ are called the next connective and the until connective, respectively. The other logical and temporal connectives are defined as usual: $\bot \triangleq \neg\top$, $\varphi_1 \wedge \varphi_2 \triangleq \neg(\neg\varphi_1 \vee \neg\varphi_2)$, $\varphi_1 \Rightarrow \varphi_2 \triangleq \neg\varphi_1 \vee \varphi_2$, $\Diamond\varphi \triangleq \top \,\mathcal{U}\, \varphi$, $\Box\varphi \triangleq \neg(\Diamond\neg\varphi)$ and $\varphi_1 \rightsquigarrow \varphi_2 \triangleq \Box(\varphi_1 \Rightarrow \Diamond\varphi_2)$. The temporal connectives $\Diamond$, $\Box$ and $\rightsquigarrow$ are called the eventually connective, the always connective and the leads-to connective, respectively.

A labeled Kripke structure (LKS) [4] lK is a 6 tuple $\langle lS, lI, lE, lP, lL, lT \rangle$, where lS is a set of states, $lI \subseteq lS$ is the set of initial states, $lE \subseteq U$ is a set of events, $lP \subseteq U$ is a set of atomic state propositions such that $lP \cap lE = \emptyset$, lL is a labeling function whose type is $lS \rightarrow 2^{lP}$, and $lT \subseteq lS \times lE \times lS$ is a total ternary relation. An element $(s, e, s') \in lT$ may be written as $s \rightarrow_e s'$ and referred as a transition labeled with e (or a labeled transition e or simply a transition e). There is an event $\iota \in lE$ such that $(s, \iota, s') \notin lT$ for any $s, s' \in lS$. For each event $e \in lE$, we suppose that there exists the atomic state proposition enabled$(e) \in lP$ and for each state $s \in lS$ enabled$(e) \in lL(s)$ iff $(s, e, s') \in lT$ for some state $s' \in lS$. A labeled transition e can be applied in a state s iff enabled$(e) \in lL(s)$. The syntax of a formula $l\varphi$ in State/Event-based Linear Temporal Logic (SE-LTL) for lK inherits all from LTL and also has $e \in lE$. The semantics of SE-LTL is defined over infinite sequences of $lE \times lS$, while the semantics of LTL is defined over infinite sequences of S. The semantics of SE-LTL, however, is defined mostly as expected as the semantics of LTL. The only difference is as follows: $lK, l\pi \models e$ iff $e = 1 \bullet l\pi(0)$, where $l\pi$ is an infinite sequence of $lE \times lS$ and $1 \bullet l\pi(0)$ is the first element of the first pair in $l\pi$. It is possible to conveniently express fairness assumptions in SE-LTL. Weak fairness of a labeled transition e is expressed as $(\Diamond \Box \text{enabled}(e)) \Rightarrow (\Box \Diamond e)$ and strong fairness of a labeled transition e is expressed as $(\Box \Diamond \text{enabled}(e)) \Rightarrow (\Box \Diamond e)$. Let WF$(e)$ and SF(e) refer to the two formulas, respectively.

For an LKS lK, the events-embedded-in-states KS (EES-KS) K_{ees} of lK is a KS denoted as $\langle S_{\text{ees}}, I_{\text{ees}}, P_{\text{ees}}, L_{\text{ees}}, T_{\text{ees}} \rangle$ such that $S_{\text{ees}} = \{(e, s) \mid e \in lE, s \in lS\}$ (that is $lE \times lS$), $I_{\text{ees}} = \{(\iota, s) \mid s \in lI\}$, $P_{\text{ees}} = lP \cup lE$, $L_{\text{ees}}((e, s)) = \{e\} \cup lL(s)$ for each $e \in lE$ and each $s \in lS$, and $T_{\text{ees}} = \{((e, s), (e', s')) \mid e, e' \in lE, s, s' \in lS, (s, e', s') \in lT\}$. A state of K_{ees} consists of an event and a state of lK. Infinite state sequences of K_{ees} are infinite sequences of $lE \times lS$ as those of lK and an event of lK becomes an atomic state proposition in K_{ees}.

We have a property preservation theorem between LKSs and EES-KSs [3]. For an arbitrary LKS lK, let K_{ees} be the EES-KS of lK, and then for an arbitrary SE-LTL formula $l\varphi$ for lK that is also an arbitrary LTL formula for K_{ees}, $lK \models l\varphi$

iff $K_{\text{ees}} \models l\varphi$. The theorem makes it possible to use an existing specification language, such as Maude, and an existing LTL model checker, such as the Maude LTL model checker, to specify EES-KSs and model check SE-LTL formulas. The research described in the present paper uses Maude and the Maude LTL model checker.

There are multiple possible ways to express states. In this paper, a state is expressed as an associative-commutative collection of name-value pairs, where a name may have parameters. Associative-commutative collections and name-value pairs are called soups and observable components, and then states are expressed as observable component soups. The juxtaposition operator is used as the constructor of soups. Let oc_1, oc_2, oc_3 be observable components, and then $oc_1\ oc_2\ oc_3$ is the soup of those three observable components. Note that the order is irrelevant due to associativity and commutativity.

Let us consider the EES-KS K_{ees} of an LKS lK and an LTL formula in the form $(f_1 \wedge \ldots \wedge f_n) \Rightarrow \varphi$, where f_i is a fairness assumption for $i = 1, \ldots, n$ and φ is a liveness property. A set of LTL formulas is abused as the conjunction of the LTL formulas. For example, $\{f_1, \ldots, f_n\}$ is treated as $f_1 \wedge \ldots \wedge f_n$ in $\{f_1, \ldots, f_n\} \Rightarrow \varphi$, and then $\{f_1, \ldots, f_n\} \Rightarrow \varphi$ is treated as the same as $(f_1 \wedge \ldots \wedge f_n) \Rightarrow \varphi$. Let qf_j be an LTL formula for $j = 1, \ldots, m$, F_1 be a subset of $\{f_1, \ldots, f_n\}$, and $F_{j'+1}$ be a subset of $\{f_1, \ldots, f_n\} \cup \{qf_1, \ldots, qf_{j'}\}$ for $j' = 1, \ldots, m-1$ such that $K_{\text{ees}} \models F_j \Rightarrow qf_j$ for $j = 1, \ldots, m$. Then, $K_{\text{ees}} \models (f_1 \wedge \ldots \wedge f_n) \Rightarrow (qf_1 \wedge \ldots \wedge qf_m)$. Let QF be a subset of $\{f_1, \ldots, f_n\} \cup \{qf_1, \ldots, qf_m\}$. If $K_{\text{ees}} \models QF \Rightarrow \varphi$, then $K_{\text{ees}} \models (f_1 \wedge \ldots \wedge f_n) \Rightarrow \varphi$. Hence, $(f_1 \wedge \ldots \wedge f_n) \Rightarrow \varphi$ can be divided into $F_j \Rightarrow qf_j$ for $i = 1, \ldots, m$ and $QF \Rightarrow \varphi$, and it suffices to (model) check $K_{\text{ees}} \models F_j \Rightarrow qf_j$ for $j = 1, \ldots, m$ and $K_{\text{ees}} \models QF \Rightarrow \varphi$ to (model) check $K_{\text{ees}} \models (f_1 \wedge \ldots \wedge f_n) \Rightarrow \varphi$. qf_j is called a quasi-fairness assumption for $j = 1, \ldots, m$. The approach is called a divide & conquer approach to liveness model checking under fairness assumptions [3].

3   A Ride-sharing System

Although the main players in the system are persons and cars, we need to consider an area (or a map) in which the service provided by the system is available. Persons and cars are located at some points in such an area. Such an area can be regarded as a fragment of the two dimensional continuous space, but we deal with it as a directed graph. An area typically has multiple landmarks, such as train stations and hospitals, which are treated as nodes in a directed graph. Persons and/or cars that are located at a landmark or near to the landmark are treated to be located in the node corresponding to the landmark. Given two landmarks lm_1, lm_2, if there is a direct route from lm_1 to lm_2 without going through any other landmarks, there is an edge from n_1 to n_2 corresponding to lm_1 to lm_2, respectively, in a graph. Although there may be two or more direct routes from lm_1 to lm_2, we treat them as one edge from n_1 to n_2. Even if there is a direct route from lm_1 to lm_2, any cars may not be permitted to directly go to lm_1 from lm_2, say, due to one-way traffic. Therefore, an area is treated as a

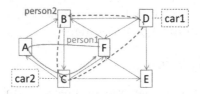

Fig. 1. A map on which there are 2 persons and 2 cars

directed graph. Since there may be and usually are cycles in an area, a graph that models the area is not acyclic (namely that a graph is not a DAG). We do not describe how to obtain a directed graph from an actual map, but suppose that directed graphs are given. We know how important it is to obtain directed graphs from actual maps but would like to concentrate on how to formally specify a ride-sharing system and model check that the system enjoys some desired properties in the present paper. We do not, however, want to have multiple formal specifications for multiple maps (or directed graphs) and then will describe how to make it sufficient to have one formal specification even for multiple maps in the next section. We suppose that for any two different nodes n, n' there is always a path from n to n' (and vice versa as well) because it would be unlikely realistic that there is no path from one landmark to another one in the real world. Therefore, there is always at least one shortest path from n to n' (and vice versa as well). We also suppose that each edge is given the same weight 1.

Each person's destination may change from time to time, and his/her source and final destination must be naturally different. We suppose that each person has one or more intermediate destinations, the order in which way the person visits the destinations is always the same and the source and final destination are always the same. That is to say, each person always visits multiple intermediate destinations in some specific order and goes back to the same place, which is repeated. When a person gets to the next destination n by a car, he/she always gets out of the car there and asks the system to deliver a car to move to the next destination of n. We can interpret each person in the system as a group of individuals such that their trips constitute a single long trip such that there are intermediate destinations and the final destination is the same as the departure node.

A car may have two or more passengers in the real world, but we suppose that each car can carry at most one passenger in the paper, although we can interpret one passenger as a group of individuals. Each car is idle, in service or reserved. An idle car stays in the current node until it is reserved. When an idle car c has been reserved by a person p, if the c's location n_1 is different from the p's location n_2, then c moves to n_2 through one of the shortest paths from n_1 to n_2. When c is in service for p, c moves to the next destination n_3 found in the p's trip route through one of the shortest paths from n_2 to n_3.

Figure 1 shows a map with six nodes and 10 edges on which two persons and two cars are located. car1 and car2 are located in node D and node C, respectively. person1 and person2 are located in node A and node C, respectively.

The person1's trip route is C, F and A, and the person2's trip route is D, B and C. Let the graph show in Fig. 1 be called Map6.

4   Formal Specification

In our formal specification of the system, directed graphs modeling maps (or areas) are treated as parameters of the specification. If a directed graph as it is is used in the specification, it is necessary to calculate one of the shortest paths from a node to another one each time we need to know it while performing model checking experiments, which must crucially affect model checking performance negatively. Therefore, we precompute with the Dijkstra's Algorithm one of the shortest paths for every directed pair (n, n') of nodes. Note that every directed pair (n, n') of nodes has at least one shortest path because of our assumption.

For example, one of the shortest paths from node C to node D on Map6 is C, A, B and D. The shortest path is expressed as the following term:

```
dbentry(nc,nd,routeentry(nc | na | nb | nd | empty,3) | empty)
```

nx for $x =$ a, b, c, etc. denotes node X for $X =$ A, B, C, etc. dbentry takes a source node n, a destination node n' and a list of route entries, where a route entry is routeentry(sp, l) such that sp is a shortest path from n to n' and l is the length of the path. The reason why the third parameter of dbentry is a list is that there may be two or more shortest paths from n to n'. In this paper, however, one shortest path for every directed pair (n, n') of nodes is taken into account. There are actually two shortest paths from nc to nd in Map6, but one of them is only used.

A directed graph is expressed as a collection of such dbentries. A soup is used as such as collection. Let routedb-m6 be the soup of dbentries that expresses Map6, which is defined as follows:

```
eq routedb-m6 =
  d6nana d6nanb d6nanc d6nand d6nane d6nanf d6nbna d6nbnb d6nbnc
  d6nbnd d6nbne d6nbnf d6ncna d6ncnb d6ncnc d6ncnd d6ncne d6ncnf
  d6ndna d6ndnb d6ndnc d6ndnd d6ndne d6ndnf d6nena d6nenb d6nenc
  d6nend d6nene d6nenf d6nfna d6nfnb d6nfnc d6nfnd d6nfne d6nfnf .
```

where the juxtaposition operator __ that is associative and commutative is used as the constructor of soups. Each element is a dbentry, and the definition of d6ncna is what you have already seen. The other dbentiries are defined likewise.

A person ID is expressed as pid(x), where x is a natural number. We prepare a special person ID pidnone that denotes nobody. We suppose that each person is in one of the four statuses: pidle, prequest, pwait and pride, meaning that the person does not want to use the system, wants to use the system, waits for a car and is being served, respectively. Each person has his/her ID, status, current position, next destination and trip route. When a person is being served, he/she is given the ID of the car that carries the person. For example, person1 on Map6 in the initial state is expressed as the following term:

```
person(pid(1),pidle,nf,na,cidnone,(na | nc | nf | empty))
```

The person1's ID is `pid(1)`. He/she is initially idle. His/her current position is **nf** and next destination is **na**. Since he/she is not being served, **cidnone** that denotes no-car is given to him/her as the car ID. His/her trip route is **na | nc | nf | empty** saying that he/she repeatedly visits **na**, **nc** and **nf** in this order.

A car ID is expressed as $cid(x)$, where x is a natural number. We prepare a special car ID **cidnone** that denotes no-car as we have already seen. We suppose that each car is in one of the three statuses: **cidle**, **creserved** and **cservice**, meaning that the car is neither reserved nor in service, has been reserved and be in service, respectively. Each car has its ID, status, current position and next destination. When a car is in service, it is given the ID of the person being served by the car. Otherwise, it is given **pidnone** as the ID of a person. For example, car1 on Map6 in the initial state is expressed as the following term:

```
car(cid(1),cidle,nd,nd,pidnone)
```

The car1's ID is `cid(1)`. It is initially idle. Its current position is **nd** and next destination is **nd**, meaning that it stays in **nd**. Since it is not in service, **pidnone** is given to it as the ID of a person.

To express each state of the system we use four observers: (cars: cs), (ps: ps), (ds: $bdes$) and (tran: e), where cs is the soup of cars participating in the system, ps is the soup of persons participating in the system, $dbes$ is the soup of dbentries that represents the directed graph modeling a map (or an area) in which the service provided by the system is available and e is the event (or transition) taken most recently. Each state is expressed as the soup of the four observable components:

```
(cars: cs) (ps: ps) (ds: bdes) (tran: e)
```

Transitions are specified in terms of rewrite rules, which can be described regardless of any instances of cs, ps and $bdes$. That is to say, cs, ps and $bdes$ can be regarded as the parameters of the formal specification. In the initial state of the system in which Map6 is used, $bdes$ is **routedb-m6**, cs is the soup of two cars car1 and car2 whose initial states can be understood from Fig. 1, ps is the soup of the two persons person1 and person2 whose initial states can be understood from Fig. 1 and e is **notran** meaning ι. Let **im6c2p2** equal the term denoting the initial state of the system in which Map6 is used.

A person can change his/her status to **prequest** if the status is **pidle** and his/her current position and next destination are different, which is specified as the following rewrite rule:

```
crl [startreq] :
 (ps: (person(PID,pidle,N1,N2,CID,DL) PS)) (tran: T)
  =>
 (ps: (person(PID,prequest,N1,N2,CID,DL) PS)) (tran: startreq)
if not(N1 == N2).
```

What are written in all capitals, such as PID and N1, are Maude variables. In the successor state, the observable component `tran:` holds `startreq` as its value because the rewrite rule labeled `startreq` has been just taken.

If a person is in `prequest` and there is a vacant car available, the person can book it, which is specified as the following rewrite rule:

```
crl [book] :
 (ps: (person(PID,prequest,N,N1,cidnone,DL) PS))
 (cars: (car(CID,cidle,N2,N3,pidnone) CS)) (db: RDB)
 (tran: T)
 =>
 (ps: (person(PID,pwait,N,N1,CID,DL) PS))
 (cars: (car(CID,creserved,N2,N,PID) CS)) (db: RDB )
 (tran: book(CID))
if car(CID,cidle,N2,N3,pidnone) \in
   (nearestvacant N of (car(CID,cidle,N2,N3,pidnone) CS) on RDB).
```

nearestvacant *n* **of** *c* **on** *dbes* calculates the soup of vacant cars available that are located nearest to the node *n*. The powerful associative-commutative pattern matching functionalities provided by Maude are used in the rewrite rule. Because the value of the observable component `cars:` is a soup of cars, `car(CID,creserved,N2,N,PID)` is an arbitrarily chosen vacant car among the soup. Note that the order in which the elements are enumerated is irrelevant because of associativity and commutativity. The condition checks if the arbitrary chosen vacant car is one of the vacant cars available that are located nearest to the node N in which the person is located. If that is the case, the person's status changes to `pwait` and the car has been reserved for the person, being changed to `car(CID,creserved,N2,N,PID)` in the successor state. In the successor state, the value of the observable component `tran:` is `book(CID)`. The reason why CID is used as the parameter of `book` is because the present paper takes into account fairness assumptions from a car point of view.

If a car has been reserved by a person and is located in the node that is different from the node where the person is located, it gets nearer to the person's location, which is specified as the following rewrite rule:

```
crl [rsvmove] :
 (cars: (car(CID,creserved,N,N1,PID) CS) ) (db: RDB) (tran: T)
 =>
 (cars: (car(CID,creserved,nexthop(N,N1,RDB),N1,PID) CS))
 (db: RDB ) (tran: rsvmove(CID))
if not (N == N1).
```

`nexthop(N,N1,RDB)` calculates the next node of the node N where the car concerned is now located. This can be straightforwardly done because RDB maintains the shortest paths for every directed pair of nodes in the map concerned.

When a car reserved by a person gets to the place where the person is located, the person gets into the car and the car gets in service, which is specified as the following rewrite rule:

```
rl [ridesvc] :
 (cars: (car(CID, creserved, N, N, PID) CS))
 (ps: (person(PID, pwait, N, N1, CID, DL) PS))
 (tran: T)
 =>
 (cars: (car(CID, cservice, N, N1, PID) CS))
 (ps: (person(PID, pride, N, N1, CID, DL) PS))
 (tran: ridesvc(CID)).
```

In the successor state, the car's next destination is the same as the person's one N1.

If a person is being served by a car, both the person and the car move to the next node of the current one in the shortest path to the destination, which is specified as the following rewrite rule:

```
crl [svcmove] :
 (cars: (car(CID,cservice,N,N1,PID) CS))
 (ps: (person(PID,pride,N,N1,CID,DL) PS))
 (db: RDB) (tran: T)
 =>
 (cars: (car(CID,cservice,nexthop(N,N1,RDB),N1,PID) CS))
 (ps: (person(PID,pride,nexthop(N,N1,RDB),N1,CID,DL) PS))
 (db: RDB) (tran: svcmove(CID))
if not (N == N1).
```

nexthop(N,N1,RDB) calculates the next node of the current one N in the shortest path to the destination N1, where the shortest path can be found in RDB.

If a person being served by a car gets to the next destination, the person gets out of the car, being in idle, which is specified as the following two rewrite rules:

```
crl [getoff] :
 (cars: (car(CID,cservice,N,N,PID) CS))
 (ps: (person(PID,pride,N,N,CID,DL) PS))
 (tran: T)
 =>
 (cars: (car(CID,cidle,N,N,pidnone) CS))
 (ps: (person(PID,pidle,N,nextdest(DL,N),cidnone,DL) PS))
 (tran: getoff(CID))
if not (nextdest(DL,N) == emptynode).

crl [getoff2] :
 (cars: (car(CID,cservice,N,N,PID) CS))
 (ps: (person(PID,pride,N,N,CID,DL) PS))
 (tran: T)
 =>
 (cars: (car(CID,cidle,N,N,pidnone) CS))
 (ps: (person(PID,pidle,N,top(DL),cidnone,DL) PS))
```

```
(tran: getoff2(CID))
if (nextdest(DL,N) == emptynode).
```

The first rewrite rule `getoff` deals with the case when the current node is not the final one of the person's trip route DL, where `nextdest(DL,N)` is the next destination of the trip route. The second rewrite rule `getoff2` deals with the case when the current node is the final one of the person's trip route DL. If that is the case, `nextdest(DL,N)` returns `emptynode` meaning no destination any more in the trip route and `top(DL)` that is the top node of the trip route DL is used as the next destination.

Those are the S_{ees}, I_{ees} and T_{ees} parts of the EES-KE K^{rsc}_{ees} formalizing the system, which are specified as a rewrite theory specification in Maude. The P_{ees} and L_{ees} parts will be described in the next section.

5   Model Checking

We have model checked several safety properties and liveness properties as the desired properties the system should enjoy for multiple maps including Map6. In the present paper, we take two safety properties and two liveness properties among them. The informal descriptions of the two safety properties are as follows:

- No Double Booking (NoDB)
- Idle Car has no Person (ICnoP)

The informal descriptions of the two liveness properties are as follows:

- Request Person will eventually Ride (RPweR)
- Vacant Car will eventually Serve (VCweS)

To formalize the two safety properties NoDB and ICnoP, we define the three atomic propositions `isidle`(cid), `hasperson`(cid) and `doublebook`(cid) for each car ID cid:

```
ops isidle hasperson doublebook : Cid -> Prop.
eq (cars: (car(CID,cidle,N,N1,PID) CS)) S
 |= isidle(CID) = true.
eq (cars: (car(CID,CST,N,N1,PID) CS)) S
 |= isidle(CID) = false [owise].
ceq (cars: (car(CID,CST,N,N1,PID) CS)) S
 |= hasperson(CID) = true
if not (PID == pidnone).
eq (cars: (car(CID,CST,N,N1,PID) CS)) S
 |= hasperson(CID) = false [owise].
ceq (ps: (person(PID,PSTAT,N,N1,CID,DL)
          person(PID2,PSTAT2,N2,N3,CID2,DL2) PS)) S
```

```
|= doublebook(CID) = true   if (CID == CID2).
eq  (ps: (person(PID,PSTAT,N,N1,CID,DL)
          person(PID2,PSTAT2,N2,N3,CID2,DL2) PS)) S
 |= doublebook(CID) = false [owise].
```

isidle(*cid*) holds iff the status of the car whose ID is *cid* is cidle.
hasperson(*cid*) holds iff the person's ID given to the car whose ID is *cid* is
not pidnone. doublebook(*cid*) holds iff there are two different persons who are
given *cid* as their car IDs.

Then, the two safety properties NoDB and ICnoP are formalized as follows:

```
ops nodb icnop : Cid -> Formula.
eq nodb(CID)  = ([] ~(doublebook(CID)) ).
eq icnop(CID) = ([] (isidle(CID) -> ~(hasperson(CID)))).
```

where [] _, _->_ and ~_ denote □, ⇒ and ¬, respectively.

To formalize the two liveness properties RPweR and VCweS, we define the
two atomic propositions reserving(*pid*) and riding(*pid*) for each person ID
pid:

```
ops reserving riding : Pid -> Prop.
ops isvacant inservice : Cid -> Prop.
eq (ps: (person(PID,prequest,N,N1,CID,DL) PS)) S
 |= reserving(PID) = true.
eq (ps: (person(PID,PSTAT,N,N1,CID,DL) PS)) S
 |= reserving(PID) = false [owise].
eq (ps: (person(PID,pride,N,N1,CID,DL) PS)) S
 |= riding(PID) = true.
eq (ps: (person(PID,PSTAT,N,N1,CID,DL) PS)) S
 |= riding(PID) = false [owise].
eq (cars: (car(CID,cidle,N,N1,PID) CS)) S
 |= isvacant(CID) = true.
eq (cars: (car(CID,CST,N,N1,PID) CS)) S
 |= isvacant(CID) = false [owise].
eq (cars: (car(CID,cservice,N,N1,PID) CS)) S
 |= inservice(CID) = true.
eq (cars: (car(CID,CST,N,N1,PID) CS)) S
 |= inservice(CID) = false [owise].
```

reserving(*pid*) holds iff the status of the person whose ID is *pid* is prequest.
riding(*pid*) holds iff the status of the person whose ID is *pid* is pride.
iscacant(*cid*) holds iff the status of the car whose ID is *cid* is cidle.
inservice(*cid*) holds iff the status of the car whose ID is *cid* is cservice.

Then, the two liveness properties RPweR and VCweS are formalized as follows:

```
op rpwer : Pid -> Formula.
```

```
op vcwes : Cid -> Formula .
eq rpwer(PID) = (reserving(PID) |-> riding(PID)) .
eq vcwes(CID) = (isvacant(CID) |-> inservice(CID)) .
```

where _|->_ denotes ⤳.

To model check NoDB for the system in which Map6 is used, all we need to do is to reduce

```
modelCheck(im6c2p2,nodb(cid(1)) /\ nodb(cid(2)))
```

where _/_ denotes ∧. To model check ICnoP for the system in which Map6 is used, all we need to do is to reduce

```
modelCheck(im6c2p2,icnop(cid(1)) /\ icnop(cid(2)))
```

Either model checking experiment does not find any counterexamples. Therefore, the system in which Map6 is used enjoys the two safety properties.

To model check RPweR for the system in which Map6 is used, all we need to do is to reduce

```
modelCheck(im6c2p2,rpwer(pid(1)) /\ rpwer(pid(2)))
```

To model check VCweS for the system in which Map6 is used, all we need to do is to reduce

```
modelCheck(im6c2p2,vcwes(cid(1)) /\ vcwes(cid(2)))
```

Each model checking experiment finds a counterexample. We cannot, however, immediately conclude that the system in which Map6 is used enjoyed neither RPweR nor VCweS. It is often the case to find such a counterexample when model checking liveness properties for concurrent and/or distributed systems. The ride-sharing system is such a system. The reason why such a counterexample is found is that unfair schedules are not excluded. We need to exclude all unfair schedules and only use some fair schedules. To this end, we can use fairness assumptions. We use both weak and strong fairness of each transition from a car point of view. Let wfair(cid) be the conjunction of wf(stratreq), wf(book(cid)), wf(rsvmove(cid)), wf(ridesvc(cid)), wf(svcmove(cid)), wf(getoff(cid)) and wf(getoff2(cid)), and wfair (the weak fairness assumption used) be the conjunction of wfair(1) and wfair(2), where wf denotes WF. sfair(cid) and sfair (the strong fairness assumption used) are defined likewise.

To model check RPweR and VCweS under wfair for the system in which Map6 is used, all we need to do is to reduce

```
modelCheck(im6c2p2,wfair -> rpwer(pid(1)) /\ rpwer(pid(2)))
modelCheck(im6c2p2,wfair -> vcwes(cid(1)) /\ vcwes(cid(2)))
```

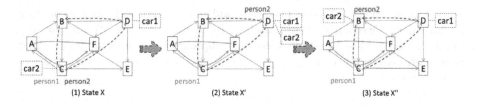

Fig. 2. A fragment of a counterexample VCweS under `wfair`

No counterexample is found when model checking RPweR under `wfair`. We expected that no counterexample would be found when model checking VCweS under `wfair`, either. A counterexample is, however, found for VCweS even under `wfair`. Figure 2 shows a fragment of the counterexample found. State X in Fig. 2 is reachable from `im6c2p2`, in which both person1 and person2 are located in node C and so is car2 and then car2 is the nearest one to person2. When car2 carries person2 to node D, person2, car1 and car2 are located in node 2 (see State X' in Fig. 2). Therefore, both car1 and car2 are the nearest ones to person2. Either car can be chosen for person2. Let us suppose that car2 is chosen and carries person2 to node B, when car2 is the nearest one to person2, while car1 is not (see State X" in Fig. 2). That is to say, there is a scenario in which car1 will be never chosen under `wfair` because even if car1 becomes the nearest one to person2, car1 may not keep on being the nearest to person 2 continuously.

To model check VCweS under `sfair` for the system in which Map6 is used, all we need to do is to reduce

```
modelCheck(im6c2p2,sfair -> vcwes(cid(1)) /\ vcwes(cid(2)))
```

No counterexample is found when model checking VCweS under `sfair`.

Note that although VCweS holds for the system in which Map6 is used under `sfair`, there are some maps that make VCweS unsatisfied by the system even under `sfair`. For example, such a map is as follows: there is a node that will never be visited by any persons, a car is initially located in the node and the car will never be the nearest one to any persons. Such a car will never serve any persons and then is useless. VCweS can be regarded as a property of a map as well as the system. For a given map, model checking VCweS for the system in which the map is used allows us to check if there exists such a car in the system or the map. Such a car should be avoided and then VCweS is worth checking. If there exists such a car, we should reduce the number of cars and/or modify the initial location of each car so that VCweS can hold for the system in which a map is used under `wfair`.

6   Improvement of Model Checking Performance Deteriorated by Fairness

It takes about 7.7 h to model check VCweS under `sfair` with an SGI computer that uses 3.20 GHz microprocessor, 256 GB memory and SUSE Linux Enterprise

Server. Only when one more person is added to Map6, any model checking attempts for VCweS under `sfair` fail because of stack overflow. To mitigate the situation, we could use a divide & conquer approach to liveness model checking under fairness assumptions [3].

Let F_0 be the set

```
{sf(startreq), sf(book(cid(1))), sf(rsvmove(cid(1)) ),
 sf(ridesvc(cid(1))), sf(svcmove(cid(1))), sf(getoff(cid(1))),
 sf(getoff2(cid(1))), sf(book(cid(2))), sf(rsvmove(cid(2))),
 sf(ridesvc( cid(2))), sf(svcmove(cid(2))), sf(getoff(cid(2))),
 sf(getoff2(cid(2)))}.
```

Such a set is treated as the formula obtained by combining all elements in it with conjunction. Therefore, F_0 -> vcwes(cid1)) /\ vcwes(cid(2)) is equivalent to `sfair` -> vcwes(cid(1)) /\ vcwes(cid(2)). For each event e, SF(e) $\Rightarrow$ WF(e) for all LKSs and then all EES-EKs. We use this fact. Let F_1 be the set obtained by replacing each element in F_0 with its weak fairness counterpart. For example, `sf(rsvmove(cid(1)))` is replaced with `wf(rsvmove(cid(1)))`.

We conjecture one hypothesis: For each car whose ID is cid, if `sf(book(`cid`))` and `wf(startreq)` hold, then the car will eventually be reserved by a person. The conclusion part is formalized as follows:

```
eq vcwebr(CID) = isvacant(CID) |-> reserved(CID).
```

where the atomic proposition `reserved(`cid`)` holds iff the status of the car whose ID is cid is `creserved`. `vcwebr` stands for "Vacant Car will eventually be Reserved." We model check the hypothesis by reducing the term:

```
modelCheck(im6c2p2,
   wf(startreq) /\ sf(book(cid(1))) /\ sf(book(cid(2)))
   -> vcwebr(cid(1)) /\ vcwebr(cid(2)) )
```

No counterexample is found. It takes about 3 s to perform this model checking experiment with the SGI computer. Let F_2 be the set that consists of all conjuncts in the premise, and then $F_2 \subseteq F_0 \cup F_1$. We then conduct the following model checking experiment:

```
modelCheck(im6c2p2,
   wf(rsvmove(cid(1))) /\ wf(rsvmove(cid(2))) /\
   wf(ridesvc(cid(1))) /\ wf(ridesvc(cid(2))) /\
   vcwebr(cid(1)) /\ vcwebr(cid(2)) -> vcwes(cid(1)) /\ vcwes(cid(2)))
```

No counterexample is found, either. It also takes about 3 s to perform this model checking experiment with the SGI computer.

Let F_3 be the set that consists of all conjuncts in the premise, and then $F_3 \subseteq F_0 \cup F_1 \cup \{\text{vcwebr(cid(1)),vcwebr(cid(2))}\}$. $F_0 \Rightarrow F_1$ from the fact. $F_0 \cup F_1 \Rightarrow F_3$ from the first model checking experiment. $F_3 \Rightarrow$

vcwes(cid(1)) /\ vcwes(cid(2))) from the second model checking experiment. Therefore, $F_0 \Rightarrow$ vcwes(cid(1)) /\ vcwes(cid(2))). Consequently, we can conclude that there is no counterexample for

modelCheck(im6c2p2,sfair -> vcwes(cid(1)) /\ vcwes(cid(2)))

from the two model checking experiments. We could say that it totally takes about 6 s to conduct this model checking experiment with the divide & conquer approach, while it takes about 7.7 h to straightforwardly do so.

Moreover, we have refined the assumption under which VCweS holds. We do not need full strong fairness of each transition, but it suffices to assume sf(book(cid)), wf(startreq), wf(rsvmove(cid)) and wf(ridesvc(cid)) for each cid. book(cid) is the only transition to which we need to give strong fairness, while it is sufficient to give weak fairness to startreq, rsvmove(cid) and ridesvc(cid). In addition, we do not need to give any fairness assumptions to svcmove(cid), getoff(cid) and getoff2(cid).

When one more person is added to Map6, it takes about 5 s and 3 m 38 s to conduct the first and second sub model checking experiments, respectively. Then, it totally takes about 3 m 43 s to conduct the liveness model checking experiment under fairness with the divide & conquer approach, while it is infeasible to straightforwardly do so due to stack overflow.

Note that the present paper does not propose the divide & conquer approach to liveness model checking under fairness assumptions but reports on a different case to which the approach can be effectively applied than the cases described in [3]. This is like that many papers, such as the present one, report on cases to which model checking can be effectively applied but do not propose model checking. The latter cases must be worth reporting and so must be the former cases.

7 Related Work

d'Orey, Fernandes and Ferreira [5] have conducted a research in which they simulate but not formally verify a dynamic and distributed taxi-sharing system. Computer simulation is another important technology to make it likely that a taxi-sharing system or a ride-sharing system achieves desired goals, but we also believe that it would be necessary to use formal verification, such as model checking, to make it more likely to do so. Among researches on simulation of autonomous vehicles are [6–8].

The First Workshop on Formal Verification of Autonomous Vehicles was held in Turin, Italy on Sep. 19, 2017 (arxiv.org/html/1709.02126). One paper presented at the workshop is on implementation and formal verification of crucial components of an autonomous vehicle (AV) [9]. The authors are interested in an AV capable of navigation, such as obstacle avoidance, obstacle selection (when a crash is unavoidable) and vehicle recovery. They implement such functionalities as intelligent or rational agent plans in the GWENDOLEN agent programming language. Those plans can be simulated in a simulated automotive environment implemented in Java. Desired properties are expressed in LTL and model checked for those plans with the AJPF verification tool, an extension of JPF, which is conducted within the MCAPL framework. Mitsch, et al. [10] have conducted a similar research, although their targets are ground robots. Autonomous vehicles, however, could be regarded as ground robots. Formal verification of obstacle avoidance is also important but independent from ours in the present paper.

The EES-KS of an LKS originates in the Meseguer's work on localized fairness [11]. Model checkers dedicated to liveness properties under fairness assumption have been developed. One of them is the Bae-Meseguer model checker [12]. We tried to use the model checker to model check RPweR and VCweS for the system concerned but were not able to use it for our purpose.

8   Conclusions and Future Work

8.1   Conclusions

We have formally specified a ride-sharing system in Maude and model checked that the system enjoys desired properties with the Maude LTL model checker. In our approach to formal systems specification, a map, a collation of cars and a collection of persons are treated as parameters, which makes it sufficient to prepare one formal systems specification of one ride-sharing system, which can be used for multiple instances of maps, car collections and person collections. The approach requires to use rich data structures, which is supported by Maude that is equipped with an LTL model checker. We doubt whether most existing LTL model checkers, such as Spin, could be at least straightforwardly used to implement our approach because they do not support rich data structures. Some smart researchers and/or engineers may come up with some non-trivial encoding of the rich data structures used in our approach with a limited set of data structures, such as bounded arrays and integers, but who guarantees that such non-trivial encoding faithfully represents rich data structures? It would be necessary to formally verify that non-trivial encoding faithfully represents rich data structures [13].

We have also demonstrated that a divide & conquer approach to liveness model checking under fairness can alleviate the situation in which model checking liveness properties under fairness assumptions become very slower and even infeasible and can refine the fairness assumptions under which liveness properties hold. The approach makes the slow liveness model checking under fairness (about 7.7 h) faster (about 6 s) and the infeasible one feasible and reasonably fast (about 3 m 43 s). The divide & conquer approach can refine the assumptions under which liveness properties hold, which has been demonstrated as well.

In addition to the two safety and two liveness properties, we have model checked some more safety and liveness properties for the system concerned. Moreover, we have used some more maps to conduct model checking experiments and measured time taken for each model checking experiment. We will describe them in an extended version of the present paper.

8.2 Future Work

One interesting point we have found about model checking performance is that times taken for model checking experiments are not crucially affected by the sizes of maps. This seems because we precompute with the Dijkstra's Algorithm the shortest path for every directed pair (n, n') of nodes. We will investigate this issue more profoundly.

In our formal specification of the ride-sharing system, each person always visits multiple intermediate destinations in some specific order and goes back to the same place, which is repeated. We could change it as follows: each person decides his/her destination on the fly every time he/she asks the system to deliver a car. For example, the term representing person1 on Map6 in the initial state is revised as follows:

```
person(pid(1),pidle,nf,nonode,cidnone)
```

where nonode means that person1 does not have any destinations to visit. Then, rewrite rule startreq is revised as follows:

```
crl [startreq1] :
 (ps: (person(PID,pidle,N1,nonode,CID,DL) PS))
 (dst[PID]: (N | Ns)) (tran: T)
  =>
 (ps: (person(PID,prequest,N1,D,CID,DL) PS))
 (dst[PID]: Ns) (tran: startreq)
if not(N1 == N).

crl [startreq2] :
 (ps: (person(PID,pidle,N1,nonode,CID,DL) PS))
 (dst[PID]: (N | Ns)) (tran: T)
  =>
 (ps: (person(PID,pidle,N1,nonode,CID,DL) PS))
 (dst[PID]: Ns) (tran: startreq)
if N1 == N.
```

where (dst[PID]:...) is a new observable component that holds a soup of nodes that are possible destinations of PID's. For example, the observable component initially may hold na na nd ne, the soup that consists of na twice, nd once and ne once. If that is the case, PID will visit na at most twice, nd once and ne once. The order in which PID will visit those places are nondeterministically chosen. Implementation of this way to choose each person's next destination is another piece of our future work.

References

1. Newcomb, D.: You won't need a driver's license by 2040. https://www.wired.com/2012/09/ieee-autonomous-2040/ (2012)
2. Clavel, M., et al.: All About Maude. LNCS, vol. 4350. Springer, Heidelberg (2007). https://doi.org/10.1007/978-3-540-71999-1
3. Ogata, K.: A divide & conquer approach to liveness model checking under fairness & anti-fairness assumptions. Front. Comput. Sci. **13**, 51–72 (2019)
4. Chaki, S., Clarke, E.M., Ouaknine, J., Sharygina, N., Sinha, N.: State/event-based software model checking. In: Boiten, E.A., Derrick, J., Smith, G. (eds.) IFM 2004. LNCS, vol. 2999, pp. 128–147. Springer, Heidelberg (2004). https://doi.org/10.1007/978-3-540-24756-2_8
5. d'Orey, P.M., Fernandes, R., Ferreira, M.: Empirical evaluation of a dynamic and distributed taxi-sharing system. In: 15th IEEE ITSC, pp. 140–146 (2012)
6. Kristensen, T., Ezeora, N.J.: Simulation of intelligent traffic control for autonomous vehicles. In: IEEE ICIA 2017, pp. 459–465 (2017)
7. Choi, S., Yeo, H.: Framework for simulation-based lane change control for autonomous vehicles. In: IEEE IV 2017, pp. 699–704 (2017)
8. Zhang, C., Liu, Y., Zhao, D., Su, Y.: RoadView: a traffic scene simulator for autonomous vehicle simulation testing. In: 17th IEEE ITSC, pp. 1160–1165 (2014)
9. Fernandes, L.E.R., Custodio, V., Alves, G.V., Fisher, M.: A rational agent controlling an autonomous vehicle: implementation and formal verification. In: 1st FVAV. EPTCS, vol. 257, pp. 35–42 (2017)
10. Mitsch, S., Ghorbal, K., Vogelbacher, D., Platzer, A.: Formal verification of obstacle avoidance and navigation of ground robots. Int. J. Robot. Res. **36**, 1312–1340 (2017)
11. Meseguer, J.: Localized fairness: a rewriting semantics. In: Giesl, J. (ed.) RTA 2005. LNCS, vol. 3467, pp. 250–263. Springer, Heidelberg (2005). https://doi.org/10.1007/978-3-540-32033-3_19
12. Bae, K., Meseguer, J.: Model checking linear temporal logic of rewriting formulas under localized fairness. Sci. Comput. Program. **99**, 193–234 (2015)
13. Ogata, K., Futatsugi, K.: Comparison of Maude and SAL by conducting case studies model checking a distributed algorithm. IEICE Trans. Fundam. **90-A**, 1690–1703 (2007)

Model Checking Python Programs
with MSVL

Xinfeng Shu[1], Fengyun Gao[1], Weiran Gao[1], Lili Zhang[1], Xiaobing Wang[2(✉)],
and Liang Zhao[2(✉)]

[1] School of Computer Science and Technology,
Xi'an University of Posts and Telecommunications, Xi'an 710061, China
shuxf@xupt.edu.cn, weirangao@foxmail.com, z_hanglili@163.com
[2] Institute of Computing Theory and Technology and ISN Laboratory,
Xidian University, Xi'an 710071, China
{xbwang,lzhao}@mail.xidian.edu.cn

Abstract. To verify the correctness of Python programs, a novel approach for model checking Python programs with MSVL (Modeling, Simulation and Verification Language) is advocated. To this end, the rules for decoding the object-oriented semantics of Python with the process-oriented semantics of MSVL are defined, and the technique for automatically rewriting a Python program into its equivalent MSVL program is formalized, which in turn can be verified with the model checking tool MSV. In addition, an example is given to illustrate how the approach works. The approach fully utilizes the powerful expressiveness of MSVL to verify Python programs in a direct way, and helps to improve the quality of the software system.

Keywords: MSVL · Python · Program verification · Model checking

1 Introduction

Python [1] is an interpreted, high-level, general-purpose programming language, which has been ranked the third most popular programming language in the TIOBE Programming Community Index since December 2018. It supports multiple programming paradigms, including procedural, object-oriented, and functional programming, and features a comprehensive standard library and a large number of third-party libraries covering networking, multithreading, web frameworks, database, scientific computing, text processing, etc. Besides, Python interpreters (e.g., CPython, Jython and PyPy) are available for many operating systems, including Windows and most modern Unix-like systems. Python is commonly used in developing web applications, image processing tools, mathematical softwares, artificial intelligence softwares and so on.

This research is supported by the Science and Technology Research Project of Xianyang (No. 2017K01-25-8), and NSFC Grant No. 61672403 and No. 61972301.

© Springer Nature Switzerland AG 2020
H. Miao et al. (Eds.): SOFL+MSVL 2019 Workshop, LNCS 12028, pp. 205–224, 2020.
https://doi.org/10.1007/978-3-030-41418-4_15

Facing the massive softwares written in Python, how to ensure their correctness and reliability is of grand challenge to computer scientists as well as software engineers. To solve the problem, software testing has been developed for many years and a variety of tools has been developed to verify software systems with success. However, the method has its innate limitation, i.e., it can only prove the presence of errors but never their absence. In contrast, formal verification, which is based on the mathematical theories, can prove the correctness of the software and become an important means to verify software systems.

As an automatic formal verification approach, model checking [2] can exhaustively search each execution path of the system model to be verified, and check whether the desired property holds. Once the property fails, it can provide a counterexample path helping engineers to locate and fix the error, and hence is welcomed by both the academia and industry. In the early days, the research on model checking mainly focuses on verifying the analysis and designment of hardware and software systems, The kernel process of the verification is to model the system with a specific modeling language (e.g., Promela [3] and NuSMV [4]), which usually need to be finished by verifiers manually. For complex system, it is very difficult to create the model and guarantee its correctness.

In recent years, some methods for model checking C programs have been advocated, and a number of model checking tools have been developed (e.g., SLAM [5], BLAST [6], MAGIC [7] and ESBMC [8]) and employed to verify device drivers, secure communication protocols, and real-time operating system kernels with success. These tools directly take C programs as input, and often use techniques of predicate abstraction, static analysis or runtime analysis to obtain the finite state model of the program as well as alleviate the state explosion problem, and complete the verification with the model checking algorithm. Within the field of object-oriented programs, Java Pathfinder (JPF) [9] is developed based on Java Virtual Machine for directly model checking Java bytecode. The available program model checking tools mainly focus on verifying the process-oriented C programs and cannot be directly employed to verify the object-oriented ones. Besides, the current tools can only check the safety property and dead lock of the system, but cannot verify the liveness property.

In addition to the above methods, model checking C programs and Java programs with MSVL (Modeling, Simulation and Verification Language) are two important approaches [10,11]. MSVL [12], a process-oriented logic programming based on the Projection Temporal Logic (PTL)[13], is a useful formalism for specification and verification of concurrent and distributed systems [14–22]. It provides a rich set of data types (e.g., char, integer, float, struct, pointer, string, semaphore), data structures (e.g., array, list), as well as powerful statements [23,24]. Besides, MSVL supports the function mechanisms [25] to model the complex system. Further, Propositional Projection Temporal Logic (PPTL), the propositional subset of PTL, has the expressiveness power of the full regular expressions [26], which enable us to model, simulate and verify the concurrent and reactive systems within a same logical system [27].

To solve problem of formal verifying Python programs, we are motivated to extend the MSVL-based model checking approaches of C/Java programs to Python programs. To this end, the rules for decoding the object-oriented semantics of Python language with the process-oriented semantics of MSVL are defined, and the techniques for automatically rewriting a Python program into its equivalent MSVL program are formalized. Thus, the Python program can be indirectly verified by model checking the corresponding MSVL program with the specific model checking tool MSV.

The rest of this paper is organized as follows. In the next section, the unified model checking approach with MSVL, PPTL, and Java is briefly presented. In Sect. 3, the rules and the algorithms for converting Python programs to MSVL programs are introduced. In Sect. 4, an example is given to illustrate the transformation progress from the partial Python program to MSVL program. Finally, the conclusion is given in Sect. 5.

2 Preliminaries

2.1 Modeling, Simulation and Verification Language

Modeling, Simulation and Verification Language (MSVL) is an executable subset of PTL with frame and used to model, simulate and verify concurrent systems. With MSVL, expressions can be regarded as the PTL terms and statements as treated as the PTL formulas. In the following, we briefly introduce the kernel of MSVL. For more deals, please refer to literatures [12].

Data Type. MSVL provides a rich set of data types [23]. The fundamental types include unsigned character (char), unsigned integer (int) and floating point number (float). Besides, there is a hierarchy of derived data types built with the fundamental types, including string (string), list (list), pointer (pointer), array (array), structure (struct) and union (union).

Expression. The arithmetic expressions e and boolean expressions b of MSVL are inductively defined as follows:

$$e ::= n \mid x \mid \bigcirc x \mid \ominus e \mid e_0 ope_1 (op ::= + \mid - \mid * \mid / \mid \%)$$
$$b ::= true \mid false \mid e_0 = e_1 \mid e_0 < e_1 \mid \neg b \mid b_0 \wedge b_1$$

where n is an integer and x is a variable. The elementary statements in MSVL are defined as follows:

(1) Immediate Assign $x \Leftarrow e \overset{\text{def}}{=} x = e \wedge p_x$

(2) Unit Assignment $x := e \overset{\text{def}}{=} \bigcirc x = e \wedge \bigcirc p_x \wedge skip$

(3) Conjunction $S_1 \text{ and } S_2 \overset{\text{def}}{=} S_1 \wedge S_2$

(4) Selection $S_1 \text{ or } S_2 \overset{\text{def}}{=} S_1 \vee S_2$

(5) Next $next \ S \overset{\text{def}}{=} \bigcirc S$

(6) Always $always \ S \overset{\text{def}}{=} \Box S$

(7) Termination $empty \overset{\text{def}}{=} \neg \bigcirc true$

(8) Skip $skip \overset{\text{def}}{=} \bigcirc \varepsilon$

(9) Sequential $S_1 ; S_2 \overset{\text{def}}{=} (S_1, S_2) \, prj \, \varepsilon$

(10) Local $exist \ x : S \overset{\text{def}}{=} \exists x : S$

(11) State Frame $lbf(x) \overset{\text{def}}{=} \neg af(x) \rightarrow \exists b : (\ominus x = b \wedge x = b)$

(12) Interval Frame $frame(x) \overset{\text{def}}{=} \Box(\overline{\varepsilon} \rightarrow \bigcirc(lbf(x)))$

(13) Projection $(S_1, \ldots, S_m) \, prj \, S$

(14) Condition $if \, b \, then \, S_1 \, else \, S_2 \overset{\text{def}}{=} (b \rightarrow S_1) \wedge (\neg b \rightarrow S_2)$

(15) While $while \, b \, do \, S \overset{\text{def}}{=} (b \wedge S)^\star \wedge \Box(\varepsilon \rightarrow \neg b)$

(16) Await $await(b) \overset{\text{def}}{=} \bigwedge_{x \in V_b} frame(x) \wedge \Box(\varepsilon \leftrightarrow b)$

(17) Parallel $S_1 || S_2 \overset{\text{def}}{=} ((S_1 ; true) \wedge S_2) \vee (S_1 \wedge (S_2 ; true))$
$\vee (S_1 \wedge S_2)$

where x is a variable, e is an arbitrary expression, b is a boolean expression, and $S_1, \ldots, S_m, S$ are all MSVL statements. The immediate assignment $x \Leftarrow e$, unit assignment $x := e$, $empty$, $lbf(x)$ and $frame(x)$ are basic statements, and the left composite ones.

For convenience of modeling complex software and hardware systems, MSVL takes the divide-and-conquer strategy and employs functions as the basic components like C programming language does. The general grammar of MSVL function is as follows [25]:

$function \ \text{funcName}(in\_type_1 \ \text{x}_1, \ldots, in\_type_m \ \text{x}_m,$
$\qquad\qquad out\_type_1 \ \text{y}_1, \ldots, out\_type_n \ \text{y}_m, return\_type \ \text{RValue})$
$\{ \ S \ \} \qquad\quad //\text{Function body}$

The grammar of function call is $funcName(v_1, \ldots, v_n)$. Parameter passing in MSVL is similar to that in C, i.e. all function arguments are passed by values (call-by-value). With call-by-value, the actual argument expression is evaluated, and the resulting value is bound to the corresponding formal parameter in the function. Even if the function may assign new values to its formal parameters, only its local copies are assigned and anything passed into a function call is unchanged in the caller's scope when the function returns. Furthermore, the pointer type is also supported by MSVL, which allows both caller and callee will be able to access and modify a same variable.

2.2 Python Programming Language

Python is a multi-paradigm programming language which supports procedural, object-oriented, and functional programming. The language uses dynamic typing, and a combination of reference counting and a cycle-detecting garbage collector for memory management. It has a comprehensive standard library covering regular expressions, networking, multithreading, GUI, database, etc. Besides, Python is highly extensible for providing a rich set of APIs and tools that allow programmers to easily write extension modules using the C, C++ or other languages, as well as directly utilize the rich third-party libraries. In the following, we briefly introduce the grammar of the subset of Python to verify.

Data Type. Despite being dynamically typed, Python is strongly typed programming language. The built-in types of Python include bool (Boolean), int (Integer), float (Float), string (String), list (List), set (Set), frozenset (Frozen Set) and dict (Dictionary), where dict, list and set are mutable data types whereas the others are immutable ones. Besides, Python allows programmers to define their own types using classes.

Expression. Let d be a constant, x a variable, cls a class, obj an object and $attr$ an attribute of a class (object) respectively. The arithmetic expressions e and boolean expressions b of Python are inductively defined as follows:

Table 1. The elementary statements of Python

Statements		Statements	
(1)Assignment	$x=e \mid obj.att = e$	(4) Sequential	S_1
(2)Object creation	$obj = className(e_1, \ldots, e_n)$	statement	S_2
(3) If statement	**if** b_1 :	(5) While	**while** b:
	S_1	statement	S
	[**elif** b_2 :	(6) Function	**def** $funcName(v_1, \ldots, v_n)$:
	S_2]	definition	S #Function body
	.....		**return** [e]
	[**else** :	(7) Function	$fun(e_1, \ldots, e_n) \mid$
	S_n]	call	$obj.fun(e_1, \ldots, e_n)$

$$e ::= d \mid x \mid cls.attr \mid obj.attr \mid e_1 \ op_1 \ e_2 \ (op_1 ::= + \mid - \mid * \mid / \mid // \mid \% \mid)$$
$$b ::= True \mid False \mid not \ b \mid e_1 \ op_2 \ e_2 \ (op_2 ::= > \mid < \mid == \mid > = \mid < = \mid ! =)$$
$$b_1 \ op_3 \ b_2(op_3 ::= and \mid or)$$

where op_1 denotes the traditional arithmetic operators, op_2 are the relational operators and op_3 the logical operators.

Elementary Statement and Function Definition. Let x be a variable, obj an object, $e, e_1, \ldots, e_n$ and $b, b_1, \ldots, b_n$ arithmetic expressions and boolean expressions respectively. The elementary statements of Python are inductively defined in Table 1, where S, S_1, S_2 are any Python statements, and single-line comment of Python begins with a hash (#) symbol. As the default, each statement needs to be written in one line, and it can also be written in multiple lines by using line continuation character (\). Besides, the block of a compound statement (e.g., the body of a function or a loop or class) starts with indentation, and the indentation must be same for each statement inside the block.

Class Definition. The object-oriented programming of Python supports polymorphism, operator overloading, and multiple inheritance. The grammar for defining a class is as follows:

> **class** $className(superClass_1, \ldots, superClass_n)$:
> $attr = e$
> $\ldots\ldots$
>   **def** __init__$(self, v_1, \ldots, v_n)$:   # Constructor of the class
> S # Function body
>   [@dec]
>   **def** $func(v_1, \ldots, v_n)$:
> S # Function body
>   **return** [e]

where, $superClass_1, \ldots, superClass_n$ $(n \geq 0)$ are the super classes; member function __init__$(\ldots)$ is the constructor of the class; @dec is the decorator indicating the type of the method $func$, i.e., it is @$staticmethod$ denoting $func$ is a static method, whereas it is missed meaning $func$ is an instance method by default. A static method can be invoked by the class name directly while an instance one can only be accessed by a class instance, and the former may have no parameters, whereas the latter must have at least one parameters of which the first parameter, usually named by $self$, is the reference of the class instance invoking the method.

3   Model Checking Python Program

In this section, the method for model checking Python programs is presented. The basic idea is to convert the Python program into an equivalent MSVL program and then perform model checking on the MSVL program obtained.

3.1   Strategy for Converting Python Program into MSVL

Since Python provides both process-oriented and object-oriented programming whereas MSVL only supports the former one, we need to decode the object-oriented semantics of Python programs with the process-oriented semantics of MSVL. The conversion rules from Python to MSVL are defined as follows:

R1. For each Python function $fun(v_1, \ldots, v_n)$, we define an MSVL function $fun(type_1\ v_1, \ldots, type_n\ v_n)$, where $type_i(1 \le i \le n)$ is the data type of parameter's. Besides, if the function fun has a return value of type $rtnType$, add a new parameter Ret with the MSVL type corresponding to $rtnType$ to the tail of the parameter list of the MSVL function. The translation rules for data types between Python and MSVL are depicted in Table 2, and the data type of a Python variable can be identified with Rule 14.

R2. For each Python class cls, we define an MSVL struct with the same name cls to the class.

R3. For each parent class par of a Python class cls, we add a new member $\_parent\_par$ with the type $struct\ par$ to the MSVL struct cls.

R4. For each class attribute $att = e$ in a Python class cls, we convert it to a global variable of MSVL with the name cls_att to keep its value, which is declared and initialized int the front of the result MSVL program.

R5. For every assignment statement $self.att = e$ in each constructor $\_init\_$ $(self, v_1, \ldots, v_n)$ of a Python class cls, we define a member $attr$ in the corresponding MSVL struct cls.

R6. For each instance method $fun(self, v_1, \ldots, v_n)$ of a class cls, we define an MSVL function $cls\_fun(struct\ cls * self, type_1\ v_1, \ldots, type_n\ v_n)$. Besides, if fun has a return value of type $rtnType$, add a new parameter Ret with the MSVL type corresponding to $rtnType$ to the tail of the parameter list of cls_fun. The class methods can be treated similarly without considering the parameter $self$.

R7. For each overload method fun of a class cls, we define a MSVL function named with the concatenation of "cls_fun" and the type name with the suffix "$\_$" of each parameters of fun in sequence. The parameters and return value of the function are handled identical to rule R6.

R8. The translation rules for elementary expressions and statements between Python and MSVL are given in Table 3. For any statement $stmt$ containing an expression $obj.attr$ accessing the attribute $attr$ of object obj, an instance of class cls, if $stmt$ locates in a general (member) function fun and obj is a parameter of the function, let $preName = \text{"}obj \rightarrow\text{"}$, otherwise $preName = \text{"}obj.\text{"}$. Further, we replace all the occurrence of $obj.attr$ in the corresponding statement of MSVL with the expression $preName$ concatenated with the result of algorithm $find\_InstAttr(cls, attr)$.

R9. For any statement containing an expression $cls.attr$ accessing the attribute $attr$ of class cls, we replace all the occurrence of $cls.attr$ in the corresponding statement of MSVL with the result of algorithm $find\_ClassAttr(cls, attr)$.

R10. For any instance method call statement $x = obj.fun(e\_1, \ldots, e\_n)$ (w.r.t. $obj.fun\ (e\_1, \ldots, e\_n)$) and obj is an instance of class cls, replace the statement in the corresponding MSVL function with the result of algorithm $find\_MemFun(cls, \text{"}obj\text{"}, \text{"}fun\text{"}, parTypeList)$ connected with the expression "$e\_1, \ldots, e\_n, \&x$)" (w.r.t. "$e\_1, \ldots, e\_n$)"), where $parTypeList$ is the data type list of the parameters $e\_1, \ldots, e_n$.

Table 2. Translation rules of data types

Python	MSVL	Python	MSVL
int	int	float	float
bool	boolean	string	string
tuple	list	list	list
set	list	dict	list

R11. For any static method call statement $x = cls.fun(e\_1, \ldots, e\_n)$ (w.r.t. $cls.fun(e\_1, \ldots, e\_n)$), replace the statement in the MSVL function with the result of algorithm $find\_StatFun(cls, \text{``} fun\text{''}, parTypeList)$ connected with the expression $(\text{``} e\_1, \ldots, e\_n, \& x\text{''})$ (w.r.t. $\text{``} e\_1, \ldots, e\_n\text{''})$, where $parTypeList$ is the data type list of the parameters $e\_1, \ldots, e_n$.

R12. For each return statement $return\ e$ in a general (member) function fun, replace the statement in the corresponding MSVL function with $*Ret := e$.

R13. For the object creation statement $obj = cls(e_1, \ldots, e_n)$, we replace it in the MSVL with a variable declare statement $struct\ cls\ obj$ and initialize the struct variable obj by calling the MSVL function corresponding to the constructor of class cls if it has, otherwise, initialize the inherited struct member $\_cls\_par$ with the function corresponding to the constructor of each parent class par. Besides, the data type of variable obj is the MSVL $struct\ cls$ corresponding to class cls.

R14. The data type of a Python variable, attribute or parameter can be identified by checking the data type of the expression assigned to it. For the assignment $v = e$ (w.r.t. $obj.att = e$), if e is a constant of boolean, integer, float or string, the data type of v (w.r.t attribute att) can be identified as bool, int, float or string. Further, if e is a composed expression based on variables with known data types, the data type of v (w.r.t attribute att) can be recognized by the computing rule of Python, e.g., let $v = a/b$, if a and b are both integer variables, the data type of v is float.

Among the above transition rules, R1 translates a general Python function into an MSVL function; R2 keeps the object data of Python with the struct of MSVL; R3 decodes the inherent attributes as the members of child class' MSVL struct; R4 handles the class attributes of Python classes with MSVL global variables; R5 deals with instance attributes initialized in the constructors of Python class as the member of corresponding MSVL struct; R6 decodes the encapsulation of instance methods of Python classes into MSVL functions keeping the ability to access the instance attributes as well as to take back the computing result; R7 treats with the overload of methods of Python classes; R8 and R9 decode the access of instance attributes and class ones; R10 and R11 handle the invocation of instance methods and class methods; R12 handles the return values; R13 deals with the dynamic creating objects; R14 gives the strategy to identify the data type of a variable, attribute or parameter. According to the semantics of

Table 3. Translation rules of expressions and statements

Type	Python	MSVL
Arithmetic expression	x [+ | - | * | / | % | != | == | > | <] y	x [+ | - | * | / | % | != | = | > | <] y
Boolean expression	b1 and b2 | b1 or b2 | not b	b1 and b2 | b1 or b2 \| !b
Assignment statement	$x = e$	$x := e$
	$obj.att = e$	$obj.att := e$
Sequential statement	S1	Stmt2M(S1);
	S2	Stmt2M (S2)
If statement	if b1:	if (b1) then
	S1	{ Stmt2M(S1) }
	[elif b2:	[else if (b2)
	S2]	{ Stmt2M(S2) }]
	.....	.....
	[else :	[else
	S3]	{ Stmt2M(S3) }]
While statement	while b:	while(condition)
	S	{ Stmt2M(S) }

Python, it is trivial to formalize the algorithms $find\_InsAttr$, $find\_Memfunc$, $find\_ClassAttr$ and $find\_Statfunc$ employed in Rules R8~R10 to compute the appropriate instance attribute, instance function, class attribute and static method respectively, so their details are omitted here.

For instance, as shown in Fig. 1, the Python program in left side consists of two classes A and B, and A is the super class of B. According to the R2 and R5, the MSVL defines two structs A and B in correspond with, and the instance attribute $count$ of class A is also the member of MSVL struct A. Subsequently, the super class A of B is represented as the member $\_parent\_A$ of struct B (R3). Further, the class attribute sm of A is regarded as the global variable A_sm of MSVL program (R4). Moreover, the overload functions sum of class B are named with different function names according to R6 and R7. Since the two function sum have return values, a new parameter Ret is added to the tail of the MSVL functions' parameters list respectively. Besides, the access of attribute $count$ in function $\_\_init\_\_$ of class A is replaced with the access of the member of MSVL struct, i.e., $self-> count$ (R8), and the return statement $return\ self.count$ in function sum is transformed into $*Ret := self-> \_parent\_A.count$ (R12). In addition, the object creation statement $obj = B()$ is handled as the definition MSVL variable obj of $struct\ B$, and calling the MSVL function $A\_init\_\_$ to initialize the variable (R13). Finally, the function call $sum = obj.sum(10, 20)$ is replace with the MSVL function call statement $B\_sum\_int\_int(\&obj, 10, 20, \&sum)$ (R10).

According to the transition rules above, the process for model checking a Python program is shown in Fig. 2. For a given Python program, firstly we analyze the source code by lexical analysis and obtain the Object-Oriented

Python program	struct A {	MSVL program
class A:	int count	
sm = 0	};	
def __init__(self):	struct B{	
count = 0	struct A _parent_A	
...	};	
class B(A):	function A__init__(struct A *self){	
def sum(self, m):	self->count :=0;	
...	...	
def sum(self, m, n):	};	
...	function B_sum_int(struct B *self, int m){	
return self.sm	...	
obj = B()	};	
sum = obj.sum(10, 20)	function B_sum_int_int(struct B *self, int m, int n, *Ret){	
	...	
	*Ret := self->sum	
	};	
	frame(A_sm, obj, sum) and (	
	int A_sm and A_sm <==0;	
	struct B obj and A__init__(&(B->A_parent_A));	
	int sum;	
	B_sum_int_int(&obj, 10, 20, &sum)	
	)	

Fig. 1. Example of transforming Python program into MSVL

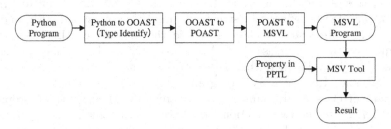

Fig. 2. Process of model checking Python program

Abstract Syntax Tree (OOAST) of the program; then transform the OOAST to the Process-Oriented Abstract Syntax Tree (POAST) and POAST to the MSVL program in sequence; finally verify the MSVL program on MSV platform. In the following subsections, we introduce the key techniques of each step in the process.

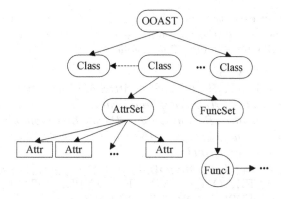

Fig. 3. Structure of Object-Oriented Abstract Syntax Tree

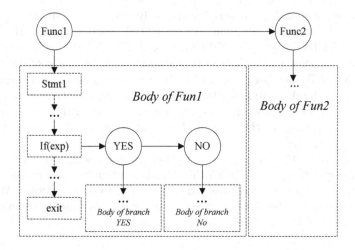

Fig. 4. Structure of Hierarchical Syntax Chart

3.2 Python Program to OOAST

In order to convert Python program into MSVL, we introduce the Object-Oriented Abstract Syntax Tree (OOAST) [28] to analyze the syntax of Python programs. The strategy of OOAST representing the syntax of Python program can be depicted as the figure in Fig. 3. The OOAST of Python program is the set of classes, and each class consists of the set of attributes, the set of member functions, and the possible inherent relations to its super classes. Besides, the technique of Hierarchical Syntax Chart (HSC) [29] is introduced to describe the syntax of each member functions. The structure of HSC is shown in Fig. 4. In first level, the HSC is the sequence of compound statements of functions, and the function body, a compound statement, is the sequence of statements in the function body. If the compound statement includes if, while or for statements, their corresponding execution breaches are also organized as the sequence of compound statements, e.g. the *if* statement in the body of function *Fun*1.

According to the above OOAST is as follows:

$$
\begin{aligned}
OOAST \quad &::= \ <ClassSet> \\
Class \quad &::= \ <name, [ParClassSet], AttrSet, FunSet> \\
Attr \quad &::= \ <[static], type, varName, [value]> \\
Fun \quad &::= \ <[static], RetType, name, ParamList, CompStmt> \\
Param \quad &::= \ <paramType, paramName> \\
CompStmt \ &::= \ <name, StmtList> \\
Stmt \quad &::= \ <StmtType, simpStmt> \ | \ <StmtType, CompStmtList> \\
StmtType \ &::= \ \text{TYPE\_COM} - \text{TYPE\_IF} - \text{TYPE\_SWITCH} \\
&\qquad - \text{TYPE\_LOOP} - \text{TYPE\_EXIT}
\end{aligned}
$$

where *type* and *RetType* are Python date types; *Fun* is a HSC which the compound statement *compStmt* describing the body of the function; *stmtType* indicates the statement is a common (TYPE_COM), branch (TYPE_IF), switch (TYPE_SWITCH), loop (TYPE_LOOP) or Exist (TYPE_EXT) statement. Within the *ClassSet*, a default class is defined to keep the syntax of the process-oriented part of Python program, which the general functions are recognized as the methods of the class, and the global variables are kept as the attributes of the class. Note that we suppose the Python program to be verified have no syntax errors, so the visibility of the Python classes, attributes and member functions are omitted in OOAST.

To create the OOAST for the given Python program, we first need to perform lexical parsing of the program with the Python's internal parser module, which provides the interface to access the parse trees of a Python program. With the syntax tree generated by Python compiler, it is not hard to write the algorithm to create the OOAST, so the details are omitted here.

3.3   Conversion from OOAST to POAST

Once the OOAST of a Python program is obtained, we then transform it into the Process-oriented Abstract Syntax Tree (POAST) which precisely describes the syntax of the MSVL program. As shown in Fig. 5, the structure of POAST is similarly to that of OOAST except that Python class is replaced with MSVL struct and the member functions in each Python class are transformed into the MSVL functions. Moreover, the syntax of MSVL functions are also described in HSC. The formal definition of POAST is as follows:

$$
\begin{aligned}
POAST \quad &::= \ <GlobalVarSet, StructSet, FunSet> \\
GlobalVar \ &::= \ <type, name> \\
Struct \quad &::= \ <name, MemberSet> \\
Member \quad &::= \ <type, name> \\
Fun \quad &::= \ <name, ParamsList, CompStmt> \\
Param \quad &::= \ <type, varName> \\
CompStmt \ &::= \ <name, StmtList> \\
Stmt \quad &::= \ <StmtType, simpStmt> \ | \ <StmtType, CompStmtList>
\end{aligned}
$$

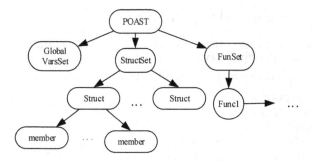

Fig. 5. Structure of Process-Oriented Abstract Syntax Tree

where *type* is a MSVL data type and *simpStmt* is elementary statement of MSVL.

According to the transition rules in Subsect. 3.1, the algorithm for converting OOAST into POAST consists of 10 functions whose relations are shown in Fig. 6. Function OOASTtoPOAST is the entry of the algorithm, and it traverse each class nodes in the OOAST. For each class node *cls*, function OOAST-toPOAST first calls functions Handle_Class, Handle_Parent, Handle_DynaAtts, Handle_StaticAtts to add a struct node *cls* (R2), deal with the inherited attributes (R3), deal with instance attributes (R5) and class attributes (R4) respectively, and then calls function Handle_HSC to process the HSC of the each general functions and member functions of classes. For each function's HSC, function Handle_HSC calls functions *Handle_FuncName*, *Replace_Vars*, *Handle_FuncCall* and *Change_RetValue* in sequence to handle the function header (R6, R7), replace the access of class' attributes with members of MSVL struct (R8, R9), handle the function call (R10, R11, R13) as well as deal with the return statement (Rule R12) respectively. The code of the functions is trivial and hence skipped here.

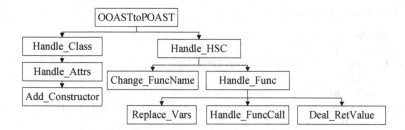

Fig. 6. Algorithm for converting OOAST into POAST

3.4 Conversion from POAST to MSVL

Now the left work is to convert the POAST to MSVL program. The pseudocode of the algorithm POASTtoMSVL is formalized as follows, where the code of function HSC2MSVL can be found in literature [29].

```
POASTtoMSVL(POAST *ast){
    string msvlCode;
    //deal with struct
    foreach cls in ast->StructSet{
        msvlCode +=  "\n struct " + cls.name + "{";
        foreach mem in cls.MemberSet{
            msvlCode += mem.type +" "+ mem.name + " and "
        }
        msvlCode +=  "};"
    }
    foreach fun in ast->FunSet{
        msvlCode +=  HSC2MSVL(fun);
    }
    return msvlCode;
}
```

4 Case Study

In following, we give an example to illustrate how our method works in verifying a Python program. Kaprekar's problem is a interesting question in number theory. It asserts that for any given 4-digit number x which the digits cannot be the same one, if we rearrange the 4 digits to get a maximum 4-digit number m and a minimum one n, and then update x with $m - n$, i.e., let $x = m - n$. If we repeatedly apply the calculating rule to x, then x must eventually equals a fix number 6174. The implementing of Kapreka problem can be depicted as the following Python program.

```python
class Number:
    numLen = 4
    def __init__(self): #Constructor
        self.num = 0
        self.arr = [0,0,0,0]
    def sort(self): #Sort the 4 digits in ascend order
        i = 0
        while i < self.numLen:
            j = 0
            while j < self.numLen - i - 1:
                if self.arr[j] > self.arr[j + 1]:
                    tmp = self.arr[j + 1]
                    self.arr[j + 1] = self.arr[j]
                    self.arr[j] = tmp
```

```
                j = j + 1
            i = i + 1
def deNum(self): #Compute the 4 digits in the number num
    ......              # and keep them in the array arr.
def checkValid(self): #Validating the given 4-digit number
    ......
def minNum(self): #Get the min-number with the 4 digits
    tmp = 0
    i = 0
    while i < self.numLen:
        tmp = tmp * 10 + self.arr[i]
        i = i + 1
    return tmp
def maxNum(self): #Get the max-number with the 4 digits
    ......              #Similar to function minNum
def run(self, n): #Implementing the Kapreka problem
    self.num = n
    val = self.checkValid()
    if not val :
        print("Not a valid nmber")
        return
    found = False
    while not found:
        self.deNum()
        self.sort()
        max = self.maxNum()
        min = self.minNum()
        diff = max - min
        if diff != self.num :
            self.num = diff
        else :
            found = True
    print(self.num)
numObj = Number()
m = input("Please input a 4-digit number: ")
n = int(m)
numObj.run(n)
```

Firstly, we analyze the lexical and syntax of the Python program to generate OOAST as shown in Fig. 7, where we only give the member function *sort* of class Number. In the figure, the *Default* class is employed to keep syntax tree of the process-oriented part of the Python program, include the object *numObj* and the variable *m* and *n*. Then, we employ algorithm OOASTtoPOAST to transform the OOAST into the POAST as shown in Fig. 8. The object-oriented semantics of the Python program is decoded with the MSVL semantics. Subsequently, we use algorithm POASTtoMSVL to transform the POAST into MSVL program and the result is as follows, where code of MSVL functions Number_deNum, Number_checkValid, Number_minNum and Number_maxNum is omitted here.

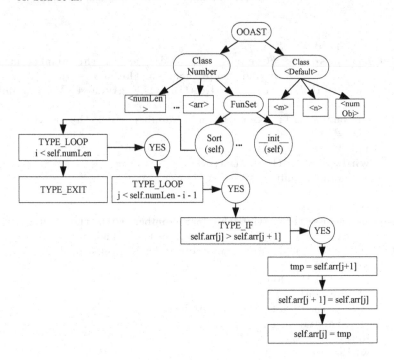

Fig. 7. OOAST of the Python program

```
frame(Number_numLen) and (
    Number_numLen <== 4 and skip;
    struct Number{
        int num and
        int arr[4]
    };
    function Number_init_(struct Number *self){
        self->num<==0 and skip
    };
    function Number_sort(struct Number *self){
        frame(i, j, tmp) and (
        int i and i<==0 and skip;
        while(i<Number_numLen){
            int j and j<==0 and skip;
            while(j<Number_numLen−i−1){
                if(self->arr[j]>self->arr[j+1])then{
                    int tmp and tmp<==self->a[j+1] and skip;
                    self->arr[j+1]<==self->arr[j] and skip;
                    self->arr[j]<==tmp and skip;
                };
                j:=j+1 and skip;
            };
            i:=i+1
```

```
        }
    )
};
```

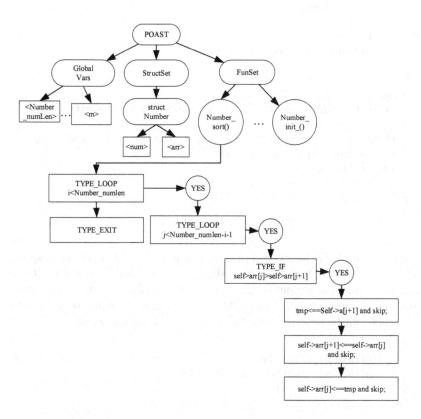

Fig. 8. POAST of the Python program

```
......
function Number_run(struct Number *self,int n){
    frame(val, found, max, min, diff) and (
        this.num:=n and skip;
            bool val and Number_checkValid(self,&val)and skip;
        if( !val )then{
            Output("Not a valid number") and skip;
            return
        };
        bool found and found<==false and skip;
        while(!found){
            Number_deNum(self) and skip;
                Number_sort(self) and skip;
            int max and Number_maxNum(self, &max) and skip;
            int min and Number_minNum(self, &min) and skip;
```

```
                int  diff  and  diff <== max − min  and  skip;
                if( diff!=self−>num)then{
                    self−>num :=  diff
                } else{
                    found :=true
                }
            };
            Output(self−>num) and  skip
        )
    };
    frame(numObj, m, n) and(
        struct Number numObj and Number__init__(&numObj) and
            skip;
        Output("Please input a 4−digit integer: ") and skip;
        int m and input(m) and skip;
        int n and n:=m;
        Number_run(&numObj, n) and skip
    )
)
```

We now can verify the Python program by model checking the corresponding
MSVL program with MSV tool. According to the Kaprekar's problem, it is easy
to figure out that the property "given a 4-digit number m, after finite steps of
calculation, the final result of $numObj− > num$ must be equal to 6174" always
holds, which can be describe with the following PPTL formulas:

```
</
    define p: m >= 1000 ;
    define q: numObj−>num = 6174 ;
    alw(p−>stims q)
/>
```

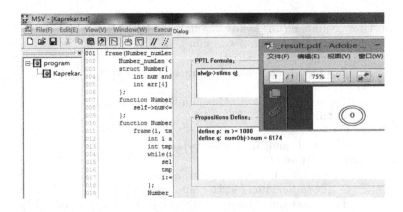

Fig. 9. Verification result of the program

Model checking the MSVL program obtained on the MSV with the input integer 2019, an empty LNFG with no edge is produced as shown in Fig. 9. Thus, the property holds.

5 Conclusion

In this paper, a novel model checking method for verifying Python programs is presented, which transforms a Python program into its equivalent MSVL program, and then verifying whether the expected property holds on the MSV platform. Compared to existing model checking method of Python, the method proposed can check more properties expressed in PPTL such as safety and liveness, etc. But the work of this paper only concerns the basic part of the Python language. In the near future, we will extend the work to more Python features, such as such as override, multi-thread, etc.

References

1. Sanner, M.F.: Python: a programming language for software integration and development. J. Mol. Graph. Model. **17**(1), 57–61 (1999)
2. Clarke, E.M.: Model checking. Lect. Notes Comput. Sci. **164**(2), 305–349 (1999)
3. Holzmann, J.: The model checker SPIN. IEEE Trans. Softw. Eng. **23**(5), 279–295 (1997)
4. Cavada, R., Cimatti, A., Jochim, C.A.: NuSMV 2.5 User Manual. http://nusmv.fbk.eu/NuSMV/userman/v25/nusmv.pdf
5. Ball, T., Rajarnani, S.K.: The SLAM project: debugging system software via static analysis. In: POPL 2002, pp. 1–3 (2002)
6. Henzinger, T.A., Jhala, R., Majumdar, R., Sutre, G.: Software verification with BLAST. In: Ball, T., Rajamani, S.K. (eds.) SPIN 2003. LNCS, vol. 2648, pp. 235–239. Springer, Heidelberg (2003). https://doi.org/10.1007/3-540-44829-2_17
7. Chaki, S., Clarke, E., Groce, A., et al.: Modular verification of software components in C. In: International Conference on Software Engineering, pp. 385–395 (2003)
8. Cordeiro, L., Morse, J., Nicole, D., Fischer, B.: Context-bounded model checking with ESBMC 1.17. In: Flanagan, C., König, B. (eds.) TACAS 2012. LNCS, vol. 7214, pp. 534–537. Springer, Heidelberg (2012). https://doi.org/10.1007/978-3-642-28756-5_42
9. Brat, G., Havelund, K., Visser, W.: Java PathFinder-Second Generation of a Java Model Checker (2000)
10. Yu, Y., Duan, Z., Tian, C., Yang, M.: Model checking C programs with MSVL. In: Liu, S. (ed.) SOFL 2012. LNCS, vol. 7787, pp. 87–103. Springer, Heidelberg (2013). https://doi.org/10.1007/978-3-642-39277-1_7
11. Shu, X., Luo, N., Wang, B., Wang, X., Zhao, L.: Model checking Java programs with MSVL. In: Duan, Z., Liu, S., Tian, C., Nagoya, F. (eds.) SOFL+MSVL 2018. LNCS, vol. 11392, pp. 89–107. Springer, Cham (2019). https://doi.org/10.1007/978-3-030-13651-2_6
12. Duan, Z., Yang, X., Koutny, M.: Framed temporal logic programming. Sci. Comput. Program. **70**(1), 31–61 (2008)
13. Duan, Z.: Temporal Logic and Temporal Logic Programming. Science Press, Beijing (2005)

14. Duan, Z., Tian, C., Zhang, L.: A decision procedure for propositional projection temporal logic with infinite models. Acta Informatica **45**(1), 43–78 (2008)

15. Zhang, N., Duan, Z., Tian, C.: A cylinder computation model for many-core parallel computing. Theoret. Comput. Sci. **497**, 68–83 (2013)

16. Tian, C., Duan, Z., Duan, Z.: Making CEGAR more efficient in software model checking. IEEE Trans. Softw. Eng. **40**(12), 1206–1223 (2014)

17. Zhang, N., Duan, Z., Tian, C.: A complete axiom system for propositional projection temporal logic with cylinder computation model. Theoret. Comput. Sci. **609**, 639–657 (2016)

18. Duan, Z., Tian, C.: A practical decision procedure for propositional projection temporal logic with infinite models. Theoret. Comput. Sci. **554**, 169–190 (2014)

19. Tian, C., Duan, Z., Zhang, N.: An efficient approach for abstraction-refinement in model checking. Theoret. Comput. Sci. **461**, 76–85 (2012)

20. Duan, Z.: Modeling and Analysis of Hybrid Systems. Science Press, Beijing (2004)

21. Wang, M., Duan, Z., Tian, C.: Simulation and verification of the virtual memory management system with MSVL. In: CSCWD 2014, pp. 360–365 (2014)

22. Shu, X., Duan, Z.: Model checking process scheduling over multi-core computer system with MSVL. In: Liu, S., Duan, Z. (eds.) SOFL+MSVL 2015. LNCS, vol. 9559, pp. 103–117. Springer, Cham (2016). https://doi.org/10.1007/978-3-319-31220-0_8

23. Wang, X., Tian, C., Duan, Z., Zhao, L.: MSVL: a typed language for temporal logic programming. Front. Comput. Sci. **5**, 762–785 (2017)

24. Shu, X., Duan, Z.: Extending MSVL with semaphore. In: Dinh, T.N., Thai, M.T. (eds.) COCOON 2016. LNCS, vol. 9797, pp. 599–610. Springer, Cham (2016). https://doi.org/10.1007/978-3-319-42634-1_48

25. Zhang, N., Duan, Z., Tian, C.: A mechanism of function calls in MSVL. Theoret. Comput. Sci. **654**, 11–25 (2016)

26. Tian, C., Duan, Z.: Expressiveness of propositional projection temporal logic with star. Theoret. Comput. Sci. **412**(18), 1729–1744 (2011)

27. Duan, Z., Tian, C.: A unified model checking approach with projection temporal logic. In: Liu, S., Maibaum, T., Araki, K. (eds.) ICFEM 2008. LNCS, vol. 5256, pp. 167–186. Springer, Heidelberg (2008). https://doi.org/10.1007/978-3-540-88194-0_12

28. Shu, X., Wang, M., Wang, X.: Extending UML for model checking. In: Tian, C., Nagoya, F., Liu, S., Duan, Z. (eds.) SOFL+MSVL 2017. LNCS, vol. 10795, pp. 88–107. Springer, Cham (2018). https://doi.org/10.1007/978-3-319-90104-6_6

29. Shu, X., Li, C., Liu, C.: A Visual modeling language for MSVL. In: Liu, S., Duan, Z., Tian, C., Nagoya, F. (eds.) SOFL+MSVL 2016. LNCS, vol. 10189, pp. 220–237. Springer, Cham (2017). https://doi.org/10.1007/978-3-319-57708-1_13

Software Analysis and Evolution

Prediction of Function Removal Propagation in Linux Evolution

Lei Wang$^{(\boxtimes)}$, Guoxiong Chen, and Liang Li

School of Computer Science and Engineering, Beihang University,
Beijing 100191, China
wanglei@buaa.edu.cn

Abstract. Software studies on the function level, which is inherently different than coarse-grained investigations, contributes to the deep understanding of the laws of software internal evolution. This paper focuses on the life cycle distribution and the propagation behaviour of removed functions in Linux kernels. After an in-depth analysis of 300 Linux kernels, from Version 2.6.12-rc2 to 3.7-rc6, we found that most removed functions have relatively low life cycles, which indicates that many functions are likely to be removed between two consecutive versions. Our experimental results also show that function removal propagation is closely related to the file containing the functions, function call dependency, and historical information. This motivated us to propose a few heuristics to predict function removal propagation, which are based on the file position, call graph, and historical information in *git*. Furthermore, we analyzed the impact of removed functions on software structure and found that Linux kernel has a strong resistance to function removal. The life cycle feature and the prediction heuristics presented in this paper can be utilized to facilitate the maintenance of large-scale complex software systems.

Keywords: Removal propagation · Linux · Function life cycle

1 Introduction

Software systems continue to evolve to meet various new requirements such as introducing new features, extending original functions and repairing bugs, otherwise they will suffer from aging [17]. There have been many software evolution studies over the past decades. Most of them investigated the problem from the perspective of the whole system [12] or the whole module [20]. We, however, focus on the fine-grained function level, which can provide more specific guidance on software development and maintenance. We analyze the life cycle and removal propagation of functions in software evolution. In our research, the life cycle of a function is defined as the number of continuous versions where the function exists. For example, function A appears in version one and is removed in version four. Assuming that natural numbers are used to denote different versions and the first version start from one, the life cycle of function A is three. The life

© Springer Nature Switzerland AG 2020
H. Miao et al. (Eds.): SOFL+MSVL 2019 Workshop, LNCS 12028, pp. 227–242, 2020.
https://doi.org/10.1007/978-3-030-41418-4_16

cycle of a function is similar to the age of a human being. Of course, for software functions, we use versions instead of years to measure their life cycle.

We found that the number of functions in Linux 2.6.12 is 121,511 and that becomes 334,443 in Linux 3.7. Namely, 96,612 functions, which accounts for 79% and 28% in these two versions respectively, are removed. Therefore, it is meaningful to study the behaviour of function removal propagation. Software change propagation analysis is important for maintaining continuously-evolving software because inconsistent changes may lead to bugs [2, 3, 13, 21, 22]. Several heuristics were proposed to predict software change propagation in [7]. However, since the proposed heuristics were devised to work for general software changes, they might not lead to the best result from the viewpoint of function removal propagation. We focuses on function removal propagation in Linux because Linux is widely used and has excellent version control. To predict how function removal propagates, we proposed some heuristics based on file position, call graph and historical information.

The major contributions of this paper are presented as follows:

Firstly, we used the file position, call graph, and historical information extracted from every commit to predict function removal propagation in Linux. We also studied the heuristics, which combine history information with file position and call graph, to predict function removal propagation. We found that the prediction of function removal propagation achieved comparable recall rate and higher precision rate (19.2% and 23.5% for the heuristics based on call graph and file position respectively), which is very different than the experimental results corresponding to general software changes [7].

Then, we analyzed the characteristics and impacts of removed functions on software structure from the perspective of call graph. It was found that, among the removed functions, the number of functions that have a minor impact on software structure with only out-degree, or without both in-degree and out-degree account for 43.6%. Among the removed functions with only in-degree, or with both in-degree and out-degree, the renamed functions and the short functions (less than three lines) that also have a minor impact on software structure account for 30%. The experimental results indicated that Linux kernel has a strong resistance to function removal.

The rest of this paper is organized as follows. Section 1 introduces the data set in this paper. The life cycle of functions in Linux kernel is analyzed in Sect. 2. Section 3 describes the removal propagation prediction model. The prediction heuristics based on file position, call graph and historical information are presented in Sect. 4. Section 5 covers the related work briefly. The paper closes with our conclusions in Sect. 6.

2   Linux Data Extraction

In this paper, the data are all from Linux Kernel revision control tool *git* or dependency file generated from compiling Linux kernel. We get 1,540,138 commit information through *git* for Linux Kernel from 2.6.12-rc3 to 3.7-rc6 total of 300 versions [10]. From our statistics, it was found that a total of 96,097 function were removed while only 61,660 of them are Full-tracked (historical information include its birth and death modification record). Thus, we only collected the life cycle and commit distribution of 61,660 removed functions. In addition, according to the version numbering scheme of Linux kernel, the version number suffixed with "rc" is release candidate version. Number without rc is official version. Every official version experiences several rc versions before its release. Thus, we collected the call graphs from dependency file by compiling Linux kernel from 2.6.0 to 2.6.39 total of 40 official versions. In our research, for clarity, we assigned sequence numbers to these Linux kernel versions according to the chronological order.

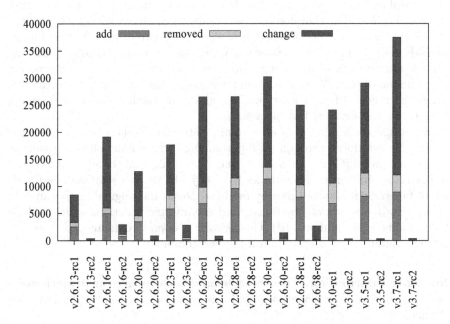

Fig. 1. Add, removed and changed functions and its proportion

2.1 Data for Function Life Cycle

ctags [5] is a static analysis tool for source code to generate an index file. We make use of *ctags* to analyze Linux kernel to extract the life cycle of functions. We use function name to identify existence of function. Even though we won't analyze removal propagation involving rc version, we still add rc version when we calculate life cycle of function because we can get a more smooth curve. The process is as follows:

(1) Get function name of every source file suffixed with *c* and head file suffixed with *h* in a version by *ctags*. (2) Repeat Step 1 to finish all 300 versions. (3) Get life cycle of all removed functions.

2.2 Data for Prediction of Function Removal Propagation

In Linux kernel, the first rc version of Linux kernel namely rc-1 always merges a large number of new feature from other branches and successive rc versions contain a few modification. Figure 1 describes the great difference between the first rc version and other rc version in aspect of the number of functions that added, removed and changed compared with its previous version. Thus, for simplicity, we don't analyze function removal propagation between rc version, but analyze removal propagation between successive official version.

Commits of Functions. Commit in *git* means a submission to *git* server. The *git* will generate a unique ID for this commit (Commit number) to identify source code state after that commit. We analyzed commit with only one father commit (previous commit) because the commit with two or more father commit is mostly used to merge code (merge), which has no code revision. A commit may contain revisions of many functions. The number of commits of a function is the number of commits that contain revisions of this function in its entire life. A removed function has at least two commits in its birth and death. Commits of Functions was extracted as follows:

(a) Obtain Hash number of all commits between two successive version. (b) Get *diff* file (produced through *git diff* command whose function is the same as Linux command *diff*) of each commit, and extract file name of affected files and modified line number in affected files from *diff* file. (c) Get start and end position of functions in affected files by modified *ctags* (the original *ctags* can only generate start position of functions), find the affected functions which include those modified line number. (d) Through *git checkout* command to switch to another commit. Goto Step (b) until the last commit.

Developer Information. There is log information in each commit which stores the email address of developer. We used this email address to identify developer information.

Call Graph of Linux Kernels. *codeviz* [4] is a patch for GCC [1], the GCC patched with *codeviz* will dump extra information including function name and call graph when compiling software source code. We used gcc 3.4.1 patched with *codeviz* 1.0.3 to compile Linux kernel from 2.6.0 to 2.6.39 total of 40 official versions.

3 Removal Propagation Prediction Model

Figure 2 illustrates the prediction model of function removal propagation according to Ref. [7]. There exist an initial removed function because of a request for a new feature, a feature enhancement, or the need to fix a bug. Once the initial entity is removed, the developer then analyzes the source code to determine the

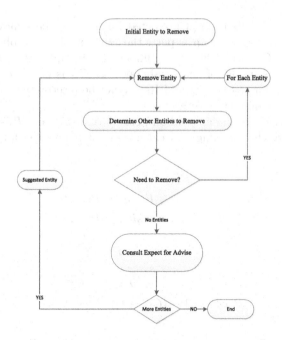

Fig. 2. Removal propagation prediction model

other functions which must be removed due to propagation. Then proceeding continue to remove those entities and propagation process is repeated for them. When the developer cannot locate other entities to remove, he has to consult an expert and gets a function that must be removed if it exists. The developer regards this function as another initial function and repeats propagation. This continues until all appropriate functions have been removed. At the end of this process, the developer has determined the removed set for the new requirement at hand. Ideally all appropriate functions should have been removed to ensure consistent assumptions throughout the system.

The expert can be a senior developer, a software development tool, or a suite of tests. So developers would like to minimize their dependence on an expert. They need software development tools that enable them to confidently determine the need to propagate removed functions without having to seek the assistance of expert [7].

Prediction performance mainly consider about the precision and recall. We define the total set of predicted functions to be removed as the Predicted set (P). The set of functions that needed to be predicted will be called the Occurred set (O). We define N as the number of removed functions between successive versions, and PO as the number of elements in the intersection set of the prediction set and the occurred set. According to the above definitions, Recall and Precision can be defined as Eqs. (1) and (2). To facilitate understanding, we introduce another variable CC. When the removal propagation prediction completes, we will get some isolate subgraph of predicted functions to be removed. For each additional consultation with an expert, the number of subgraph will increase by one. We use CC to represent the number of subgraph and r_i represent the number of elements in one of those subgraph s_i. CC is equal to the times we consult experts. As a result, PO and Recall can be interpreted as Eqs. (4) and (5), CC is the determinant of recall.

O and PO is easy to understand and calculation. CC and P is not obvious, so we will analyze the meaning and calculation of P and CC for each specific prediction heuristic.

$$Recall = PO/O \tag{1}$$
$$Precision = PO/P \tag{2}$$
$$P = \sum_{i=1}^{CC} r_i \tag{3}$$
$$PO = N - CC \tag{4}$$
$$Recall = 1 - (CC - 1)/(N - 1) \tag{5}$$

4 Heuristics for Removal Propagation Prediction

There exist some relevance between functions removed. We can use certain rules to find other function through an initial removed function. Rules can be such as call relationship because removal of the callee may cause removal of the caller. Modular design is a basic strategy of software design, interrelated functions often appear in the same folder or the same file, so the file position of functions can be used to predict removal propagation. Moreover, due to capability and interest of developer, removal propagation may happen among all function developed by the same developer.

Consequently, in this paper, we use file position, call graph and historical information of function to predict function removal propagation.

4.1 File Position Heuristic

Although there exist subjective factors in software code layout, developer will put functions which have close relationship with each other in the same file for maintenance and reading. So if some of them should be removed, other functions in the same file is probable to be removed. Different modules in Linux kernel are relatively independent between each other, so removal propagation behavior may also be different. We selected six modules which exist since the initial Linux version as net, arch, drivers, fs, kernel, mm to analyze.

Guided by the removal propagation prediction model, we have an initial removed function f_i in file ff_i and the removal will propagate to all function that are added into d_i in ff_i. Obviously CC is equal to the number of files

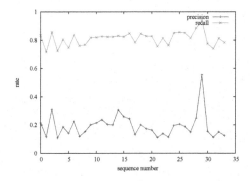

Fig. 3. Precision and recall of file position heuristic

Table 1. Average recall and precision of different modules

	Recall	Precision
net	0.68	0.09
arch	0.76	0.27
drivers	0.83	0.19
fs	0.69	0.08
kernel	0.73	0.07
mm	0.57	0.03

that contain removed function, because propagation process will stop when no function need be removed in a file ff_i and we must ask an expert.

Figure 3 depicts prediction precision and recall rate by using file position heuristic, X axis is version number, Y axis represents the percentage of recall rate and precision. On average, removal probability of functions in the same file at the same version is 25.5%.

The average result is list in Table 1.

4.2 Call Graph Heuristic

Call graph represents the interdependence between functions, if the function A calls function B, it is reasonable to predict the removal of function A if function B is removed. Some studies have found that call graph is not a good prediction heuristic for software change propagation [7] while we get different results when apply it on the prediction of function removal propagation.

Guided by the removal propagation prediction model, we have an initial removed function f_i and the removal will propagate to all function called by f_i and caller of f_i will be added into d_i.

The value of CC depends on clustering of removed functions through call relation. The worst case is that there are no call relation between removed function. CC is equal to N, the best case is that all removed function were in a graph

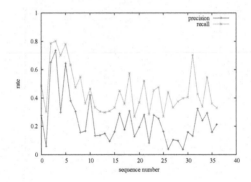

Fig. 4. Precision and recall of call graph heuristic

when prediction completed. CC is equal to one. Therefore CC falls between N and one under deferent circumstances.

Figure 4 shows the precision and recall rate of call graph heuristic. On the whole, the predicting precision of call graph heuristic is higher than that of file position heuristic, but the recall rate is lower than that of file position heuristic.

Characteristics of Removed Functions. Functions in call graph can be classified into four kinds by existence of in-degree and out-degree. They are functions with only in-degree, or out-degree, functions without degree, and functions having both in-degree and out-degree (short for IN, OUT, ZERO and BOTH respectively). Figure 5 shows that the majority of removed functions are OUT and BOTH accounting for average 36.8% and 47.4%, IN and ZERO accounting for average 8.9% and 6.7%.

We found some characteristics of them depending on the analysis of removed functions from version 2.6.13 to 2.6.14.

* ZERO: These functions are featured with empty or short (not more than three line) body, some of them act as function pointer. Such as *dummy_inode_post_symlink*, it is a default safety function pointer when there is no other security module. In 2.6.14 *dummy_inode_post_symlink* is removed. ZERO functions always like an island on call graph, removal of them will not directly affect the kernel structure.
* IN: These functions are featured with the short body. Most of them are removed because they are absorbed directly into their caller. For example in 2.6.13, slab allocator function *ac_entry* become an attribute entry of its caller *array_cache* in 2.6.14.
* OUT: In call graph, OUT functions have no in-degree because most of them act as function pointer. As we known, function pointer is a design strategy for easy replacement. It is widely used in VFS. Removed function *w1_default_read_name* is used as a function pointer.
* BOTH: There exist short functions which were removed the same as IN. Some of them were renamed with little change on the name of variable. Some

of them are refactored such as *expand_fd_array* which has 69 lines of code expanding file descriptor table in 2.6.13. According to the call relationships and code similarity, we find that it becames *expand_fdtable* in 2.6.14. Their caller are *expand_files*. Some of them were removed because significant changes of their caller, such as *get_pci_port* with 60 lines of code called by *serial_register* with 48 lines of code which were used to register the serial port on the PCI card in 2.6.13. After refactory in 2.6.14 *serial_register* shrink to 14 lines of code and *get_pci_port* were removed.

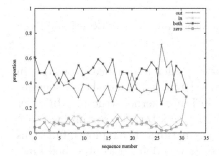

Fig. 5. Proportion of in, out, zero and both

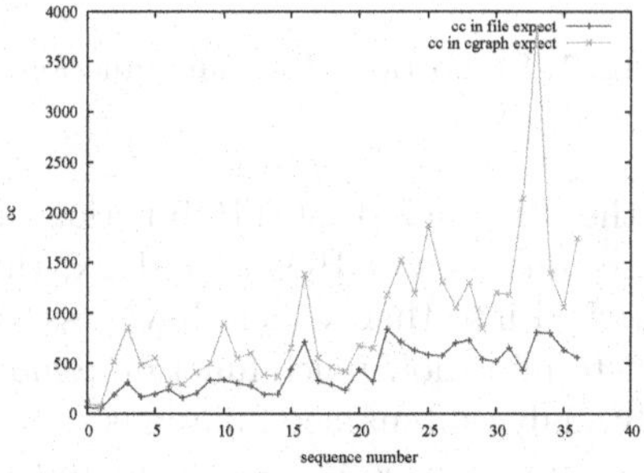

Fig. 6. *CC* of file position and call graph

Recall Rate Analysis. As we known, *CC* is the determinant of recall rate. The larger *CC* is, the lower recall rate will be. It is known that recall rate of file position heuristic is great than that of call graph. Figure 6 describes the difference on *CC* between file position and call graph, X axis represents the version number and Y axis represents the number of *CC*. From Fig. 6, we can see that *CC* of file position is always smaller than that of call graph, which indicates that removed functions tend to cluster in the same file, not call graph. The main reason is that ZERO and OUT function account for a large part (45.7%) of removed functions (See Fig. 5). For the removed functions of OUT type, 82% of them can not be predicted from other removed functions because they do not connect with other removed functions.

Function Removal Impact on Software Structure. Usually function change has impact on the structure of a software while the software with good design should be less affected. We study how function removal affects software structure.

In call graph, ZERO and OUT functions clearly have less impact on software architecture because removal of them will not affect other functions directly. Removal of BOTH and IN functions tend to affect more functions because they are usually complex structured. In one hand, IN functions have more callers.

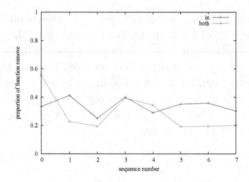

Fig. 7. Proportion of rename functions and absorbed functions in BOTH and IN

In the other hand BOTH functions have both caller and callee. However, in those functions of BOTH and IN, the renamed functions and short functions absorbed into their callers have less impact on Linux kernel structure. In order to determine how much function removal affects Linux kernel structure, we carefully analyzed renamed functions and absorbed functions. The removed functions whose function body has not more than three line is defined as absorbed function. We identify renamed functions from two aspect including longest common string (lcs) and code line difference (loc) according to Ref. [9].

$$Dloc = min(loc(f_r, f_n))/max(loc(f_r, f_n)) \tag{6}$$

$$Rlcs = lcs(f_r, f_n)/min(len(f_r), len(f_n)) \tag{7}$$

$$Similarity = Rlcs * Dloc \tag{8}$$

here f_r is a removed function and f_n is a new function in one version. We use the value of similarity between two functions to determine whether they are rename from one to another. With carefully observation, we think 0.7 is a appropriate threshold value, because at this point, the changes only happen on the name of some variables.

We look for renamed functions from the new functions. Moreover in order to reduce the time complexity, we only calculate similarity between removed functions and new functions whose first and second directory are the same.

Figure 7 describes the proportion of rename functions and absorbed functions in BOTH and IN. From Fig. 7, We found they account for about 30% in BOTH and IN.

All case including OUT, ZERO, and the above two considered, removed functions with minor impact on Linux kernel account for approximately 60%. This means most function removal don't affect the structure of Linux kernel. Namely Linux kernel has a strong resistance for functions removal.

4.3   Historical Information Heuristic

We collected historical information including developer information and commit information. A commit has a owner who submit this commit. When developer information used as prediction heuristic, all functions owned by a developer will be propagated when one of his/her functions were removed. When commit information used as prediction heuristic, all functions in one commit will be propagated. Obviously prediction set of commit information is the subset of that of developer information.

Suppose that function A was modified in different commits by different developers, D_A is the propagation prediction set by developer heuristic, F_A is the propagation prediction set by commit information. F_A will not be great than D_A because there may exist developers who submit two or more commits. As a result, the prediction set of developer information will be great than that of commit information while CC is less than that of commit information. Therefore the precision of commit information will be higher than that of developer information, while recall rate of commit information will be less than that of developer information.

Even though we will not analyze removal propagation between rc versions, commit information between them will be added to historical information as a whole.

Developer Information. We use developer information because we think function owned by the same developer may have close correlation. Linux kernel is a very complex software consist of a lot of functions. A developer can only focus on a very small part of them.

According to the removal propagation prediction model, we have an initial removed function f_i whose developer is a_i and the removal will propagate to all functions a_i owned added into d_i. Special attention should be paid that f_i may be modified by more than one developer, we will add all functions owned by those developer to prediction set. Due to some functions that no longer exists in the current versions, these functions will not be added to prediction set.

Theoretically the largest value of CC is N when every removed function was owned by different developer. In fact, a developer often owns many functions and a function may be owned by more than one developer. There is a great probability that CC is far less than N.

Figure 8 shows precision and recall of developer information heuristic. The average precision is 0.0346 and average recall rate is 0.658. The reason why the precision is too low is that we get many developers when a function with more than one owner is removed.

In addition, due to the lack of historical information, the recall rate is low at the beginning. Then, the recall rates in later versions become normal.

Analysis of Recall Rate and Precision. Similar to the recall analysis of call graph, we study the value of CC to find why the recall rate of developer

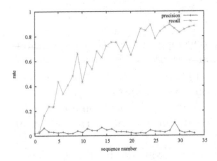

Fig. 8. Precision and recall of prediction with developer information heuristic

Fig. 9. Average number of functions owned by per developer

Table 2. Number of effective ownership record of some developers till 3.6

Modified the number of functions	Developer E-mail
17594	jeffrey.t.kirsher@intel.com
13045	tiwai@suse.de
9851	joe@perches.com
7975	gregkh@suse.de
5815	viro@zeniv.linux.org.uk
5467	tglx@linutronix.de

information heuristic is high. In the worst case, every removed function is isolate and owned by only one developer, so CC is equal to the number of removed functions. In the best case, the removed functions construct a connected graph through ownership, and CC is equal to one. Specifically if functions are owned by the same developer, we think they are connected directly. Besides a function often has more than one developer, it is possible that all the removed functions exist in one connected graph.

The initial number of developers is 674 in version 2.6.12, it become 7,958 in version 3.6. The number of effective ownership record grow from at the beginning to the end of 552,303. Ownership record is two-tuples (email address, function name and its directory).

Figure 9 describes changes of the average number of ownership record per developer along with version number increase. It can be seen that the average number of ownership keep stable at about 40 after initial rapid grow up. From Table 2, the distribution is extremely uneven, the largest number of ownership record (jeffrey.t.kirsher@intel.com) is 17,594 while the least is only one. That is to say if one of the function owned by jeffrey.t.kirsher@intel.com was removed, removal propagation will spread to all function he owned. If the function has more than one owner, the process will repeat without increase of CC.

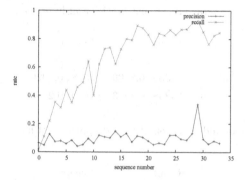

Fig. 10. Precision and recall of commit information heuristic

Commit Information. Generally, we can get a specific purpose from the log in commit. If some functions were modified in the same commit, it is reasonable to assume that they will be removed at the same time.

According to the removal propagation prediction model, we have an initial removed function f_i which are modified in commit c_i and the removal will propagate to all functions modified in c_i. It is noteworthy that f_i may be modified in more than one commit in history. We will add functions with f_i in all commits to predicted set.

The value of CC depends on the number of commits per removed function and functions in each commit.

The average precision of commit information heuristic is 0.0940 which is three times lager than that of developer information. That means removed functions tend to cluster due to modification, not ownership. The average recall rate is 0.625, which is a litter less than that of developer information. The reason is that the prediction set of commit information heuristic is the subset of developer information's.

Unlike file position heuristic and call graph heuristic, the richness of historical information affected precision and recall rate of prediction severely. For example, function F will be removed and no modified record about F exist in historical information, the propagation will stop which lead to lower precision and recall rate.

We collect historical information beginning at version 2.6.12, so historical information is incomplete for these early versions of *git*. This leads to the low recall rate of removal propagation prediction in these version. From our statistics, even though 61,660 out of 96,097 removed function are full-tracked.

4.4   Hybrid Heuristic

File position heuristic and call graph heuristic only used current information. Result may be improved when combine historical information with current information. According to previous result, the historical information heuristic has a

Table 3. Average recall and precision of hybrid approach

	Recall		Precision	
	Yes	No	Yes	No
file	0.7835	0.8109	0.2558	0.1926
cgraph	0.4858	0.4483	0.1950	0.2353

Table 4. Average recall and precision of hybrid approach of file position and commit on different modules

	Recall		Precision	
	Yes	No	Yes	No
drivers	0.8159	0.8370	0.2491	0.1994
fs	0.6465	0.6954	0.1314	0.0878
kernel	0.6540	0.7358	0.1216	0.0765
mm	0.4461	0.5733	0.0519	0.0301
arch	0.7369	0.7648	0.3446	0.2702
net	0.6344	0.6803	0.1495	0.0966

relatively high prediction precision and recall rate. Thus, we combined commit information with other two methods to predict function removal propagation.

File position heuristic prediction has higher precision and recall, and we hope to use commit information to further improve the precision. Prediction set of this hybrid method is intersection set of their prediction set. Note that if removed functions have no commit heuristic prediction set, we use only file heuristic prediction set. We also apply this hybrid method on different modules of Linux kernel. In order to improve recall rate of call graph heuristic, we combined with commit heuristic.

Table 3 describes the result of hybrid heuristic ("Yes" means hybrid heuristic). Table 3 shows that precision of hybrid heuristic of file position and commit increases by 6% while the recall rate declines by 4%. The precision and recall rate of call graph and commit are falling and rising by 4% respectively. Table 4 shows that the result of different modules in Linux ("Yes" means hybrid heuristic). The recall rate of all modules decreases while the precision rate increases. The increase of precision rate in drivers and arch modules is greater than the decline of their recall rate while kernel, mm modules are on the contrary. Changes of recall and precision rate in net and fs modules are equivalent.

5   Related Work

In this section, we present the related work on software prediction and evolution.

5.1 Bug Prediction

Bug prediction has also been widely studied [6,8,14]. Nagappan and Ball used code churn, which measures the amount of changes made to a component over a period of time, to predict system bug [15]. Martin et al. use developer-related histories to predict bugs [18]. Ostrand et al. predict fault based on the code of the file in the current release, and fault and modification history of the file from previous releases [16]. Kim et al. analyzed four kinds of bug locality from version history of 7 software system and proposed a bug prediction model called FixCache based on those locality. FixCache can achieve high accuracy in file level and entity level [11].

5.2 Software Evolution

Software evolution has been largely studied from many aspect. Lehman and Ramil firstly showed the clear linear growth of the OS/360 operating system over a number of releases [12]. Parnas fully analyze causes and preventive medicine of aging problems in the process of software evolution [17]. Modeling software evolution is useful to study software maintenance. Rajlich and Bennett promote a staged model to describe Software life cycle from the aspect of software maintenance [19].

6 Conclusions

Our experimental results on function removal propagation showed that the proposed heuristics based on call graph, file position, and historical information led to different precision rates in descending order while the heuristics based on historical information, file position, and call graph resulted in varied recall rates in descending order. We also studied a few hybrid heuristics based on multiple types of information and found that the hybrid heuristics can not improve the precision and recall rate simultaneously.

Acknowledgments. This work was supported by National Natural Science Foundation of China (No. 61672073).

References

1. GCC 3.4: GCC 3.4 release series (2006). http://gcc.gnu.org/gcc-3.4/
2. Bohner, S.A.: Impact analysis in the software change process: a year 2000 perspective. In: Proceedings of the International Conference on Software Maintenance, pp. 42–51 (1996)
3. Bohner, S.A.: Software change impacts-an evolving perspective. In: Proceedings of the International Conference on Software Maintenance, pp. 263–272 (2002)
4. Codeviz: Codeviz – freecode (2008). http://freshmeat.sourceforge.net/projects/codeviz/
5. Ctags: Exuberant ctags (2009). http://ctags.sourceforge.net/

6. Hassan, A.E.: Predicting faults using the complexity of code changes. In: Proceedings 31th International Conference on Software Maintenance, pp. 78–88 (2009)
7. Hassan, A.E., Holt, R.C.: Predicting change propagation in software systems. In: Proceedings of the International Conference on Software Maintenance, pp. 284–293 (2004)
8. Hata, H., Mizuno, O., Kikuno, T.: Bug prediction based on fine-grained module histories. In: Proceedings 34th International Conference on Software Engineering, pp. 200–210 (2012)
9. Hirschberg, D.S.: Algorithms for the longest common subsequence problem. J. ACM **24**, 664–675 (1997)
10. Kernel, L.: The linux kernel archives (2018). https://www.kernel.org/
11. Kim, S., Zimmermann, T., Whitehead, E., Zeller, A.: Predicting faults from cached history. In: Proceedings of 29th International Conference on Software Engineering, pp. 489–498 (2007)
12. Lehman, M.: Laws of software evolution revisited. Lect. Notes Comput. Sci. **1149**(1996), 108–124 (1996)
13. Maia, M.C.O., Bittencourt, R.A., de Figueiredo, J.C.A., Guerrero, D.D.S.: The hybrid technique for object-oriented software change impact analysis. In: Software Maintenance and Reengineering (CSMR), pp. 252–255 (2010)
14. Nagappan, N.: Static analysis tools as early indicators of pre-release defect density. In: Proceedings of the 27th International Conference on Software Engineering, pp. 580–586 (2005)
15. Nagappan, N., Ball, T.: Use of relative code churn measures to predict system defect density. In: Proceedings of the 29th International Conference on Software Engineering, pp. 284–292 (2005)
16. Ostrand, T., Weyuker, E., Bell, R.: Predicting the location and number of faults in large software systems. IEEE Trans. Softw. Eng. **31**(10), 340–355 (2005)
17. Parnas, D.L.: Software aging. In: Proceedings of the International Conference on Software Maintenance, pp. 279–287 (1994)
18. Pinzger, M., Nagappan, N., Murphy, B.: Can developer-module networks predict failures? In: Proceedings of the 16th ACM SIGSOFT International Symposium on Foundations of Software Engineering (2008)
19. Rajlich, V.T., Bennett, K.H.: A staged model for the software life cycle. In: IEEE Compute, pp. 2–8 (2000)
20. Svetinovic, D., Godfrey, M.: Architecture, evolution, and cloning of linux device drivers: a case study (2007). citeseer.ist.psu.edu/745737.html
21. Vora, U.: Change impact analysis and software evolution specification for continually evolving systems. In: Software Engineering Advances (ICSEA), pp. 238–243 (2010)
22. Wilkerson, J.W.: A software change impact analysis taxonomy. In: Proceedings of the International Conference on Software Maintenance, pp. 625–628 (2012)

Regression Models for Performance Ranking of Configurable Systems: A Comparative Study

Yuntianyi Chen, Yongfeng Gu, Lulu He, and Jifeng Xuan$^{(\boxtimes)}$

School of Computer Science, Wuhan University, Wuhan, China
{yuntianyichen,yongfenggu,luluhe,jxuan}@whu.edu.cn

Abstract. Finding the best configurations for a highly configurable system is challenging. Existing studies learned regression models to predict the performance of potential configurations. Such learning suffers from the low accuracy and the high effort of examining the actual performance for data labeling. A recent approach uses an iterative strategy to sample a small number of configurations from the training pool to reduce the number of sampled ones. In this paper, we conducted a comparative study on the rank-based approach of configurable systems with four regression methods. These methods are compared on 21 evaluation scenarios of 16 real-world configurable systems. We designed three research questions to check the impacts of different methods on the rank-based approach. We find out that the decision tree method of Classification And Regression Tree (CART) and the ensemble learning method of Gradient Boosted Regression Trees (GBRT) can achieve better ranks among four regression methods under evaluation; the sampling strategy in the rank-based approach is useful to save the cost of sampling configurations; the measurement, i.e., rank difference correlates with the relative error in several evaluation scenarios.

Keywords: Regression methods · Performance prediction · Sampling · Software configurations

1 Introduction

A highly configurable system integrates many configuration options (i.e., a configurable feature of a system) to provide choices for system administrators and end users. For instance, a web server, such as Apache Http Server, supports the configuration of server performance to adapt to the resource limit or particular hardware platforms. Given a configurable system, many configurations may result in performance issues, e.g., the resource consumption of a compiler or the response time of a web server [14]. Due to the large search space of examining all configurations, it is expensive to find out the optimal configuration for a complicated system [8]. A highly configurable system contains numerous configuration options; in a large configurable system, even examining one configuration

© Springer Nature Switzerland AG 2020
H. Miao et al. (Eds.): SOFL+MSVL 2019 Workshop, LNCS 12028, pp. 243–258, 2020.
https://doi.org/10.1007/978-3-030-41418-4_17

may be time-consuming, e.g., deploying and rebooting a web server. This makes manually examining all configurations impossible.

Existing studies have introduced machine learning methods to predict the performance of a configuration [6,14]. The predicted performance of a configuration serves as a reference to the user. This prediction can be used to assist the choice of configurations. A general way of performance prediction is to use a regression method to approximate an exact performance value. Such a regression method evaluates the predicted performance with the relative error of performance [8–10,14–16]. The Classification And Regression Tree (CART) is viewed as one of the state-of-the-art methods for the regression on performance prediction [10,15]. An ideal result is that the regression method can predict performance for all configurations. However, the user of performance prediction may not care about the performance of all the configurations. Instead, choosing a configuration with the best performance is practical. Nair et al. [8] revisited the goal of performance prediction: getting the (near) optimal configuration for users. Therefore, the original regression problem is treated as a ranking problem: ranking configurations based on their predicted performance and choosing a "good" configuration rather than predicting performance for all configurations. Such a method is called a *rank-based approach*. A rank-based approach evaluates the result with the *rank difference*, which is defined as the actual rank for a configuration that is predicted as the best.

The study by Nair et al. [8] also revealed an important problem of performance prediction, i.e., the number of sampled configurations for machine learning. A user cannot collect many configurations with known performance since examining the actual performance of configurations is costly. Nair et al. [8] used an iterative sampling method to reduce the number of sampled configurations in the rank-based approach. This sampling method is considered to shorten the cost of sampling configurations in real-world applications.

In this paper, we conducted a comparative study on the rank-based approach of configurable systems with four regression methods, including Classification And Regression Tree (CART), Support Vector Regression (SVR), Gaussian Process Regression (GPR), and Gradient Boosted Regression Trees (GBRT). Methods in the study are compared on 21 evaluation scenarios of 16 real-world configurable systems. We designed three Research Questions (RQs) to investigate the impacts of different methods on the rank-based approach. In the study, we evaluated the result of each regression method via learning a model from known configurations and measured the result with the rank difference and the Mean Magnitude of Relative Error (MMRE). Each experiment is repeated for 50 times to reduce the disturbance of randomness. We find that among four regression methods under evaluation, the decision tree method CART and the ensemble learning method GBRT can achieve better ranks while SVR and GPR can save more sampled configurations; the sampling strategy in the rank-based approach is useful to the reduction of sampled configurations; the measurement, i.e., rank difference correlates with the relative error in several evaluation scenarios.

This paper makes the following major contributions:

- We compared four different regression methods for the problem of performance ranking of configurable systems on 21 evaluation scenarios of 16 real-world systems.
- We empirically studied the saved cost of sampling configurations and the correlation between evaluation measurements.

The rest of this paper is organized as follows. Section 2 presents the background of this study. Section 3 shows the study setup, including three research questions and the data preparation. Section 4 describes the results of our comparative study. Section 5 lists the threats to the validity. Section 6 presents the related work and Sect. 7 concludes.

2   Background and Motivation

Accurately predicting the performance of configurations is challenging due to the time cost of sampling and the accuracy of building performance models.

2.1   Problem Formalization

In this paper, we followed Nair et al. [8] to adopt the rank-based approach. In this approach, a regression model is learned from a training set of configurations and then is used to predict the performance for each configuration in the test set. The rank-based approach sorts all configurations in the test set in terms of the predicted performance. We call the sorting results a *predicted sequence*, denoted as ps; let ps_k denote the top-k configurations in ps.

Let X be the search space of all configurations in a dataset. Denoting the number of configuration options as n and one configuration as x, we can define a configurable option in a configuration as x_i and $x = \{x_1, x_2, ..., x_n\}$. The domain of x_i is defined as $D(x_i)$. Thus $X \subseteq D(x_1) \times D(x_2) \times ... \times D(x_n)$. Let $perf(x)$ be the performance of a configuration x. Then we denote the actual performance of x as $perf_a(x)$ and the predicted performance that is calculated by a regression method as $perf_p(x)$.

Previous studies of performance prediction generally employs the Mean Magnitude of Relative Error (MMRE) to evaluate the accuracy of performance prediction [14,15]. MMRE is defined as follow,

$$\text{MMRE} = \frac{1}{n} \sum_{x \in X} \frac{|perf_a(x) - perf_p(x)|}{perf_a(x)}$$

Nair et al. [8] introduced the rank difference to evaluate the actual rank of configurations that are predictively ranked as the top. The rank difference can be defined as the minimum of actual rank values of the top-k configurations, i.e., $MAR(k)$. The rank difference $MAR(k)$ can be used to pick a configuration out from the predicted sequence. We use $MAR(k)$ to evaluate the ability of ranking configurations to the top of the predicted sequence.

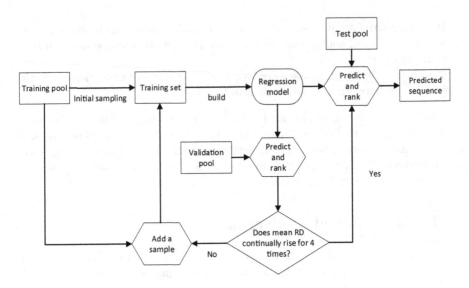

Fig. 1. Overview of the rank-based approach.

2.2 Rank-Based Approach

The state-of-the-art approach to solve the ranking problem of software configurations is called the rank-based approach by Nair et al. [8]. They considered
ranking as the ultimate goal of performance prediction and claimed that users
concerned ranks rather than exact performance. They adopted a rank-based sampling method to reduce the number of training samples for building regression
models. To evaluate the ranking deviation of a configuration, they introduced a
measurement *rank difference*, which means the rank distance between the predicted rank and the actual rank of a configuration. We denote a predicted rank
as $rank_p(x)$ and an actual rank as $rank_a(x)$.

$$RD(x) = |rank_a(x) - rank_p(x)|$$

Figure 1 shows the overview of the rank-based approach by Nair et al. [8]. The
rank-based approach employs an iterative sampling strategy to collect a training
set. At the beginning of sampling, they randomly select a certain number of
samples from the training pool as the training set. The training set is used to
build a regression model and to predict the performance on the validation pool.
Then, the mean of rank differences RD is calculated for all configurations to
decide whether the iterative sampling process terminates. Once the mean RD
continually rises for a pre-defined number of times, the iteration ends. Otherwise,
a new sampled configuration is added into the training set from the training pool.
Finally, a regression model is learned from the training set and is used to predict
and rank the test pool. The result we get after ranking is called the predicted
sequence of the test pool.

2.3 Motivation

Highly configurable systems are common in our daily lives. A software usually contains a large number of configuration options. For instance, Project lrzip is a compression software for large files. As for performance related configuration options, we can identify 19 features, which lead to 432 configurations [13]. A user could tune these configuration options to change the performance, namely the compression time in Project lrzip. Rich choices of configuration can facilitate the functions of systems, but may hide faults and performance issues [14, 16–18]. Due to the large number of configurations, manual examination on all configurations is arduous. Thus, it is feasible to predict the performance for configurations with unknown performance via machine learning algorithms [6].

Learning a regression model requires sampled configurations, which are selected by users and examined by deploying the system with the configurations. However, sampling is time-consuming. Existing studies have proposed several sampling strategies to reduce the number of sampled configurations [9, 12, 14, 20]. In this paper, we expect to evaluate the cost of learning a regression model, i.e., the number of configurations that contain known performance.

There are many regression methods in machine learning. The CART serves as the state-of-the-art method in performance prediction [6, 8–10, 12, 16, 20]. In this paper, we expect to find out which regression method is the best on performance ranking. Can the CART reduce the number of configurations with known performance in learning regression models? In this paper, we comprehensively compare the result of performance ranking with four regression methods.

3 Study Setup

We describe the data preparation, four regression methods, and three RQs in this section.

3.1 Dataset Preparation and Evaluation Setup

In this paper, we empirically evaluate the performance ranking on 16 subject systems with 21 evaluation scenarios. A *evaluation scenario* is a subject system deployed on a particular running environment.

One subject system may contain one or more evaluation scenarios. For instance, *wc-6d-c1-obj1* and *wc-6d-c1-obj2* are two evaluation scenarios that use the same subject system and hardware environments, but different performance indicators: *wc-6d-c1-obj1* measures performance with throughput while *wc-6d-c1-obj2* measures performance with latency [7]. Table 1 presents the details of 21 evaluation scenarios in our study.

The performance of configurable systems can be measured with different indicators. For example, the performance is measured by throughput in *wc-6d-c1-obj1*. That is, the larger the value is, the better the performance is. In *BerkeleyC*, the performance is defined as the response time. For the sake of unification, we

Table 1. Configurations of 21 evaluation scenarios in 16 subject systems.

Scenario	Options	Configurations	Performance	Ref.
AJStats	19	30, 256	Analysis time	[13]
Apache	9	192	Max response rate	[13]
BerkeleyC	18	2, 560	Response time	[13]
BerkeleyJ	26	180	Response time	[13]
clasp	19	700	Solving time	[13]
Dune	11	2, 304	Solving time	[8]
HSMGP_num	14	3, 456	Average time	[8]
lrzip	19	432	Compression time	[8]
noc	4	259	Runtime	[21]
snw	3	206	Throughput	[21]
spear	14	16, 384	Solving time	[13]
SQL	39	4, 553	Response time	[13]
wc+rs-3d-c4-obj1	3	196	Throughput	[7]
wc+rs-3d-c4-obj2	3	196	Latency	[7]
wc-6d-c1-obj1	6	2, 880	Throughput	[7]
wc-6d-c1-obj2	6	2, 880	Latency	[7]
wc-c1-3d-c1-obj1	3	1, 343	Throughput	[7]
wc-c1-3d-c1-obj2	3	1, 343	Latency	[7]
WGet	16	188	Main memory	[8]
x264	16	2, 047	Encoding time	[13]
XZ	16	1, 078	Execution time	[16]

pre-processed the raw data. For instance, we transferred the throughput value tp in *wc-6d-c1-obj1* into $100/tp$.

In our study, the whole dataset is randomly divided into three parts, including the training pool, the test pool, and the validation pool, which respectively account for 40%, 40%, and 20% of the total number of configurations. Each regression method is evaluated on the same division of the dataset and with the same random seed. The experiment is repeatedly run for 50 times to count the average.

We evaluate the results with two measurements, $MAR(k)$ and $MMRE(k)$, which denote the minimum of actual ranks for the top-k ranking and the mean magnitude of relative errors of the performance prediction for the top-k ranking, respectively.

We also measure the correlation between $MAR(k)$ and $MMRE(k)$ with the *Pearson correlation coefficient*. We repeated running each experiment for fifty times and collected each 50 pairs of $MAR(k)$ and $MMRE(k)$. Let Y and X be the vectors of $MAR(k)$ and $MMRE(k)$ values. Then the Pearson correlation coefficient between $MAR(k)$ and $MMRE(k)$ is calculated as follows,

$$\rho(X,Y) = \frac{\mathrm{cov}(X,Y)}{\sigma_X \sigma_Y}$$

where $\rho(X,Y)$ and $\mathrm{cov}(X,Y)$ are the correlation coefficient and the covariance between X and Y, σ_X and σ_Y are the standard deviation of X and Y, respectively.

Our experiment is implemented with Python 3.7.3. We use the Python package *scikit-learn* to build regression models and to predict the performance of configurations. Our running environment is a PC with Intel Core i7 Quad CPU 2.60GHz and 8GB RAM memory.

3.2   Regression Methods

In this paper, we selected four regression methods: three basic regression methods, Classification and regression tree (CART), Support Vector Regression (SVR), and Gaussian Process Regression (GPR), and one ensemble method, Gradient Boosted Regression Trees (GBRT). In our evaluation, we do not assume that there is a specific function between the performance and configurations of a scenario.

CART is a classic decision tree algorithm, which builds a classification or regression model within a tree structure [1]. The decision tree iteratively partitions into branches to generate a decision rule. Leaf nodes of the tree contain the prediction result. *SVR* is the regression model of the support vector machine algorithm [2]. SVR uses a hyperplane to discriminate samples and sets a tolerance for the loss function. In our study, we chose the Radial Basis Function (RBF) as the kernel algorithm of SVR because we assume configuration data are non-linear. *GPR* is a non-parametric regression model that uses probability distribution to predict results [11]. We also use the RBF as the kernel. *GBRT* is an ensemble learning algorithm of multiple decision trees, i.e., CART [3]. GBRT uses multiple weak learners to fit a strong learner. GBRT iteratively finds decision trees to turn down the value of loss functions.

3.3   Research Questions

Our experiments are designed to compare the ranking ability of four different regression methods. We aim at investigate the performance ranking via answering three RQs:

- RQ1. Which Regression Method Can Achieve Better Ranking for the Performance Ranking?
- RQ2. How Many Configurations are Sampled in the Rank-Based Performance Ranking?
- RQ3. Does the Rank Difference in Performance Ranking Correlate with the Relative Error in Performance Prediction?

In RQ1, we check which regression method can perform well in the performance ranking of configurable systems. The CART method is considered as a state-of-the-art method [8]. Then what is the effectiveness of other typical regression methods? We plan to evaluate the four regression methods on the performance ranking via two measurements, the minimum of actual ranks and the relative error.

In RQ2, we aim at evaluating the number of sampled configurations for learning a rank-based model. Nair et al. [8] employed an iterative strategy to sample configurations for the model learning. We focused on the number of sampled ones by different regression methods.

In RQ3, we use the Pearson correlation coefficient to measure the relevance between two measurements. We collect results from fifty repeated experiments and calculate the correlation between the minimum of actual ranks $MAR(k)$ and the mean magnitude of relative error $MMRE(k)$. The correction is evaluated by checking $k = 1$, $k = 5$, and $k = 10$, respectively, i.e., the measurements of top-1, top-5, and top-10.

4   Comparative Study

We conducted a comparative study on using four regression methods in the performance ranking. These regression methods are evaluated with experiments on 21 evaluation scenarios of 16 subject systems.

4.1   RQ1. Which Regression Method Can Achieve Better Ranking for the Performance Ranking?

We followed the rank-based approach by Nair et al. [8] to use an iterative strategy of sampling. This strategy samples the training set from a given training pool and then a regression model is learned from the training set. All configurations in a validation pool are used to validate the prediction by the learned regression model. The sampling process repeats until a pre-defined threshold reaches. In the training pool, configurations that are not sampled can be viewed as configurations without known performance. Then the sampling strategy can save the effort of examining the actual performance of configurations. If the sampling strategy terminates, the learned regression model is used to predicted performance for all configurations in the test set. According to the predicted performance, configurations in the test set are sorted and measured with two defined measurements $MAR(k)$ and $MMRE(k)$ in Sect. 3.1.

Table 2 shows the minimum of actual ranks, i.e., $MAR(k)$, on 21 evaluation scenarios of four regression methods, CART, SVR, GBRT, and GPR. We compared the minimum of actual ranks for top-1, top-5, and top-10 configurations in the predicted sequence.[1] As shown in Table 2, CART can obtain the best rank in 7 out of 21 evaluation scenarios for top-10 configurations; GBRT can obtain the best rank in 11 scenarios; SVR and GPR obtain the best rank in one and two

---

[1] Ranks in the experiment are zero-based; that is, the MAR value of the best configuration is zero.

scenarios, respectively. CART and its enhanced method GBRT could achieve better rank than the other methods. The difference among four regression methods is not slight. For instance, in top-10 of Scenario AJStats, the rank of GBRT is 689.62 while the rank of GPR is 6514.96; in top-10 of Scenario XZ, the rank of GBRT is 18.46 while the rank of GPR is 10.98. In top-10, four regression methods can nearly rank the actually optimal configuration to the top for several evaluation scenarios, e.g., Apache, BerkeleyJ, noc, snw, and wc+rs-3d-c4-obj1.

Table 2. Minimum of actual ranks on 21 evaluation scenarios of 4 regression methods

Scenario	Top-1				Top-5				Top-10			
	CART	SVR	GBRT	GPR	CART	SVR	GBRT	GPR	CART	SVR	GBRT	GPR
AJStats	4381.56	4159.68	**3920.20**	9611.40	**949.62**	1985.46	1219.68	7630.66	739.48	1254.20	**689.62**	6514.96
Apache	5.52	6.54	**2.66**	4.78	1.02	1.30	**0.32**	0.32	0.36	0.50	**0.14**	0.18
BerkeleyC	122.70	161.82	**83.14**	110.52	**35.34**	73.08	47.18	39.10	24.82	49.38	29.98	**18.54**
BerkeleyJ	11.30	15.86	**10.92**	17.34	3.56	4.60	**3.36**	7.48	**1.52**	2.68	1.54	2.98
clasp	17.08	38.84	**6.20**	54.34	4.86	16.80	**1.64**	21.64	1.76	8.22	**0.46**	14.98
Dune	161.74	**87.06**	110.10	276.38	55.52	**27.42**	31.22	119.92	37.88	18.58	**18.58**	83.52
HSMGP_num	88.42	29.46	**14.60**	71.92	23.92	10.48	**2.28**	16.62	12.10	7.58	**1.26**	13.08
lrzip	**10.80**	35.34	13.68	27.80	**3.16**	19.72	3.30	8.80	**1.42**	11.76	1.62	6.60
noc	6.50	3.60	**1.66**	27.18	0.80	1.46	**0.04**	2.24	0.18	0.94	**0.02**	1.86
snw	3.66	4.32	**1.30**	20.04	0.52	0.40	**0.12**	3.58	0.32	0.18	**0.00**	2.02
spear	**1072.44**	1360.02	1237.38	1335.10	**246.9**	776.60	646.78	549.14	**204.34**	651.74	444.7	378.26
SQL	749.38	**589.60**	590.74	682.52	288.48	237.08	**212.36**	271.84	123.34	155.80	**106.22**	128.72
wc+rs-3d-c4-obj1	13.94	26.94	**5.74**	21.92	2.66	6.24	**1.86**	5.94	0.84	4.08	**0.16**	3.56
wc+rs-3d-c4-obj2	**4.56**	16.08	18.74	49.52	**1.00**	6.40	4.78	23.36	**0.42**	3.84	1.92	10.06
wc-6d-c1-obj1	268.60	395.60	**261.06**	499.56	**56.20**	150.82	103.18	339.24	**26.28**	94.72	45.70	201.44
wc-6d-c1-obj2	**80.58**	225.50	209.58	395.46	**34.42**	106.80	116.88	296.38	**18.78**	86.10	83.56	247.50
wc-c1-3d-c1-obj1	56.36	102.68	**31.74**	494.58	16.26	**4.58**	5.12	440.70	7.88	2.20	**1.70**	400.86
wc-c1-3d-c1-obj2	82.46	94.84	**64.62**	481.22	16.20	18.58	**16.02**	450.64	11.38	8.62	**8.18**	380.94
WGet	**25.48**	30.92	26.38	47.50	7.34	8.64	**6.96**	23.04	**3.70**	4.06	3.78	11.36
x264	92.42	72.06	**17.60**	300.90	25.84	16.00	**3.28**	129.32	14.22	9.72	**1.82**	86.94
XZ	86.84	93.60	134.84	**85.04**	**17.14**	27.10	37.88	26.26	11.52	14.56	18.46	**10.98**

We also present the results of MMRE in Table 3. In top-10, CART reaches the best MMRE in 7/21 evaluation scenarios; SVR can obtain the best MMRE values in 3/21 scenarios; GBRT achieves the best MMRE in 11/21 scenarios; GPR cannot obtain the best MMRE in these scenarios.

We consider the results across Tables 2 and 3. For Scenario XZ, CART performs the best for all MMRE values in Table 3 while GPR performs the best for top-1 and top-10 for MAR values in Table 2. This observation reveals that the MAR value may not correlate with the MMRE value. We study such correlation in Sect. 4.3.

4.2 RQ2. How Many Configurations are Sampled in the Rank-Based Performance Ranking?

The iterative strategy of sampling in the rank-based approach [8] can save the effort of examining actual performance of configurations. In RQ2, we evaluate the sampling via the number of sampled configurations, denoted as #samples. In

Table 3. Mean magnitude of relative errors on 21 evaluation scenarios of 4 regression methods

Project	Top-1				Top-5				Top-10			
	CART	SVR	GBRT	GPR	CART	SVR	GBRT	GPR	CART	SVR	GBRT	GPR
AJStats	0.02	**0.02**	0.03	0.85	0.02	**0.02**	0.03	0.84	0.02	**0.02**	0.03	0.84
Apache	0.10	0.76	**0.06**	0.14	0.09	0.69	**0.05**	0.11	0.09	0.63	**0.05**	0.11
BerkeleyC	**0.15**	1.08	0.98	4.86	**0.15**	1.29	0.91	3.75	**0.15**	1.36	0.83	3.15
BerkeleyJ	0.06	0.47	**0.06**	0.65	0.05	0.46	**0.05**	0.59	0.05	0.45	**0.04**	0.53
clasp	0.05	0.41	**0.03**	0.29	0.06	0.40	**0.04**	0.28	0.06	0.40	**0.04**	0.28
Dune	0.18	0.40	**0.14**	1.00	0.18	0.40	**0.13**	0.89	0.18	0.38	**0.12**	0.83
HSMGP _num	0.19	1.67	**0.16**	1.59	0.21	1.43	**0.14**	1.35	0.22	1.31	**0.14**	1.20
lrzip	**0.09**	2.04	0.69	2.52	**0.10**	1.97	0.57	1.92	**0.10**	1.94	0.47	1.47
noc	0.03	0.11	**0.02**	0.20	0.03	0.09	**0.02**	0.11	0.04	0.08	**0.02**	0.09
snw	0.08	0.38	**0.06**	3.04	0.07	0.31	**0.06**	1.90	0.07	0.26	**0.05**	1.26
spear	**0.46**	27.68	8.69	9.15	**0.51**	28.61	8.16	6.02	**0.50**	28.36	8.37	4.84
SQL	0.08	**0.04**	0.08	0.99	0.08	**0.04**	0.08	0.99	0.08	**0.04**	0.08	0.99
wc+rs-3d-c4-obj1	0.28	0.44	**0.24**	3345.07	**0.26**	0.49	0.27	1937.15	0.24	0.49	**0.24**	1245.09
wc+rs-3d-c4-obj2	**0.12**	165.99	108.94	1997.79	**0.11**	93.29	107.11	1469.57	**0.15**	76.28	67.58	1638.20
wc-6d-c1-obj1	**0.35**	0.83	1.27	450.99	**0.35**	0.74	1.19	407.35	**0.34**	0.77	1.10	380.17
wc-6d-c1-obj2	**0.17**	14.49	27.16	504.66	**0.20**	11.07	21.70	348.91	**0.20**	10.22	20.78	334.28
wc-c1-3d-c1-obj1	0.08	**0.07**	0.07	4.53	0.07	0.09	**0.06**	4.12	0.07	0.10	**0.06**	3.84
wc-c1-3d-c1-obj2	0.10	0.16	**0.08**	8.59	0.09	0.21	**0.09**	8.13	0.10	0.22	**0.08**	7.75
WGet	**0.04**	0.08	0.14	0.86	0.07	**0.05**	0.11	0.83	0.07	**0.05**	0.09	0.81
x264	0.07	0.16	**0.04**	0.74	0.07	0.17	**0.04**	0.73	0.07	0.16	**0.04**	0.72
XZ	**0.59**	2.78	1.33	0.85	**0.64**	3.12	1.25	0.86	**0.67**	3.00	1.08	0.83

the rank-based approach, *#samples* counts all configurations that have known actual performance, including both the training set and the validation pool. Table 4 shows the number of sampled configurations by four regression methods. For the sake of space, we only show the MAR results of top-10 and remove the MMRE results.

As presented in Table 4, iterative sampling can save nearly up to half of samples compared with the *No sampling* method, especially for projects with a large number of configurations like Projects AJStats and spear. As for four regression methods, SVR and GPR can respectively obtain the least samples in 12 and 7 scenarios. The difference between CART and GBRT is slight: both have relatively more samples than the other two methods and can achieve the least samples in only one scenario. For instance, in Scenario wc-6d-c1-obj1, CART has 617.66 samples on average and its MAR is 26.28. SVR and GPR have 606.34 and 602.28 samples on average but their MARs are 94.72 and 201.44, which are much higher than the MAR of the CART.

4.3 RQ3. Does the Rank Difference in Performance Ranking Correlate with the Relative Error in Performance Prediction?

As mentioned in Sect. 4.3, the rank-based approach can be measured with MAR and MMRE. We investigate whether there exists correlation between the values of MAR and MMRE.

Table 4. Number of sampled configurations for top-10 results on 21 evaluation scenarios by four regression methods. *No sampling* denotes the number of all configurations without sampling.

| Project | Iteratively sampling | | | | | | | | No sampling |
| | CART | | SVR | | GBRT | | GPR | | |
	MAR	#Samples	MAR	#Samples	MAR	#Samples	MAR	#Samples	#Samples
AJStats	739.48	6088.48	1254.20	6080.46	**689.62**	6089.28	6514.96	**6073.56**	12102
Apache	0.36	73.18	0.50	**64.28**	**0.14**	69.32	0.18	70.40	76
BerkeleyC	24.82	557.36	49.38	**546.32**	29.98	561.08	**18.54**	562.20	1024
BerkeleyJ	**1.52**	68.46	2.68	62.84	1.54	64.72	2.98	**59.34**	72
clasp	1.76	190.26	8.22	**171.56**	**0.46**	182.60	14.98	181.60	280
Dune	37.88	500.66	**11.80**	495.08	18.58	497.22	83.52	**490.98**	921
HSMGP_num	12.10	**733.48**	7.58	734.86	**1.26**	737.52	13.08	752.16	1382
lrzip	**1.42**	124.98	11.76	**114.86**	1.62	129.30	6.60	121.96	172
noc	0.18	91.68	0.94	**80.36**	**0.02**	89.56	1.86	82.42	103
snw	0.32	76.46	0.18	**65.38**	**0.00**	74.94	2.02	68.74	82
spear	**204.34**	3310.18	651.74	3311.72	444.70	**3308.46**	378.26	3327.34	6553
SQL	123.34	943.42	155.80	**934.00**	**106.22**	949.52	128.72	935.24	1821
wc+rs-3d-c4-obj1	0.84	73.56	4.08	**62.32**	**0.16**	75.64	3.56	62.62	78
wc+rs-3d-c4-obj2	**0.42**	71.24	3.84	**62.56**	1.92	68.90	10.06	62.66	78
wc-6d-c1-obj1	**26.28**	617.66	94.72	606.34	45.70	616.84	201.44	**602.28**	1152
wc-6d-c1-obj2	**18.78**	630.96	86.10	**601.92**	83.56	607.18	247.50	601.94	1152
wc-c1-3d-c1-obj1	7.88	308.08	2.20	**293.34**	1.70	313.80	400.86	297.22	537
wc-c1-3d-c1-obj2	11.38	305.36	8.62	296.36	**8.18**	307.78	380.94	**295.26**	537
WGet	**3.70**	74.42	4.06	62.32	3.78	67.06	11.36	**60.36**	75
x264	14.22	453.94	9.72	**427.26**	**1.82**	468.04	86.94	432.38	818
XZ	11.52	248.98	14.56	250.82	18.46	249.54	**10.98**	**243.82**	431

Table 5. Pearson correlation coefficient on 21 scenarios of four regression methods. The mark * denotes the coefficient has p-value < 0.05.

| Project | Top-1 | | | | Top-5 | | | | Top-10 | | | |
	CART	SVR	GBRT	GPR	CART	SVR	GBRT	GPR	CART	SVR	GBRT	GPR
AJStats	0.1929	-0.3878*	**0.8760***	0.3400*	0.2882*	-0.3500*	**0.6025***	0.4193*	0.1209	-0.1834	0.3132*	0.5578*
Apache	0.2363	-0.5089*	0.3028*	**0.7257***	0.2577	-0.2406	0.1390	0.4475*	0.1507	-0.1594	0.1255	0.5294*
BerkeleyC	**0.6092***	-0.2703	0.0192	-0.2037	0.2650	-0.2635	0.0769	-0.0721	-0.0761	-0.2365	0.0526	-0.0594
BerkeleyJ	0.4720*	-0.5279*	**0.7545***	0.3710*	0.3415*	-0.5902*	0.3960*	0.3766*	0.1297	-0.5623*	0.1247	0.3543*
clasp	**0.7202***	-0.7174*	0.0626	0.8735*	0.6506*	-0.5339*	0.1743	0.7088*	0.5672*	-0.4681*	0.2322	0.6332*
Dune	0.3255*	-0.9613*	0.7844*	0.2381	0.4888*	-0.6208*	0.2781	0.3103*	**0.6569***	-0.3618*	0.1407	0.4032*
HSMGP_num	-0.0163	-0.8033*	0.2286	-0.1414	0.4586*	-0.5325*	0.1049	-0.0743	0.4032*	-0.5314*	-0.1091	-0.0395
lrzip	0.6610*	-0.4326*	0.3091*	-0.0281	0.2278	-0.2810*	0.2769	0.1778	0.2602	-0.2354	0.1424	0.1828
noc	0.6121*	-0.2536	0.0248	0.8451*	0.5143*	-0.1117	N/A	0.8481*	0.2964*	-0.1327	N/A	0.8905*
snw	0.2423	-0.5291*	-0.2146	-0.0768	0.1591	-0.3073*	0.0480	0.2994*	0.0847	-0.0889	N/A	0.1206
spear	0.2691	-0.2080	-0.0716	-0.5949*	-0.1824	-0.1299	-0.0437	-0.4684*	-0.2601	-0.1335	-0.1131	-0.4651*
SQL	0.1724	0.2529	**0.8438***	0.1353	0.1438	-0.1746	0.6293*	-0.0827	0.1952	-0.1272	0.5459*	0.2039
wc+rs-3d-c4-obj1	0.5080*	-0.2223	0.3822*	-0.209	0.5200*	-0.6263*	0.4198*	-0.0922	0.5343*	-0.5536*	0.0040	-0.1581
wc+rs-3d-c4-obj2	**0.6604***	-0.4572*	-0.2554	-0.6365*	0.6475*	-0.3564*	-0.1413	-0.5552*	0.4188*	-0.3014*	-0.0684	-0.2407
wc-6d-c1-obj1	0.2732	-0.4223*	0.1438	-0.1919	0.2342	-0.3863*	0.2297	-0.1120	-0.0327	-0.2669	0.0694	-0.0013
wc-6d-c1-obj2	0.4586*	-0.3422*	-0.2649	-0.5077*	0.244	-0.2266	-0.184	-0.4362*	0.4112*	-0.2421	-0.1593	-0.4416*
wc-c1-3d-c1-obj1	0.3199*	0.3387*	0.2233	-0.0751	0.0664	-0.3066*	0.0856	0.2208	0.3260*	-0.3595*	-0.0887	0.3529*
wc-c1-3d-c1-obj2	0.1695	-0.3289*	**0.812***	-0.5458*	0.2465	-0.3552*	0.5888*	-0.4455*	-0.0588	-0.3955*	**0.7149***	-0.2672
WGet	0.3138*	**0.6341***	**0.6819***	0.3722*	0.3934*	-0.2516	0.3587*	0.2987*	0.4472*	-0.0445	0.3907*	0.1540
x264	0.2806*	-0.5289*	0.4741*	**0.6381***	0.5089*	-0.3099*	0.4471*	0.5058*	0.3811*	-0.3079*	0.3384*	0.4681*
XZ	-0.0780	-0.3862*	-0.2468	-0.1039	0.3236*	-0.5986*	-0.1742	0.0054	0.2098	**-0.6915***	-0.1401	-0.1965

Each experiment repeated for 50 individual runs. Then we collected the values of MAR and MMRE and calculated the Pearson correlation coefficient. The absolute value of the coefficient shows the strength of the correlation. A positive value means that one measurement increases with the other; a negative value means that one measurement increases when the other decreases. Table 5 shows the Pearson correlation coefficient between MAR and MMRE for the top rankings. We labeled the significant values (p-value < 0.05) with * and highlighted the values whose absolute values of correlation coefficients are higher than 0.6, which means strong correlation between MAR and MMRE.

As presented in Table 5, the top-1 configuration has stronger correlation than the top-5 and top-10 configurations. The more configurations we take from predicted sequences, the less number of scenarios of strong correlation we would have. For instance, CART has five scenarios of strong correlation in top-1 but only has two and one in top-5 and top-10. In top-1, CART, SVR, GBRT, and GPR have 5, 4, 6, and 5 scenarios of strong correlation out of 21 evaluation scenarios, respectively. It means MAR and MMRE may not have strong correlation for regression methods. Besides, SVR has a negative correlation between MAR and MMRE for most of significant scenarios, which is different from the other three regression methods.

Summary. From three RQs, we can understand the reason that many existing studies used CART as their regression method in performance prediction of software configurations. However, our study shows that all four regression methods can behave well in several evaluation scenarios. The rank-based approach for the performance ranking can be further improved to reduce the ranking difference and the number of sampled configurations.

5   Threats to Validity

We discuss threats to the validity to our comparative study in the following three dimensions.

Threats to Construct Validity. Our experiments used four regression methods to check the impact on performance ranking. It is feasible to conduct a large experiment via involving other existing regression methods. The dataset in our study is selected from existing work [7,8,13,16,21]. All projects in the dataset are real-world configurable systems. However, selecting the projects may lead to the bias of favoring specific application domains. This may be a threat to the project selection in the experiment.

Threats to Internal Validity. In the experiment, we repeated individual runs for 50 times to reduce the randomness of the dataset division, i.e., dividing a dataset into three subsets, the training pool, the validation pool, and the test pool. The 50 times of repetitive experiments is used to avoid the influence of randomness. However, the randomness cannot be totally removed.

Threats to External Validity. We compared four regression methods in the study. We do not claim that the comparative results can be generalized to other projects or to other regression methods. Considering the large number of existing configurable systems, projects and regression methods can be viewed as a sample of performance ranking on real-world systems.

6 Related Work

In this paper, we studied the performance ranking with four regression methods. Previous studies on the performance of configurable systems generally focused on sampling methods and learning methods. We present the related work as follows.

Guo et al. [6] used the CART method to predict the performance of configurations. Their empirical results show that the method can reach a prediction accuracy of 94% on average based on small random samples. They claimed that prediction accuracy would robustly increase with the increasing of the sample size. Valov et al. [15] compared the predicting accuracy of four typical regression methods. They selected regressions methods, including CART, SVM, random forests, and bagging. Their results show that bagging does better in performance prediction when all configurations are evaluated with the relative errors. Siegmund et al. [13] proposed an approach that learns a performance-influence model for a configurable system. Their approach can flexibly combine both binary and numeric configuration options. Sarkar et al. [12] compared two sampling strategies, progressive sampling and projective sampling, with the prediction accuracy and the measurement effort and found that the projective sampling is better than the progressive sampling. Gu et al. [4] proposed a multi-objective optimization method for configuration sampling. This method considers both the number of configurations in the training set and the rank difference in the test set.

Zhang et al. [20] proposed a Fourier learning method to learn performance functions for configurable systems. They showed that this method can generate performance predictions with guaranteed accuracy at the confidence level. Nair et al. [9] proposed a fast spectral learner and three new sampling techniques. They conducted experiments on six real-world configurable software systems. Xuan et al. [19] designed a method genetic configuration sampling, which used a genetic algorithm to reduce the number of sampled configurations to reveal the internal system faults, which result in system crashes. Gu et al. [5] learned a predictive model to identify whether the root cause of crashing faults resides in the lines of stack traces. This model is built on the features of stack traces and faulty source code.

The rank-based approach by Nair et al. [8] reconsidered the problem of performance prediction and refined the problem as a ranking problem. Their work first used the rank difference instead of predicting accuracy as the measurement in the evaluation. They also proposed an iterative sampling strategy and conducted experiments on nine real-world systems to compare with two state-of-the-art residual-based approaches. The results show that the rank-based approach uses fewer sampled configurations than residual-based approaches and the rank-based approach is effective to find out the optimal configurations for most systems under evaluation.

7   Conclusions

It is challenging to find the optimum among numerous configurations for highly configurable systems. The rank-based approach aims to rank the optimal configurations to the top and to assist the decision by system administrators and users. To find out which regression method can rank the best configuration to the top, we compare four different regression methods in the rank-based approach. We conducted experiments on 21 evaluation scenarios of 16 real-world systems. Empirical results show that the decision tree method CART and the ensemble learning method GBRT can achieve better ranks while SVR can save more sampled configurations in the rank-based approach. Meanwhile, the results indicate that the minimum of actual ranks may not strongly correlate with the relative error.

In future work, we plan to design a new sampling strategy to maintain the predicting accuracy and reduce the number of measurements for training regression models. We also want to check other sampling strategies for the rank-based approach in the future.

Acknowledgments. The work is supported by the National Key R&D Program of China under Grant No. 2018YFB1003901, the National Natural Science Foundation of China under Grant Nos. 61872273 and 61502345, the Open Research Fund Program of CETC Key Laboratory of Aerospace Information Applications under Grant No. SXX18629T022, and the Advance Research Projects of Civil Aerospace Technology, Intelligent Distribution Technology of Domestic Satellite Information, under Grant No. B0301.

References

1. Breiman, L.: Classification and Regression Trees. Routledge, Abingdon (2017)
2. Drucker, H., Burges, C.J., Kaufman, L., Smola, A.J., Vapnik, V.: Support vector regression machines. In: Advances in Neural Information Processing Systems, pp. 155–161 (1997)
3. Friedman, J.H.: Stochastic gradient boosting. Comput. Stat. Data Anal. **38**(4), 367–378 (2002)
4. Gu, Y., Chen, Y., Jia, X., Xuan, J.: Multi-objective configuration sampling for performance ranking in configurable systems. In: Proceedings of the the 26th Asia-Pacific Software Engineering Conference (APSEC 2019), Putrajaya, Malaysia, 2–5 December 2019 (2019)
5. Gu, Y., et al.: Does the fault reside in a stack trace? Assisting crash localization by predicting crashing fault residence. J. Syst. Softw. **148**, 88–104 (2019). https://doi.org/10.1016/j.jss.2018.11.004
6. Guo, J., Czarnecki, K., Apel, S., Siegmund, N., Wasowski, A.: Variability-aware performance prediction: a statistical learning approach. In: 2013 28th IEEE/ACM International Conference on Automated Software Engineering, ASE 2013, Silicon Valley, CA, USA, 11–15 November 2013, pp. 301–311 (2013). https://doi.org/10.1109/ASE.2013.6693089

7. Jamshidi, P., Casale, G.: An uncertainty-aware approach to optimal configuration of stream processing systems. In: 24th IEEE International Symposium on Modeling, Analysis and Simulation of Computer and Telecommunication Systems, MASCOTS 2016, London, United Kingdom, 19–21 September 2016, pp. 39–48 (2016). https://doi.org/10.1109/MASCOTS.2016.17

8. Nair, V., Menzies, T., Siegmund, N., Apel, S.: Using bad learners to find good configurations. In: Proceedings of the 2017 11th Joint Meeting on Foundations of Software Engineering, ESEC/FSE 2017, Paderborn, Germany, 4–8 September 2017, pp. 257–267 (2017). https://doi.org/10.1145/3106237.3106238

9. Nair, V., Menzies, T., Siegmund, N., Apel, S.: Faster discovery of faster system configurations with spectral learning. Autom. Softw. Eng. 25(2), 247–277 (2018). https://doi.org/10.1007/s10515-017-0225-2

10. Nair, V., Yu, Z., Menzies, T., Siegmund, N., Apel, S.: Finding faster configurations using FLASH. CoRR abs/1801.02175 (2018). http://arxiv.org/abs/1801.02175

11. Rasmussen, C.E.: Gaussian processes in machine learning. In: Bousquet, O., von Luxburg, U., Rätsch, G. (eds.) ML -2003. LNCS (LNAI), vol. 3176, pp. 63–71. Springer, Heidelberg (2004). https://doi.org/10.1007/978-3-540-28650-9_4

12. Sarkar, A., Guo, J., Siegmund, N., Apel, S., Czarnecki, K.: Cost-efficient sampling for performance prediction of configurable systems (T). In: 30th IEEE/ACM International Conference on Automated Software Engineering, ASE 2015, Lincoln, NE, USA, 9–13 November, pp. 342–352 (2015). https://doi.org/10.1109/ASE.2015.45

13. Siegmund, N., Grebhahn, A., Apel, S., Kästner, C.: Performance-influence models for highly configurable systems. In: Proceedings of the 2015 10th Joint Meeting on Foundations of Software Engineering, ESEC/FSE 2015, Bergamo, Italy, 30 August–4 September 2015, pp. 284–294 (2015). https://doi.org/10.1145/2786805.2786845

14. Siegmund, N., et al.: Predicting performance via automated feature-interaction detection. In: 34th International Conference on Software Engineering, ICSE 2012, Zurich, Switzerland, 2–9 June 2012, pp. 167–177 (2012). https://doi.org/10.1109/ICSE.2012.6227196

15. Valov, P., Guo, J., Czarnecki, K.: Empirical comparison of regression methods for variability-aware performance prediction. In: Proceedings of the 19th International Conference on Software Product Line, SPLC 2015, Nashville, TN, USA, 20–24 July 2015, pp. 186–190 (2015). https://doi.org/10.1145/2791060.2791069

16. Valov, P., Petkovich, J., Guo, J., Fischmeister, S., Czarnecki, K.: Transferring performance prediction models across different hardware platforms. In: Proceedings of the 8th ACM/SPEC on International Conference on Performance Engineering, ICPE 2017, L'Aquila, Italy, 22–26 April 2017, pp. 39–50 (2017). https://doi.org/10.1145/3030207.3030216

17. Xu, Y., Jia, X., Xuan, J.: Writing tests for this higher-order function first: automatically identifying future callings to assist testers. In: Proceedings of the 11th Asia-Pacific Symposium on Internetware (Internetware 2019), Fukuoka, Japan, 28–29 October 2019 (2019)

18. Xuan, J., Cornu, B., Martinez, M., Baudry, B., Seinturier, L., Monperrus, M.: B-refactoring: automatic test code refactoring to improve dynamic analysis. Inf. Softw. Technol. 76, 65–80 (2016). https://doi.org/10.1016/j.infsof.2016.04.016

19. Xuan, J., Gu, Y., Ren, Z., Jia, X., Fan, Q.: Genetic configuration sampling: learning a sampling strategy for fault detection of configurable systems. In: Proceedings of the 5th International Workshop on Genetic Improvement (GI@GECCO 2018), Kyoto, Japan, 15–19 July 2018 (2018). https://doi.org/10.1145/3205651.3208267

20. Zhang, Y., Guo, J., Blais, E., Czarnecki, K.: Performance prediction of configurable software systems by Fourier learning (T). In: 30th IEEE/ACM International Conference on Automated Software Engineering, ASE 2015, Lincoln, NE, USA, 9–13 November 2015, pp. 365–373 (2015). https://doi.org/10.1109/ASE.2015.15
21. Zuluaga, M., Krause, A., Püschel, M.: e-pal: an active learning approach to the multi-objective optimization problem. J. Mach. Learn. Res. **17**, 1–104:32 (2016). http://jmlr.org/papers/v17/15-047.html

Combining Model Learning and Model Checking to Analyze Java Libraries

Shahbaz Ali[1,2], Hailong Sun[1,2], and Yongwang Zhao[1,2(✉)]

[1] School of Computer Science and Engineering, Beihang University, Beijing, China
[2] Beijing Advanced Innovation Center for Big Data and Brain Computing,
Beijing University, Beijing, China
{bazgikian,sunhl,zhaoyw}@buaa.edu.cn

Abstract. In the current technological era, the correct functionality and quality of software systems are of prime concern and require practical approaches to improve their reliability. Besides classical testing, formal verification techniques can be employed to enhance the reliability of software systems. In this connection, we propose an approach that combines the strengths of two effective techniques, i.e., *Model learning* and *Model checking* for the formal analysis of Java libraries. To evaluate the performance of the proposed approach, we consider the implementation of "Java.util" package as a case study. First, we apply model learning to infer behavior models of Java package and then use model checking to verify that the obtained models satisfy basic properties (safety, functional, and liveness) specified in LTL/CTL languages. Our results of the formal analysis reveal that the learned models of Java package satisfy all the selected properties specified in temporal logic. Moreover, the proposed approach is generic and very promising to analyze any software library/package considered as a black-box.

Keywords: Model learning · Model checking · Formal verification · Software testing · Active automata learning · Java library

1 Introduction

Developing a bug-free software is a challenging job, and ensuring its correctness is even more challenging. In addition to classical testing, model-based techniques are practical approaches to improve the quality of software systems. Such techniques are more suitable in the scenarios where behavior models are readily available either from requirement specifications or by the use of program analysis techniques to source code directly [8,28]. However, these techniques are inappropriate for software systems (like software libraries) which are generally distributed without access to the source code (considered as black-box). Since

This work is supported by the National Natural Science Foundation of China (NSFC) under Grant No. 61872016 and by the National Key Research and Development Program of China under Grant No. 2016YFB1000804.

© Springer Nature Switzerland AG 2020
H. Miao et al. (Eds.): SOFL+MSVL 2019 Workshop, LNCS 12028, pp. 259–278, 2020.
https://doi.org/10.1007/978-3-030-41418-4_18

the construction of behavior models is a crucial problem for black-box systems, so we find its solution from the domain of software reverse-engineering.

Model learning [27] is a reverse engineering and dynamic analysis technique to get the behavior models of hardware and software systems automatically. Recently, it has emerged as a highly effective bug-finding technique and attracted the attention of researchers, especially from the fields of testing and verification. In *model learning*, behavior models of concrete implementations are inferred automatically, but checking the conformance of complex models becomes difficult. On the other hand, *Model checking* [7,12] checks conformance of models to specifications automatically and it requires models and formalized specifications. In this paper, we propose a methodology that combines the strengths of two state-of-the-art techniques called *Model learning* and *Model checking* to analyze implementations of Java libraries.

To evaluate the effectiveness of our suggested approach, we consider the implementation, in binary form, of 'java.utility' package as a case study. Our selected package (library) for experimentation is prevalent in the developer's community and being used extensively for cost-effective and rapid development of software systems. Java utility package provides a 'Collection' framework, i.e., *java.util.collection*, which defines several classes and interfaces to represent a group of objects as a single unit. We learn the models of implementations, provided by Oracle Corporation, corresponding to three basic interfaces, i.e., Set, List, and Queue. After model learning, we verify the LTL/CTL based formalized properties using NuSMV model checker [11]. In this study, we use the NuSMV model checker since the learned models are too complex to inspect manually. Moreover, our suggested black-box approach is generic and can be used for the formal analysis of any software library (e.g., C, C++, C#, Java libraries in the form of .dll, .jar, etc.).

Perceiving a software component as a model (state machine) enables a developer (or tester) to design, document, and rigorously test the program in terms of its behavior. Models facilitate the process of verification and validation, which refer to testing that the implementation complies with the needs and requirements of the customer. The main advantage of this approach is that we analyze the "real thing (not hand-made model)" and may find bugs in implementations. The learned models are highly effective and can benefit model checking approaches.

Organization. The paper is structured as follows: Sect. 2 presents the related work in the field of model learning and model checking. Section 3 gives the background knowledge of the model learning technique. In Sect. 4, we present a learning setup based on our proposed methodology to analyze software implementations. Sections 5 and 6 explain the results of model learning and model checking, respectively. Finally, we conclude our study in Sect. 7.

2   Related Work

Peled [23] was the first one who introduced the idea of combining model checking and model learning under the name of *black-box checking*. Although the learned models can be analyzed manually [1, 13] but it is tedious, and time-consuming activity since the inferred models may be too complex to inspect manually. In a research work, Meinke and Sindhu [20] showed how the paradigm of learning-based testing could be utilized to automate specification-based black-box testing of reactive systems. They used the NuSMV model checker to analyze learned models via model learning (automata learning).

MullerOlm et al. [21] argued that obtained models by model learning of black-box components are extremely valuable and can benefit model-checking techniques. Fiterau-Brosten et al. [15] combined model learning and model checking in a case study involving Linux, Windows, and FreeBSD to analyze the implementations of TCP formally. In a similar kind of study, Fiterau-Brosten et al. [16] used model learning technique to get the behavior models of SSH security protocol and then performed model-checking using nuSMV model checker. In both studies, they found some security breaches and violations of RFC specifications. In fact, security breaches and standard violations reported in [10, 13, 14] have been observed with model learning.

Some other successful applications where model learning has been used to infer state machines include: EMV bank cards [1], Biometric passport [3], smart-card reader [10], controller of printer [25], malware detection [30], composition of components [6], unit and integration testing of black box components [24] and model-based testing of reactive systems [9].

3   Background on Model Learning

Model Learning Approaches. The goal of model learning is to learn a state model (e.g., a DFA, a Mealy machine) of a black-box system by providing inputs (tests) and observing outputs. Generally, model learning approaches can be categorized into active and passive learning.

The passive learning algorithms learn the behavior models of SUL from the available set of positive and negative traces (training data) [19, 29]. However, if a log file missed some behavior, then it is difficult to infer a conclusion, and hence the resulted model became erroneous due to this missed or unobserved behavior. To deal with this problem, a solution exists, and that is to request additional behavior traces as per the requirement from the target system. This strategy has been incorporated in *active learning* approach. In active learning [4, 5, 26], the learner interacts with the SUL continuously and performs experiments (tests) on it. By applying this process of experimentation repeatedly, a model is approximated, which represents the complete and run-time behavior of the SUL. It is the test-based and counterexample-driven approach for learning models of real-world black-box software systems fully automatically.

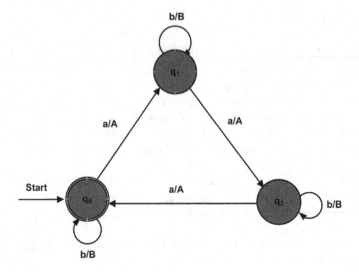

Fig. 1. A simple mealy machine

In our work, we employ an active learning approach to obtain behavior models in the form of Mealy machines. A Mealy machine is a suitable option to model input/output based systems (reactive systems). Figure 1, represents a simple Mealy machine with input alphabet $= \{a, b\}$, output alphabet $= \{A, B\}$, and q_0 as the *initial* state.

Basic Framework. Dana Angluin, in the context of active learning, proposes a query learning algorithm [5], L^* for inferring DFA, which describes regular sets. Many efficient learning algorithms have been developed since then, and mostly follow Angluin's approach of MAT framework. In her productive work, she proposes the idea of *MAT*, where the learning activity can be considered

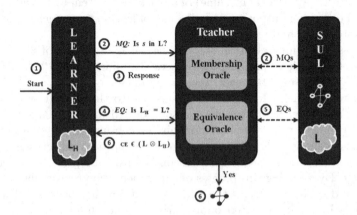

Fig. 2. Learning with MAT framework

as a game. In this game, the learning of a model involves the *'learner'* and a *'teacher'*. Here, the task of the learner is to get the model of the black-box system by putting queries to the teacher.

The learner knows the I/O alphabets of the SUL while the teacher has the complete knowledge of the behavior of the SUL. To learn a black-box automaton $\mathcal{X}$, the active learner puts queries continuously, and stores the replies in a data structure, called observation table. After some saturation of learning, the learner infers an unknown automaton (using stored results) whose behavior resembles the target SUL. During the learning process, the active learner uses two kinds of queries:

(1) Membership Query: A membership query (MQ) is a sequence of symbols from the input alphabet. The active learner puts this query to test whether it belongs to the language of SUL or not. If it belongs to the target SUL then the answer is *'Yes'*, otherwise *'No'*.

(2) Equivalence Query: The active learner uses equivalence query (EQ) to validate the hypothesis model $\mathcal{Z}$ i.e., $\mathcal{Z} \approx \mathcal{X}$. The teacher answers *'Yes'* if $\mathcal{Z} = \mathcal{X}$ otherwise it answers *'No'* in case of $\mathcal{Z} \neq \mathcal{X}$ and provides a counterexample.

A self-explanatory and general working of the active learning process using MAT framework is shown in Fig. 2.

Abstraction. Existing implementations of learning algorithms only proved useful when applied to machines with small abstract input/output alphabet symbols. Realistic systems like SSH protocol, however, typically posses large alphabets, e.g., inputs and outputs symbols contain data parameters of type string or integer.

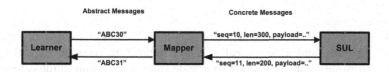

Fig. 3. Working of mapper component

To solve this problem, Aarts et al. [2] proposed the idea of *abstraction*. Abstraction, in this case, plays a key role in scaling the current model learning techniques to real-world systems. A *mapper* is a software component which plays the role of abstraction and is placed in-between the *learner* and the *SUL*. The abstract inputs of the *learner* are forwarded to the mapper component. The mapper component transforms these abstract messages into concrete inputs and sends them to the *SUL*. On receiving the concrete outputs/responses from the SUL, the mapper component transforms back to abstract outputs/messages and returns to the *learner*. A graphical overview of the working of the mapper component is shown in Fig. 3.

4   Proposed Methodology

From our literature survey, which is described in Sect. 2, it is clear that, in recent years, *model learning* has emerged as a highly effective bug-finding technique. Model learning provides behavior models of software implementations automatically, but the conformance checking of these models becomes difficult. On the other hand, model checking can perform conformance checking of these models to specifications automatically. Therefore, by considering strengths and limitations of two techniques, we propose a methodology, for formal analysis of Java libraries (taken as black-box), which combines the strengths of two state-of-the-art technologies, i.e., model learning and model checking, as shown in the Fig. 4.

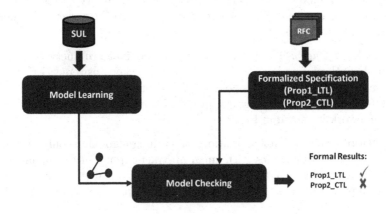

Fig. 4. Proposed methodology

The proposed approach learn the accurate behavior models of software library, efficiently and automatically. It is pertinent to mention here that our proposed approach can be applied to a wide range of software implementations because they are being treated as black-boxes (binary files available in the form of .jar, .dll, etc.).

4.1   Approach

In this section, we describe our approach used for the formal analysis of Java libraries. It mainly consists of model learning and model checking phases, as shown in Fig. 5. In the following subsections, we explain these phases one by one.

4.1.1   Model Learning

The model learning phase returns the models of SUL to be analyzed further by the model checking phase. It consists of the following core components:

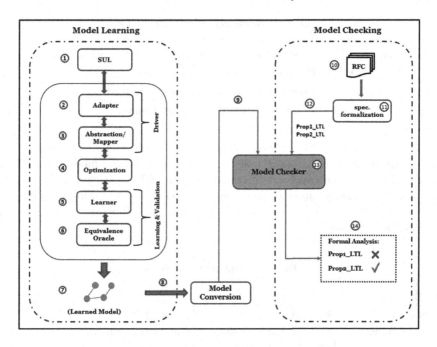

Fig. 5. Experimental setup

System Under Learning (SUL). To evaluate the effectiveness of our app-roach, we consider 'java.util' package as a case study. It provides a wide range of interfaces for implementations. The Java 'Collection' interface, provided by java.util package, is one of the root interfaces of the 1Java Collection API'. The JDK does not provide any direct implementations of this interface: it provides implementations of more specific sub-interfaces. The sub-interfaces which extend the Java collection interface include List, Set, SortedSet, NavigableSet, Queue, and Deque. The 'Collection' interface just defines a set of methods (behaviors) that each of these collection sub-types shares. For performance evaluation of our approach, we only consider the implementations of List, Queue, and Set provided by Oracle Corporation, as shown in Table 1. However, the same methodology can be used to formally analyze all the implementations (one by one) of remaining interfaces provided by 'java.util' package/library.

First, we consider one of the implementations of Set (i.e., Java.util.HashSet), learn its models via model learning, and then formally analyze the obtained models to find bugs (if any). Later, we shall consider implementations of List and Queue, and compare their formal results in a table.

The Adapter Module. In the active learning approach, the learner interacts with the SUL via an adapter (interface component) module. It bridges the gap of communications between learner and SUL. This component is SUL dependent. From the available documentation of the SUL (java.util package[1]), we develop an adapter module for SUL (Set) in Java.

---

[1] https://docs.oracle.com/javase/8/docs/api/java/util/Collection.html.

Table 1. Systems under learning (SULs)

S.No	Interface	Super interfaces	Selected implementation (SUL)
1	List	Collection, Iterable	java.util.stack
2	Queue	Collection, Iterable	java.util.LinkedList
3	Set	Collection, Iterable	java.util.HashSet

The Mapper Module. As discussed in Sect. 3, the mapper module translates abstract input (AI) messages into concrete input (CI) messages, and concrete output (CO) messages into abstract output (AO) messages. More specifically, parameters contained in messages are mapped from a concrete to an abstract domain, and vice versa.

Table 2. Alphabets for SULs

SUL	I	O	$(|\Sigma|)$
java.util.stack	$\{pu0, pu1, size, pop\}$	$\{empty, ful\}$	6
java.util.HashSet	Not fixed. For experiment having three elements, it is: $\{add1, add2, add3, remov1, remov2, remov3, size\}$	$\{empty, ful, Tru, Fls\}$	Variable
java.util.Linked-List	$\{ofer0, ofer1, pol, size\}$	$\{tru, nul, ful\}$	7

To develop mapper modules, we define input/output alphabets for selected SULs, as shown in Table 2. In the table, 'I' represents the input alphabet, 'O' represents the output alphabet, and $(|\Sigma|)$ represents the alphabet length. For learning models of 'List' and 'Queue' implementations, which allow duplication of elements, we learn their models by changing the sizes of stack and queue but keeping fixed input/output alphabets. And, for the set implementation, which do not allow duplication of elements, we perform experiments by varying the sizes of input/output alphabets. After defining input/output alphabets, we define our mapper module, which perform the role of transformations, as shown in Table 3.

Optimization Module. The required time to learn a model of real-world implementation can be very long. The learning complexity mainly depends upon equivalence queries, membership queries, and the length of counter-example generated during the equivalence checking phase. To optimize the learning process, we develop an optimization module that eliminates duplicated queries. To refine it further, we also use the optimization techniques provided by the LearnLib[2] library.

---

[2] https://learnlib.de/.

Table 3. Mappings of alphabets for SULs

AI + Meaning	CI	CO	AO
Mapper definition for list implementation			
'pu0'. Push '0' on the stack	stackObj.push(0)	0 if $size < fixsize$	'0' or 'ful' if size = fixsize
'pu1'. Push '1' on the stack	stackObj.push(1)	1 if $size < fixsize$	'1' or 'ful' if size = fixsize
'pop'. Pop item from the stack	stackObj.pop()	Last inserted value (LIFO)	'0' or '1'
'size'. Return size of the stack	stackObj.size()	size of the stack	stack size (0 to 16)
Mapper definition for set implementation			
'add1'. Add '1' in the set	setObj.add(1)	'true' if 1 is not already in set otherwise 'false'	'Tru' or 'Fls'
'add2'. Add '2 in the set	setObj.add(2)	'true' if 2 is not already in set otherwise 'false'	'Tru or 'Fls'
'add3'. Add '3 in the set	setObj.add(3)	'true' if 3 is not already in set otherwise 'false'	'Tru or 'Fls'
'remov1'. Remove '1' from the set	setObj.remove(1)	'true' if set contains '1' otherwise 'false'	'1' if set contains '1', else 'Fls'
'remov2'. Remove '2' from the set	setObj.remove(2)	'true' if set contains '2' otherwise 'false'	'2' if set contains '2', else 'Fls'
'remov3'. Remove '3' from the set	setObj.remove(3)	'true' if set contains '3' otherwise 'false'	'3' if set contains '3', else 'Fls'
'size'. Return the size of the set	setObj.size()	size of the set	set size (0 to 10)
Mapper definition for queue implementation			
'ofer0'. Add '0' in the queue	queueObj.offer(0)	'true' if the element was added to this queue, else 'false'	'tru' or 'ful'
'ofer1'. Add '1' in the queue	queueObj.offer(1)	'true' if the element was added to this queue, else 'false'	'tru' or 'ful'
'pol'. Poll the item from the queue	queueObj.poll()	the 'head' of this queue, or 'null' if this queue is empty	First inserted value (0 or 1)
'size'. Return the size of the set	queueObj.size()	size of the queue	queue size (3 to 16)

The Learner and Tester. In our experimental setup, we use LearnLib and AutomataLib[3] libraries. These libraries have been implemented in Java and provide the provision of graph-based modeling formalisms (like Mealy machines). These libraries also provide optimized implementations of various learning and equivalence checking algorithms. We select and modify the 'ExtensibleL-StarMealy' [18,22], a L* based learner for learning Mealy machines. To validate the learned models, we select 'MealyWpMethodEQOracle' [17] (and also 'RandomWalkEQOracle' to cross-check the final model) as equivalence checking algorithms (equivalence oracles), and adapt them as per the requirements.

4.1.2 Model Checking

The model learning phase provides Mealy models of SULs in DOT format. The resulted models can be viewed by a visualizer. Dot tool, for example, from GraphVIZ[4] can be used for visualization and manual analysis. In our experimental setup, we select NuSMV[5] model checker to formally analyze the models. As NuSMV require models in the form of .smv format, so we convert .dot models into .smv format. For this, we customize the conversion module, which was used and developed for the formal analysis of SSH protocol [16].

5 Model Learning Results

We use the approach described in Sect. 4 to learn models of the list, queue, and set implementations provided by Java.util package. The learning and testing statistics for the 'Set' implementation has been shown in Table 4. The statistics include the information like (1) set size (capacity to hold elements), (2) the number of states in the learned model, (3) the number of learning and testing queries, (4) the number of hypotheses built during the learning process, and (5) the time spent during model learning and searching the counter-example. For learner queries (MQs), we record two types of queries, namely: (1) total queries posed by the learner during model learning, i.e., 'queries from learner', and (2) 'queries to SUL' refined by optimization module after filtering out redundant queries. For test queries, we only consider those queries which are run on the last hypothesis.

We learn the models of 'Set' implementation with different sizes ranging from 2 to 10. Here, due to space limitation, we consider only the learned model of size (capacity) 3 and discuss its behavior model. As other learned models (in dot format) are too large to present here, so we place them on a repository[6] created on GitHub.

Figure 6 represents the learned model, i.e., a Mealy model having eight states and size equal to 3, for set implementation. To improve readability, we have

---

[3] https://learnlib.de/projects/automatalib/.

[4] https://www.graphviz.org.

[5] http://nusmv.fbk.eu/.

[6] https://github.com/bazali/SATE2019.

Table 4. Learning and testing statistics for SET implementation

Size	States	MQs (resets)		EQs (Hyps)	TQs	Time (ms)	
		Queries from learner	Queries to SUL			Learning	Searching (CE)
2	4	125	100	1	914	9	51
3	8	455	392	1	8031	17	69
4	16	1449	1296	1	47684	31	137
5	32	4235	3872	1	222775	48	349
6	64	11661	10816	1	890478	88	953
7	128	30735	28800	1	3196865	169	3274
8	256	78353	73984	1	10617288	291	9281
9	512	194579	184832	1	631726200	626	597765
10	1024	473109	451584	1	2087451080	1202	31 min

edited the obtained model slightly. The learned model has been obtained from binary code files of set implementation, i.e., by treating the SUL (Set) as black-box. It represents the complete run-time behavior (i.e., it contains the information of every possible combination of states and input values with corresponding output values and next states) of the SUL. In the learned model, the initial state, representing the empty set, is labeled with '0'. As the set is empty, so it remains in the same state for queries R1 (i.e., remove 1 from the set), R2 (remove 2), R3 (remove 3), and S (size) with outputs E (representing Empty set) and 0 (representing size at initial state). To understand the behavior of this learned model, we consider an MQ query, i.e., 'R1A1A1'. On receiving this query, the system moves to state '1' on input A1 and output 'T' (representing 'true', and it means 1 has been added successfully into the set). For the second word 'A1' of input query R1A1A1, the system remains in state 1 and outputs 'F' (indicating 'false', it means that '1' cannot be added because it is already present in the Set). And for the third word 'R1' of this query, the system moves back to the initial state by outputting 'T' (indicating that 1 has been removed from the set successfully).

To make sure that the response of every query is independent of others, the learner 'ExtensibleLStarMealy' *resets* the SUL after each query. For example, another query 'A2A3A1' moves the SUL from the *initial state* (not from the previous state where it was on the last query) to state 7 that represents the size of the set equal to 3 (indicating full set). The learner exhaustively tests the SUL on every state by posing every possible query and records the responses in a data structure called *observation table*. From Table 4, it is clear that to learn this model, the learner takes 17 ms to pose 455 queries, which are further refined to 392 by optimization module. Our adapted equivalence oracle poses 8031 test queries in 69ms to validate the hypothesis. As it finds no counter-example during this time, so it returns the current hypothesis as the final model and terminates the learning experiment successfully.

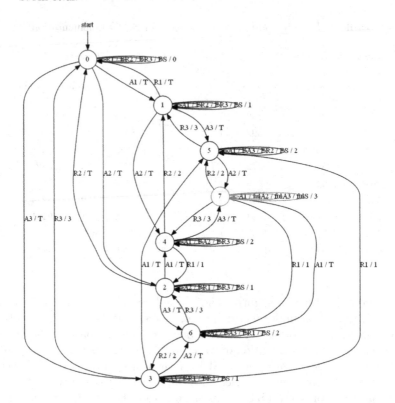

Fig. 6. Learned model for set implementation (size = 3). To improve the readability of the model, we use abbreviations instead of whole words. For example, we use 'A' for adding, 'R' for removal, 'S' for size, 'E' for empty, 'ful' for full, 'T' for true and 'F' for false.

Next, we discuss the learning and testing results for queue implementation provided by the same Java library, i.e., Java.util.*. The queue is a dynamic structure that exhibits FIFO behavior. We modify our developed modules (adapter, mapper, optimization, etc.) according to the specification documentation of queue and learn its behavior models by considering its various sizes (ranging from 3 to 16), as shown in Table 5. The table includes statistical information like that of Table 4 with additional information regarding testing queries (TQs). Here, in addition to queries that are run on the last hypothesis, we also consider testing queries to the last hypothesis. In this table, 'Lt' represents the learning time and 'CEt' represents the counterexample searching time.

Figure 7 represents the learned model for queue implementation, having fifteen states and size equal to 3. As it represents the complete run-time behavior of the SUL (queue), so we can visualize its various behaviors and get confidence about the correctness of the obtained model, for example, the FIFO behavior can be easily checked from the model. From Table 5, it is clear that to learn this model, the learner takes 30 ms to pose 566 queries, which are further refined

Table 5. Learning and testing statistics for queue implementation

Size	States	MQs (resets)		EQs (Hyps)	TQs		Time (ms)	
		Queries from learner	Queries to SUL		Tests to last hyp	Tests on last hyp	Lt	CEt
3	15	566	383	3	678	4747	30	55
5	63	2780	1606	5	6194	30594	57	119
9	1023	55496	23444	9	214685	831492	299	1475
12	8191	529167	182109	12	2407927	27641969	2089	47661
13	16383	1120180	362754	13	5275850	59232497	4625	117 s
14	32767	2366729	723677	14	11469111	126353163	11321	7 min
15	65535	4989722	1445105	15	24773009	1002450824	24394	48 min
16	131071	10496499	2887489	16	49413615	2116543123	65298	104 min

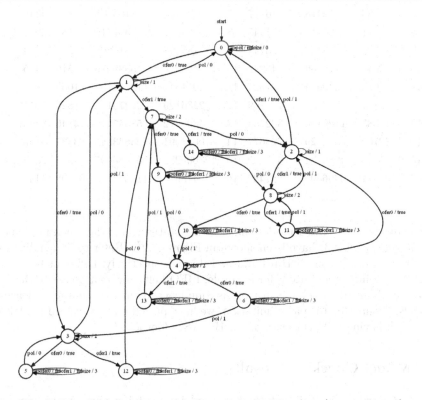

Fig. 7. Learned behavior model of queue implementation (queue size = 3)

to 383 by optimization module. Our adapted equivalence oracle validates the hypothesis by posing 678 test queries to reach the final hypothesis and further pose 4747 queries in 55 ms to search a counter-example. The learning statistics for queue implementation has been shown in Table 5. Moreover, all the learned models with sizes ranging from 5 to 16 have been placed on GitHub.

Table 6. Learning and testing statistics for stack implementation

Size	States	MQs (resets)		EQs	TQs		Time (ms)	
		Queries from learner	Queries to SUL		Tests to last hyp	Tests on last hyp	Lt	CEt
3	12	566	383	3	617	4686	30	56
4	31	1287	805	4	2029	12251	44	84
5	63	2780	1606	5	5772	30127	63	114
6	127	5889	3141	6	14929	71057	71	205
7	255	12418	6117	7	36464	163005	112	434
8	511	26219	11945	8	86462	367416	183	893
9	1023	55496	23444	9	189398	816205	295	1934
10	2047	117669	46249	10	452284	5885916	510	9435
11	4095	249614	91627	11	1011347	12754784	1055	21756
12	8191	529167	182109	12	2236129	27470171	1828	50112
13	16383	1120180	362754	13	4898772	58855419	3846	2 min
14	32767	2366729	723677	14	10648991	125533043	3837	5 min
15	65535	4989722	1445105	15	23002282	1000680097	24948	38 min
16	131071	10496499	2887489	16	49413615	2116543123	65298	114 min

Similarly, the learned model and learning statistics for the stack implementation (of capacity 3) have been shown in Figure A.2[7]. (Refer to Appendix A of APPENDICES file on GitHub) and in Table 6, respectively. Different behaviors of the stack implementation, for example, LIFO behavior, can be easily checked from the obtained model, which gives us confidence about the accuracy of learned models. Again, due to space limitation, we have placed all the learned models of the stack having different sizes on GitHub (See footnote 6).

6   Model Checking Results

Model Checking [7,12] is a formal method for verifying if an abstract representation of a system (i.e., model) is correct relative to a formal specification describing the desired/expected system behavior. We select the NuSMV model checker to analyze the learned models formally. As the obtained models are in the .dot format, so we must convert them into the language of the NuSMV model checker.

---

[7] https://github.com/bazali/SATE2019/tree/master/APPENDICES

6.1 Model Conversion (.dot Model to .smv Model)

In the NuSMV model, the state of the model is specified by a set of finite variables and a transition-function that describes changes in these variables. We specify the requirements to be checked in LTL and CTL temporal logic. NuSMV will check whether the formal properties hold or not. It provides a counter-example if a certain specification is not true. The automatic generation of NuSMV models from the learned models is straightforward. The states of .dot model are directly translated to states of the NuSMV model. NuSMV model contains two variables, one for the input alphabet, and the other for the output alphabet. Also, the NuSMV transitions are generated by taking a combination of a state and an input-word (from input alphabet) and defining an output-word (from output alphabet) and the next state for the considered combination.

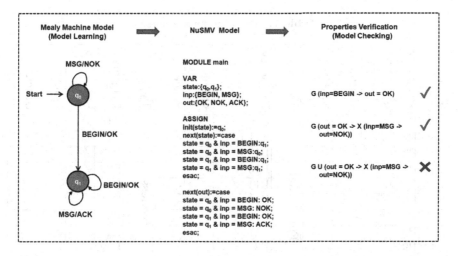

Fig. 8. Conversion of .dot model to .smv model. Figure adapted from a figure in [16].

Figure 8 gives the graphical overview of the model conversion process by considering a trivial Mealy model consisting of two states q_0 and q_1. By using our model conversion module, we convert all learned models (in .dot format) to .smv models (.smv format) and place them on GitHub[8].

6.2 Formal Specification of Properties

Now we define and formalize the properties to be verified in LTL/CTL temporal logic. We group our selected properties into safety (something bad never happens), functional (basic functions that the system *should/or must* offer), and liveness (something good will eventually happen) properties. The formalized

---

[8] https://github.com/bazali/SATE2019/tree/master/SMVModels.

properties corresponding to Set, Queue, and Stack have been shown in Tables B.1, B.2, and B.3, respectively (Refer to Appendix B of APPENDICES file on GitHub).

6.3 Model Checking

Table 7 presents model checking results for Set, Queue and Stack implementations provided by Java.util.* library. The tick-mark symbols in the columns of 'Set' indicate that the *safety* properties (range from P1 to P9), *functional* properties (range from P10 to P17), and *liveness* properties (range from P18 to P21), which are defined and formalized in Table B.1 (Refer to our repository on GitHub), all satisfy the Set implementation. In other words, for this group of properties, we have found no bug/error in the implementation of the

Table 7. Model checking results

Type	Property	Set	Queue	Stack	Type	Property	Set	Queue	Stack	Type	Property	Set	Queue	Stack
Safety	P1	✓	-	-	Functional	P10	✓	-	-	Liveness	P18	✓	-	-
	P2	✓	-	-		P11	✓	-	-		P19	✓	-	-
	P3	✓	-	-		P12	✓	-	-		P20	✓	-	-
	P4	✓	-	-		P13	✓	-	-		P21	✓	-	-
	P5	✓	-	-		P14	✓	-	-		P40	-	✓	-
	P6	✓	-	-		P15	✓	-	-		P41	-	✓	-
	P7	✓	-	-		P16	✓	-	-		P42	-	✓	-
	P8	✓	-	-		P17	✓	-	-		P43	-	✓	-
	P9	✓	-	-		P31	-	✓	-		P62	-	-	✓
	P22	-	✓	-		P32	-	✓	-		P63	-	-	✓
	P23	-	✓	-		P33	-	✓	-		P64	-	-	✓
	P24	-	✓	-		P34	-	✓	-		P65	-	-	✓
	P25	-	✓	-		P35	-	✓	-		-	-	-	-
	P26	-	✓	-		P39	-	✓	-		-	-	-	-
	P27	-	✓	-		P54	-	-	✓		-	-	-	-
	P28	-	✓	-		P55	-	-	✓		-	-	-	-
	P29	-	✓	-		P56	-	-	✓		-	-	-	-
	P30	-	✓	-		P57	-	-	✓		-	-	-	-
	P31	-	✓	-		P58	-	-	✓		-	-	-	-
P44 to P53		-	-	✓		P59	-	-	✓		-	-	-	-
		-	-	✓		P60	-	-	✓		-	-	-	-
		-	-	✓		P61	-	-	✓		-	-	-	-
		-	-	✓		-	-	-	-		-	-	-	-
		-	-	✓		-	-	-	-		-	-	-	-

Set interface. Moreover, it is pertinent to mention here that each property has been formally checked on all sizes of learned models. For example, the formalized property 'P60' has been checked for all 'Stack' models having states ranging from 12 (simple model) to 131071 (more complex model).

From the formal analysis results, it is clear that for our selected set of properties, the three chosen implementations provided by Oracle Corporation are stable and bug-free. In our study, we have selected and analyzed three modules of Java package. However, by using the same approach, we can perform a formal analysis of remaining modules, like SortedSet, NavigableSet, Deque, etc., of the 'Collection' interface. Likewise, we can formally analyze implementations of different packages/libraries including java.lang, java.io, java.net, etc., provided by Java Oracle Corporation as well as by third-party vendors. Moreover, the suggested approach is generic and takes the implementation under testing as black-box, so any software library (in the form of .dll, .jar, etc.) can be analyzed formally.

6.4   An Example

In the last section, we observed that for our selected set of properties, there is no bug in the implementation of the Java utility package. To give some more confidence in the effectiveness of the proposed approach, we consider another but a small example. First, we formally analyze the behavior model of a bug-free source code module. In the next step, we intentionally induce an error in the code (as an implementation error) and detect this induced faulty behavior by the proposed approach. This complete example including implementation, learned models and results have been placed on the GitHub repository (See footnote 6).

Let us consider the behavior of a 'login utility' that does not allow a user to 'login' until he creates a user account first, as shown in the Fig. 9a. After learning and transforming the model of login utility, we checked the property that 'a user cannot login without having an account first' i.e., $LTLSPEC\ NAME\ spec1 := inp = LogIn- > out = nok$. This specification represents the scenario that initially, if the user tries to login (i.e., input is LogIn), then the system should deny (i.e., the output must be 'not ok'). As there is no implementation error, so the NuSMV model checker verifies this property (as per our expectation). Next, we introduced an error (let user was granted access by mistake without creating its account first) in the implementation that was detected in the learned model (highlighted with dotted red line), as shown in Fig. 9b. And, this time, the same specified property $(LTLSPEC\ NAME\ spec1 := inp = LogIn- > out = nok)$ was not verified and a counterexample was generated by the model checker. So, this small example proves the fact that the proposed approach has the full potential to capture any faulty behavior (if present) of the implementation.

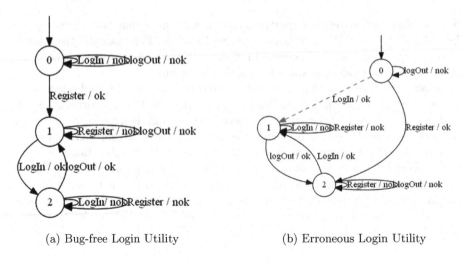

(a) Bug-free Login Utility   (b) Erroneous Login Utility

Fig. 9. Behavior models of login utility

7   Conclusions

We have proposed an approach that combines the strengths of two emerging techniques, i.e., *model learning* and *model checking* for the effective formal analysis of Java libraries. To validate our approach, we have considered 'java.util' package (in binary form) as a case study. First, we learned the models of three core interfaces, i.e., Set, List, and Queue, using model learning with abstraction technique. Then, we formalized several safety, liveness, and functional properties, drawn from Java documentation, in LTL and CTL languages. We have used the NuSMV model checker to formally verify the properties on the learned models. Our formal analysis results showed that the learned models of Java library satisfy all the selected properties. In this study, we have performed a formal analysis of three modules, but following the same approach, we can perform a formal analysis of the whole library. Moreover, our proposed approach is generic and very auspicious for the formal analysis of any library considered as black-box.

Future Work

In this study, we selected the implementation of "java.util.*" the library provided by Oracle Corporation and performed its formal analysis. The implementations of the same library have been provided by many third-party vendors, for example, google.guava.collection, Apache Commons Collections, fastutil, Trove, GS collection, HPPC, etc. These third-party implementations are also popular among the community of software developers. One of the future works is to formally test these implementations and compare their formal analysis results.

Acknowledgment. We are thankful to Mr. Markus Frohme from TU Dortmund University for constructive discussion on LearnLib and AutomataLib libraries. We are also grateful to Mr. Paul Fiterau-Brostean for assisting in converting the learned model (.dot format) to NuSMV format (.smv).

References

1. Aarts, F., De Ruiter, J., Poll, E.: Formal models of bank cards for free. In: 2013 IEEE Sixth International Conference on Software Testing, Verification and Validation Workshops (ICSTW), pp. 461–468. IEEE (2013)
2. Aarts, F., Jonsson, B., Uijen, J.: Generating models of infinite-state communication protocols using regular inference with abstraction. ICTSS **6435**, 188–204 (2010)
3. Aarts, F., Schmaltz, J., Vaandrager, F.: Inference and abstraction of the biometric passport. In: Margaria, T., Steffen, B. (eds.) ISoLA 2010. LNCS, vol. 6415, pp. 673–686. Springer, Heidelberg (2010). https://doi.org/10.1007/978-3-642-16558-0_54
4. Aarts, F.D.: Tomte: bridging the gap between active learning and real-world systems. [Sl: sn] (2014)
5. Angluin, D.: Learning regular sets from queries and counterexamples. Inf. Comput. **75**(2), 87–106 (1987). https://doi.org/10.1016/0890-5401(87)90052-6
6. Arbab, F.: Reo: a channel-based coordination model for component composition. Math. Struct. Comput. Sci. **14**(3), 329–366 (2004)
7. Baier, C., Katoen, J.P.: Principles of Model Checking. MIT Press, Cambridge (2008)
8. Ball, T., Rajamani, S.K.: The SLAM project: debugging system software via static analysis. In: ACM SIGPLAN Notices, vol. 37, pp. 1–3. ACM (2002)
9. Broy, M., Jonsson, B., Katoen, J.-P., Leucker, M., Pretschner, A. (eds.): Model-Based Testing of Reactive Systems. LNCS, vol. 3472. Springer, Heidelberg (2005). https://doi.org/10.1007/b137241
10. Chalupar, G., Peherstorfer, S., Poll, E., De Ruiter, J.: Automated reverse engineering using lego®. In: WOOT 2014, pp. 1–10 (2014)
11. Cimatti, A., et al.: NuSMV 2: an OpenSource tool for symbolic model checking. In: Brinksma, E., Larsen, K.G. (eds.) CAV 2002. LNCS, vol. 2404, pp. 359–364. Springer, Heidelberg (2002). https://doi.org/10.1007/3-540-45657-0_29
12. Clarke, E.M., Grumberg, O., Peled, D.: Model Checking. MIT Press, Cambridge (1999)
13. De Ruiter, J., Poll, E.: Protocol state fuzzing of TLS implementations. In: USENIX Security Symposium, pp. 193–206 (2015)
14. Fiterău-Broştean, P., Janssen, R., Vaandrager, F.: Learning fragments of the TCP network protocol. In: Lang, F., Flammini, F. (eds.) FMICS 2014. LNCS, vol. 8718, pp. 78–93. Springer, Cham (2014). https://doi.org/10.1007/978-3-319-10702-8_6
15. Fiterău-Broştean, P., Janssen, R., Vaandrager, F.: Combining model learning and model checking to analyze TCP implementations. In: Chaudhuri, S., Farzan, A. (eds.) CAV 2016. LNCS, vol. 9780, pp. 454–471. Springer, Cham (2016). https://doi.org/10.1007/978-3-319-41540-6_25
16. Fiterău-Broştean, P., Lenaerts, T., Poll, E., de Ruiter, J., Vaandrager, F., Verleg, P.: Model learning and model checking of SSH implementations. In: Proceedings of the 24th ACM SIGSOFT International SPIN Symposium on Model Checking of Software, pp. 142–151. ACM (2017)

17. Fujiwara, S., Bochmann, G.V., Khendek, F., Amalou, M., Ghedamsi, A.: Test selection based on finite state models. IEEE Trans. Softw. Eng. **17**(6), 591–603 (1991)

18. Hungar, H., Niese, O., Steffen, B.: Domain-specific optimization in automata learning. In: Hunt, W.A., Somenzi, F. (eds.) CAV 2003. LNCS, vol. 2725, pp. 315–327. Springer, Heidelberg (2003). https://doi.org/10.1007/978-3-540-45069-6_31

19. Lorenzoli, D., Mariani, L., Pezzè, M.: Automatic generation of software behavioral models. In: Proceedings of the 30th International Conference on Software Engineering, pp. 501–510. ACM (2008)

20. Meinke, K., Sindhu, M.A.: Incremental learning-based testing for reactive systems. In: Gogolla, M., Wolff, B. (eds.) TAP 2011. LNCS, vol. 6706, pp. 134–151. Springer, Heidelberg (2011). https://doi.org/10.1007/978-3-642-21768-5_11

21. Müller-Olm, M., Schmidt, D., Steffen, B.: Model-checking. In: Cortesi, A., Filé, G. (eds.) SAS 1999. LNCS, vol. 1694, pp. 330–354. Springer, Heidelberg (1999). https://doi.org/10.1007/3-540-48294-6_22

22. Niese, O.: An integrated approach to testing complex systems. Ph.D. thesis, Technical University of Dortmund, Germany (2003)

23. Peled, D., Vardi, M.Y., Yannakakis, M.: Black box checking. J. Autom. Lang. Comb. **7**(2), 225–246 (2002)

24. Shahbaz, M.: Reverse engineering enhanced state models of black box software components to support integration testing. Ph.D. thesis (2008)

25. Smeenk, W.: Applying automata learning to complex industrial software. Master's thesis, Radboud University Nijmegen (2012)

26. Steffen, B., Howar, F., Merten, M.: Introduction to active automata learning from a practical perspective. In: Bernardo, M., Issarny, V. (eds.) SFM 2011. LNCS, vol. 6659, pp. 256–296. Springer, Heidelberg (2011). https://doi.org/10.1007/978-3-642-21455-4_8

27. Vaandrager, F.: Model learning. Commun. ACM **60**(2), 86–95 (2017). https://doi.org/10.1145/2967606. http://dl.acm.org/citation.cfm?doid=3042068.2967606

28. Walkinshaw, N., Bogdanov, K., Ali, S., Holcombe, M.: Automated discovery of state transitions and their functions in source code. Softw. Test. Verif. Reliab. **18**(2), 99–121 (2008)

29. Walkinshaw, N., Bogdanov, K., Holcombe, M., Salahuddin, S.: Reverse engineering state machines by interactive grammar inference. In: 14th Working Conference on Reverse Engineering, WCRE 2007, pp. 209–218. IEEE (2007)

30. Xiao, H.: Automatic model learning and its applications in malware detection (2017)

Data Provenance Based System for Classification and Linear Regression in Distributed Machine Learning

Muhammad Jahanzeb Khan[1], Ruoyu Wang[1,3], Daniel Sun[2,3], and Guoqiang Li[1,2(✉)]

[1] School of Software, Shanghai Jiao Tong University, Shanghai 200240, China
{jahanxb_khan,wang.ruoyu,li.g}@sjtu.edu.cn
[2] Enhitech Co. Ltd., Shanghai 200241, China
[3] University of New South Wales, Sydney 2745, Australia

Abstract. Nowadays, data provenance is widely used to increase the accuracy of machine learning models. However, facing the difficulties in information heredity, these models produce data association. Most of the studies in the field of data provenance are focused on specific domains. And there are only a few studies on a *machine learning (ML)* framework with distinct emphasis on the accurate partition of coherent and physical activities with implementation of ML pipelines for provenance. This paper presents a novel approach to usage of data provenance which is also called *data provenance based system for classification and linear regression in distributed machine learning (DPMLR)*. To develop the comprehensive approach for data analysis and visualization based on a collective set of functions for various algorithms and provide the ability to run large scale graph analysis, we apply StellarGraph as our primary ML structure. The preliminary results on the complex data stream structure showed that the overall overhead is no more than 20%. It opens up opportunities for designing an integrated system which performs dynamic scheduling and network bounded synchronization based on the ML algorithm.

Keywords: Data provenance · Machine learning · StellarGraph · Pipeline · Distributed computing

1 Introduction

The global data volume is stretching up to billion terabytes due to the manifold advancements in technology and is expected to increase further [1]. Data evaluation and storage at such scales is a modern-day challenge attributed to the cost and time. To achieve viable inputs, scholars have been varying the data that justifies the regulatory models. Fewer software approaches have been implemented to reuse the knowledge acquired in previous executions. In doing so, the size and

© Springer Nature Switzerland AG 2020
H. Miao et al. (Eds.): SOFL+MSVL 2019 Workshop, LNCS 12028, pp. 279–295, 2020.
https://doi.org/10.1007/978-3-030-41418-4_19

structure of the data get extensively complex, where machine learning provides an adequate solution with its quick data accumulation and processing features.

A raw and basic data feed will not suffice the proper functioning of an ML model, it rather has to be meaningful and evocative. The data needs to be evaluated for its provenance to determine its feasibility for amalgamation with other datasets and incorporation into models. The provenance and attribution of data play a vital role in its restoration and authenticity evaluation, debugging and workflow troubleshooting [3].

Consistency, dependability, accuracy and scalability are the prominent aspects of data provenance workflows that need to be checked and cared for, termed as key features for data analytics [6,9]. As it helps the data analytics in rationalizing the proper data warehousing through systematic storage and inventory including the data concealed in inventories.

Data reliability, originality and identifiable origin provenance have several hindrances to face, though they are of vital prominence to the analytics in pipeline debugging and error removals [16]. [5] focused on the usage of the provenance-based systems and particular on the integrity of meta-data provenance. Moreover, data delineation is considered to be a key factor for machine learning models productivity. [4] mentioned the positive outcomes of data provenance usage with machine learning saying that processes can be embedded to capture data provenance in pipeline analytics and different scaling mechanisms to increase performance specifically on parallel computing architectures such as Hadoop [2].

In [7], the challenges of the objects in metadata that can be used to determine attributes which establishes the relationship between objects are mentioned. [8] uses an approach to facilitate consumption of provenance by semantics and data entities which represent provenance artifacts, a flexible approach to capture data provenance and visualize within analytics software. But this approach causes a loss of data fidelity for processes, lacks the granularity and has not outperformed comprehensive performance evaluation.

This study is based on the proposal of orthodox prearrangement that facilitates the data provenance amalgamation with various machine learning models, named as data provenance based system for classification and linear regression in distributed machine learning (DPMLR). It will facilitate researchers in the agglomeration of complex unachievable utilities like the enhancement of homogenate machinated assessment into more versed in and tested models. DPMLR provides optimal reliability by assessing the results obtained and evaluation of the pipeline paths through proper scoring systems.

The contributions associated with the framework proposed in this study are as follow: (i) handling the meta-data and pedigree of the prehistoric infrequencies along with the provision of a section point for the queries associated with continuous meta-data. Moreover, it can benignant the exempted ML models through incorporation of provenance minimizing the time required in reorientation of these models; (ii) Data provenance model has proved broad reliability, attributed to the evaluation of obtained results along the assessment and scoring of the pipelines paths employed in obtaining those results; (iii) The scoring system is based on the ELO methodology which computes the data processed in a specific path [3]. Once the final scores have been complied for various paths, they are compared for the data processed and time consumed along the data reliability by pipeline monitoring (PM); (iv) Quantifying the precision augmentation achieved by groups over a period of time striving towards a certain ML ambition, like representing the evaluation and classification of precipitate outcomes over longer durations accomplished through pipelines.

The proposed framework will enable researchers of efficacious provisory inspection of their established models. Moreover, it provides an initial stage to researchers for the segregation of research data from the rudimentary reflections employed in ML pipelines, which are based on the principle of typifying multifaceted elemental variation chains constituted of discrete work units.

Each pipeline can serve as the halfway and log event storage concurrently. The probe timing remains nearly perpetual in the original system, being associated with these log events which are entrenched with the ElasticSearch [10]. It has been instigated in various systems and frameworks like Map-Reduce, Hadoop ES and Apache Pig [2,11,14].

However, provenance can enhance the efficiency of ML models attributed to its capability of minimizing the process time and resources required for its development. This performance optimization of ML models through provenance come in terms of cost reduction, enhanced accuracy and consistent data origin traceability. StellarGraph [13], being developed in python has opted as the key framework for this study.

The rest of the paper is organized as follows. Section 2 provides the overview of architecture and design. Section 3 has the functionalities and implementation. Section 4 provides brief description of the experiments performed. Section 5 provides the evaluation of experiments. Section 6 contains the review on related work. Finally, Sect. 7 enlightens the conclusion and future work.

2   Overview of Architecture and Design

In DPMLR, pipeline monitoring is the central base of the system with extensions provided for data services and ElasticSearch through Restful APIs. Pipeline monitor inspects the user pipelines and then collects the information and handles the data storage when it receives the logs. Then, PM evaluates the generated data and the processing units which gives a Boolean result to check the outcome from the pipeline. Figure 1 illustrates the architecture of the provenance system and the pipe-lining. User pipelines are organized in Pig Latin [6,9] and use the UDF (User Defined Function) provided by the provenance system. The pipeline refers to a set of steps of data processing which is an executable entity for each step that refers to both intermediate and final data. UDFs generate event logs to the pipeline monitors and then feed it to data dumps in the Data service. The developed system has following steps:

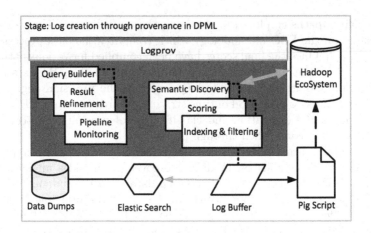

Fig. 1. Creating log semantics and data dumping procedure

1. Pipeline monitors (PM) collect the context information. Then, after each pipeline accomplishes its tasks the system inspects the user pipelines and then stores the data received from the logs.
2. PM assigns a unique indexing for these data instances which will be embedded into the logs.
3. PM evaluates both data and processing units on the involved paths by applying *Oracle*() function [6].
4. Data Service (DS) handles the storing process of the data into memory and keeps data repositories and mapping.
5. ElasticSearch could fetch the semantics from logs. Based on Pipeline Monitoring, logs and histories can be retrieved and queried by reviewing the pipeline specification through Restful APIs.
6. The trustworthiness score is computed, and then it updates the newly added logs by embedding the scores. Finally, it moves the logs to the ElasticSearch.
7. The Distributed Machine Learning is based on PySpark SQL queries which communicate with ES to generate specific portion of the datasets by semantics that keeps the record of the data logs.
8. PySpark Containers are modified on Parameters through workers and schedulers to increase the accuracy rate.

Whenever a request is generated to provide data again, DS queries the ElasticSearch for data context and then fetches the input data to repeat the processing. Figure 2 shows that after moving the logs to ES, the queries are collected by data dumps which send the data streams to StellarGraph. Spark Cluster handles the processing units which are required for running an ML model on the StellarGraph. We propose the capabilities of DPMLR by providing a framework for data streams to send to StellarGraph via Log Provenance and using the distributed computing environment to further process and train models on Spark Clusters.

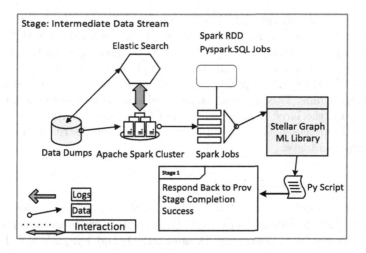

Fig. 2. Intermediate data stream and PySparkSQL procedural calls to ElasticSearch

3   Functionalities and Implementation

This section lies in the representation of detailed functionality and implementation of the provenance architecture and data pipelines. Furthermore, we present the interaction between distributed clusters and machine learning model. We modify different components such as PM, DS that are obtained from provenance [6,9,24] for distributed machine learning [25], parameter server models and container method [14,17].

3.1   Pipeline Inspection

Logs are passively monitored by PM through Pig runtime script which ensures that it is responding to the reports of logs and the data into PM. Pig UDFs are created to customize the user pipelines written in Pig Latin. Logs and intermediate data are generated and dumped by the UDFs, and then ES handles those logs. Finally, it processes the logs or data into data dumps which are used by the Spark RDD (Resilient Distributed Datasets) over the HDFS (Hadoop Distributed File System) through custom job handling task scripts.

3.2   Data Control

We apply ES-Hadoop [15] to collect data from the map-reduce steps over the HDFS since it's possible to refine provenance grain in DPMLR. Pig Scripts are used to dump and store intermediate data generated from data pipelines. We also predefine the format and the terminology for the sake of reversibility and extendibility.

Query. ElasticSearch supports ES-Hadoop [15] infrastructure which provides the interface for integrating our logs for semantic retrievals and SQL such as queries in PySpark Script through Restful APIs. These queries transform and load the data into data dumps and create data pipelines for models. We specified the log lines by the specific operations on data [6,9], and it is equivalent to graph traverse algorithms. This information retrieval process is used in the temporary pipe-lining for the large datasets since the PM becomes complex while the log buffer size is increased. To overcome this problem, we distribute data after a specific threshold level.

3.3 StellarGraph on PySpark

To train the models, we select the StellarGraph as a library framework. We embedded Spark containers to the StellarGraph which reads and generates data logs through Resilient Distributed Dataset (RDD) and PySpark SQL from the data dumps created by ES.

These PySpark SQL queries communicate with ES to generate specific portion that is read by semantics. This semantic keeps the record of the data logs and it makes the DPMLR efficiently and faster compared with its application comes to distributed machine learning.

If the node size is more than the threshold level, PySpark job is to directly load data logs directly into RDD which streams the files to the spark streaming. Consequently, in both intermediate or static ways. Figure 3 illustrates the processing mechanism on semantics over ES which receives queries back and forth from StellarGraph. However, in terms of graph processing, we adopted two mechanisms for the system to generate graphs. If the node size is more than 10K, StellarGraph shifts the graph processing on spark streams.

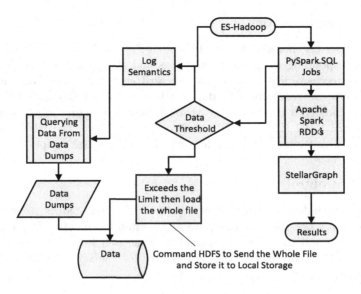

Fig. 3. Interaction of queries with semantics and StellarGraph

Schedulers. The scheduling system enables model-parallelism to control the model parameters which are updated by worker machines. It is performed by user-defined scheduling function *schedule*(), which outputs a set of parameters for each worker. The scheduler sends the identities of these parameters to workers via the scheduling control channel, while the actual parameter values are delivered through the parameter server system.

Several common patterns for schedule design are extremely important such as fixed-scheduling dispatches model parameters A in a predetermined order; static, round-robin schedules fit; the scheduling fixed model [25]. Dependency-aware scheduling allows re-ordering of variable/parameter updates to accelerate model-parallel ML algorithms.

Workers. StellarGraph on PySpark methods intentionally does not enforce a data abstraction. Hence, any data storage system could be used.

In Data-parallel stochastic algorithms [25], workers sample single data point at a time while in batch algorithms, worker could pass through all data points within one iteration.

Each worker node receives parameters data updated from *schedule*() and then runs parallel update functions on Data. The model states can be properly synchronized with the parameters during execution. If workers finish the scheduling, the scheduler may use the new model state to generate future scheduling decisions.

4 Experiments

In this section, we conduct a series of experiments on our clusters. Data filtering and analytics pipelines are to provide various fragments of provenance. We do not explore all the possible solutions in our provenance system, but we also conducted our experiments on a large dataset. This is a fair evaluation since the overhead problem is less visible to long data processing time.

4.1 Datasets

Our datasets are obtained from Yelp Data challenges 2016 originated from Kaggle [12] under the license agreement of Yelp. Our dataset has 2.7 million reviews and 649 K tips by 687 K users and 86 K businesses with 566 K business attributes e.g., hours, parking availability, ambiance. A social network of 687 K users for a total of 4.2M social edges with aggregated check-ins over time for each of the 86 K businesses. We only considered 687 K users and 86 K businesses.

4.2 Environment Setup

For experimental setup, we implemented provenance on Physical multi-nodes Hadoop clusters equipped with ES and Apache Pig. Apache Spark is also

deployed on the cluster since Spark can work on top of Yarn. PySpark and
GraphX libraries are also deployed to work on Spark. A summary of experiment
environment is listed in Table 1.

Table 1. Experimental environment

Instances	1 master and 2 Slaves
Operating system	Ubuntu 16.04 LTS
VCPUs	v2. each (can be 1 CPU)
Memory	8 GB each
Disk	915.83 GB each
Hadoop	2.7.2
Pig	0.16.0
ElasticSearch	5.5.1
Apache spark	2.4.0
PySpark	2.4.0

4.3   Methodology

We have conducted our experiments on recommendation systems for Yelp [19]
that are based on collaborative filtering algorithms on top of Spark layer to
provide distributed system utilization using StellarGraph. The methodology that
we adopted for our system is based on the [18] to filter out content and feed the
data on the intermediate data pipelines. StellarGraph fetches data streams on
the pipelines and then utilizes the streams on run-time providing the results on
each data query run by the user.

Data Filtering and Preprocessing. For this large dataset, we wrote a UDF
in the Provenance system that is going to create data dumps for distinct user_ids
and business_ids that share the same city, state, and country, and users who have
reviewed those businesses. PySpark.sql container job will deliberately fetch all
the data and store it temporarily and then distinct an ID that is associated with
a user and split the entire business data into smaller subsets into nine major
cities:

- USA→ Charlotte
- USA→ Las Vegas
- USA→ Phoenix
- USA→ Pittsburgh
- USA→ Urbana

- CA → Montreal
- USA→ Madison
- UK→ Edinburgh
- DE → Karlsruhe

Collaborative Filtering Based Recommendation Using Spark MLlib.
We implemented a collaborative filtering algorithm based on Low Rank Matrix
factorization, which is widely used for recommendation systems as Collaborative
filtering based algorithm has low-rank factorization for fast results and proto-
type. We use SparkMLib for ALS-based collaborative model and tune the best
rank and filter user inputs keywords to prune user preferences.

By factorization, we extract useful information and do the assessment for
finding the missing nodes or values and perform a cross-validation check to take
the best rank that leads to a minimal Residual Mean Squared Error (RMSE).
We assume that user ratings are the results of only a few factors related to the
business. The entries in the matrix are populated by explicit and implicit user
evaluations of the items.

To visualize clearly, we adopted two simple strategies: out of all the edges
in a city, we either randomly selected 1% to 2% of all the edges, or sequentially
selected the first (1% to 2%) of all edges. Even if we randomly select only 2%
of the entire edges, the generated networks still have the power to reveal many
insights about a city, if we dig deeper. We briefly go over three cities: Charlotte
(US), Edinburgh (UK), and Montreal(Canada) and collected few samples as
shown in Figs. 4, 5 and 6.

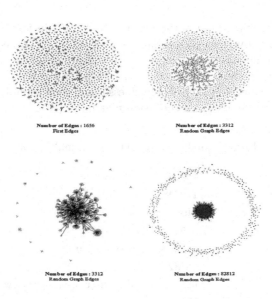

Fig. 4. Randomly selected edges on US: Charlotte, 1% to 2% of the total edges

We focus mainly on the explicit ratings since implicit evaluations correspond
to information gathered through user actions, whereas explicit evaluations correspond to feedback from the users.

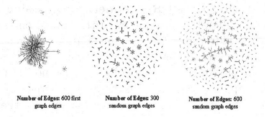

Fig. 5. Randomly selected edges on UK: Edinburgh , 1% to 2% of the total edges

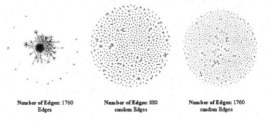

Fig. 6. Randomly selected edges on Canada: Montreal , 1% to 2% of the total edges

Binary Classification. Using the features described in the previous section, we used an extended version Graph-Sage Algorithm [21,22] called Hinsage Algorithm. For recommendation system, we predict the best business options for the users based on the reviews generated by the *'elite'* status holding users. Table 2 specifies the nodes and edges types of businesses and corresponding users. Table 3 shows the number of nodes in a confusion matrix.

Table 2. StellarGraph: undirected multigraph

Nodes	43936
Edges	174248
	Node types
Business	5154
Edge types	business → review → user
User	38782
Edge types	user → friend → user, user → review → business
	Edge types
business → review→user	129631
user → friend → user	44617

Table 3. Test set metrics (confusion matrix)

Metrics	Values
Number of nodes	29087
Confusion matrix	29087
Binary prediction	[[True]...]]
Weighting loss	[0.01, 1.0]

Prediction is based on the binary classification, as after classifying nodes, it is easy to generate such results. Pipeline sends responses back to the spark job, which triggers the UDF to respond to provide such data stream so that intermediate data can reload and log into the pipeline. The data processing is much faster to streamline the analysis phase compared to the legacy methods [23], and it seemed more efficient and accurate. Table 4 shows the binary accuracy; Table 5 shows the average score recorded on precision, recall, and F1 score.

Table 4. Timespan estimation approaches of binary accuracy

Epoch	Time(s)	Loss	Binary accuracy
1/10	174	0.0212	0.8937
2/10	17	0.0220	0.9104
3/10	12	0.0152	0.9111
4/10	12	0.0126	0.9135
5/10	12	0.0120	0.9152
6/10	12	0.0117	0.9167
7/10	12	0.0113	0.9174
8/10	12	0.0111	0.9179
9/10	12	0.0109	0.9182
10/10	12	0.0107	0.9183

Table 5. Average score recorded on the model precision, accuracy and recall

Accuracy	Precision	Recall	F1 Score
0.9132	0.915	0.918	0.916

5   Evaluation

To evaluate the results through a baseline method to compare the performance of data provenance on a recommendation system, we query several outcomes based on different cities. Complex queries often require a lot of preprocessing steps for baseline, especially for large datasets. As in any provenance system, delays may happen when dealing with large amount of data. To evaluate provenance, we check the logging performance of the system.

Table 6. Timespan estimation on multiple levels

Component	A	B	C	D	E
Time (ms)	1870	1840	2034	1811	1790

To test the spanning time, the logs are processed in ElasticSearch and fetched to the model trainer from the start of the log generation till its end. As in [6,9], in our system it also turns out to have constant value where the approximation was near to 1.8 min for collecting data dumps on different levels, shown in Table 6.

The results of the overhead are near to constant and cannot be impacted by the number of slave machines if to take data provenance into account. However, speaking of fast processing of Spark jobs and graph processing, the number of slaves does increase the performance. Since more data requires more time for storing and transferring, it is not difficult to find the overhead, which is mainly caused by non-blocking [6]. It is still not more than 10% to 20%. However, increasing more physical memory, adding more HDFS I/O speed and more power to machines can generally be used to reduce the overall overhead.

Table 7. Overhead with different size of datasets

Data Size	264.12	483.48	931.70	1022.48	1426.0
Without LPV(s)	196	197	205	216	217
With LPV(s)	202	210	231	239	246
Intermediate data (MB)	224.70	394.13	797.47	847.63	1185.03
Writing to HDFS (ms)	28	53	67	95	142
Overhead blocking (%)	12.22	40	58.07	83.42	85.06
Overhead non-blocking	1.88	5.93	17.63	18.75	4.08

The overhead value changes as well as the size of data that is read from the datasets does. The more precise and selective the query is in Pig Script, the less the data size. As shown in the Table 7. We also list some query examples in Table 7 to check the response time of simple queries, whether it is shorter as compared to the complex queries. In ES [15], the response time can be clashed by what we queried and the number of logs and memory size that are available. It's response time is directly proportional to the size of the logs that can fit into the memory [20].

Table 8. Querying the intermediate data and the time duration

Query string	Time duration (ms)
(empty)	2
sourceVar==raw	30
destvar== filtered	250
sourceVar==splitcity & & destvar=distcity	380
sourceVar==users & & destvar==distcity	434
userID==buzID & & destvar==userCity	391
sourceVar==splitcity & & (userID == reviewUserID || operator == Combining)	247

In Table 8, we show a sample of intermediate data of how after each operation the data is stored. If the reading size is small, the actual amount of data should be stored from the start to end. However, in case of broad data, we filtered out some general information from the number of K lines that we proposed that may vary to the size of the actual size of the data. We examined provenance up to some certain level of possibilities and use cases and tried to show the promising applications of it in the data provenance and machine learning systems.

5.1 Performance and Speed

DPMLR system design supports a variety of ML programs and improves the performance by faster convergence rate than single-machine baselines. In system design, we exploited model dependencies and error tolerance to make it run faster and reach larger model sizes than other programmable platforms because it stores ML Program variables in an optimized and distributed level (on the parameters and scheduler). It uses the model techniques from Spark, adopts them into StellarGraph and performs twice fast than Graph-Lab. It operates only one worker on each city node adjacent to the business.

5.2 Model Size

DPMLR is faster and supports much larger models than baseline. It constructs a 'lineage graph' to preserve its full strict fault recovery. Fault recovery can be performed with lower overhead through periodic checkpoints. For scalability, it divides the model across the clusters and sets the parameters in minimal storage overhead. We show that DPMLR can support larger models on the same cluster specifications. Figure 7 shows the running time on a fixed number of machines and compares it with model size. DPMLR converges faster than the generic Spark framework and GraphLab. DPMLR flexibility is the result of the factors it derived from PETUUM lightweight parameters server with minimal storage overhead and the model parallelism model which divides model across machines for model scalability. Compared to generic Spark RDD, DPMLR consumed less memory to store model variables.

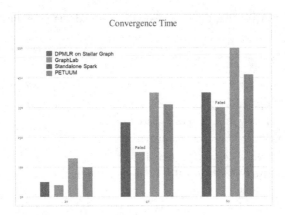

Fig. 7. Matrix factorization: convergence time: DPMLR On StellarGraph vs GraphLab vs standalone spark vs PETUUM

6   Related Work

Provenance has been followed by many production systems. Provenance for big data can be challenging, and its provenance graph can be quite complex. Taverna is a domain-independent workflow management system that provides features for data provenance and creates graphs of provenance from the data cycle [26]. Same Provenance model is also provided in OPM [24] (Open provenance model) which emphasis is on improved intractability. This model is represented by directed graph abstract mainly on graph datasets.

Another common platform is Dremio [27], which is a Data-as-a-Service platform that utilizes data lineage using raw, aggregation, and data reflections, it maintains a dependency graph (DAG) that defines the order of data reflections. It makes use of multiple compression options for storing Data reflections, including dictionary, run-length, and delta encoding. Dremio provides SQL functions for managing Data reflections. Manta [28] is an interactive tool for data lineage that maps the entire data and provides end-to-end lineage which can be used to generate provenance by methods that automatically report the differences between current and previous revisions. There has been a discussion that data lineage can derive data origins and where it moves over time as it records the data life cycle in ETL (Extract Transform Load) systems. It can describe the data transformation as it goes through diverse processes and can provide analytics pipelines and error tracking.

Big data creates many challenges for machine learning algorithms; the distributed machine learning algorithms provide an advance approach for massive data scale and large model size. The data parallelism and model parallelism approaches have been discussed various times, and many solutions have been proposed. One of them is Parallel ML System (PETUUM) [25] which is based on two main mechanisms; (1) the Parameter Server, (2) Scheduler. The key-value parameter server is a distributed shared memory system that allows the model parameters to be shared between workers globally. The schedulers are responsible for analyzing the ML model structure for optimized execution order and provide supports for parallel model ML-algorithms.

GraphLab [29] also provides distributed computing environment for graph-based models. It supports asynchronous execution and ensures the program can run in parallel for large and power-law graphs through edge-cutting partitioning. For Graph Correctness, it specifies more fine-grained constraints for ML algorithms. Tensorflow Fold [30] and MXNet [31] provide support for dynamic task graphs; they utilize both GPU and CPU efficiently but have limited support to modify the DAG during execution when it comes to task progress and fault tolerance.

Frameworks for concurrent distributed systems are Orleans [32] and Akka [33], but they provide less support for data recovery and are pruned to fault tolerance. Compared to our system, they provide at-most-once semantics while DPMLR provides fault tolerance and semantics; the performance of our applications does not affect as clearly seen in the experiments.

7   Conclusion and Future Work

This paper discusses the importance of data provenance for machine learning problems. We explored a few possibilities of data provenance in machine learning that can extract and analyze the data pipelines and test the trustworthiness of the pipelines before sending the data streams for model testing and classification. It aims to provide a precise system to solve collective ML-based problems through provenance.

We only explore a few possibilities to test the functionality of our current domain and improved the provenance system to provide substantial data provenance. The accomplishments that we achieve on provenance level is the constant performance overhead under 20%; as this extensive system flows back and forth from pipelines to Spark streams, we consider this overhead to be reasonable and acceptable. We noticed the overhead tends to be larger from an average threshold level on complex queries.

The future work is to propose a better solution to optimize performance overhead and keeping the overhead to a minimum, provide asynchronous executions for graphs based models, and specify fined-grained constraints.

Acknowledgement. This work is supported by Shanghai Pujiang Program with No. 19pj1433100 and the Key R&D Project of Zhejiang Province with No. 2017C02036.

References

1. Big data to turn 'mega' as capacity will hot 44 zettabytes by 2020, DataIQ News, Oct. 2014. https://tinyurl.com/bigdata-hit-44-zettabytes-2020
2. Apache hadoop. https://hadoop.apache.org/
3. Elo, A.: The rating of chessplayers past and present. Arco Pub (1978). https://books.google.com.au/books?id=8pMnAQAAMAAJ

4. L'Heureux, A., Grolinger, K., Elyamany, H.: Machine learning with big data: challenges and approaches. IEEE Access **5**, 7776–7797 (2017). https://doi.org/10.1109/ACCESS.2017.2696365

5. Wang, X., Zeng, K., Govindan, K., Mohapatra, P.: Chaining for securing data provenance in distributed information networks. In: MILCOM 2012 - 2012 IEEE Military Communications Conference, Orlando, FL, pp. 1–6 (2012)

6. Wang, R., Sun, D., Li, G., Atif, M., Nepal, S.: LogProv: logging events as provenance of big data analytics pipelines with trustworthiness. In: 2016 IEEE International Conference on Big Data (Big Data), Washington, DC, pp. 1402–1411 (2016)

7. Bechhofer, S., Goble, C., Buchan, I.: Research objects: towards exchange and reuse of digital knowledge (2010).(August 2017)

8. Xu, S., Rogers, T., Fairweather, E., Glenn, A., Curran, J., Curcin, V.: Application of data provenance in healthcare analytics software: information visualisation of user activities. AMIA Joint Summits Transl. Sci. Proc. **2017**, 263–272 (2018)

9. Wang, R., Sun, D., Li, G., Wong, R., Chen, S.: Pipeline provenance for cloud-based big data analytics. Softw. Pract. Exper.,1–17 (2019). https://doi.org/10.1002/spe.2744

10. ElasticSearch. https://www.elastic.co

11. Apache Pig. https://pig.apache.org

12. Kaggle Yelp Dataset. https://www.kaggle.com/yelp-dataset/yelp-dataset/version/9

13. StellarGraph. https://www.stellargraph.io/

14. PySpark API. https://spark.apache.org/docs/2.2.1/api/python/pyspark.html

15. ES-Hadoop. https://www.elastic.co/guide/en/elasticsearch/hadoop/current/index.html

16. Bertino, E., Lim, H.-S.: Assuring data trustworthiness: concepts and research challenges. In: Proceedings of the 7th VLDB Conference on Secure Data Management service, SDM 2010, pp. 1–12 (2010)

17. Schelter, S., Boese, J.H., Kirschnick, J., Klein, T., Seufert, S.: Automatically tracking metadata and provenance of machine learning experiments. In: Machine Learning Systems workshop at NIPS (2017)

18. Yelper Recommendation System. http://tinyurl.com/yxff5f4r

19. Yelp Site. https://www.yelp.com/

20. Log Search. http://www.logsearch.io/blog/2015/05/performance-testing-elasticsearch.html

21. GraphSAGE: Inductive Representation. http://snap.stanford.edu/graphsage/

22. Hamilton, W.L., Ying, R., Leskovec, J.: Inductive representation learning on large graphs. arXiv:1706.02216 [cs.SI] (2017)

23. Recommender System for Yelp Dataset - Northeastern University. www.ccs.neu.edu/home/clara/resources/depaoliskaluza_CS6220.pdf

24. http://openprovenance.org/

25. Xing, E.P., et al.: Petuum: a new platform for distributed machine learning on big data. In: Proceedings of the 21th ACM SIGKDD International Conference on Knowledge Discovery and Data Mining (KDD 2015), pp. 1335–1344. ACM, New York (2015). https://doi.org/10.1145/2783258.2783323

26. https://taverna.incubator.apache.org/

27. Dremio. https://www.dremio.com

28. https://getmanta.com/

29. graphLab. https://turi.com/

30. Tensorflow Fold. https://github.com/tensorflow/fold

31. MxNet. https://mxnet.apache.org/
32. Bykov, S., Geller, A., Kliot, G., Larus, J.R., Pandya, R., Andthelin, J.: Orleans: cloud computing for everyone. In: Proceedings of the 2nd ACM Symposium on Cloud Computing, p. 16. ACM (2011)
33. Akka. https://akka.io/

Software Analysis and Testing

Metamorphic Testing in Fault Localization of Model Transformations

Keke Du, Mingyue Jiang$^{(\boxtimes)}$, Zuohua Ding, Hongyun Huang, and Ting Shu

School of Information Science, Zhejiang Sci-Tech University, Hangzhou 310018, China
{mjiang,shuting}@zstu.edu.cn, zouhuading@hotmail.com

Abstract. Model transformations are cornerstone elements of Model Driven Engineering (MDE), and their quality directly affects the successful application of MDE in practice. However, due to the characteristics of model transformation programs, the debugging of model transformations faces the oracle problem. In this paper, we propose an approach of debugging model transformations by using the technique of metamorphic testing (MT). Our approach leverages MT to alleviate the oracle problem, and integrates MT with spectrum-based fault localization technique to locating faulty rules of model transformations. We conduct experiments to evaluate our approach by using open-source model transformation programs, and compare the effectiveness of our approach with that of a fault localization technique using constraint-based oracles. Both of the experimental analysis and the comparison study show that our approach is of promising effectiveness, suggesting that MT can be a good support for debugging model transformations.

Keywords: Model transformation · Metamorphic testing · Fault localization

1 Introduction

Model transformations play a key role in Model Driven Engineering (MDE) [16]. They support the manipulation and transformation of models, and are the cornerstones of building software systems in MDE. Because of this, the quality of the resulting system is highly related with the quality of model transformations. Therefore, effective debugging techniques for model transformations is critical to the successful application of MDE in practice.

A model transformation is a program implemented by some model transformation languages (such as ATL, QTV, etc.). Generally, it takes a *source model* as input, and produces a *target model* as output after processing the source

This work was supported in part by the National Natural Science Foundation of China (NSFC) under grant numbers 61210004, 61170015, 61802349 and Zhejiang Provincial Natural Science Foundation of China under Grant numbers LY17F020033, LY20F020021 and by the Fundamental Research Funds of Zhejiang Sci-Tech University under Grant numbers 17032184-Y, 2019Q041, 2019Q039.

© Springer Nature Switzerland AG 2020
H. Miao et al. (Eds.): SOFL+MSVL 2019 Workshop, LNCS 12028, pp. 299–314, 2020.
https://doi.org/10.1007/978-3-030-41418-4_20

model using some transformation rules. Models handled by model transformations can be very complex, and the size of models and model transformations may be varying. Due to this, the testing and debugging of model transformations face several challenges. Among them, one common challenge refers to the difficulty of checking the correctness of the output model produced by model transformations, which is known as the *oracle problem* [5].

In order to test or debug model transformations, different categories of strategies have been proposed to alleviate the oracle problem, such as the use of a reference transformation, the use of a reverse transformation, the use of an expected output model, and the use of constraint-based oracles [2]. Among these strategies, the constraint-based oracle is most commonly adopted [5,6,19]. This category of strategies always checks the target model produced by a model transformation against some constraints, including the pre-conditions that should be satisfied by the source models, the post-conditions on the target model, the invariants between source and target models. Constraints are specified by different languages (for example, OCL, ECL). Although the constraint-based oracle is helpful for checking the correctness of model transformations, its effectiveness is still restricted by its scope and the expressive capability of the language used to specify the constraint [2].

This paper proposes to apply the technique of *metamorphic testing* (MT) to alleviate the oracle problem of debugging model transformations. MT is a technique that has been successfully applied to alleviate the oracle problem in various application domains [7,8,22]. Our previous work has applied MT to test model transformation programs, and also demonstrated that MT can both alleviate the oracle problem and achieve satisfactory testing effectiveness [12]. In this paper, we go one step forward to investigate MT-based debugging method for model transformation programs. We first integrate MT with the spectrum-based fault localization technique to locating faulty rules of model transformation programs. Then, we conduct a series of experiments to demonstrate the overall fault localization effectiveness of our approach. Furthermore, we conduct comparison analysis by investigating the effectiveness of our approach with that of another novel fault localization method using a different oracle mechanism. Our experimental results show that our approach is effective for locating faulty rules of model transformations, and the comparison analysis further reveals that our approach outperforms the method under comparison for the subject programs studied.

The rest of this paper is organized as follows. Section 2 gives a brief introduction to basics of our approach. Section 3 presents the details of our approach. Section 4 describes the experimental design and presents our experimental analysis results. Section 5 summarizes related work, and Sect. 6 concludes the paper.

2   Background

This section presents some basics to understand our approach. We first introduce some concepts of model transformations, followed by an explanation of how

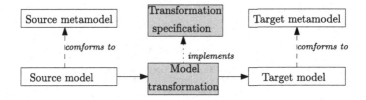

Fig. 1. The paradigm of model transformation

to test model transformations by MT. Then, we explain the basic rationale of spectrum-based fault localization.

2.1 Model Transformation

Model transformations are core elements of MDE, which automatically transform models into other models [16]. Figure 1 shows the paradigm of a typical model transformation. Basically, a model transformation is a program that takes a *source model* as input and produces a *target model* as output. Source and target models conform to *source metamodel* and *target metamodel*, respectively. That is, the source (target) metamodel specifies the structure and constraints for a series of source (target) models, and as a result, each source (target) model is an instance of the source (target) metamodel. For the sake of simplicity, in this paper, we use SM and TM to represent the source and target models, respectively. To convert SMs into TMs, the transformation specification, which consists of descriptions defining correspondences between source and target metamodels, will be identified and then be implemented by model transformations. Model transformations are programs written in model transformation languages. Up to now, there are various model transformation languages, such as ATL, QVT, JTL, etc.

This paper focuses on ATL model transformations, because ATL is one of the most popular model transformation languages used in both industry and academia. An ATL transformation is composed of a series of *rules*, each of which specifies the way of converting some elements of the SM to some elements of the TM. Figure 2 shows an example ATL transformation, that is, the *Class2Relational* transformation [1]. There are two rules: *Class2Table* and *DataType2Type*, where the former one will convert a *class* of a SM into a *Table* of a TM, and the latter one specifies the way of transforming a *DataType* into a *Type* of a TM.

2.2 Testing Model Transformations with Metamorphic Testing

The correctness of model transformations is critical to the quality of the software system developed in a model-driven way. However, due to the nature of model

```
19  rule Class2Table {
20      from
21          c : Class!Class
22      to
23          out : Relational!Table (
24              name <- c.name,
25              col <- Sequence {key}->union
26              (c.attr->select(e | not e.multiValued)),
27              key <- Set {key}
28          ),
29          key : Relational!Column (
30              name <- 'objectId',
31              type <- thisModule.objectIdType
32          )
33  }
34  rule DataType2Type {
35      from
36          dt : Class!DataType
37      to
38          out : Relational!Type (
39              name <- dt.name
40          )
41  }
```

Fig. 2. Excerpt of the *Class2Relational* ATL transformation.

transformations, the testing of model transformations faces the oracle problem, which is one of the main challenges to model transformation based applications [5].

MT [7,8] is a methodology that has successfully alleviated the oracle problem in various application domains. MT makes use of properties encoding the intended program's functionality, which are specified via relations among inputs and outputs of multiple executions of the program. Such relations are known as *metamorphic relations* (MRs). The key difference between MT and the traditional testing methods is that instead of checking the correctness of individual outputs, MT checks the relations among inputs and outputs of multiple executions against MRs. In this way, MT can be applied regardless of the existence of oracles.

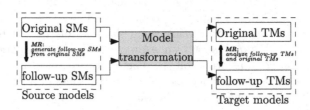

Fig. 3. Testing model transformation by metamorphic testing.

MT has been applied to test model transformation programs and reported with promising effectiveness [10,12,19]. The general procedure of applying MT to model transformations is shown in Fig. 3. Given some original SMs (these original SMs can be obtained by applying some existing strategies of generating

SMs for model transformations) and an MR, MT constructs their corresponding follow-up SMs according to the MR. In this context, a SM and its relevant TM associated with an MR is called a *metamorphic test group* (MTG). By executing SMs of an MTG on the model transformation program, their TMs can be collected. After that, relations among SMs and TMs of an MTG are checked against the relevant MR: the MTG is said to be non-violating if the MR is satisfied and is said to be violating otherwise. A violating MTG suggests that the model transformation under test is faulty. When using MT to test model transformations, several TMGs will be used and the model transformation is regarded to be faulty if there is at least one violating MTG.

The key step of applying MT to model transformations is the identification of MRs. To identify MRs for model transformations, we can refer to the model transformation specification, and MR identification methods used for conventional software programs can also be adopted. As an example for illustration, consider the *Class2Relational* transformation as shown in Fig. 2. One possible MR for this program can be: *The follow-up SM is constructed by adding one DataType into the original SM, then the total number of Types in the follow-up TM should be greater than the total number of Types in the original TM.*

Currently, more progresses have been made to support the application of MT to model transformations. For example, He et al. [10] apply MT to test bidirectional model transformations; Troya et al. [19] propose an automatic way of generating MRs for model transformations.

2.3   Spectrum-Based Fault Localisation

Spectrum-based fault localization (SBFL) [3] is a popular technique used for locating faults in software programs. Basically, SBFL makes use of two types of information, namely, program spectrums and test results, to predict the statements' likelihood of being faulty. A program spectrum records runtime information of the program during test. There are various types of program spectrums, one commonly used category of which is the code coverage information related to individual test cases.

For a program having m statements and tested by n test cases ($m \geq 1, n \geq 1$), the coverage information used by SBFL can be represented by a coverage matrix and an error vector, which are displayed in Table 1. In Table 1, cells with light gray color constitute the coverage matrix, where a cell with value 1 means that the statement of the row is executed by the test case of the column, and a cell with 0 means that the statement of the row is not executed by the test case of the column. Cells with dark gray color of the table constitute the error vector, with P and F representing the results of passing and failing, respectively.

Based on the coverage matrix, a large number of risk evaluation formulas [21] can be applied to calculate the suspiciousness scores, which indicates the probability of being faulty, for each statement. A larger suspiciousness score suggests a higher probability of being faulty. Given a statement s, we use n_{ep} and n_{ef} to represent the number of passing and failing test cases that execute s, and use n_{np} and n_{nf} to represent the number of passing and failing test cases

Table 1. The coverage matrix and error vector used by SBFL.

Statements	t_1	t_2	...	t_n
s_1	1	0	...	1
s_2	0	1	...	0
.		.		
.			.	
.			.	
s_m	0	1	...	1
TR	P	F	...	P

that do not execute s, and use n_p and n_f to denote the total number of passing and failing test cases. As an example for illustration, consider the risk evaluation formula Ochiai [13]. To calculate the suspiciousness score of statement s, namely, R_s, the expression of Ochiai is $R(s) = \frac{n_{ef}}{\sqrt{(n_f) \times (n_{ef}+n_{ep})}}$. Note that the values of n_{ef} (n_{nf}), n_{ep} (n_{np}), and n_f (n_p) can all be collected by analyzing the coverage matrix and error vector together.

SBFL is widely applied because it is easy to be understood and conducted. However, it should be noted that SBFL requires the information from testing, including both the coverage information and the test result of individual test cases. That is, SBFL needs the support of oracle mechanisms.

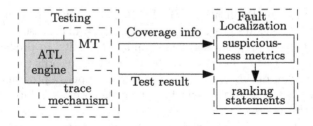

Fig. 4. Implementation of SBFL-MT.

3   Integration of MT and SBFL for Locating Faulty Rules of Model Transformations

In this section, we present our approach for locating faulty rules of model transformations. The framework of our method is depicted in Fig. 4. Our main idea is to integrate MT with SBFL such that faulty rules of model transformations can be effectively identified without the need for an oracle. Xie et al. [22] has designed the way of integrating MT with SBFL for locating faults of conventional software programs. In this study, we follow main principles proposed in [22], and adapt them to model transformation programs. In order to support SBFL, MT is applied to test model transformations, and then the execution information and test results are properly collected to construct the coverage matrix and the error vector. The general idea of integrating MT and SBFL to model transformations is summarized as below.

- *The set of rules covered by the execution of an MTG is collected.* When using MT, the basic test unit is an MTG. Therefore, the coverage information is also collected for each MTG: the set of rules covered by an MTG is the union of the sets of rules covered by executing each of its SMs.
- *The test result associated with an MTG is reported as either violating or non-violating.* As demonstrated in Sect. 2.2, a violating MTG indicates the detection of faulty rules, while a non-violating MTG fails to detect any faulty rules.

Table 2. The coverage matrix and error vector used to locating faulty rules of model transformations.

Transformation Rules	mtg_1	mtg_2	...	mtg_n
r_1	1	0	...	1
r_2	0	1	...	0
.		.		
.		.		
.		.		
r_m	0	1	...	1
TR	N	V	...	N

Given a model transformation program M_p that contains a set of rules $\{r_1, r_2, ..., r_m\}$ $(m \geq 1)$, we first must identify MRs based on the transformation specification, and also construct original SMs by following the source metamodel. Let $MR = \{mr_1, mr_2, ..., mr_x\}$ $(x \geq 1)$ be the set of MRs identified for M_p, and $OSM = \{osm_1, osm_2, ..., osm_y\}$ $(y \geq 1)$ be the set of original SMs constructed. Then, the follow-up SM fsm_j^i can be generated from osm_j by applying mr_i $(0 \leq i \leq x, 0 \leq j \leq y)$, with osm_j and fsm_j^i constituting an MTG of mr_i. By using all MRs and original SMs, a series of MTGs, $MTG = \{mtg_1, mtg_2, ..., mtg_n\}$, will be constructed. The test result of each MTG can be collected by conducing MT, and the rules covered by each model transformation execution can be collected and analyzed by using the trace mechanism of ATL [19]. As a result, a coverage matrix and an error vector for locating faulty rules of model transformations can be obtained, as shown in Table 2.

Table 3. Subject programs information.

Transformation name	#Rules	#MRs	#Mutants
Class2Relational [1]	6	6	15
PetriNet2PNML [19]	4	5	14
Families2PersonsExtended [19]	10	7	14
UML2ER [18]	8	7	18

In Table 2, the coverage matrix is highlighted with light gray color, where 1 (0) indicates the rule of the row is (not) executed by the MTG of the column, and the error vector is highlighted with dark gray color, with V and N representing the test results of violating and non-violating, respectively. Based on the information, different risk evaluation formulas can be further applied to calculate the suspiciousness scores for individual rules, and finally the ranked list of suspicious transformation rules can be constructed.

4   Empirical Evaluation

In order to evaluate our approach, we conducted a series of experiments. In this section, we first introduce our experimental setup, and then analyze experimental results to demonstrate the effectiveness of our approach.

4.1   Experimental Setup

Research Questions. In order to investigate the effectiveness of our approach, we consider the following two Research Questions (RQs):

RQ1: *How effective is our approach for locating faulty rules of model transformations?* When applying our approach, it is MRs that are used to check relations among input and outputs of multiple executions, in order to report the test results.

Since MRs are of weaker capabilities than oracles in terms of specifying the intended functionalities of the program, it is necessary to investigate the overall fault localization effectiveness of our approach.

RQ2: *How does our approach perform in comparison with an approach using SBFL but applying a different oracle mechanism?* Since our approach integrates MT and SBFL, we compare it with a notable fault localization technique proposed for model transformations [18], which also incorporates SBFL but uses constraint-based oracles.

Subject Programs, MRs and Original Source Models. In the empirical evaluation, we use four model transformation programs. For each subject

Table 4. MRs for PetriNet2PNML.

Category	MRs	Example
Addition	MR2, MR3	MR2:Construct SM_2 by adding a *transition* to SM_1, then TM_2.num(*pnml:transition*)= TM_1.num(*pnml:transition*)+1
Modification	MR1, MR4,MR5	MR1:Construct SM_2 by changing the *location* of first *place* of SM_1 to be '11:22-33:44', then TM_2.*pnml:Place.location*=11:22-33:44

Table 5. Risk evaluation formulas under investigation.

Name	Formula expression
Ochiai	$\dfrac{n_{ef}}{\sqrt{(n_f)\times(n_{ef}+n_{ep})}}$
Kulczynski2	$\frac{1}{2}\times\left(\dfrac{n_{ef}}{n_{ef}+n_{nf}}+\dfrac{n_{ef}}{n_{ef}+n_{ep}}\right)$
Mountford	$\dfrac{n_{ef}}{0.5\times((n_{ef}\times n_{ep})+(n_{ef}\times n_{nf}))+(n_{ep}\times n_{nf})}$
Zoltar	$\dfrac{n_{ef}}{n_{ef}+n_{nf}+n_{ep}+\frac{10000\times n_{nf}\times n_{ep}}{n_{ef}}}$
Tarantula	$\dfrac{\frac{N_{ef}}{N_f}}{\frac{N_{ef}}{N_f}+\frac{N_{es}}{N_s}}$
Klosgen	$\sqrt{\dfrac{n_{ef}}{n_f+n_s}}\max\left(\dfrac{n_{ef}}{n_{ef}+n_{es}}-\dfrac{n_f}{n_f+n_s},\dfrac{n_{ef}}{n_f}-\dfrac{n_e}{n_f+n_s}\right)$

program, we identify some MRs for it, and these MRs are further used for locating faulty rules of its mutants.

Mutants of subject programs are constructed by applying mutation operators proposed by [17]. Table 3 shows the detailed information related to each subject program, including the number of transformation rules, the number of MRs identified, and the number of mutants constructed.

When identifying MRs for model transformations, we can generally consider three categories of operations on the SMs: addition, modification and deletion [19]. For our subject programs, we utilize the former two categories of MRs. As an example for illustration, we present MRs used for PetriNet2PNML in Table 4.

To prepare original source models, we implement a random source model generator for each subject program. The random source model generator uses a random heuristics to construct elements of the source model by referring to the source metamodel. In our experiments, we randomly generate 100 source models for each subject program. Therefore, if a subject program has n MRs, $100\times n$ MTGs will be constructed and used for fault localization.

Measurement. In this study, we apply six risk evaluation formulas to calculate the suspiciousness scores. The former four formulas come from Troya et al. [18]

which are shown to be of better performance than the other formulas in locating faulty rules for model transformations. We have also used another two risk evaluation formulas, Klosgen and Tarantula, because the Klosgen outperforms other formulas for single-bug programs [15]. The information of these formulas is shown in Table 5.

In order to evaluate the fault localization effectiveness, we adopt the EXAM score, which is a measurement used by several fault localization studies [18,22]. In our study, a EXAM score represents the percentage of rules that needs to be examined until the first faulty rule is found. Obviously, a lower EXAM score value indicates that the faulty rule is closer to the front of the ranked list, thus suggesting a better fault localization effectiveness. In a ranked rule list, two or more different rules may have the same ranking index (that is, their suspiciousness values are equal). Therefore, when the faulty rule has the same ranking index with other rules, we consider three different cases: (1) In the best case (BC), the faulty rule is regarded as the first one to be examined; (2) In the worst case (WC), the faulty rule is regarded as the last one to be examined; and (3) In the average case (AC), the faulty rule will be assigned an average index position among all of these equal-index rules.

4.2   Experimental Analysis

In this section, we present our experimental results to answer our research questions. For each mutant of our subject program, we apply MT to test it such that the corresponding coverage matrix and error vector can be constructed. Next, the formulas presented in Table 5 are used to calculate suspiciousness scores for individual rules, based on which the ranked list can be constructed. At last, we calculate the EXAM score for each mutant based on its ranked list.

RQ1: We use the line diagram to present the distribution of EXAM scores of individual subject programs, which is shown in Fig. 5. Each sub-graph collects the result from all mutants of the relevant subject program in one of the three cases (namely, BC, AC, and WC), and summarizes the result in terms of different risk evaluation formulas. In a sub-graph, the horizontal axis represents the EXAM score, and the vertical axis denotes the cumulative percentage of mutants whose EXAM scores are less than or equal to the corresponding EXAM score. It is obvious that the faster a line reaches 100%, the higher effectiveness our approach has.

As can be observed from Fig. 5, these four formulas, Ochiai, Kulczynski2, Mountford and Zoltar, also perform better than the others. From the statistical data of the four formulas, we can see that the overall fault localization effectiveness of our approach is good: the faulty rules of about 50% mutants can be found by inspecting less than 30% rules of the ranked list. Specifically, in the BC, about 90% mutants' faulty rules can be identified by inspecting about 50% rules of the ranked list; in the AC, about 70% mutants' faulty rules can be identified by inspecting about 40% rules of the ranked list; and in the WC,

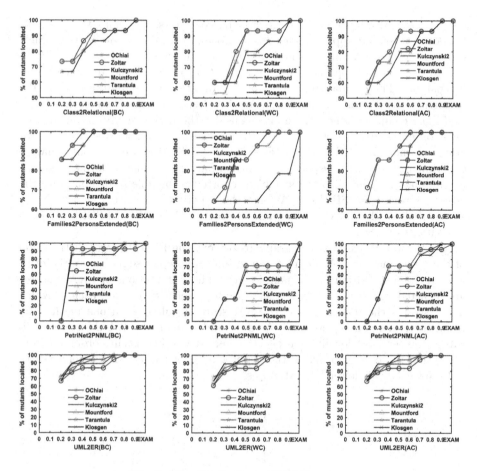

Fig. 5. The distribution of EXAM scores.

more than 70% mutants' faulty rules can be identified by inspecting about 50% rules of the ranked list. It is obvious that although the overall performance of Tarantula and Klosgen are not as good as the performance of the above four, more than 80% mutants' faulty rules can be found by inspecting about 40% rules of the ranked list in the BC. We can further find that the effectiveness varies for different subject programs, and our approach performs best for program *Families2PersonsExtended*, while performs worst for program *PetriNet2PNML*. Moreover, although the fault localization effectiveness is different when different risk evaluation formulas are used, we can find from Fig. 5 that these differences are very slight.

RQ2: In order to answer **RQ2**, we compare the fault localization effectiveness of our approach with that of one novel fault localization technique proposed for model transformations. The technique to be compared is proposed in [18], which also applies SBFL but uses the constraint-based oracles. Therefore, the main difference between our approach and this approach lies in the use of different oracle mechanisms. For the sake of simplicity, in the following analysis, we use SBFL-MT to refer to our approach and use SBFL-CS to refer to the approach under comparison. The comparison study applies statistical techniques to analyze the difference between the fault localization effectiveness of these two methods.

In the comparison study, we only consider the best case (BC), and merely focus on one subject program, *UML2ER*, because the other three subject programs are not included in the dataset of SBFL-CS. Moreover, we only analyze experimental data with respect to the former four risk evaluation formulas shown in Table 5, which are also the formulas reported to be able to demonstrate the best performance of SBFL-CS. We get the experimental data (that is, EXAM scores of all single-faulty-rule mutants of program *UML2ER*) of SBFL-CS from the dataset of [18].

Firstly, we utilize box-plot graph to present the EXAM scores distribution of these two methods. A box-plot can graphically depict some key statistics as well as the distribution of the sample data. The distributions of EXAM scores are depicted in Fig. 6. In Fig. 6, a sub-graph presents two boxes, each of which demonstrates the distribution of EXAM scores resulted from one method by using the corresponding formula. As a reminder, a smaller EXAM scores indicates a better fault localization effectiveness. It can be visually observed from Fig. 6 that for all four formulas, the application of our approach (namely, SBFL-MT) always yields lower EXAM scores.

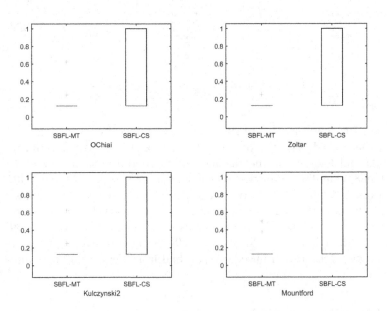

Fig. 6. The EXAM scores of program *UML2ER* in the best case.

We further apply the null-hypothesis test and the effect-size estimation to statistically analyze the difference between the effectiveness of SBFL-MT and SBFL-CS. To conduct a null-hypothesis test, we apply the Wilcoxon rank-sum test [9], because it is a nonparametric test which is suitable for independent samples regardless of the equality of sample sizes. The Wilcoxon rank-sum test is used to check whether there is a significant different between the fault localization effectiveness of SBFL-MT and SBFL-CS. In addition, we apply the $\hat{A}_{12}$ statistics, which measures the probability for one method to outperform the other one, to evaluate the effect size [20]. In the effect-size analysis, if $\hat{A}_{12} < 0.44$, it is regarded that our approach is of better effectiveness; if $\hat{A}_{12} > 0.56$, SBFL-CS is regarded to be of better effectiveness; and if $0.44 \leq \hat{A}_{12} \leq 0.56$, the two methods are regarded to be of similar effectiveness.

We conduct four comparison studies with respect to the four risk evaluation formulas. In these four comparisons, although the Wilcoxon rank-sum test dose not suggest a significant difference between the two methods under study, every of the effect-size estimation indicates the superiority of our approach over SBFL-CS (the $\hat{A}_{12}$ values are 0.4192, 0.3586, 0.3606, 0.3626, respectively). This means that our approach outperforms SBFL-CS for locating faulty rules of program *UML2ER*.

4.3   Discussion

Locating Multiple Faulty Rules for Model Transformations. In the above experiments, we only consider program mutants containing only one faulty rule. For the subject program *UML2ER*, there are also some mutants that have multiple faulty rules. Therefore, we also investigate the fault localization effectiveness of our approach in the context of multiple faulty rules. We apply our approach to mutants having multiple faulty rules, and compare the experimental results with that of applying SBFL-CS. The comparison shows that these two approaches yield comparable EXAM score distribution for about 50% of the mutants, while SBFL-CS outperforms our approach for the remainder mutants. By looking into the details of the experimental data, we find that when locating multiple faulty rules, our approach is impacted by both the selected MRs and the nature of the subject programs. For the subject program *UML2ER*, one of its characteristics is that it makes use of rule inheritance. That is, in this program, multiple rules correspond to each other with respect to the inheritance relationships. As a result, the coverage information extracted may be more vague (when a rule is executed, its super-rule is also been executed).

Factors Affecting the Fault Localization Effectiveness. Firstly, since our approach is an MT-based approach, its effectiveness is intrinsically affected by the selection of original SMs as well as the selection of MRs. The use of different original SMs and MRs may yield different coverage information for locating faults, and thereby leading to varying fault localization results. Secondly, our approach adopts SBFL risk evaluation formulas, and thus the strengths of the used formulas also have impacts on the effectiveness of our approach. As can be observed from Figs. 5 and 6, the use of different formulas always yields different fault localization results for each subject programs. Last but not least, the characteristics of the subject programs and fault patterns may also influence the fault localization results.

5   Related Work

Metamorphic Testing in Model Transformations. As a well-known technique for alleviating the oracle problem, MT has also been applied to test model transformation programs [10,12]. Moreover, according to the characteristics of model transformations, Troya et al. [19] propose a method for automatically construct MRs by analyzing the runtime information of model transformation programs. The automation of MRs generation largely facilitates and supports the automation of MT-based applications in this domain. In this study, we further extend the MT's application in the domain of model transformation from testing to debugging.

Locating Faults for Model Transformations. Generally, there are two categories of methods for locating faulty rules of model transformations: static methods and dynamic methods. Static methods identify faulty rules by conduct analysis without running the model transformation programs. One typical static fault localization approach makes use of metamodel footprints presented in the transformation rules, and utilizes constraint-based oracles to support the procedure of locating faulty rules [6]. In this approach, alignments among metamodel footprints appearing in the transformation rules and those presented in the constraint-based oracles are automatically built and matched, based on which the faulty rules are identified. Differently, dynamic approaches locate faults by executing model transformation programs. PRFL is an enhanced SBFL method that makes use of the PageRank algorithm [23]. Le et al. [4] propose a method to localize buggy programs by applying a learning-to-rank strategy and using Daikon invariants. Furthermore, they also create a multi-modal technique which combines IR-based techniques with spectrum-based techniques [14]. Forensic debugging [11] analyzes the trace information of model transformations to identify relationships between elements of source and target models and to determine the transformation logic. Based on the analysis, it further extract answers to some debugging questions. Troya et al. propose a SBFL-based approach for model transformations [18], which utilizes constraint-based oracles. The key differences between this approach and ours lies in the use of different oracle mechanisms. A comparison with this approach has been presented in Sect. 4.2, where we can observe that our approach achieves higher fault localization effectiveness for the subject programs under study.

6   Conclusion and Future Work

Fault localization of model transformations is a challenging task. In this paper, we present an approach to locate faulty rules of model transformations by integrating the technique of metamorphic testing (MT) and spectrum-based fault localization (SBFL). By leveraging MT, our approach can alleviate the oracle problem in debugging model transformations. We conduct a series of experiments to evaluate the proposed approach, including an justification of the overall fault localization effectiveness, and a comparison analysis involving a novel SBFL-based approach that use constraint-based oracles. The experimental results show that our approach is of good fault localization effectiveness for model transformations.

This study demonstrates a new application of MT in the domain of model transformations. In the future, we will do more explorations in this research direction. Further experiments will be conducted to reveal the fault localization effectiveness across different source models, different MRs, and model transformation programs with various different characteristics. Moreover, strategies that can improve the fault localization effectiveness will be investigated and integrated into the current approach, in order to achieve better effectiveness. Finally, since the proposed approach focuses on locating faulty rules, it is worthwhile to study for the approach that can provide more detailed fault localization information (for example, information for identifying faulty statements).

References

1. Atl transformations. https://www.eclipse.org/atl/atlTransformations/
2. Rahim, L.A., Whittle, J.: A survey of approaches for verifying model transformations. Softw. Syst. Model. **14**(2), 1003–1028 (2015)
3. Abreu, R., Zoeteweij, P., Golsteijn, R., van Gemund, A.J.C.: A practical evaluation of spectrum-based fault localization. J. Syst. Softw. **82**(11), 1780–1792 (2009)
4. Le, T.D.B., Lo, D., Le Goues, C., Grunske, L.: A learning-to-rank based fault localization approach using likely invariants. In: Proceedings of the 25th International Symposium on Software Testing and Analysis, ISSTA 2016, pp. 177–188. ACM (2016)
5. Baudry, B., Ghosh, S., Fleurey, F., France, R., Le Traon, Y., Mottu, J.M.: Barriers to systematic model transformation testing. Commun. ACM **53**(6), 139–143 (2010)
6. Burgueño, L., Troya, J., Wimmer, M., Vallecillo, A.: Static fault localization in model transformations. IEEE Trans. Softw. Eng. **41**(5), 490–506 (2015)
7. Chen, T.Y., Cheung, S.C., Yiu, S.M.: Metamorphic testing: a new approach for generating next test cases. Technical report HKUST-CS98-01, Department of Computer Science, Hong Kong University of Science and Technology (1998)
8. Chen, T.Y., et al.: Metamorphic testing: a review of challenges and opportunities. ACM Comput. Surv. **51**(1), 4:1–4:27 (2018)
9. Field, A.: Discovering Statistics Using IBM SPSS Statistics, 4th edn. Sage Publications, Thousand Oaks (2003)
10. He, X., Chen, X., Cai, S., Zhang, Y., Huang, G.: Testing bidirectional model transformation using metamorphic testing. Inform. Softw. Techol. **104**, 109–129 (2018)

11. Hibberd, M., Lawley, M., Raymond, K.: Forensic debugging of model transformations. In: Engels, G., Opdyke, B., Schmidt, D.C., Weil, F. (eds.) MODELS 2007. LNCS, vol. 4735, pp. 589–604. Springer, Heidelberg (2007). https://doi.org/10.1007/978-3-540-75209-7_40

12. Jiang, M., Chen, T.Y., Kuo, F.C., Ding, Z.: Testing central processing unit scheduling algorithms using metamorphic testing. In: Proceedings of the 4th IEEE International Conference on Software Engineering and Service Science, pp. 530–536 (2014)

13. Jones, J.A., Harrold, M.J., Stasko, J.: Visualization of test information to assist fault localization. In: Proceedings of the 24th International Conference on Software Engineering, ICSE 2002, pp. 467–477 (2002)

14. Le, T.D.B., Oentaryo, R.J., Lo, D.: Information retrieval and spectrum based bug localization: better together. In: Proceedings of the 2015 10th Joint Meeting on Foundations of Software Engineering, ESEC/FSE 2015, pp. 579–590 (2015)

15. Lucia, D.L., Lingxiao Jiang, F.T., Budi, A.: Extended comprehensive study of association measures for fault localization. J. Softw.: Evol. Process 26(2), 172–219 (2014)

16. Lúcio, L., et al.: Model transformation intents and their properties. Softw. Syst. Model. 15(3), 647–684 (2016)

17. Troya, J., Bergmayr, A., Burgueño, L., Wimmer, M.: Towards systematic mutations for and with ATL model transformations. In: 2015 IEEE Eighth International Conference on Software Testing, Verification and Validation Workshops (ICSTW), pp. 1–10 (2015)

18. Troya, J., Segura, S., Parejo, J.A., Ruiz-Cortés, A.: Spectrum-based fault localization in model transformations. ACM Trans. Softw. Eng. Methodol. 27(3), 1–50 (2018)

19. Troya, J., Segura, S., Ruiz-Corts, A.: Automated inference of likely metamorphic relations for model transformations. J. Syst. Softw. 136(C), 188–208 (2018)

20. Vargha, A., Delaney, H.D.: A critique and improvement of the cl common language effect size statistics of mcgraw and wong. J. Educ. Behav. Stat. 25(2), 101–132 (2000)

21. Xie, X., Chen, T.Y., Kuo, F.C., Xu, B.: A theoretical analysis of the risk evaluation formulas for spectrum-based fault localization. ACM Trans. Softw. Eng. Methodol. 22(4), 31:1–31:40 (2013)

22. Xie, X., Wong, W.E., Chen, T.Y., Xu, B.: Metamorphic slice: an application in spectrum-based fault localization. Inf. Softw. Technol. 55(5), 866–879 (2013)

23. Zhang, M., Li, X., Zhang, L., Khurshid, S.: Boosting spectrum-based fault localization using PageRank. In: Proceedings of the 26th ACM SIGSOFT International Symposium on Software Testing and Analysis, ISSTA 2017, pp. 261–272. ACM (2017)

A Fault Localization Method Based on Dynamic Failed Execution Blocks

Baoyi Pan, Ting Shu$^{(\boxtimes)}$, Jinsong Xia, Zuohua Ding, and Mingyue Jiang

School of Information Science and Technology, Zhejiang Sci-Tech University,
Hangzhou 310018, China
shuting@zstu.edu.cn

Abstract. Software fault localization is the most tedious and time-consuming activity in program debugging. Spectrum-based software fault localization (SFL) is a typical light-weight automated diagnosis technique for boosting fault localization. In the previous work, the researchers has found that although there is no optimal formula, the accuracy of a specific SFL-based method may be affected by the used program spectra at different granularity levels, e.g., statements, methods, basic blocks. In this paper, therefore, we further explore the correlation between the spectra granularity and the fault localization accuracy, and then the dynamic failed execution block (DFEB), a novel granularity for program spectra, is introduced to improve the diagnostic accuracy of a specific SFL technique. Consequently, a new method for fault localization by using DFEBs is proposed. Finally, to validate the effectiveness of our proposed method, an experimental study on 8 classic SFL techniques and 11 well-known benchmark programs including Siemens suite, space, gzip, grep, and sed, is conducted in detail. Experimental results show that the new approach is more effective in most cases, in comparison with these subject SFL methods.

Keywords: Fault localization · Program spectra · Basic block · Software testing

1 Introduction

With increasing scale and complexity of software, software testing, as a way of ensuring and improving its quality, plays a more and more important role in software development life cycle. Debugging is part of the software testing process and involves locating and correcting code faults in the program under testing. Software fault localization, which mainly focuses on identifying the specific locations of faults, is considered to be the most expensive and time-consuming activities in debugging [17]. In addition, for a large-scale program in particular, manual locating its faulty codes becomes a challenging problem due to the limitations of tester's experience and knowledge. To mitigate this problem, a number of methods [1,8], therefore, have been proposed for automatic fault localization

© Springer Nature Switzerland AG 2020
H. Miao et al. (Eds.): SOFL+MSVL 2019 Workshop, LNCS 12028, pp. 315–327, 2020.
https://doi.org/10.1007/978-3-030-41418-4_21

in academia and industry, while improving the efficiency and effectiveness of localizing faults.

Amongst the proposed approaches for software fault localization, spectrum-based software fault localization (SFL) is a typical light-weight automated diagnosis technique and relatively more efficient by reducing the debugging effort. A program spectrum is an execution profile that details dynamic program behaviour during a run. It can be used to indicate which components of a program, such as statements, conditional branches and methods, are exercised in a specific run. Intuitively, codes frequently executed in failed runs are more suspicious than those executed in passed runs. In other words, these suspicious codes are more related to the root cause of test failures. By analyzing the differences of program spectra for passed and failed runs, SFL can aid tester to localize suspicious code that is responsible for a specific test failure, reducing the search scope for faulty codes. Among these proposed SFL methods, similarity coefficient-based techniques are widely employed to compute the suspiciousness of program entities. Concretely, to identify the faulty part of program, a SFL method needs first to design and run a sufficient quantity of test cases (passed and failed test cases). Then it abstracts the program spectrum from passed and failed runs and analyzes the code coverage for each run. Next, the suspiciousness of every statement can be calculated using a predefined risk evaluation formula. Consequently, we can rank each statement to check in descending order of its suspiciousness. A study [1] has shown that SFL can pinpoint program faults up to an accuracy such that on average less than 20% of the program needs to be inspected.

For similarity coefficient-based SFL approaches, risk evaluation formulas have a decisive influence on the diagnostic accuracy. Early studies, therefore, have proposed a variety of risk evaluation formulas, e.g., Tarantula [9], Ochiai [2], DStar [16] and so on, for exploring an optimal method. However, these valuable attempts have shown that each proposed risk evaluation formula has its own advantage under different scenarios [14]. A recent study [20] of Yoo et al. also concluded that greatest risk evaluation formula does not exist. Although there is no optimal formula, researchers also found that the effectiveness of a given one is affected by the used program spectra at different granularity levels, e.g., statements [16], methods [21], basic blocks [10]. Since some correct statements with high suspiciousness scores may be excluded from high suspicious code blocks (methods or basic blocks). The existence of these statements will affect bug-revealing capabilities of the SFL methods.

Inspired by this, this paper first introduces dynamic failed execution block (DFEB) as a novel granularity for program spectra to improve the diagnostic accuracy of a specific SFL technique. DFEB can be easily constructed based on the coverage matrix obtained from test executions by grouping adjacent statements that are covered by each test case. Then we integrate the DFEB into the SFL technique using conditional probability model proposed by our previous work [13] and proposed a new method for fault localization. In our proposed method, locating faults is achieved in two steps: DFEB ranking and statement ranking. The former use the given risk formula to compute the suspiciousness for each DFEB and sort DFEBs for bug inspection according to their computed suspiciousness in descending order. Similarly, for each DFEB, the latter also use the same risk formula to implement fault localization as the traditional SFL based on statement granularity. Finally, to validate the effectiveness of the proposed method, an experimental study on 11 well-known benchmark programs including Siemens suite, space, gzip, grep, and sed are conducted in detail. Experimental results show that it is more effective on most case, in compassion with these subject SFL methods.

The rest of this paper is as follows. Section 2 introduces the fundamental concepts of SFL method and conditional probability model. Section 3 describes our new method in detail. Section 4 discusses empirical evaluation and analysis. Section 4.4 describes related work. Finally, we conclude our work in Sect. 5.

2 Preliminaries

2.1 Spectrum-Based Fault Localization

In the past two decades, a large number of similarity coefficient-based SFL methods have been proposed for single-fault and multi-fault programs. The common idea of these proposed formula is that a program entity executed by more failing tests and less passing tests is more likely to be faulty. Usually, we define four kinds of factors (a_{11}, a_{10}, a_{00}, a_{01}) to describe the correlation between program spectra and execution results. a_{11} denotes the number of times a statement is covered in failed tests; a_{10} represents the number of times a statement has been covered in successful tests; a_{00} and a_{01} represent the number of times a statement was not covered in successful tests or failed tests, respectively. In this paper, we take 8 well-known SFL techniques: Tarantula, Ochiai, Ochiai2, Op2, Kulczynski, Kulczynski2, Jaccard and Dstar as the benchmark formula, as shown in Table 1.

Table 1. 8 well-known risk evaluation formulas.

SFL methods	Formulas
Tarantula	$susp(s) = \dfrac{\frac{a_{11}}{a_{11}+a_{01}}}{\frac{a_{11}}{a_{11}+a_{01}} + \frac{a_{10}}{a_{10}+a_{00}}}$
Ochiai	$susp(s) = \dfrac{a_{11}}{\sqrt{(a_{11}+a_{01})\times(a_{11}+a_{01})}}$
Ochiai2	$susp(s) = \dfrac{a_{11}a_{10}}{\sqrt{(a_{11}+a_{10})\times(a_{00}+a_{10})\times(a_{11}+a_{01})\times(a_{01}+a_{00})}}$
Op2	$susp(s) = a_{11} - \dfrac{a_{10}}{a_{10}+a_{00}+1}$
Kulczynski	$susp(s) = \dfrac{a_{11}}{a_{01}+a_{10}}$
Kulczynski2	$susp(s) = \dfrac{1}{2} \times \left(\dfrac{a_{11}}{a_{11}+a_{10}} + \dfrac{a_{11}}{a_{11}+a_{10}} \right)$
Jaccard	$susp(s) = \dfrac{a_{11}}{a_{11}+a_{01}+a_{10}}$
Dstar	$susp(s) = \dfrac{a_{11}^{*}}{a_{01}+a_{10}}$

Jones et al. [9] first proposed the Tarantula method to calculate the suspiciousness for each statement. Ochiai [2], Ochiai2 [12], an extension of Ochiai, Jaccard [3] are generally considered to be superior to Tarantula technique. OP2 [12], in some cases, is considered as the optimal formula for single error. Wong et al. [17] extended Kulczynski [5] in the context of fault localization and proposed Dstar method. Experimental results show that Dstar surpass all compared techniques in most cases, in terms of its effectiveness at fault localization.

2.2   A Risk Formula on Conditional Probability Model

In our previous work [13], we defined a conditional probability model (CPM) for quantifying the potential relationships between program spectra and test results. For the convenience of description, the following notations are given. E and N denote an event that an entity is executed or not executed during a run, respectively. F is a failed test and T is a passed test. Therefore, two CPMs: P_{fe} and P_{ef} can be defined as follows.

Definition 1. P_{fe} **model.** *Suppose an entity is executed, the probability of program execution failure can be expressed as* $P_{fe} = P(F|E) = \frac{P(EF)}{P(E)} = \frac{a_{11}}{a_{11}+a_{10}}, a_{11} + a_{10} \neq 0$.

Obviously, for SFL methods, an entity must be covered at least once during test runs. Otherwise we can't obtain the spectrum of the program under testing. Therefore, this constraint $a_{11} + a_{10} \neq 0$ is always satisfied.

Definition 2. P_{ef} **model.** *Suppose a test is failed, the probability that a specific entity is executed can be expressed as* $P_{ef} = P(E|F) = \frac{P(EF)}{P(F)} = \frac{a_{11}}{a_{01}+a_{11}}, a_{01} + a_{11} \neq 0$.

Similarity, in order to achieve effective fault localization, test results should include at least one failure. Consequently, $a_{01} + a_{11} \neq 0$ is also always satisfied.

Based on the above two CPMs, a new risk evaluation formula has been proposed as follows.

$$susp(s) = a_{11} \times P_{fe} + a_{11} \times P_{ef} = a_{11} \times \left(\frac{a_{11}}{a_{11} + a_{10}} + \frac{a_{11}}{a_{11} + a_{01}} \right) \quad (1)$$

In this paper, we use the CPM-based technique as a basis and explore its effectiveness of the formula on different granularities in terms of locating faults.

3   The Proposed Approach

In this section, the definition of dynamic failed execution block and some related notations are first described. Then, we present our approach to improve the effectiveness of fault localization by using DFEBs. For the convenience of understanding, finally, a simple example will be given to illustrate how the proposed method works.

3.1 Dynamic Failed Execution Block

There have been various program spectra proposed on different granularities. The basic block is one of the most popular granularity, which can strike a balance between instrumentation costs and fault locating capabilities. For each test case, its execution slice is a set of statements covered by the corresponding test run. Therefore, an execution slice with respect to a failed test must contain at least one fault. If we use code blocks in a failed execution slice as the granularity to calculate their suspiciousness, some original statements with high suspiciousness at the statement granularity level may be included in less suspicious code blocks. On the example program foo presented in Fig. 1, the statements s_5 and s_6 have identical suspiciousness scores 0.556 on which they are ranked fourth and fifth based. For code blocks, however, they will be ranked seventh and eighth, respectively. Consequently, diagnostic accuracy is improved using code blocks technique.

From above observation, we introduce the concept of dynamic failed execution block to compute a new program spectrum. Unlike other basic block technologies such as dynamic basic block [4], a DFEB is constructed from the perspective of a failed execution slice, not the entire test suite. Intuitively, based on DFEBs, we can build a more efficient fault localization method. Concretely, we first give the following definition.

Definition 3. *Dynamic Failed Execution Block. Let FS be a failed execution slice and P be the program under testing. A dynamic failed execution block DFEB is the set of adjacent statements in P that are contained in a FS. Any two statements of P belong to the same DFEB, if and only if they are directly adjacent and contained in the identical FS.*

As an illustration of this concept, we can also consider the example in Fig. 1. There are 7 DFEBs in the coverage matrix of Fig. 1: $b1 = \{s1, s2, s3, s4\}$, $b2 = \{s11\}$, $b3 = \{s13\}$, $b4 = \{s17\}$, $b5 = \{s1, s2, s3, s4, s5, s6\}$, $b6 = \{s8\}$, and $b7 = \{s10\}$. Hence, DFEBs can be easily extracted from a coverage matrix by grouping adjacent statements in a failed execution slice. Since it is obvious that a failed execution slice contains some faulty codes, DFEBs can cover the error statements. Depending on whether statements contained in any two DFEBs are overlapped, their relationship can be divided into three categories: intersection, disjoint sets and set inclusion.

3.2 An Approach Using DFEBs

Our proposed approach is implemented in two phases. The first phase computes the DFEBs from coverage matrix and ranks DFEB in terms of their suspiciousness calculated by a given risk evaluation formula. In this paper, we choose the CPM-based formula (1) described in Sect. 2.2 as the host formula. Similar to traditional SFL methods, the second phase of our approach ranks each statement in DFEBs to inspect bugs in descending order of its suspiciousness.

example program P int foo (int x, int , int z)	statement	t1 (1,1,1)	t2 (0,1,1)	t3 (-1,1,1)	t4 (-1,0,1)	t5 (-1,-1,-1)	t6 (-2,-1,-2)	t7 (-1,-1,0)	sus (si)
{int w=1;	S1	1	1	1	1	1	1	1	0.5
If(x<0){ // bug, if(x<-1)	S2	1	1	1	1	1	1	1	0.5
w*=x;	S3	0	0	1	1	1	1	1	0.625
If(y<0){	S4	0	0	1	1	1	1	1	0.625
w*=-y;	S5	0	0	0	0	1	1	1	0.556
If(z<0){	S6	0	0	0	0	1	1	1	0.556
w*=(-1)*z	S7	0	0	0	0	1	1	0	0
}else if(z>0){	S8	0	0	0	0	0	0	1	1
w*=z	S9	0	0	0	0	0	0	0	0
}else{w=z;}	S10	0	0	0	0	0	0	1	1
}else if(y>0){	S11	0	0	1	1	0	0	0	0.714
w*=y;	S12	0	0	1	0	0	0	0	0
}else{w=y;}	S13	0	0	0	1	0	0	0	1
}else if(x>0){	S14	1	1	0	0	0	0	0	0
w*=x;	S15	1	0	0	0	0	0	0	0
}else{w=x;}	S16	0	1	0	0	0	0	0	0
Print("%d\n", w);}	S17	1	1	1	1	1	1	1	0.5
results	-	T	T	T	F	T	T	F	-

Fig. 1. Example program and its execution results.

Concretely, in the first phase, for each failed execution slice, DFEBs will be abstracted from the coverage matrix by grouping adjacent statements. Then, the DFEB-hit spectra are calculated to indicate whether each DFEB is covered or not during each test. Specifically, we also use four factors (A_{11}, A_{10}, A_{00}, A_{01}) similar to the statement-hit spectrum to describe the coverage of DFEBs. A_{11} and A_{10} denote the number of times a DFEB is covered in failed tests and passed tests, respectively. A_{00} and A_{01} depict the number of times a DFEB is not covered in passed tests and failed tests, respectively. Introducing these four factors into a given risk formula, the suspiciousness of each DFEB can be calculated to indicate which block is the most suspicious in the program under test. Meanwhile, the suspiciousness scores of each statements are also computed using the identical formula. Consequently, programer can examine the DFEBs one by one for locating bugs in descending order of their suspiciousness.

For each DFEB, in the second phase, all the statements are ranked to be inspected according to their suspiciousnesses from large to small. This process is similar to the traditional SFL methods. However, it is worth noting that not all the statements in a DFEB are potential objects to be detected. Since some statements in a specific block may also be included in other more suspicious DFEB, that is, they have been previously checked and hence there is no need to detect them again. To achieve this, we define a statement pool $P(s)$ to store the statements that have been examined. The specific intra-block detection algorithm is mainly divided into three steps, as described below.

Step1: For each DFEB, statements in the block are ranked in descending order of their suspiciousnesses.

Step2: Before checking, each statement first needs to be judged whether it already has been contained in $P(s)$. If not, this one will be checked and then stored in $P(s)$. Otherwise, the next statement continues to be detected.

Step3: If the current statement is found to be a buggy statement, the algorithm terminates, otherwise repeat **Step2**.

3.3   A Simple Example

Figure 1 shows an example to demonstrate the working process and effectiveness of the proposed method. The first and second columns contain the example code and its statement identifiers, respectively. Seven test cases and their corresponding execution results are denoted in the subsequent columns. The rightmost column represents the suspicious score for each statement. Bold black circle denotes the DFEB contained in failed execution slices. For this code snippet shown in Fig. 1, a bug lies in the condition expression of the statement $S2$ and the correct one should be $(x < -1)$. In this example, we take the classical Tarantula technique as the host formula to calculate the suspiciousness scores of statements and DFEBs, respectively.

According to the descending order of their suspiciousness scores calculated by using Tarantula formula, the ranked statement queue sq should be ($S8$, $S10$, $S13$, $S11$, $S3$, $S4$, $S5$, $S6$, $S1$, $S2$, $S17$,$S7$, $S9$, $S12$, $S14$, $S15$, $S16$). Therefore, before locating the bug in statement $S2$, the developer needs to inspect ten statements based on Tarantula technique. For our new method, on the statement coverage matrix in this example, we can abstract seven DFEBs: b1 = {$S1$, $S2$, $S3$, $S4$}, b2 = {$S11$}, b3 = {$S13$}, b4 = {$S17$}, b5 = {$S1$, $S2$, $S3$, $S4$, $S5$, $S6$}, b6 = {$S8$}, b7 = {$S10$}. Their suspiciousness scores are b1 = 0.625, b2 = 0.714, b3 = 1, b4 = 0.5, b5 = 0.556, b6 = 1, and b7 = 1, respectively. Hence, the ranked block queue bq should be (b3, b6, b7, b2, b1, b5, b4). The faulty statement $S2$ is both contained in the blocks b1 and b5. After examining all the statements in b3, b6, b7 and b2, the next block to be checked becomes the b1. According to intra-block detection algorithm, $S2$ will be last inspected due to its ranking in the block b1. Consequently, to locate the faulty statement $S2$, it is required to examine eight statements in the proposed method. Therefore, the DFEB-based method can narrow the scope of statement inspection. Compared with Tarantula technique, this method, in this example, can improve 20% of the accuracy of fault localization.

This simple example can intuitively illustrate that locating faults at the granularity of DFEBs is a promising way to improve the accuracy of fault localization methods. Since some correct statements with high suspiciousness scores may be excluded from high suspicious DFEBs.

4   Experiments

4.1   Subject Programs and Configuration

In order to validate the effectiveness of our proposed method, detailed experiments are conducted based on 11 well-known benchmark programs [7] including Siemens suite, space, gzip, grep, and sed. These subject programs are selected from the publicly available Software-artifact Infrastructure Repository (SIR). Table 2 shows the details of subject programs. All the considered programs provide both correct versions and multiple error versions. Some faulty versions are not suitable for the controlled experiments on SFL methods, since there are no failed test cases contained in them. we exclude these versions from our experiments: v32 of replace, v9 of schedule2, v1, v2, v32, v34 of space. In addition, some versions with problems in the compile and run phases are also discarded, such as v27 of replace, v1, v5, v6, v9 of schedule, v25, v26, v30, v35, v36, v38 of space. As a result, we used 153 faulty versions in our experiments including 125 versions of Siemens programs, 28 versions of space and 47 versions of three Unix utilities. For building multi-fault programs, a function is designed to randomly choose any two versions from subject single-fault versions, and combine them into a novel multi-fault program. Consequently, we take 113 multi- fault programs as the experimental subject.

Table 2. Subject programs.

Programs	Faulty versions	Source code lines	Test cases	Descriptions
print_tokens	7	563	4130	Lexical analyzer
print_tokens2	10	406	4115	Lexical analyzer
replace	32	563	5542	Pattern replacement
tcas	41	173	1608	Altitude separation
schedule	9	410	2650	Priority scheduler
schedule2	10	307	2710	Priority scheduler
tot_info	23	406	1052	Information measure
space	28	9127	13525	ADL interpreter
gzip	13	6571	217	Compress
grep	16	12658	470	Search for patterns in files
sed	18	14427	360	Stream editor

4.2   Experiment Design

In this section, the experiments are designed to evaluate the effectiveness of the proposed method based on 8 classical SFL techniques as shown in Table 1. The objectives of our experiments is to explore the following three research questions:

$Q1$: How does the fault localization effectiveness of our proposed method change based on different host risk evaluation formulas? $Q2$: How is the accuracy of fault localization impacted when we employ the DFEBs-based method? $Q3$: For single-fault or multi-fault programs, how does the accuracy of fault localization change?

For $Q1$, we introduce Top-N [21] as the evaluation metric to observe the difference in diagnostic accuracy between those with different risk evaluation formulas. This metric counts the number of bugs successfully located in the top-N ranked suspicious entities. Top-N is a relatively fair metric for accuary comparison, as the DFEB is deterministic for each test case in each program. In this preliminary experiment, we consider the first DFEB in the ranking list. For the subject 11 programs, Top-N scores are computed for 8 considered SFL techniques, respectively. Thus, when the identical number of buggy programs is detected, the larger the Top-N score is, more effective the method can be in practice.

To answer the question $Q2$ and $Q3$, the EXAM [16] score is used to measure the accuracy improvement of the DFEB-based method over the subject SFL approaches. The EXAM score is the percentage of statements that need to be inspected in the program under testing until find the first faulty one. According to the EXAM, the higher the percentage of defective versions found in the same code ranking percentage is, the better the defect localization effect of this method is. For single-fault and multi-fault programs, EXAM scores are respectively calculated to examine the difference in fault location capability under different test scenarios.

4.3   Experiment Results

Figure 2 illustrates the boxplot of Top-1 scores achieved by the DFEB-based methods based on CPM and other subject formulas. For single-fault programs,

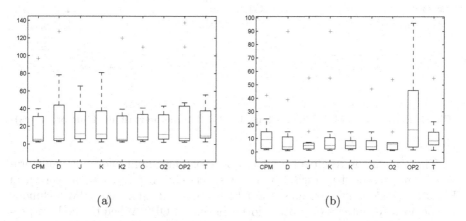

Fig. 2. Top-1 scores (a) single-fault programs (b) multi-fault programs

it can be seen from the data in Fig. 2(a) that the CPM-based approach may surpass over all the other considered formulas. From the Fig. 2(b) we can see that, for multi-fault programs, although the effectiveness of CPM-based method is similar to other methods, it is more effective than the OP2. Compared to other formulas, we therefore conclude that the DFEB-based method using the CPM has better universality for different test scenarios.

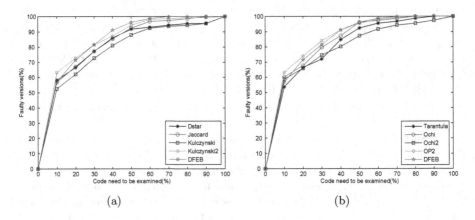

(a)   (b)

Fig. 3. EXAM scores for different fault localization methods (single-fault programs)

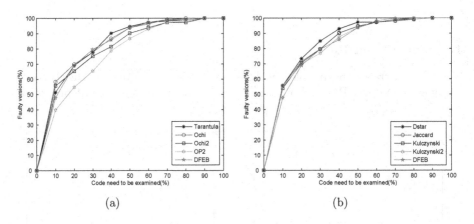

(a)   (b)

Fig. 4. EXAM scores for different fault localization methods (multi-fault programs)

The comparison results of EXAM scores for single-fault and multi-fault programs are presented in Figs. 3 and 4, respectively. In particular, as shown in Fig. 3 for single-fault programs, the DFEB approach using the CPM technique has obvious advantages over other formulas except OP2. When the code inspection ratio is between 0 and 20%, Kulczynsik2 formula is more effective than DFEB, but from 30% to 60% DFEB is better than any other formulas expect

OP2. When detecting more than 60% codes, the effectiveness of our method is the optimal.

Figure 4 illustrates the EXAM scores for multi-fault programs. Different from the single-fault test scenario, our approach is better or closer to other compared formulas expect Dstar, with respect to fault localization accuracy. Although OP2 is an optimal formula for single-fault programs, from the data shown in this Figure, it is apparent that OP2 technique has relatively poor fault location capability in terms of multi-fault programs.

Based on the above experiment results, the conclusion is drawn that the proposed method can be effectively applied to both single-fault and multi-fault test scenarios. Compared with the subject methods, our method has a more universal fault localization capability since it is based on the suitable granularity of program spectra.

4.4   Related Work

In recent years, various techniques have be proposed for improving the efficiency and effectiveness of software fault localization. Program spectrum-based methods are amongst the most lightweight and popular techniques for locating faults. Jones et al. [3] first proposed Tarantula method to calculate the suspiciousness of program statements, which is based on the intuition that program entities which are frequently executed by failing test cases and infrequently executed by passing test cases are more likely to be faulty. Inspired by the similarity formula of gene in molecular biology and the idea of cluster analysis, Abreu et al. [2] proposed Ochiai and Jaccard [3] methods respectively. Empirical research shows that Ochiai and Jaccard surpass Tarantula with respect to fault location accuracy in most case. Dallmeier et al. [6] proposed Ample, an Eclipse plug-in for identifying faulty classes in Java software. Naish et al. [12] proposed two optimal ranking formulas, Op and Op2, for single-fault program and comparison experiments on C programs are conducted to illustrate their advantages. Wong et al. [16] argue that the program execution trajectories for test cases have a pattern to follow and can assist pinpointing program bugs by analyzing the similar information between the execution trajectories of statements for failed test cases. Consequently, they extend Kulczynski formula and propose Dstar method.

To further improve the fault localization accuracy, researchers has explored new ways at different granularity levels, such as methods, slices and basic blocks [10]. Zhang et al. [22] proposed a forward and a bidirectional dynamic slicing techniques for improving fault localization. Wong et al. [18] proposed a novel method based on data dependency information between execution slices and code blocks. Wen et al. [15] proposed the PSS-SFL method by modifying the Tarantula formula by using the dynamic slice of failed test and the frequency information of the statements. Xuan et al. [19] also use the program slicing technique to seperate test cases into minimal fractions to improve spectrum-based fault localization. Mao et al. [11] proposed an approximate dynamic backward slicing technique to weigh the conflict between the size and accuracy of slices, and constructed a new risk evaluation formula. This method effectively reduce the scope of code detection for locating faults and then the fault localization effectiveness is improved. However, the additional overhead of these program-slicing based approaches becomes one of their main limitations. Due to the fact that static blocks can be indistinguishable, dynamic basic blocks (DBB) [4] is proposed to optimize an existing set of test cases based on a test-for-diagnosis criterion. A DBB is the set of statements that is covered by the same test suite. The main difference between DBBs and DFEBs is that a DBB is computed from an entire test suite, while a DEFB is only extracted from some failed execution slices. In addition, the statements in a DEFB are required to be adjacent.

5   Conclusion and Further Work

Spectrum-based fault localization is amongst the most promising methods. In this paper, we proposed a novel approach for boosting software faults localization by using DFEBs. Since DFEBs are calculated from failed execution slices, some valuable information contained in DFEBs can be used to narrow down the fault detection scope for software debugging. In order to validate the effectivenss of our proposed method, a comparison experimental study on 11 well-known bench-mark programs and 8 classic risk formulas are conducted in detail. Experimental results indicate that the proposed method is more effective than subject methods on most case.

Our further work will focus on exploring the universal applicability of our method for more large-scale programs. Furthermore, to reduce the number of DFEBs, it is also a new way for further improving the performance of the proposed method.

Acknowledgements. This research was supported by Zhejiang Provincial Natural Science Foundation of China under Grant No. LY17F020033, the National Natural Science Foundation of China (No. 61101111, 61802349) and the Fundamental Research Funds of Zhejiang Sci-Tech University (2019Q039, 2019Q041).

References

1. Abreu, R., Zoeteweij, P., Golsteijn, R., Van Gemund, A.J.: A practical evaluation of spectrum-based fault localization. J. Syst. Softw. **82**(11), 1780–1792 (2009)
2. Abreu, R., Zoeteweij, P., Van Gemund, A.J.: An evaluation of similarity coefficients for software fault localization. In: 2006 12th Pacific Rim International Symposium on Dependable Computing (PRDC 2006), pp. 39–46. IEEE (2006)
3. Artzi, S., et al.: Finding bugs in web applications using dynamic test generation and explicit-state model checking. IEEE Trans. Softw. Eng. **36**(4), 474–494 (2010)
4. Baudry, B., Fleurey, F., Le Traon, Y.: Improving test suites for efficient fault local-ization. In: Proceedings of the 28th International conference on Software Engineer-ing, pp. 82–91. ACM (2006)
5. Choi, S.S., Cha, S.H., Tappert, C.C.: A survey of binary similarity and distance measures. J. Syst. Cybern. Inf. **8**(1), 43–48 (2010)

6. Dallmeier, V., Lindig, C., Zeller, A.: Lightweight bug localization with AMPLE. In: Proceedings of the Sixth International Symposium on Automated Analysis-driven Debugging, pp. 99–104. ACM (2005)

7. Heiden, S., et al.: An evaluation of pure spectrum-based fault localization techniques for large-scale software systems. Softw. Pract. Exp. **49**(8), 1197–1224 (2019)

8. Janssen, T., Abreu, R., van Gemund, A.J.: Zoltar: a toolset for automatic fault localization. In: Proceedings of the 2009 IEEE/ACM International Conference on Automated Software Engineering, pp. 662–664. IEEE Computer Society (2009)

9. Jones, J.A., Harrold, M.J., Stasko, J.T.: Visualization for fault localization. In: Proceedings of ICSE 2001 Workshop on Software Visualization. Citeseer (2001)

10. Lucia, L., Lo, D., Jiang, L., Thung, F., Budi, A.: Extended comprehensive study of association measures for fault localization. J. Softw. Evol. Process **26**(2), 172–219 (2014)

11. Mao, X., Lei, Y., Dai, Z., Qi, Y., Wang, C.: Slice-based statistical fault localization. J. Syst. Softw. **89**, 51–62 (2014)

12. Naish, L., Lee, H.J., Ramamohanarao, K.: A model for spectra-based software diagnosis. ACM Trans. Softw. Eng. Methodol. (TOSEM) **20**(3), 11 (2011)

13. Shu, T., Huang, M.X., Ding, Z.H., Wang, L., Xia, J.S.: Fault localization method based on conditional probability model. J. Softw. **6**, 17 (2018)

14. Tang, C.M., Chan, W., Yu, Y.T., Zhang, Z.: Accuracy graphs of spectrum-based fault localization formulas. IEEE Trans. Reliab. **66**(2), 403–424 (2017)

15. Wen, W., Li, B., Sun, X., Li, J.: Program slicing spectrum-based software fault localization. In: SEKE, pp. 213–218 (2011)

16. Wong, W.E., Debroy, V., Gao, R., Li, Y.: The DStar method for effective software fault localization. IEEE Trans. Reliab. **63**(1), 290–308 (2013)

17. Wong, W.E., Gao, R., Li, Y., Abreu, R., Wotawa, F.: A survey on software fault localization. IEEE Trans. Softw. Eng. **42**(8), 707–740 (2016)

18. Wong, W.E., Qi, Y.: Effective program debugging based on execution slices and inter-block data dependency. J. Syst. Softw. **79**(7), 891–903 (2006)

19. Xuan, J., Monperrus, M.: Test case purification for improving fault localization. In: Proceedings of the 22nd ACM SIGSOFT International Symposium on Foundations of Software Engineering, pp. 52–63. ACM (2014)

20. Yoo, S., Xie, X., Kuo, F.C., Chen, T.Y., Harman, M.: No pot of gold at the end of program spectrum rainbow: greatest risk evaluation formula does not exist. RN **14**(14), 14 (2014)

21. Zhang, M., et al.: An empirical study of boosting spectrum-based fault localization via PageRank. IEEE Trans. Softw. Eng. p. 1 (2019)

22. Zhang, X., Gupta, N., Gupta, R.: Locating faulty code by multiple points slicing. Softw. Pract. Exp. **37**(9), 935–961 (2007)

Adaptive Random Testing by Bisection and Comprehensive Distance

Chengying Mao[1(✉)] , Mengting Quan[1], Zhilei Chen[1], and Tsong Yueh Chen[2]

[1] School of Software and IoT Engineering, Jiangxi University of Finance and Economics, Nanchang 330013, China
maochy@yeah.net

[2] Department of Computer Science and Software Engineering, Swinburne University of Technology, Melbourne, VIC 3122, Australia
tychen@swin.edu.au

Abstract. Adaptive random testing (ART) has been proved to be effective in improving the failure detection ability of random testing. As a lightweight ART algorithm, the ART by bisection (ART-B) can realize test case generation in a linear order of time complexity, but its ability for finding failures is not so strong. In this study, the dynamic bisection is used to generate candidates randomly from the empty regions as much as possible. For each candidate, two types of distances are taken into account. Then, a comprehensive distance metric is defined to determine the next test case from the candidate set. For the nearest neighbor query in the proposed ART by Bisection and Comprehensive Distance (ART-BCD), the distance-ware forgetting is adopted to ensure its computational cost is still in the linear order. To validate the effectiveness of ART-BCD algorithm, both simulation experiments and empirical studies are performed for comparative analysis. The experimental results show that ART-BCD is better than or comparable to the ART-B and other typical algorithms, such as the fixed-size-candidate-set ART (FSCS-ART), in most cases, especially for the block failure pattern.

Keywords: Software testing · Adaptive random testing · Failure detection ability · Dynamic bisection · Comprehensive distance metric

1 Introduction

Software quality assurance by means of testing is particularly necessary in the whole software development life-cycle [1]. The software systems without the adequate testing often cause large economic losses and even endanger personal safety. For example, the Uber self-driving crash in 2018 was a profound lesson from software failures [12]. Essentially, software testing is an effective technique of sampling the diverse, differentiated inputs from the whole input domain or configuration space to exploit the potential defects in a software system [17]. In

© Springer Nature Switzerland AG 2020
H. Miao et al. (Eds.): SOFL+MSVL 2019 Workshop, LNCS 12028, pp. 328–344, 2020.
https://doi.org/10.1007/978-3-030-41418-4_22

general, the input (or configuration) space of a software system is huge, so it is obviously impractical to select all the inputs for testing. Accordingly, how to select the test cases with strong fault-revealing ability is an important research topic in both the research and industrial community of software engineering.

Random testing (RT) [10] is one of the simplest test case selection techniques [16]. Although it can be easily implemented, its failure detection ability is usually quite limited. To overcome this problem, Chen *et al.* proposed an enhanced version of RT, namely *adaptive random testing* (ART) [5,6]. In this method, with the incremental generation of test cases, the adaptive strategy can ensure that test cases are distributed as evenly as possible. As a typical ART by dynamic partitioning [3], ART by bisection (ART-B) is one of the effective ways to reduce the computational overhead in ART, and realize a linear order of time complexity for test case generation [14,18]. However, its failure detection effectiveness is usually not so good. The underlying reason is that the algorithm cannot effectively avoid test cases clustering together.

On the other hand, the *fixed-size-candidate-set* ART (FSCS-ART for short) is a more popular and effective algorithm. It can disperse test cases as far as possible through a candidate set mechanism. To reduce its computational overhead, in our previous work, a lightweight ART method named DF-FSCS [13] is formed by combining dynamic bisection with distance-ware forgetting strategy. It not only reduces the overhead from the quadratic order to linear order, but also maintains the comparable failure-detection ability as the original FSCS-ART. Furthermore, Rezaalipour *et al.* [19] suggested that the next test case should be selected preferentially in the low-density regions in the DF-FSCS algorithm. On the other hand, Zhang *et al.* [20] proposed an iterative partition testing method. Their method divides the input domain by iteration and chooses the central point of the sub-domain as the test case to be executed. The experimental results show that this method can achieve very good failure-detection results in some cases. However, the method is too deterministic and lack of randomness in selecting test cases, which makes it difficult to cope with the change of failure patterns.

In order to distribute test cases more evenly in the input domain with less computational cost, in this study, the input space of a program is dynamically partitioned in the way of bisection. First, some (e.g., a given number s) empty grid cells are randomly selected. Subsequently, one (or two in a particular case) candidate point is randomly generated in each selected cell. To avoid selecting the next test case too close to existing ones, the distance-based candidate mechanism in the FSCS-ART is also adopted here. Besides the maximum nearest neighbor distance of a candidate, its distance to the center point of the cell which the candidate lies in is also taken into consideration for test case selection. That is to say, the above two types of distance are both considered to define a *comprehensive distance metric* for selecting candidates as the next test case. When query the nearest test case for a given candidate, the distance-ware forgetting is also used to ensure the proposed ART-BCD algorithm in the linear order of time complexity. Furthermore, the failure-detection effectiveness of the ART-BCD algorithm has been validated by both simulation experiments and empirical studies.

The remaining part of the paper is organized as follows. In the next section, the concept of failure patterns and the related ART algorithms are briefly reviewed. The basic principle and the technical details of the proposed algorithm are addressed in Sect. 3. Subsequently, the simulation analysis in three types of failure patterns is conducted in Sect. 4. Furthermore, the comparative experiments on some real-life programs are performed in Sect. 5 to further examine the advantages of the proposed algorithm in practical application scenarios. Finally, Sect. 6 concludes the paper.

2   Background

2.1   Failure Patterns

In order to select test cases in a cost-effective way, it is necessary to understand the distribution of inputs that can cause program failures. To investigate this issue, some empirical studies have been performed to summarize the distribution features of failure-causing inputs. The corresponding experimental results show that the failure-causing inputs often exhibit a clustering phenomenon, that is, these inputs are usually clustered together to form one or more small contiguous regions. Furthermore, Chen *et al.* generally classified it as three typical patterns [6]: block pattern, strip pattern, and point pattern. The features of all three failure patterns are illustrated in Fig. 1.

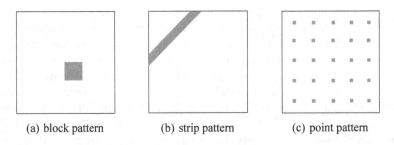

(a) block pattern   (b) strip pattern   (c) point pattern

Fig. 1. Three typical failure patterns, where the shaded area represents the failure-causing inputs.

For the block pattern, the failure-causing inputs amalgamate into one or several contiguous block regions. The corresponding failures are usually triggered by computational errors. For the strip pattern, the failure-causing inputs lie in a narrow strip. Its failures are often caused by predicate faults in a branch statement of program code. For the point pattern, the failure-causing inputs are not explicitly clustered, but are scattered throughout the input domain.

In the research community of RT, the ratio of failure-causing inputs to the whole input domain is usually defined as *failure rate* (θ) [6,9]. It is not difficult to see that the smaller failure rate of the program under test, the more difficult it is to detect the failures in it. On the contrary, it is easier to detect the failures.

2.2 ART by Bisection

Dynamic partitioning [3] is an effective way to reduce the computational cost in test case selection, thus it has been widely adopted by the lightweight ART algorithms [8,13]. Typically, there are two forms: *ART by random partitioning* (ART-RP) and *ART by bisection* (ART-B). In this study, we mainly concern with the way of bisection.

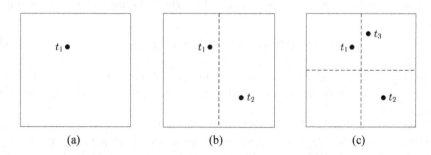

Fig. 2. The illustration of test case generation of the ART-B algorithm.

The ART-B algorithm iteratively divides the current regions into two equal parts, and then randomly generates test cases in the empty sub-regions. Take a two-dimensional (i.e., $d = 2$) space as an example, the process of test case generation in ART-B is demonstrated in Fig. 2. Initially, the first test case is randomly generated from the whole input domain (see Fig. 2(a)). Then, the input domain is divided into two parts in the X-axis direction. Thus, as shown in Fig. 2(b), the second test case is randomly generated in the empty subregion on the right side. When there are no remaining empty sub-regions, each sub-region continues to be bisected in the Y-axis direction. Subsequently, the follow-up test cases are selected from the new empty sub-regions in turn. In the example in Fig. 2(c), the third test case is generated in the empty sub-regions in the upper right corner. In this way, when four test cases are generated in the input domain, each sub-region is further bisected in the X-axis direction.

The typical feature of ART-B algorithm is that it can generate test cases at the cost of linear time complexity [18]. However, since the distances to the existing test cases are not considered when generating a new test case, the test cases are easy to close together, such as the test cases t_1 and t_3 shown in Fig. 2(c). It should be pointed out that although in the standard ART-B algorithm, the input domain is divided according to each dimension in turn, in fact, it can be bisected in all dimensions at the same time. Such partition method is also called *dynamic grid partition* [8,13].

2.3 FSCS-ART

Because the failure-causing inputs tend to be clustered together in most cases, in order to reveal failures more quickly, the selected test cases need to be distributed as evenly as possible in the input domain. As a typical and popular distance-based ART algorithm, FSCS-ART enables test cases to disperse evenly in the input domain by making them as far away from each other as possible.

In the FSCS-ART algorithm, the set TS is used for storing the test cases already generated. Similarly, the first test case is also randomly generated in the initial step. Meanwhile, $CS = \{c_1, c_2, \cdots, c_s\}$ is a set for storing the temporary candidates. In each round of test case selection, a candidate c_j $(1 \leq j \leq s)$ is determined as the next test case should follow the following distance criterion.

$$\min_{j=1}^{|TS|} dist(c_h, tc_j) \geq \min_{j=1}^{|TS|} dist(c_k, tc_j), \tag{1}$$

where tc_j $(1 \leq j \leq |TS|)$ is a test case in set TS, c_k and c_h $(1 \leq k, h \leq s)$ are elements in candidate set CS, and $dist$ refers to the Euclidean distance for numeric inputs.

The main feature of FSCS-ART algorithm is to introduce a candidate set mechanism to ensure that test cases are spread out. The experimental results have shown that the FSCS-ART is superior to many other ART algorithms in terms of the failure-detection effectiveness [5]. However, for each candidate, the distances from it to all existing test cases should be calculated. Thus, it leads to a quadratic order of time complexity, which affects the wide application of FSCS-ART algorithm [2]. According to our previous work [13], this problem can be well solved by dynamic bisection and distance-aware forgetting. In addition, the FSCS-ART algorithm has another weakness, that is, it is easy to cause test cases to appear in the boundary region with a higher probability [4]. In this study, we attempt to weaken the boundary effect by modifying the original distance metric of the nearest neighbor.

3   ART by Bisection and Comprehensive Distance

3.1   Basic Idea

In order to weaken the boundary effect of FSCS-ART algorithm, it is necessary to reduce the chance of test cases appearing at the boundary, and make them move towards the non-boundary region. On the other hand, the IPT method proposed by Zhang et al. [20] reveals a rule that when the test case tends to be at the center of the sub-region, its probability of detecting failures in the block pattern increases significantly. Based on the above clues, in order to make test cases distribute as evenly as possible, the following two constraints need to be met: (1) the distance between the candidate and its nearest neighbor test case should be as large as possible; (2) the candidate should be as close as possible to the center of its cell.

In order to realize fast nearest neighbor queries, in this study, we also adopt the *distance-aware forgetting strategy* [13] to conduct the distance computation. That is, the input domain of program is partitioned into small cells by the dynamic bisection. With the progress of testing, an increasing number of cells are dynamically generated. Then, for a given candidate, only the test cases lying in its neighborhood cells are taken into considered for distance computation. Of course, in this way, the nearest neighbor test case found for the candidate is not necessarily the actually nearest neighbor.

Besides the above approximate nearest neighbor distance, for a candidate, the distance from it to the center of its cell is also taken into account for designing a comprehensive metric for determining which candidate as the next test case. In the application of this metric, the nearest neighbor distance of the candidate should be as large as possible, and the distance to the center of its cell should be as small as possible.

3.2 Algorithm Description

Without loss of generality, the two-dimensional $(d = 2)$ input space is taken as an example to introduce the ART algorithm by bisection and comprehensive distance (**ART-BCD** for short). In the algorithm, the dynamic bisection mainly plays the following three roles: (1) It aids to implement fast nearest neighbor queries. (2) It facilitates to preferentially generate test cases in the empty regions, and ensures that one test case is in a cell. (3) The cell center is an important reference point for defining comprehensive distance metric. Compared with the original FSCS-ART, the main improvement of ART-BCD algorithm is as below: on the basis of dynamic bisection, ART-BCD combines two types of distances to form a more comprehensive metric to select the next test case from the candidate set.

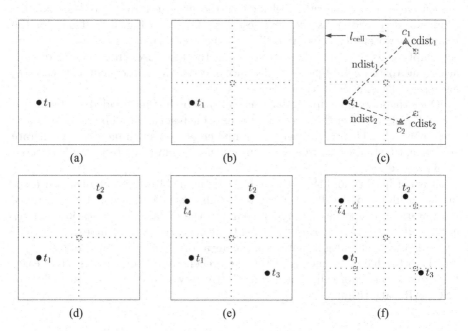

Fig. 3. The illustration of ART by bisection and comprehensive distance.

As illustrated by Fig. 3(a), the first test case is randomly generated in the whole input domain. Then, the input domain is divided by its center point to obtain 4 sub-regions (see Fig. 3(b)). For the three empty cells, we can randomly select s cells out of them. In this simple example, s is set to 2. Then, a candidate point is generated from each selected empty cell. Of course, when there is only one empty cell, two candidate points are randomly generated in it. As shown in Fig. 3(c), suppose the two cells on the right are selected, and candidates c_1 and c_2 are randomly generated from them, respectively.

Subsequently, for each candidate c_k $(1 \leq k \leq s)$, its comprehensive distance metric $(\mathrm{cdm}(c_k))$ is calculated in the following way.

$$\mathrm{cdm}(c_k) = \mathrm{ndist}(c_k) \times (2 - \mathrm{ratio}(c_k)^{\frac{1}{2}\log_2 d}) \tag{2}$$

$$\mathrm{ratio}(c_k) = \frac{\mathrm{cdist}(c_k)}{\sqrt{d} \cdot l_{\mathrm{cell}}/2} \tag{3}$$

where d is the dimension number of the input domain of a program, $\mathrm{ndist}(c_k)$ is the distance from c_k to its nearest test case neighbor, $\mathrm{cdist}(c_k)$ represents the distance from c_k to the center of the cell in which it is located, and l_{cell} is the side length of the cell. In this algorithm, we also adopt the distance-aware forgetting strategy [13] to identify the nearest test case neighbor for a candidate, that is, only the test cases in the the $3^d - 1$ neighbor cells around the candidate are taken into consideration for distance computation. Therefore, the $\mathrm{ndist}(c_k)$ is an approximate nearest distance from c_k to all executed test cases.

Based on the above computation, the candidate with the maximum comprehensive distance metric is selected as the next test case. In this example, candidate c_1 is chosen as the next test case, i.e., t_2 in Fig. 3(d). Then, for the remaining two empty cells, according to the above rule of randomly selecting the empty cells first and then determining the test cases from the candidates according to the comprehensive distance metric, the subsequent test cases t_3 and t_4 are determined in turn (see Fig. 3(e)).

Once there are no empty cells, each cell will be further divided by its central point (Fig. 3(f)). After the bisection, the existing test cases will be re-located into these new cells. Then, the newly generated empty cells will be used to generate subsequent test cases, as well as to ensure that at most one test case is selected from each cell.

It is not hard to find that, through the dynamic bisection, only the test cases in the neighborhood cells of a candidate are taken into account for distance computation. Therefore, the upper bound of the distance computation cost for each candidate is $3^d - 1$. Based on this treatment, the time complexity of ART-BCD algorithm can be guaranteed in the linear order of the number of test cases. On the other hand, by means of the comprehensive distance metric, test cases tend to the center of cell, which can effectively weaken the boundary effect of FSCS-ART algorithm.

Algorithm ART–BCD

Input: (1) The d-dimensional input domain R.

    (2) The size of candidate set, denoted as s ($s > 1$).

    (3) The initial partition number (p_0) for each dimension.

    (4) The termination condition of test case generation.

Output: The set of test cases TS.

1: Initialize $p = p_0$, $TS = \{\}$, $CS = \{\}$, and $L_{EC} = \{R\}$; //CS is the set of candidates and L_{EC} is a list for storing the empty cells

2: Randomly select a test case tc from the whole input domain R;

3: **while** (termination condition does not satisfy) **do**

4:    Add tc into TS, and remove the cell containing tc from L_{EC};

    //dynamic adjustment for grid partitioning

5:    **if** $L_{ER} = \varnothing$ **then**

6:      $p = 2p$;

7:      Re-partition each dimension of R into p equal parts, and construct a new indexing structure for the newly generated cells, the side length of cell is denoted as l_{cell};

8:      Re-locate all existing test cases in TS into the newly generated cells;

9:      Add all empty cells into L_{EC};

10:    **end if**

    //construct the candidate set by selecting the empty cells

11:    **if** $|L_{EC}| > s$ **then**

12:      Randomly select s empty cells from L_{EC} and then randomly generate one candidate from each cell, add the candidates into CS;

13:    **else if** $1 < |L_{EC}| \leq s$ **then**

14:      Randomly generate one candidate from each cell in L_{EC}, and add the candidates into CS;

15:    **else**

16:      Randomly generate two candidates from the only empty cell, and add them into CS;

17:    **end if**

    //calculate the comprehensive distance metric for each candidate

18:    **for** each candidate c_k in CS **do**

19:      According to the location of c_k, find its 3^d-1 neighbour cells, and denoted it $neig(c_k)$;

20:      Collect all test cases lying in $neigh(c_k)$ to form set $TS_{neig(c_k)}$;

21:      Calculate the nearest distance form c_k to the test cases in $TS_{neig(c_k)}$, and denoted it $ndist(c_k)$;

22:      Calculate the distance from c_k to the center point of its cell, and denote it $cdist(c_k)$;

23:      Calculate the comprehensive distance metric ($cdm(c_k)$) for c_k according to Equations (2) and (3);

24:    **end for**

25:    Find the candidate with the maximum comprehensive distance metric from CS, and set it as the next test case tc;

26: **end while**

27: **return** TS;

3.3 The ART-BCD Algorithm

Through the above description of technical details, the key steps of ART-BCD algorithm have been addressed. Here, we use pseudo-code to explain the execution process of the algorithm. The algorithm requires the following four types of input data. That is, the boundary information of input domain R and its dimensional number d, the preset size of candidate set, i.e., s, the number of initial partitions on each dimension of the input domain, and the condition for stopping test case generation. The output of algorithm is the set of the selected test cases, namely TS. In addition, the algorithm utilizes two temporary storage structures, namely, a set CS for storing candidate points and a list L_{EC} for storing empty cells.

Initially, the first test case is randomly generated from the whole input domain. Then, the test case generation process is represented by a while loop from line 3 to line 26. Only when the termination condition is satisfied, the process can be stopped. In practice, the condition can be a failure is detected or the number of the selected test cases reach to a preset number.

In the while loop, once the test case tc is executed, the cell in which it is located is removed from the list L_{EC} (see line 4). Subsequently, it is to check whether the list L_{EC} is empty. If so, the input domain R is further dichotomized in each dimension and the existing test cases are re-located into the newly generated cells. At the same time, the remaining empty cells are added to the list L_{EC} (lines 5–10). Then, at the stage shown in lines 11 to 17, a subset of no more than s cells is randomly selected from the empty cell list L_{EC}. If the number of empty cells is greater than 1, one candidate point is randomly generated from each cell to form the set CS. Otherwise, two candidates are randomly generated from the only one empty cell. At the third stage (lines 18–24), for each candidate c_k in CS, it is to calculate its comprehensive distance metric ($\text{cdm}(c_k)$) according to Eqs. (2) and (3). Specifically, lines 19–21 calculate $\text{ndist}(c_k)$ for candidate c_k by only considering the distances from it to the test cases lying in its $3^d - 1$ neighbour cells. On line 22, the distance from c_k to the center point of its cell, namely $\text{cdist}(c_k)$, is calculated. When the comprehensive distance metrics of all candidates in CS are achieved, the candidate with the maximum metric is selected as the next test case tc (line 25).

It is not hard to find that the time complexity of ART-BCD algorithm is mainly composed of the distance computation cost and the test case re-location cost. (1) *Distance computation cost.* At each step, at most s candidates are randomly generated. For each candidate, there are up to $3^d - 1$ existing test cases in its neighborhood to participate in distance computation. Then, the cost of distance computation for selecting each new test case is $O(s \cdot 3^d)$. Accordingly, to generate n test cases, the corresponding distance computation cost is $O(s \cdot 3^d \cdot n)$. (2) *Test case re-location cost.* According to the analysis in [13], we can know that the total cost of test case re-location in the process of generating n test cases will not exceed $2n$. Thus, the cost of test case re-location is in the order of $O(n)$. Taken together, the time complexity of ART-BCD algorithm can be expressed as $O(s \cdot 3^d \cdot n)$, which is linear with the number of test cases.

4   Simulation Analysis

4.1   Experimental Setup

As mentioned earlier, software failure patterns can be principally classified into three types: block, strip, and point. Without loss of generality, in the simulation analysis, we validated the failure detection effectiveness of the proposed ART-BCD algorithm by the three failure patterns respectively. In the experiment, the interval of each dimension was set to -5000 to 5000, and the input domains of two to four dimensions were examined emphatically. To simulate the block failure pattern, a small square (or cube) was randomly placed in the input domain as a failure region. For the strip pattern, a narrow strip with arbitrary angle was used to simulate the failure region. For the point pattern, 25 very small non-overlapping squares (or cubes) were randomly distributed into the input domain.

In the context of random testing, the expected number of test cases to detect the first failure is usually taken as an indicator for measuring the effectiveness of a test case generation algorithm, and is denoted as F-measure [7]. In addition, the F-measure of random testing is usually used as a baseline to define a relative measure for testing effectiveness, that is, F-ratio $= F_{ART}/F_{RT}$, where F_{ART} and F_{RT} are the F-measures of the ART method and the RT method, respectively. In theory, $F_{RT} = 1/\theta$. In order to investigate the failure detection ability of each ART algorithm under various failure rates, we changed the failure rate (θ) from 0.01 to 0.0001.

In our algorithm, the dynamic bisection is used to reduce the computational cost of the nearest neighbor query for a candidate. Meanwhile, similar to the ART algorithms based on dynamic partitioning, the ART-BCD algorithm ensures that a test case is selected from each sub-region. For comparison, ART-B and ART-RP are regarded as two typical representatives of dynamic partitioning-based ART algorithms. In addition, the distance between two test cases is also seen as an important indicator of their dispersion degree in our ART-BCD algorithm. For this reason, FSCS-ART [6] is also run in the comparative experiments. In the experiments, the number of repeated trials for each algorithm under each failure rate was set to 5000, the size of candidate set (i.e., s) was set to 10.

4.2 Experimental Results

In the simulation experiments, we want to investigate whether the ART-BCD algorithm shows an advantage to the other three algorithms, namely ART-RP, ART-B, and FSCS-ART, in the three failure patterns. The experimental results in the case of block failure pattern are listed in Table 1. When $d = 2$, the F-ratio of ART-RP algorithm increases slightly with the decrease of θ, while the F-ratio of ART-B algorithm is basically stable at around 73.5%. In contrast, the F-ratio of ART-BCD algorithm is significantly lower than those of ART-RP and ART-B algorithms at each value of θ. Meanwhile, the F-ratio of ART-BCD algorithm decreases obviously with the decrease of θ value. Therefore, the advantages of ART-BCD algorithm over the ART-RP and ART-B algorithms are significantly enhanced with the decrease of θ value. On the other hand, although the F-ratio of FSCS-ART algorithm decreases obviously with the decrease of θ, the corresponding value of ART-BCD algorithm is always lower than that of

FSCS-ART, but the advantage of ART-BCD algorithm reduces with the decrease of θ value.

Table 1. F-ratio comparison in the case of block failure pattern (unit: %)

Failure rate θ	$d = 2$				$d = 4$			
	ART-RP	ART-B	FSCS-ART	ART-BCD	ART-RP	ART-B	FSCS-ART	ART-BCD
0.01	76.70	74.70	67.43	64.54	86.54	87.79	106.98	93.34
0.005	76.66	73.54	66.10	61.44	86.95	88.93	101.05	90.85
0.001	78.54	74.33	63.80	61.88	89.96	87.88	90.92	85.39
0.0005	79.48	73.76	63.41	61.64	90.13	88.84	87.88	81.79
0.0001	78.79	73.13	61.56	60.63	94.34	89.10	85.02	81.69

When $d = 4$, the F-ratio of ART-RP algorithm increases obviously with the decrease of failure rate, while the F-ratio of ART-B algorithm fluctuates slightly at about 89%. Compared with ART-BCD algorithm, the F-ratios of both algorithms are smaller than that of the ART-BCD algorithm when θ is greater than 0.005. However, when θ reaches to 0.001, the F-ratio of ART-BCD algorithm is significantly lower than those of the two algorithms. Similarly, with the decrease of failure rate, ART-BCD algorithm has more obvious advantages than both ART-RP and ART-B. While considering the FSCS-ART algorithm, although the change trend of F-ratio value is similar to that of ART-BCD algorithm, that

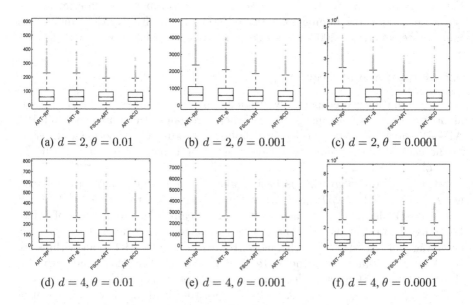

(a) $d = 2$, $\theta = 0.01$ (b) $d = 2$, $\theta = 0.001$ (c) $d = 2$, $\theta = 0.0001$

(d) $d = 4$, $\theta = 0.01$ (e) $d = 4$, $\theta = 0.001$ (f) $d = 4$, $\theta = 0.0001$

Fig. 4. The F-measure distribution of four ART algorithms.

is, the F-ratio decreases gradually with the decrease of θ value, but the ART-BCD algorithm is always better than FSCS-ART algorithm in terms of failure detection ability. Specifically, when $\theta = 0.01$, the F-ratio of ART-BCD is lower than that of FSCS-ART about 14 %. When θ is reduced to 0.0001, the F-ratio of ART-BCD algorithm is still 3 % lower than that of FSCS-ART.

In addition, we further analyze the F-measure distribution of four ART algorithms, and the results are shown in Fig. 4. It is easy to see that the F-measure distribution range of ART-BCD algorithm is narrower than that of the other three algorithms except for the case of $d = 4$ and $\theta = 0.01$. And with the decrease of θ, the advantage of ART-BCD algorithm is more obvious. The above results show that ART-BCD algorithm performs better in most cases of block failure pattern. Meanwhile, for programs with low failure rate, the failure detection ability of ART-BCD algorithm is more stable.

For the strip failure pattern, the F-ratio results of four algorithms are shown in Table 2. In the case of $d = 2$, the F-ratios of the four algorithms are basically not significantly different. Only when $\theta = 0.01$, the F-ratio of ART-BCD algorithm is about 3 % lower than those of other three algorithms. In the case of $d = 4$, the F-ratio of each algorithm increases by a small margin with the decrease of θ, and the range of increase is about 2 to 5 %. According to the F-ratio results in this case, there is no significant difference in failure detection ability between the four ART algorithms.

Table 2. F-ratio comparison in the case of strip failure pattern (unit: %)

Failure rate θ	$d = 2$				$d = 4$			
	ART-RP	ART-B	FSCS-ART	ART-BCD	ART-RP	ART-B	FSCS-ART	ART-BCD
0.01	94.64	93.50	93.62	90.84	98.93	98.57	97.42	96.73
0.005	96.86	93.36	95.36	95.69	99.02	99.04	98.64	97.49
0.001	100.17	99.10	96.49	96.78	98.17	100.06	98.69	98.80
0.0005	97.75	98.95	95.15	98.91	99.64	99.85	100.22	100.23
0.0001	98.58	98.66	99.85	98.89	101.81	99.99	99.70	100.32

For the point failure pattern, there are no very significant differences in the F-ratio results of the four algorithms in the case of $d = 2$ (Table 3). For the first three algorithms, namely, ART-RP, ART-B, and FSCS-ART, their F-ratios do not change significantly with the change of failure rate. By contrast, the F-ratio of ART-BCD algorithm has a very small decrease with decreasing θ value. When $d = 4$, the F-ratio of ART-RP algorithm has a decrease of about 2 % from its value in the case of $d = 2$, while the F-ratio of ART-B algorithm remains substantially stable. The F-ratios of FSCS-ART and ART-BCD algorithms are both significantly higher than their values in the case of $d = 2$. Thus, in the case of $d = 4$, the failure detection ability of these two algorithms is lower than those of ART-RP and ART-B. As far as these two algorithms are concerned, the failure detection ability of our ART-BCD algorithm is significantly stronger than the FSCS-ART algorithm. However, the F-ratio of the two algorithms decreases with the decrease of θ value, and the difference between them is gradually narrowing.

Table 3. F-ratio comparison in the case of point failure pattern (unit: %)

Failure rate θ	$d = 2$				$d = 4$			
	ART-RP	ART-B	FSCS-ART	ART-BCD	ART-RP	ART-B	FSCS-ART	ART-BCD
0.01	96.80	97.63	98.87	99.79	94.11	98.91	129.37	114.86
0.005	98.01	97.72	98.90	98.00	95.15	96.84	121.89	104.30
0.001	98.01	97.34	98.45	97.17	97.69	97.06	113.70	103.49
0.0005	98.57	100.26	98.49	95.20	95.31	98.38	111.55	100.91
0.0001	99.69	95.98	96.21	96.71	96.26	99.48	108.34	101.54

Findings: According to the above simulation experiments, we can observe that the ART-BCD algorithm outperforms the other three algorithms in most cases of the block failure pattern. In the strip pattern, the failure detection abilities of the four algorithms are comparable. For the point pattern, the ART-BCD algorithm has always been superior to the FSCS-ART algorithm, which is comparable to ART-RP and ART-B in the low-dimensional case. In the high-dimensional case, the ART-BCD failure detection effectiveness is lower than ART-RP and ART-B, but the gap is significantly reduced as the failure rate decreases.

5   Empirical Study

5.1   Programs Under Test

Although the failure regions simulated above can represent all kinds of possible failure cases, it is not the reflection of actual faults in the program after all. Therefore, in this section, we use some real-life programs containing faults to analyze and compare the failure detection abilities of the four ART algorithms mentioned above. As shown in Table 4, the first 12 programs are the widely-used subject programs in the existing ART researches. In our experiments, we set up them with the same faults and input domains as the empirical studies in [6,13,15]. In addition, the last program perpendicular was taken from the program package prepared by Zhou et al. [21], and the fault in it was seed by the mutation operator CRP (constant replacement) [11] in a manual way.

The dimension number of the input domains of all 13 programs varies from 1 to 4. The number of the seeded faults in them is between 1 and 9, and the corresponding failure rate is within the range from 0.0003 to 0.002. In this empirical study, the repeated trials for each subject program were also set to 5000, and the average of F-measures of all trials is used as the effectiveness metric for comparing the four ART algorithms.

Table 4. The details of 13 programs under test

Program	Dim. d	Input domain		Total faults	Failure rate θ
		From	To		
airy	1	−5000	5000	1	0.000716
bessj0	1	−300000	300000	5	0.001373
erfcc	1	−30000	30000	4	0.000193
probks	1	−50000	50000	4	0.000104
tanh	1	−500	500	4	0.001817
bessj	2	(2, −1000)	(300, 15000)	4	0.001298
gammq	2	(0, 0)	(1700, 40)	4	0.000830
sncndn	2	(−5000, −5000)	(5000, 5000)	5	0.001623
golden	3	(−100, −100, −100)	(60, 60, 60)	5	0.000550
plgndr	3	(10, 0, 0)	(500, 11, 1)	5	0.000368
cel	4	(0.001, 0.001, 0.001, 0.001)	(1, 300, 10000, 1000)	3	0.000332
el2	4	(0, 0, 0, 0)	(250, 250, 250, 250)	9	0.000690
perpendicular	4	(−50, −50, −50, −50)	(50, 50, 50, 50)	1	0.001085

5.2 Experimental Results

The F-measure results of four ART algorithms for all 13 programs are shown in Table 5. For the five programs with 1-dimensional inputs, the failure detection effectiveness of ART-BCD is significantly better than those of ART-RP and ART-B algorithms, and is comparable to the FSCS-ART algorithms. In the case of 2-dimensional input domain, the F-measure of ART-BCD is obviously less than those of ART-RP and ART-B for programs bessj and gammq, and is comparable to the FSCS-ART. For the program sncndn, ART-BCD is also comparable to other three algorithms in terms of failure detection effectiveness.

In the case of 3-dimensional inputs, the failure detection ability of ART-BCD is significantly stronger than those of other three ART algorithms for program golden. For program plgndr, the F-measure of ART-BCD is still significantly less than those of ART-RP and ART-B. Compared with FSCS-ART algorithm, ART-BCD's F-measure is less about 40. For the first two programs with 4-dimensional inputs, namely, cel and el2, the F-measure of ART-BCD is significantly less than those of ART-RP and ART-B, but it is significantly higher than that of FSCS-ART algorithm. For another program perpendicular, the F-measure of ART-BCD is obviously less than those of all other three ART algorithms.

Findings: Based on the results of empirical study, it is can be found that ART-BCD outperforms ART-RP and ART-B in terms of failure detection ability, and is comparable to FSCS-ART algorithm in most cases.

Table 5. The average F-measures of four algorithms for the 13 programs

Program	F-measure			
	ART-RP	ART-B	FSCS-ART	ART-BCD
airy	938.49	791.51	796.20	745.66
bessj0	526.89	526.61	446.36	458.67
erfcc	3446.83	3543.91	2865.97	2967.63
probks	6549.39	6863.23	5643.45	5825.45
tanh	369.89	372.80	311.03	318.29
bessj	692.69	739.05	441.32	466.72
gammq	1180.15	1143.68	1058.69	1014.83
sncndn	617.75	632.31	633.87	626.65
golden	1578.95	1595.40	1584.71	1352.31
plgndr	3144.66	2716.06	1612.69	1570.66
cel	3765.38	3044.33	1577.30	3033.35
el2	1730.01	1431.54	701.55	1257.31
perpendicular	931.12	946.40	981.81	840.37

6   Concluding Remarks

As an enhanced version of random testing, ART shows a stronger failure detection ability. The traditional partition-based ART algorithms, such as ART-RP and ART-B, can achieve a lightweight test case generation, but they are difficult to avoid test cases clustering together. FSCS-ART algorithm promotes test cases to be dispersed as far as possible through distance computation, but the distance computation often causes heavy computational overhead. Meanwhile, it is easy to cause boundary effect. In this paper, we adopt the dynamic bisection and distance-aware forgetting to speed up the nearest test case query for a given candidate. At the same time, by using the candidate mechanism of empty cells, the randomly generated candidates are ensured to be dispersed as far as possible and far away from the existing test cases. More importantly, the comprehensive distance metric is defined to avoid the test cases being too easy to fall in the boundary region of input domain. Based on the above treatments, a new bisection-based ART algorithm named ART-BCD is developed.

Both simulation and empirical experiments have been performed to validate the effectiveness of the proposed ART-BCD algorithm, the experimental results show that ART-BCD has stronger or comparable failure detection ability than other three ART algorithms (i.e., ART-RP, ART-B, and FSCS-ART) in most cases. The advantage is especially obvious in the case of block failure pattern.

Acknowledgments. This work was supported in part by the National Natural Science Foundation of China (Grant No. 61762040) and the Natural Science Foundation of the Jiangxi Province (Grant Nos. 20162BCB23036 and 20171ACB21031).

References

1. Ammann, P., Offutt, J.: Introduction to Software Testing, 2nd edn. Cambridge University Press, Cambridge (2016)
2. Arcuri, A., Briand, L.: Adaptive random testing: an illusion of effectiveness? In: Proceedings of the 2011 International Symposium on Software Testing and Analysis (ISSTA 2011), pp. 265–275, July 2011
3. Chen, T.Y., Eddy, G., Merkel, R., Wong, P.K.: Adaptive random testing through dynamic partitioning. In: Proceedings of the 4th International Conference on Quality Software (QSIC 2004), pp. 79–86, September 2004
4. Chen, T.Y., Huang, D.H., Tse, T.H., Yang, Z.: An innovative approach to tackling the boundary effect in adaptive random testing. In: Proceedings of the 40th Annual Hawaii International Conference on System Sciences (HICSS 2007), pp. 262–271, January 2007
5. Chen, T.Y., Kuo, F.C., Merkel, R.G., Tse, T.H.: Adaptive random testing: the ART of test case diversity. J. Syst. Softw. 83(1), 60–66 (2010)
6. Chen, T.Y., Leung, H., Mak, I.K.: Adaptive random testing. In: Maher, M.J. (ed.) ASIAN 2004. LNCS, vol. 3321, pp. 320–329. Springer, Heidelberg (2004). https://doi.org/10.1007/978-3-540-30502-6_23
7. Chen, T.Y., Kuo, F.C., Merkel, R.: On the statistical properties of testing effectiveness measures. J. Syst. Softw. 79(5), 591–601 (2006)
8. Chow, C., Chen, T.Y., Tse, T.H.: The ART of divide and conquer: an innovative approach to improving the efficiency of adaptive random testing. In: Proceedings of the 13th International Conference on Quality Software (QSIC 2013), pp. 268–275, July 2013
9. Gutjahr, W.J.: Partition testing vs. random testing: the influence of uncertainty. IEEE Trans. Softw. Eng. 25(5), 661–674 (1999)
10. Hamlet, R.: Random testing. In: Marciniak, J.J. (ed.) Encyclopedia of Software Engineering, 2nd edn, pp. 1507–1513. Wiley, Chichester (2002)
11. Jia, Y., Harman, M.: An analysis and survey of the development of mutation testing. IEEE Trans. Softw. Eng. 37(5), 649–678 (2011)
12. Levin, S.: Uber crash shows 'catastrophic failure' of self-driving technology, experts say, 22 March 2018. https://www.theguardian.com/technology/2018/mar/22/self-driving-car-uber-deathwoman-failure-fatal-crash-arizona/
13. Mao, C., Chen, T.Y., Kuo, F.C.: Out of sight, out of mind: a distance-aware forgetting strategy for adaptive random testing. Sci. China Inf. Sci. 60, 092106:1–092106:21 (2017)
14. Mao, C., Zhan, X.: Towards an improvement of bisection-based adaptive random testing. In: Proceedings of the 24th Asia-Pacific Software Engineering Conference (APSEC 2017), pp. 689–694, December 2017
15. Mao, C., Zhan, X., Tse, T.H., Chen, T.Y.: KDFC-ART: a KD-tree approach to enhancing fixed-size- candidate-set adaptive random testing. IEEE Trans. Reliab. 68(4), 1444–1469 (2019)
16. Mariani, L., Pezz, M., Zuddas, D.: Recent advances in automatic black-box testing. Adv. Comput. 99, 157–193 (2015)
17. Mathur, A.P.: Foundations of Software Testing, 2nd edn. Addison-Wesley Professional, Boston (2014)
18. Mayer, J., Schneckenburger, C.: An empirical analysis and comparison of random testing techniques. In: Proceedings of the 2006 ACM/IEEE International Symposium on Empirical Software Engineering (ISESE 2006), pp. 105–114, September 2006

19. Rezaalipour, M., Talebsafa, L., Vahidi-Asl, M.: Arselda: an improvement on adaptive random testing by adaptive region selection. In: Proceedings of the 8th International Conference on Computer and Knowledge Engineering (ICCKE 2018), pp. 73–78, October 2018

20. Zhang, X.F., Zhang, Z.Z., Xie, X.Y., Zhou, Y.C.: An approach of iterative partition testing based on priority sampling. Chin. J. Comput. **39**(11), 2307–2323 (2016). (in Chinese)

21. Zhou, M., Cheng, X., Guo, X., Gu, M., Zhang, H., Song, X.: Improving failure detection by automatically generating test cases near the boundaries. In: Proceedings of the IEEE 40th Annual Computer Software and Applications Conference (COMPSAC 2016), pp. 164–173, June 2016

CMM: A Combination-Based Mutation Method for SQL Injection

Jing Zhao[1,2](✉), Tianran Dong[1,3], Yang Cheng[1,3], and Yanbin Wang[4]

[1] Software Engineering, Dalian University of Technology, Dalian, China
zhaoj9988@dlut.edu.cn
[2] Cyberspace Security Research Center, Peng Cheng Laboratory, Shenzhen, China
[3] Department of Computer Science and Technology,
Harbin Engineering University, Harbin, China
{dongtianran,chengyangheu}@hrbeu.edu.cn
[4] Department of Industrial Engineering, Harbin Institute of Technology,
Harbin, China
wangyb@hit.edu.cn

Abstract. With the rapid development of Web applications, SQL injection (SQLi) has been a serious security threat for years. Many systems use superimposed rules to prevent SQLi like backlists filtering rules and filter functions. However, these methods can not completely eliminate SQLi vulnerabilities. Many researchers and security experts hope to find a way to find SQLi vulnerabilities efficiently. Among them, mutation-based fuzzing plays an important role in Web security testing, especially for SQLi. Although this approach expands the space for test cases and improves vulnerability coverage to some extent, there are still some problems such as mutation operators cannot be fully covered, test cases space explosions, etc. In this paper, we present a new technique Combinatorial Mutation Method (CMM) to generate test set for SQLi. The test set applies *t-way* and variable strength Combinatorial Testing. It makes the mutation progress more aggressive and automated and generates test cases with better *F-measure Metric* and *Efficiency Metric*. We apply our approach to three open source benchmarks and compare it with *sqlmap*, *FuzzDB* and *ART4SQLi*. The experiment results demonstrate that the approach is effective in finding SQLi vulnerabilities with multiple filtering rules.

Keywords: SQL injection · Mutation method · Combinatorial Testing (CT) · *t-way* Combinatorial Testing (*t-way* CT) · Variable Strength Combinatorial Testing (VSCT)

1 Introduction

Database-driven Web applications have been rapidly adopted in a wide range of areas including on-line stores, e-commerce, etc. However, this popularity makes them more attractive to attackers. The number of reported Web attacks is growing sharply [8]: for instance, a recent Web application attack report observed an

© Springer Nature Switzerland AG 2020
H. Miao et al. (Eds.): SOFL+MSVL 2019 Workshop, LNCS 12028, pp. 345–361, 2020.
https://doi.org/10.1007/978-3-030-41418-4_23

average increase of around 17% in different types of Web attacks over the nine-month period from August 1, 2013 to April 30, 2014.

Within the class of Web based vulnerabilities, SQL injection (SQLi) vulnerabilities have been labeled as one of the most dangerous vulnerabilities by the Open Web Application Security Project (OWASP). Although the cause and mechanism of SQLi is single, the number of SQLi attack events increased continuously. To solving SQLi problems, static analysis is a traditional security mechanism with trivial process, in which hybrid constraint solver would be used when an SQL query is submitted. Therefore, dynamic testing methods such as black-box testing have become a popular choice. For example, mutation-based fuzzy testing [22] can automatically generate mutations and analyze them.

There have been many studies devoted to detecting SQLi vulnerabilities [9,12,23]. Adaptive Random Testing (ART) [1] is an improvement based on random testing. Researchers believe that software bugs are continuous and can be reflected in the input domain. If the test cases are evenly distributed across the input field, they will have strong error detection capabilities. Therefore, ART4SQLi [25] selects the farthest test case from the selected one. ART4SQLi uses this method to trigger SQLi vulnerabilities as quickly as possible, i.e. the smallest possible F-measure (this metric will be detailed later).

Nowadays, multiple filtering rules can pick out many statements with sensitive characters, so a mutated test case will be dropped if the sensitive part remains after the mutation operation. Meanwhile the types of mutation operator increasing is causing the test space explosion. We integrate the other black box testing with the mutation approach to reduce the probability of the test case being filtered and decrease its space. In addition, we focus on generating test cases by integrating the Combinatorial testing (CT) with the mutation method and detecting potential SQLi vulnerabilities by generating more effective test cases. The goal of the CT is to select a small number of test cases from the huge combined space, and detect the faults that may be triggered by the interaction of various factors. This method reduces the size of the test cases set and will have a good F-measure and efficiency.

In this paper, we present a new input mutation method CMM aimed at increasing the likelihood of triggering vulnerabilities beyond filtering rules. We import the original mutation methods from *sqlmap*[1], and classify them into five groups according to their mutation behavior. Motivated by CT, we want to find the best combination of mutation operators with the least test cases during the test. Then we build a CT model for these mutation methods. The model is input into a combinatorial test generation tool *ACTS* [24], and a combined object is generated using *t-way* and variable strength CT, which is simply a symbol array. Every row of the generated array is used to output a test case. We use the array to instruct our test cases mutation progress. The experiment result demonstrated that the better efficiency and effectiveness in triggering vulnerabilities of our method when there are multiple filtering rules. This paper is structured as follows. Section 2 provides background information on SQLi vulnerabilities and CT.

---

[1] http://sqlmap.org/.

Section 3 discusses in detail our approach, followed by Sect. 4 where we introduce our experiments and results. Section 5 concludes this paper and discusses future work.

2 Background and Related Work

2.1 Background

SQLi Vulnerabilities. Two major cause fro SQL injections are the ignorance towards filtering out user-input, and framing SQL queries dynamically using string data type by concatenating SQL code and user-input during runtime [6]. For example, a SQL statement is formed as Fig. 1 (a simplified example from one of our Web applications): The user's input is stored in the string variable *$id*. After being filtered by the filter function *tsFilter*, *$id* will be concatenated with the rest of the SQL statement. The SQL statement will be send to database server to be executed. If the filter function is not strong enough, the SQLi Vulnerabilities will be easily exploited.

```
1  $id = $_GET['$id'];
2  $id = tsFilter($id);
3  $getid = '' SELECT first_name, last_name FROM users WHERE
          user_id='$id' ";
4  $result = mysqli_query($getid) or die(mysqli_error());
```

Fig. 1. Example of an SQLi vulnerability

Combinatorial Testing (CT). Combinatorial testing is motivated by the selection of a few test cases in such a manner that good coverage is still achievable, while for a general treatment of the field of CT we refer the interest reader to the recent survey of [17]. The combinatorial test design process can be briefly described as follows:

(1) Model the input space. The model is expressed in terms of parameter and parameter values.
(2) The model is input into a combinatorial design procedure to generate a combinatorial object that is simply an array of symbols.
(3) Every row of the generated array is used to output a test case for a System Under Test (SUT).

One of the benefits of this approach is that steps 2. and 3. can be completely automated. In particular, we used the *ACTS* combinatorial test generation tool. Currently, *ACTS* supports *t-way* test set generation for $1 \leq t \leq 6$. In addition, *ACTS* also supports VSCT, We refer to two definitions from as follows:

Definition 1. *(t-way Covering Arrays): For the SUT, the n-tuple $(v_{n_1}, ..., v_{n_t}, ...)$ is called a t-value schema $(t > 0)$ when some t parameters have fixed values and the others can take on their respective allowable values, represented as "-". When $t = n$, the n-tuple becomes a test case for the SUT as it takes on specific values for each of its parameters. It is based on the fact that a test set covering all possible t-way combinations of parameter values for some t is very effective in identifying interaction faults. t usually takes a value from 2 to 6 [10,14].*

Definition 2. *(Variable Strength Covering Arrays): $VSCA(N; t, v_1, v_2, ..., v_k, \{C\})$ is a $N \times k$ CA of strength t containing C. Here C is a subset of the k columns having strength $t' > t$ and can be CA. A VSCA can have more than one C, each having same or different strength [5]. For instance, consider a VSCA $(27; 2, 3^9 2^2, CA(27; 3, 3^3)^3)$. It has total 11 parameters: 9 parameters each having 3 values and 2 parameters each having 2 values. The strength of the MCA is 2 and the number of rows is 27. Of these 11 parameters, there exists three subsets C having 3 parameters each having 3 values. The strength of the C is 3. Thus, the VSCA should cover all the 2-way interactions among 11 parameters and 3-way interactions among 3 parameters of subset C [20].*

2.2   Related Work

Researchers have proposed a series of techniques to prevent SQL injection vulnerabilities. Many existing techniques, such as input filtering, static analysis and security testing can detect and prevent a subset of the vulnerabilities that lead to SQLi [21].

The most important reason of SQLi vulnerabilities is insufficient input validation of data and code in dynamic SQL statements [7]. Thus, the most straightforward way is to set up an input filtering proxy in front of Web applications. A novel approach for detection of SQLIA is proposed by Bisht et al. [2], for mining programmer-intended queries with dynamic evaluation of candidate input. However, implementation of this method is not always feasible. Specifically, in a highly accessible web-application in which verification of a run-time query needs to retrieve its programmer intent or application constraint.

More and more researchers applied software testing technology to Web application security. Static analysis focus is to validate the user input type in order to reduce the chances of SQLi attacks rather than detect them. While the dynamic analysis method do not need to modify the web applications. However, the vulnerabilities found in the web application pages must be fixed manually and not all of them can be found without predefined attack codes. So the combination of static and dynamic analysis techniques are used as the basis of a preventative solution [15].

Random testing is one of the dynamic analysis and Adaptive Random Testing (ART) is its improvement [4]. ART is based on the observation that test cases revealing software failures tend to cluster together in the test cases domain.

Inspired by this, we realize that effective payloads tend to cluster in the payload space and proposed a new method ART4SQLi to accelerate the SQLi vulnerability discovery process [25]. ART4SQLi selects the farthest payload from all the evaluated ones. But in some test scenarios, the test cases would not distributed evenly. So ART may not perform as expected [18].

Mutation testing has been proposed and studied extensively [13] as a method of evaluating the adequacy of test suites where the program under test is mutated to simulate faults. While detecting software vulnerabilities, it can also measure the detection capability of the test set. Because of these unique advantages, mutation testing has been rapidly developed in network security and is widely used. Shahriar and Zulkernine [22] defined SQLi specific mutation operators to evaluate the effectiveness of a test suite in finding SQLi vulnerabilities. Holler et al. [11] proposed an approach LangFuzz to test interpreters for security vulnerabilities, and it has been applied successfully to uncover defects in Mozilla JavaScript and PHP interpreter. However, there are still some problems. First, as the type of mutation increases, the test cases space will produce a combined explosion. Second, the output of some mutation operators could be filtered because of sensitive characters. But CT can detect failures triggered by interactions of parameters in the SUT with a covering array test suite generated by some sampling mechanisms [17].

Kuhn et al. [14] found that the faulty combinations are caused by the combination of no more than 6 parameters. Three or fewer parameters triggered a total of almost 90% of the failures in the application. Nie [3] gave a different coverage definition, which also shows only the coverage definition of the k-value schema and does not reflect the importance of failure-causing schema in the test cases set. Qi [19] indicated that variable strength reachability testing reaches a good tradeoff between the effectiveness and efficiency. It can keep the same capability of fault detection as exhaustive reachability testing while substantially reducing the number of synchronization sequences and decreasing the execution time in most cases. Therefore, to solve the problem of mutation testing mentioned above, we propose the CMM technique in combination with the characteristics of CT and mutation method.

3   Approach

3.1   A Simple Example of SQL Injections

SQL injections come from a lack of encoding/escaping of user-controlled input when included in SQL queries. For example, a SQL statement is formed as follows:

A simplified example of one of our web applications is shown in Fig. 1. The *user_id* is an input provided by users, which is concatenated with the rest of the SQL statement and then stored in the string variable *$id*. For instance, the id value entered by the user is *'OR '1'='1'*, then the query generated by passing the value of id into the SQL statement, which is: "SELECT first_name, last_name FROM users WHERE user_id = ' ' OR '1'='1'". The query logic of the SQL statement has been changed, because the statement after the OR operation of the query will always return true. Then the function *mysqli_query* sends the SQL statement to the database server, and return all the first_name and last_name information in the users table. The information obviously exceeds the query permission of users and the data table has been leaked. But nowadays, there is always a filter function (such as, $id = tsFilter(\$id)$) between line 1 and line 2 of Fig. 1 to solve this kind of problems. So from the point of view of penetration testers or attackers, it is necessary to enhance the mutation of the SQL statement to prevent it from being filtered, then further to access the system information for attacking.

3.2   Test Case Mutation Methods

Sqlmap is an open source penetration testing tool that automates the process of detecting and exploiting SQLi flaws and taking over of database. We import the mutation methods from *sqlmap*, and classify them into five groups according to their behavior:

- Comment: This method attach a SQL comment command at the back of the input test case, there are four comments: "–", "#", "%00", "and '0having'='0having'". These comments can make the SQL statement followed the input be valid or change the structure of the whole SQL. Example like this: the original input may be "1 and 1=1", after the mutation it would be "1 and 1=1 %00".
- Stringtamper: This kind of mutation method is aimed at changing the appearance of original input, it will cheat the target system as a normal input. However, the input is a malicious code. There are eight kinds of methods: "between", "bluecoat", "greatest", "lowercase", "nonrecursivereplacement", "randomcase", "randomcomments", "symboliclogical".
- Space2: This kind of mutation method is aimed at changing the space in the input, because the target system will not allow a space in the input. There are fourteen kinds of methods: "halfversionedmorekeywords", "modsecurityversioned", "modsecurityzeroversioned", "multiplespaces", "overlongutf8", "space2c", "space2dash", "space2morehash", "space2mssqlblank", "space2randomblank", "space2hash", "space2mssqlhash", "space2mysqlblank", "space2mysqldash", "space2plus".
- Apostle: This kind of mutation method is aimed at changing the apostle in the input. There are two kinds of methods: "apostrophemask", "apostrophenullencode".
- Encoding: This kind of mutation method is aimed at changing the encoding of the original statement. there are five kinds of methods: "base64encode", "chardoubleencode", "charencode", "charunicodeencode", "percentage".

Algorithm 1 introduces the detailed process of the test case mutation methods. Given an valid test case input, the apply_MO function randomly applies one or more mutation operators to mutate this test case. Because the input values are

Algorithm 1. Test Case Mutation Method

Input: I:A set of Legal input.
Output: TS:Test case space.
1: $T = \{ \ \}$
2: **for** each input in I **do**
3:      **while** $not \ max\_tries$ **do**
4:          $t = $ apply_MO(input)
5:          **if** t not in T **then**
6:              Add t into TS
7:          **end if**
8:      **end while**
9: **end for**
10: **return** TS

Table 1. A input model of CT

Parameter	Input	Comment	Stringtamper
Value	1: "1' or 1=1 or" 2: "1 or 1=1"	0:Not be capable 1: "–" 2: "#" 3: "%00" 4: "'0having'='0having'" '	0:Not be capable 1: "between" 2: "bluecoat" ... 8: "symboliclogical"
Parameter	Space2	Apostle	Encoding
Value	0:Not be capable 1: "halfversionedmorekeywords" 2: "modsecurityversioned" ... 14: "space2randomblank"	0:Not be capable 1: "apostrophemask" 2: "apostrophenullencode"	0:Not be capable 1: "base64encode" 2: "chardoubleencode" ... 5: "percentage"

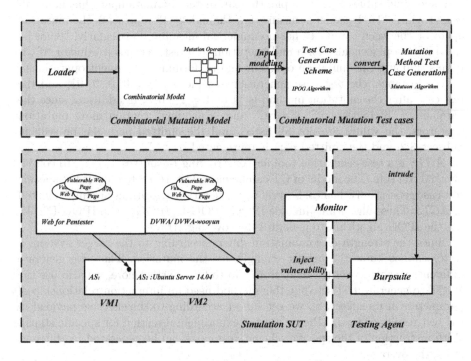

Fig. 2. SQLi vulnerability detection based on the combinatorial mutation testing

diverse and specific, so the mutation operator may not always be effective. For example, the SQL statement would not be changed if a mutation operator just converts the single quotes to the double quotes. So before adding the mutated SQL statement into the test set TS, checking for repeatability is needed. After using a series of mutation methods, the expanded original test cases TS can be obtained from the input value set I, which could cover more vulnerabilities.

3.3   Combinatorial Mutation Method

As the number of mutation operators increases, the space explosion problem will be highlighted. The CT could reduce the number of test cases while ensuring coverage. Therefore, we propose a new CT-based mutation method to detect vulnerabilities, which is *Combinatorial Mutation Method*. It contains two main steps: (1) Produce test case generation scheme; (2) Output test set with the given scheme.

CT-Based Test Case Generation Scheme. Since the target system may have multiple filtering rules for the input, only one mutation method is not enough for attackers or penetration testers. Firstly, we parameterize the mutation methods to output the test case generation scheme.

Table 1 shows the input model of CT including the Six parameters and their corresponding values. For example, the parameter "Stringtamper" has nine values, of which "1: "between"" means that the index "1" represents the mutation operator "between", and "1" has no numerical meaning. Particularly, "0:not be capable" is a placeholder for a null operation. If a test case has a value of "0", it means skipping this mutation operator and performing subsequent operations.

For instance, the test case generation scheme is {2, 3, 0, 0, 0, 0}, and the test case after the mutation method is "1 or 1 = 1% 00". In addition, since the parameters "Stringtamper" "Space2" and "Encoding" contain more mutation operators, the values are not all listed, and the omitted part can be seen in Subsect. 3.2, and the omitted part is represented by "...".

ACTS is a test generation tool for constructing *t-way* (t = 1, 2, ..., 6) combinatorial test sets. The model of CT can be passed to *ACTS* to output the specific test case generation schemes. Several test generation algorithms are implemented in *ACTS*. These algorithms include IPOG, IPOG-D, IPOG-F and IPOG-F2. We use the IPOG algorithm to generate the covering array.

Since the strength of combination differs according to the target system, a tester cannot know the proper strength for the mutation. Thus, we generate different strength covering array from two to five. Furthermore, we also use the VSCT to generate test set, but this method need an interaction relationship of parameters in its subset. So we get subset according to the effective payload in the test results of *t-way* (Please see the experimental section for specific steps). With instruction of the specific scheme, test cases can be generated by different strength coverage.

Algorithm 2. IPOG-based t-way CMM

Input: The parameter $f_1, f_2, ... f_n$ of the system S
Input: k: The strength of t-way CT
Input: The corresponding value set P ($P_1, P_2, ..., P_n$) of parameter $f_1, f_2, ... f_n$
Output: TS': Test cases space.
1: $T = \{\ \}$
2: $TS = \{(v_1, v_2, ..., v_k) | v_1 \in P_1, v_2 \in P_2, ..., v_k \in P_k\};$
3: **if** n==k **then return end if**
4: **for** P_i(i=k+1,...,n) **do**
5:     let π be the set of k-way combinations of values involving parameter P_i and $k-1$ parameters among the first $i-1$ parameters
6:     **for** each test (o=$v_1, v_2, ..., v_{i-1}$) in TS **do**
7:         choose a value v_i of P_i and replace o with $o' = v_1, v_2, ..., v_{i-1}, v_i$ so that o' covers the most number of k-way of values in P_i
8:         remove from P_i the combinations of values covered by o'
9:     **end for**
10:     **while** TS does not cover the value pairs formed by P_i and $P_1, P_2, ..., P_{i-1}$ **do**
11:         Add a new test for the parameters $P_1, P_2, ..., P_i$ to the TS, remove from π the k-way of values covered by TS
12:     **end while**
13: **end for**
14: **for** each input in TS **do**
15:     **while** *not max_tries* **do**
16:         $t = $ apply_MO(input)
17:         **if** t not in T **then** Add t into TS' **end if**
18:     **end while**
19: **end for**
20: **return** TS'

CMM-Based Test Set Generation. A set of test case generation schemes is parsed into test set with specific mutations. Algorithm 2 lists the IPOG-based *t-way* CMM process: the test case generation algorithm needs to pass the model's parameter CM and the coverage strength k to the test case set generation module according to the CT model. Then the IPOG algorithm (line 2–16) [16] is used to generate TS set. Next, for each legal input, the test case mutation algorithm apply_MO is executed according to the index of the cover set TS. Similarly, VSCT also generates CMM test cases based on the IPOG algorithm, as shown in Algorithm 3. The difference between those two algorithms is that VSCT is based on the 2-way CT (line 2–16) test set TS, and the subset C has the *t-way* ($t > 2$) interaction (line 17–21) relationship sample S'. Then we remove the combinations of values covered by S' from TS, and the rest combinations are merged with S' to generate a new test set S.

After the process, we pass the test cases set to the Web Security Auditing and Scanning tool *Burpsuite*[2], then the intruder mode in *Burpsuite* is applied to inject SQL vulnerabilities into Simulation SUT to get the request statement. The SQLi vulnerability detection process based on the combinatorial mutation testing is shown in Fig. 2.

---

[2] https://portswigger.net/burp.

Algorithm 3. IPOG-based variable strength CMM

Input: The parameter $f_1, f_2, ...f_n$ of the system S
Input: k: The variable strength of subset $C \subseteq \{C_1, C_2, C_{n-1}\}$
Input: The corresponding value set P $(P_1, P_2, ..., P_n)$ of parameter $f_1, f_2, ...f_n$
Output: TS': Test cases space.
1: $T = \{ \}$
2: $TS = \{(v_1, v_2)|v_1 \in P_1, v_2 \in P_2\}$;
3: **if** n==2 **then return end if**
4: **for** P_i(i=3,4,...,n) **do**
5:     let π be the set of i-way combinations of values involving parameter P_i and $i-1$ parameters
        among the first $i-1$ parameters
6:     **for** each test (o=$v_1, v_2, ..., v_{i-1}$) in TS **do**
7:         choose a value v_i of P_i and replace o with $o' = v_1, v_2, ..., v_{i-1}, v_i$ so that o' covers the most
            number of k-way of values in π
8:         remove from π the combinations of values covered by o'
9:     **end for**
10:     **while** TS does not cover the value pairs formed by P_i and $P_1, P_2, ..., P_{i-1}$ **do**
11:         Add a new test for the parameters $P_1, P_2, ..., P_i$ to the TS, remove from π the k-way of
            values covered by TS
12:     **end while**
13: **end for**
14: **while** C_i(i=1,2,...,n-1) **do**
15:     $S' = IPOG(k, C_i)$
16:     remove from TS the combinations of values covered by S'
17:     $S = TS \cup S'$
18: **end while**
19: **for** each input in S **do**
20:     **while** not max_tries **do**
21:         $t=$ apply_MO(input)
22:         **if** t not in T **then** Add t into TS' **end if**
23:     **end while**
24: **end for**
25: **return** TS'

4   Experiment and Results

4.1   Experiment Framework

In the experiment, Web server is deployed on a virtual machine, the operating system is Ubuntu14.04, as shown in the Fig. 3. We set three open source vulnerable Web applications on the server as the target system: *Web For Pentester*[3], *DVWA*[4], *DVWA-WooYun*[5]. Testing tool is set on the host, the OS is Windows7.

We visit the vulnerable pages on the server and then hijack the Web request by *Burpsuite* which is an integrated platform for performing security testing of Web applications. The mutated input is loaded in intruder mode of *Burpsuite*, some important parameters in the request which are input of users are injected with our mutated input.

When a malicious input is successfully injected, these vulnerable Web applications will reply with a response page containing a list of users and passwords. Then we judge whether the injection point can be injected based on response pages. Here we choose these vulnerable Web applications because they have a high coverage of SQLi types, at the same time, there are different filter functions.

---

[3] https://www.pentesterlab.com/.
[4] http://www.dvwa.co.uk/.
[5] http://sourceforge.net/projects/dvwa-wooyun/.

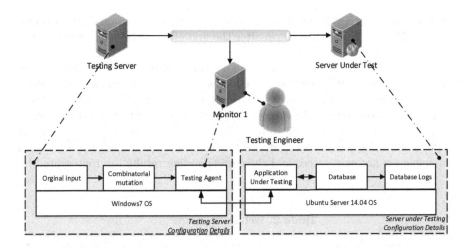

Fig. 3. Experiment framework

Pentester lab is one of the basics training for Web testing and summary of the most common vulnerabilities. This platform show how to manually find and exploit the vulnerabilities, which contains SQLi. *Web For Pentester* has 9 SQLi pages with different filter functions, but the last two pages are about how to use the vulnerability.

DVWA is a PHP/MySQL Web application that is damn vulnerable. Its main goals are to provide a legal environment for security experts to test their technology and tools, to help Web developers better understand the security issues of Web applications. In SQLi part, it contains general injection and blind injection with security level of low, medium and high. Low level has SQLi vulnerability, medium level has filter functions which want to protect the system, while high level is a standard safe programming paradigm.

DVWA-WooYun is a Wooyun OpenSource project based on DVWA project. It is based on real bug reported on *wooyun.org*. Each vulnerable page has a "View Source" button to show the php source code, which can help people understand the vulnerability.

4.2 Metrics

In our experiments, we use the *F-measure* (represented by F in tables), *Efficiency* (represented by E in tables) to demonstrate the capabilities of different approaches.

– *F-measure Metric*: *F-measure* calculates the expected number of payloads required to detect the first SQLi vulnerability. In other words, a lower *F-measure* value means fewer tests are used to accomplish the task. Therefore, if a testing strategy yields a lower *F-measure* value, it is considered to be more effective. Obviously the metric is affected by the order of the test cases, but in our experiment the order is random, so it is not enough to evaluate the CMM. As *sqlmap* would stop after the first effective test case were found, if *sqlmap* cannot stop after.

- *Efficiency Metric*: The *Efficiency* is a very common test case evaluation standard that reflects the percentage of effective test cases. It can effectively evaluate the quality of the test case when detecting vulnerability. The formula is expressed as follows: $Efficiency(\%) = (X/N) * 100\%$, where X is the number of test cases that can trigger vulnerabilities, and N is the size of test set. As *sqlmap* would stop after the first effective test case were found, the *Efficiency* of *sqlmap* is not calculated, and the corresponding results are represented by "-".

Table 2. Web for Pentester

	Example 1		Example 2		Example 3		Example 4		Example 5		Example 6		Example 7	
	F	E	F	E	F	E	F	E	F	E	F	E	F	E
1-way	0	0.00%	0	0.00%	0	0.00%	7	13.33%	7	26.67%	0	0.00%	9	6.67%
2-way	14	5.19%	26	3.70%	0	0.00%	12	5.93%	8	20.74%	19	3.70%	15	1.48%
3-way	14	6.38%	14	3.39%	211	0.14%	16	6.68%	8	18.73%	26	3.53%	26	3.26%
4-way	2	6.46%	10	3.44%	63	0.14%	4	5.96%	4	17.06%	45	3.62%	9	1.74%
5-way	11	5.13%	92	2.65%	2805	0.08%	7	4.62%	1	15.60%	1	3.37%	30	1.74%
$VSCA_1$	20	8.14%	45	4.65%	71	0.33%	15	8.14%	4	25.25%	15	1.16%	13	1.83%
$VSCA_2$	13	7.45%	23	5.25%	129	1.03%	5	8.46%	5	26.73%	12	0.85%	9	1.69%
sqlmap	40	–	44*	–	58*	–	40	–	41	–	80	–	–	–
FuzzDB	25	6.64%	42	0.47%	42	0.47%	17	1.42%	17	1.42%	17	1.42%	0	0.00%

4.3   Results

As a comparison, we conduct a series of experiment with *sqlmap*, *FuzzDB*[6] and our method. Our method is a mutation method to generate aggressive test cases.

Table 3. DVWA

	SQLi(low)		SQLi(blind)(low)		SQLi(medium)		SQLi(blind)(medium)	
	F	E	F	E	F	E	F	E
1-way	0	0.00%	0	0.00%	7	13.33%	7	13.33%
2-way	26	4.44%	26	4.44%	12	5.93%	12	5.93%
3-way	14	5.29%	14	5.29%	16	6.78%	16	6.78%
4-way	2	5.78%	2	5.78%	4	5.96%	4	5.96%
5-way	11	4.09%	11	4.09%	7	4.62%	7	4.62%
$VSCA_1$	45	5.65%	45	5.65%	49	5.48%	49	5.48%
$VSCA_2$	46	5.41%	46	5.41%	54	5.25%	54	5.25%
sqlmap	46	–	104	–	40	–	102	–
FuzzDB	25	7.11%	25	7.11%	17	1.42%	17	1.42%

---

[6] https://github.com/fuzzdb-project/fuzzdb.

Table 4. DVWA wooyun-I

	Sqli QUERY_STRING		Sqli filter #02-once		Sqli Mysql #01		No [Comma] Sqli	
	F	E	F	E	F	E	F	E
1-way	0	0.00%	0	0.00%	7	20.00%	0	0.00%
2-way	58	2.22%	26	2.96%	15	18.52%	26	4.44%
3-way	8	2.71%	14	4.48%	8	16.82%	14	6.38%
4-way	143	1.83%	2	4.22%	18	13.71%	2	7.29%
5-way	1	1.61%	11	2.87%	1	12.56%	11	5.45%
$VSCA_1$	6	2.82%	45	4.32%	4	19.44%	45	5.65%
$VSCA_2$	8	3.05%	46	4.06%	8	20.30%	68	5.41%
sqlmap	–	–	73*	–	380	–	–	–
FuzzDB	0	0.00%	25	6.16%	17	1.90%	25	6.64%

Table 5. DVWA wooyun-II

	Sqli using[Slashes]		Sqli filter #02-80sec		Sqli filter#01		No [Space] Sqli	
	F	E	F	E	F	E	F	E
1-way	0	0.00%	14	6.67%	13	6.67%	0	0.00%
2-way	0	0.00%	15	7.41%	58	1.48%	26	3.70%
3-way	0	0.00%	16	6.78%	16	1.63%	14	4.48%
4-way	0	0.00%	27	6.37%	18	1.83%	5	4.81%
5-way	0	0.00%	1	5.71%	1	1.78%	11	3.39%
$VSCA_1$	0	0.00%	13	3.99%	8	1.16%	45	5.65%
$VSCA_2$	0	0.00%	21	4.91%	45	1.18%	45	4.40%
sqlmap	–	–	–	–	–	–	2626	–
FuzzDB	0	0.00%	17	1.90%	33	0.47%	25	4.74%

The automated SQLi tool *sqlmap* requires manual judgment and implementation, and may need to try many times. *FuzzDB* is an open source database of attack patterns, predictable resource names, regex patterns for identifying interesting server responses and documentation resources, which is hosted at Google Code. We only choose the cross platform SQLi part of the dictionary.

In addition to using *t-way* $(1 < t < 6)$ combination approach, we also consider combination method of variable strength to generate test sets to trigger more vulnerabilities. We analyze the *Efficiency* of the 3-way, 4-way, 5-way test set of the three benchmarks and the effective payload (effective test cases) in the experimental results, and find three parameter sets: {input, stringtamper, space2}, {comment, space2, apostle}, {input, comment, apostle}, in which the interaction relationships can make the payload more efficient. To balance the effectiveness and flexibility of the mutation-force combination method, the number of test cases should be set between the number of 2-way test cases and the number of 3-way test cases. In order to achieve this goal, the six parameters based on the 2-way CT generate test set. Then respectively add two subset {{input, stringtamper, space2}, {input, comment, apostle}}, {{input, stringtamper, space2}, {comment, space2, apostle}}. these subsets have the 3-way $(t > 2)$

interaction relationship. Using 3-way CT, parameters in the subset generate test cases S'. Then we remove the combinations of values covered by S' from TS, and the rest combinations are merged with S' to generate a new test set $VSCA_1$, $VSCA_2$, the gray part of these tables are $VSCT$.

To prove the validity of our method, we calculate the average time cost of t-way. The number of test cases generated by different methods is different and constant. 1-way takes less than 0.01 s to generate 15 test cases. 2-way takes 0.45 s to generate 135 test cases. 3-way takes 14.8 s to generate 737 test cases. 4-way takes 417.8 s to generate 2181 test cases. 5-way takes 2158.4 s to generate 5287 test cases. $VSCA_1$ takes 43.0 s to generate 602 test cases. $VSCA_2$ takes 42.0 s to generate 591 test cases. The evaluation of effectiveness in Tables 2, 3, 4 and 5, where the total number of test cases for each way is derived from test cases sets given above.

We perform an average of 10 experiments on t-way as the test results to prevent the randomness of the conclusion and to verify the method more accurately. As can be seen in Table 2, in most cases there are better F-measure and $Efficiency$ for 2-way and above than the other two methods, especially Example 4, Example 5 and Example 7. In addition, $sqlmap$ can exploit this vulnerability only if it implements manual judgment and specifies mutation methods in Example 2 and Example 3 (marked with * in the table). Composite-based test case generation methods perform better than other methods in testing these pages. In Example 7, the other two methods are invalid, but t-way works well and has a superiority in the discovery of potential vulnerabilities under multiple filtering rules.

As shown in Table 3, t-way and $VSCT$ can ignore the type of injection, whether it is normal or blind. Although there are some fluctuations, t-way still has advantages over $sqlmap$ and $FuzzDB$ on the whole, especially in $SQLi(medium)$ and $SQLi(blind)(medium)$ with better $Efficiency$. Although $VSCT$'s F-measure and $Efficiency$ decrease slightly with difficulty, their $Efficiency$ is still higher than $FuzzDB$. It shows that t-way is good at exploring vulnerabilities when there are interaction between the various factors.

In Tables 4 and 5, with different filtering rules from real bug reports, t-way also works better than the other two methods. But the page $Sqli$ using[Slashes] may have some problems in the application.

Seen as a whole, Example 2, 4, 5, 6, 7 in Table 2, t-way t-way and $VSCT$ have a better efficiency than $FuzzDB$, especially in Example 5. $VSCT$ is better than t-way and $FuzzDB$ in terms of F-measure and $Efficiency$ in Example 1 and 2. For Table 3, 4 and 5 considering F-measure, the number of payload and $Efficiency$, CMM are irreplaceable by $sqlmap$ and $FuzzDB$.

Above all, combined with Tables 2, 3, 4 and 5, if we have requirements for both evaluation criteria F-measure and $Efficiency$, the high-way ($4 \leq t \leq 5$) covering array is undoubtedly a good choice. But for all Benchmarks, $VSCT$ is more efficient than any t-way. That is, if we want to improve the quality of test cases and enhance the reliability of Web applications, we need to find the subset

Table 6. Comparison with ART4SQLi

	Web for Pentester SQLi Example 1		DVWA wooyun sql query string		DVWA wooyun sql filter 01	
	F	E	F	E	F	E
1 way	0	0.00%	0	0.00%	9	6.67%
2 way	12	2.22%	41	2.22%	41	1.48%
3 way	23	6.38%	13	2.71%	93	1.63%
4 way	8	6.52%	62	1.82%	52	1.79%
5 way	15	5.12%	30	1.59%	46	1.83%
$VSCA_1$	13	8.14%	6	2.82%	13	1.16%
$VSCA_2$	15	7.29%	14	3.05%	87	1.18%
ART4SQLi	49	1.58%	1359	0.04%	1183	0.06%

relationship between the parameters based on the *t-way*'s effective test cases or professional test experience to further generate the variable strength test set.

In order to compare with our previous work, ART4SQLi, we conduct experiments under the same conditions in the ART4SQLi experiment and showed them in Table 6. In addition, ART4SQLi generated 76105 test cases. As can be seen in Table 6, although 1-way cannot successfully inject in Web for Pentester SQLi Example 1 and DVWA wooyun sql query string, it still performs good in DVWA wooyun sql filter 01 with only 15 test cases. In other pages and *t-ways* and *VSCTs* perform much better than *ART4SQLi*. *ART4SQLi*'s strategy of selecting the farthest test case from the selected onetest is talented. But the test cases set of *ART4SQLi* is too large (76105 test cases) and it lacks of function to filter out invalid mutants, which leads to bad *F-measure* and *Efficiency*.

5   Conclusion

SQL injections have been ranked as one of the most dangerous Web application vulnerabilities. Researchers have proposed a wide range of techniques to address the problem of detecting SQL injections. In this paper, we introduce a new technique CMM to detect vulnerabilities for SQLi. CMM first establish a CT modeling base on mutation operators of *sqlmap*. After that, test case generation schemes can be generated by specific methods, such as *t-way* CT and VSCT. Then the schemes are converted into mutation sets. Finally, we use the Web Security Auditing and Scanning tool to inject SQL vulnerabilities into Simulation SUT.

The experiments adopt three open source SQLi benchmarks, and the results show that high-way ($4 \leq t \leq 5$) covering arrays are undoubtedly better than the others, considering the *F-measure* and *Efficiency*. But only for *Efficiency*, variable strength is also a good choice, if we know the constraint relationship between parameters in advance. The CMM approach is effective in finding SQLi vulnerabilities with multiple filtering rules. In the future, we also expect to apply CMM to other Web application vulnerabilities, such as XSS.

Acknowledgement. We would like to thank anonymous reviewers for their invaluable comments and suggestions on improving this work. This work is supported by National Natural Science Foundation of China (NSFC) (grant No. 61572150), and the Fundamental Research Funds for the Central Universities of DUT (No. DUT17RC(3)097).

References

1. Appelt, D., Nguyen, C.D., Briand, L.C., Alshahwan, N.: Automated testing for SQL injection vulnerabilities: an input mutation approach. In: Proceedings of the 2014 International Symposium on Software Testing and Analysis, pp. 259–269. ACM (2014)
2. Bisht, P., Madhusudan, P., Venkatakrishnan, V.: Candid: dynamic candidate evaluations for automatic prevention of SQL injection attacks. ACM Trans. Inf. Syst. Secur. (TISSEC) **13**(2), 14 (2010)
3. Nie, C., Leung, H.: A survey of combinatorial testing. ACM Comput. Surv. **43**(2), 1–29 (2011)
4. Chen, J., et al.: An adaptive sequence approach for OOS test case prioritization. In: IEEE International Symposium on Software Reliability Engineering Workshops (2016)
5. Cohen, M.B., Gibbons, P.B., Mugridge, W.B., Colbourn, C.J.: Constructing test suites for interaction testing. In: Proceedings of the 25th International Conference on Software Engineering, pp. 38–48. IEEE Computer Society (2003)
6. Deepa, G., Thilagam, P.S.: Securing web applications from injection and logic vulnerabilities: approaches and challenges. Inf. Softw. Technol. **74**, 160–180 (2016)
7. Deshpande, V.M., Nair, D.M.K., Shah, D.: Major web application threats for data privacy & security-detection, analysis and mitigation strategies. Int. J. Sci. Res. Sci. Technol. **3**(7), 182–198 (2017)
8. Fossi, M., et al.: Symantec global internet security threat report. White Paper, Symantec Enterprise Security 1 (2009)
9. Gu, H., et al.: DIAVA: a traffic-based framework for detection of SQL injection attacks and vulnerability analysis of leaked data. IEEE Trans. Reliab. (2019)
10. Hagar, J.D., Wissink, T.L., Kuhn, D.R., Kacker, R.N.: Introducing combinatorial testing in a large organization. Computer **48**(4), 64–72 (2015)
11. Holler, C., Herzig, K., Zeller, A.: Fuzzing with code fragments. In: Presented as Part of the 21st USENIX Security Symposium (USENIX Security 2012), pp. 445–458 (2012)
12. Huang, Y., et al.: A mutation approach of detecting SQL injection vulnerabilities. In: Sun, X., Chao, H.-C., You, X., Bertino, E. (eds.) ICCCS 2017. LNCS, vol. 10603, pp. 175–188. Springer, Cham (2017). https://doi.org/10.1007/978-3-319-68542-7_15
13. Jia, Y., Harman, M.: An analysis and survey of the development of mutation testing. IEEE Trans. Softw. Eng. **37**(5), 649–678 (2011)
14. Kuhn, D.R., Kacker, R.N., Lei, Y.: Introduction to Combinatorial Testing. CRC Press, Boca Raton (2013)
15. Lee, I., Jeong, S., Yeo, S., Moon, J.: A novel method for SQL injection attack detection based on removing SQL query attribute values. Math. Comput. Model. **55**(1), 58–68 (2012)
16. Lei, Y., Kacker, R., Kuhn, D.R., Okun, V., Lawrence, J.: IPOG: a general strategy for t-way software testing. In: IEEE International Conference & Workshops on the Engineering of Computer-based Systems, ECBS 2007 (2010)

17. Nie, C., Leung, H.: A survey of combinatorial testing. ACM Comput. Surv. (CSUR) **43**(2), 11 (2011)
18. Nie, C., Wu, H., Niu, X., Kuo, F.C., Leung, H., Colbourn, C.J.: Combinatorial testing, random testing, and adaptive random testing for detecting interaction triggered failures. Inf. Softw. Technol. **62**, 198–213 (2015)
19. Qi, X., He, J., Wang, P., Zhou, H.: Variable strength combinatorial testing of concurrent programs. Front. Comput. Sci. **10**(4), 631–643 (2016)
20. Sabharwal, S., Aggarwal, M.: Variable strength interaction test set generation using multi objective genetic algorithms. In: 2015 International Conference on Advances in Computing, Communications and Informatics (ICACCI), pp. 2049–2053. IEEE (2015)
21. Sadeghian, A., Zamani, M., Manaf, A.A.: A taxonomy of SQL injection detection and prevention techniques. In: 2013 International Conference on Informatics and Creative Multimedia (ICICM), pp. 53–56. IEEE (2013)
22. Shahriar, H., Zulkernine, M.: Music: Mutation-based SQL injection vulnerability checking. In: The Eighth International Conference on Quality Software 2008, QSIC 2008, pp. 77–86. IEEE (2008)
23. Simos, D.E., Zivanovic, J., Leithner, M.: Automated combinatorial testing for detecting SQL vulnerabilities in web applications. In: Proceedings of the 14th International Workshop on Automation of Software Test, pp. 55–61. IEEE Press (2019)
24. Yu, L., Yu, L., Kacker, R.N., Kuhn, D.R.: ACTS: a combinatorial test generation tool. In: IEEE Sixth International Conference on Software Testing (2013)
25. Zhang, L., Zhang, D., Wang, C., Zhao, J., Zhang, Z.: ART4SQLi: the ART of SQL injection vulnerability discovery. IEEE Trans. Reliab. **68**, 1470–1489 (2019)

Author Index

Printed in the United States
by Bookmasters

Printed in the United States
By Bookmasters